6396.
344.010

0 2 APR 2001

EMPLOYMENT LAW
AND THE HUMAN RIGHTS ACT 1998

D0294549

0 2 APR 2001

EMPLOYMENT LAW
AND THE HUMAN RIGHTS ACT 1998

Declan O'Dempsey
Barrister
Cloisters
1 Pump Court

Andrew Allen
Barrister
Coram Chambers
4 Brick Court

Susan Belgrave
Barrister
9 Gough Square

Jill Brown
Barrister
Coram Chambers
4 Brick Court

JORDANS
2001

Published by
Jordan Publishing Limited
21 St Thomas Street
Bristol BS1 6JS

Copyright © Jordan Publishing Limited 2001

All rights reserved. No part of this publication may be reproduced, stored in a
retrieval system, or transmitted in any way or by any means, including photocopying
or recording, without the written permission of the copyright holder, application for
which should be addressed to the publisher.

British Library Cataloguing-in-Publication Data
A catalogue record for this book is available from the British Library.

ISBN 0 85308 503 X

Typeset by Mendip Communications Ltd, Frome, Somerset
Printed by MPG Books Ltd, Bodmin, Cornwall

PREFACE

The Human Rights Act 1998 is set to have a tremendous impact upon many aspects of our domestic law and this is especially true in the area of employment.

Following implementation of the Act on 2 October 2000, rights contained in the European Convention on Human Rights are directly enforceable through any level of the UK courts and, as anyone studying the Convention case-law will quickly appreciate, employment law has already presented the Strasbourg institutions with several controversial and difficult problems.

We very much hope that this book will provide employment law practitioners and human resources professionals with everything they require to familiarise themselves with these important new rights and apply them in the domestic courts.

DECLAN O'DEMPSEY
ANDREW ALLEN
SUSAN BELGRAVE
JILL BROWN

March 2001

CONTENTS

TABLE OF CASES

References are to paragraph numbers.

TABLE OF STATUTES

References are to paragraph numbers.

TABLE OF STATUTORY INSTRUMENTS

References are to paragraph numbers.

TABLE OF EUROPEAN MATERIALS

References are to paragraph numbers.

TABLE OF INTERNATIONAL MATERIALS

References are to paragraph numbers.

TABLE OF NATIONAL STATUTES ETC

References are to paragraph numbers.

TABLE OF ABBREVIATIONS

ACAS	Advisory, Conciliation and Arbitration Service
CAC	Central Arbitration Committee
the Commission	the European Commission of Human Rights
the Convention	the Convention for the Protection of Human Rights and Fundamental Freedoms
CPR 1998	Civil Procedure Rules 1998, SI 1998/3132
CPS	Crown Prosecution Service
DDA 1995	Disability Discrimination Act 1995
DPA 1998	Data Protection Act 1998
EAT	Employment Appeal Tribunal
ECtHR	European Court of Human Rights
ECJ	European Court of Justice
ERA 1996	Employment Rights Act 1996
ESA	European Space Agency
ETA 1996	Employment Tribunals Act 1996
GMC	General Medical Council
HRA 1998	Human Rights Act 1998
ICCPR	International Covenant on Civil and Political Rights
ILO	International Labour Organisation
LCD Consultation Paper	Lord Chancellor's Department Consultation Paper, *Human Rights Act 1998: Rules & Practice Directions*, March 2000
RIPA 2000	Regulation of Investigatory Powers Act 2000
RRA 1976	Race Relations Act 1976
SDA 1975	Sex Discrimination Act 1975
TULR(C)A 1992	Trade Union and Labour Relations (Consolidation) Act 1992
UDHR	Universal Declaration of Human Rights

Chapter 1

THE EUROPEAN CONVENTION AND THE INTERNATIONAL COMMON LAW OF HUMAN RIGHTS

1.1 ORIGINS OF THE CONVENTION

The Convention for the Protection of Human Rights and Fundamental Freedoms (the Convention)[1] is one of many treaties promulgated under the aegis of the Council of Europe, which was established in 1949 in the aftermath of World War II and has now expanded to include 41 Member States, all of which have ratified the Convention.[2]

The title given to the White Paper 'Rights Brought Home'[3] does have some basis in fact. British lawyers were involved in the drafting of the Convention, which drew upon a great number of sources including the Magna Carta (1215) and the English Bills of Rights (1688 and 1689).[4] The most important direct source for the Convention was the United Nations Universal Declaration of Human Rights (1948), and the development of the United Nations (UN) human rights system also had substantial British involvement. In their turn, the constitutional packages imposed upon former British colonies contained protections of fundamental rights very closely modelled on the Convention.

The Convention was drafted following the post-war constitutional reconstruction of Western Europe and during the cold war. The courts, rather than elected representatives, were seen as the most effective bulwark against future tyranny. Civil and political rights were emphasised over economic, cultural and social rights which have never gained the same status under the Council of Europe.[5]

The UK signed the Convention on 4 November 1950 and was the first country to ratify it on 8 March 1951. The UK did not, however, ratify the Articles recognising the jurisdiction of the European Court of Human Rights (ECtHR),[6] or the right of individual petition[7] until 14 January 1966. The Convention entered into force on 3 September 1953.

---

1 The Convention was signed on 4 November 1950 and came into force on 3 September 1953.
2 The founding Statute of the Council of Europe in Article 3 enjoins every Member State to accept 'the principles of the rule of law and of the enjoyment by all persons within its jurisdiction of human rights and fundamental freedoms'.
3 *Rights Brought Home: The Human Rights Bill* (Cm 3782) October 1997.
4 Although the French Declaration of the Rights of Man (1789) was much more influential.
5 The European Social Charter was signed in 1961 but does not have a similar enforcement mechanism.
6 [Former Article 46].
7 [Former Article 25].

The procedural provisions of the Convention, although not the substantive rights themselves, have been substantially amended by the 11th Protocol, which came into force on 1 November 1998.[8]

1.2   FRAMEWORK

1.2.1   Main Treaty, Protocols, Reservations

Articles 2 to 12 contain the substantive rights; Article 13 the right to an effective remedy; Article 14 provides for non-discrimination in the provision of the rights; Article 15 permits and regulates derogations in emergencies; Article 16 permits restrictions on the political activity of aliens; Article 17 prohibits the abuse of rights; and Article 18 limits restrictions on rights.

Eleven Protocols have been added to the Convention since its inception. The 2nd, 3rd, 5th, 8th, 9th and 10th Protocols were concerned with procedure and have been repealed following the 11th Protocol. The UK has signed and ratified the 1st (protection of property, right to education, right to free elections) and 6th (abolition of the death penalty) Protocols, which are in force. It has signed the 4th Protocol (no debtors' prisons, freedom of movement, protection from arbitrary expulsion) but has not ratified it. It has not yet signed the 7th Protocol (right of criminal appeal, right to compensation for wrongful conviction, freedom from double jeopardy, equality between spouses).

The UK Government indicated in its *Review of Human Rights Instruments (Amended)*,[9] published on 27 October 1999, that it was not possible to ratify the 4th Protocol at this stage because of concerns about compatibility with UK immigration legislation but that it intends to sign and ratify the 7th Protocol when certain inconsistencies with UK family law have been removed.

The UK has entered a reservation in respect of Article 2 of the 1st Protocol[10] and has derogated from Article 5(3) relating to the powers under the Prevention of Terrorism Act 1989 to extend the period of detention of persons suspected of terrorism connected with the affairs of Northern Ireland for up to seven days.[11]

The Human Rights Act 1998 (HRA 1998) is concerned with the rights protected by Articles 2 to 12 and 14 of the Convention; Articles 1 to 3 of the 1st Protocol and Articles 1 and 2 of the 6th Protocol as read with Articles 16 to 18 of the Convention.

---

8   References in the text and footnotes to the provisions of the Convention are to the revised text with a reference to the original text in square brackets where appropriate.
9   http://www.homeoffice.gov.uk/hract/amrevrhi.htm
10   See **1.3.15** below.
11   See **1.2.8** and **1.3.4** below.

1.2.2   The Institutions of the Council of Europe[12]

(1)   Parliamentary Assembly of the Council of Europe[13]

The Parliamentary Assembly of the Council of Europe elects the judges of the ECtHR. Each Member State submits a list of three judges and the Parliamentary Assembly elects one for each State.

(2)   The Committee of Ministers of the Council of Europe[14]

The Committee of Ministers was established under the Statute of the Council of Europe (1949) and part of its executive role relates to the Convention. It comprises the foreign ministers of the Member States and, although its judicial role has been eliminated by the 11th Protocol, it still has an administrative part to play in the Convention mechanisms. The Committee alone can request advisory opinions[15] and it supervises the execution of the judgments of the ECtHR.[16] Ultimately, the Committee could suspend a Member State from membership of the Council of Europe.[17]

(3)   The Secretary General of the Council of Europe

The Secretary General must be kept informed of measures taken by Member States exercising the right to derogate in times of emergency and the reasons therefor. The Secretary General must also be informed when the measures have ceased to operate.[18] In addition, the Secretary General can request any Member State to furnish an explanation of the manner in which its international law ensures the effective implementation of any of the provisions of the Convention.[19]

(4)   The Directorate of Human Rights

The Directorate of Human Rights provides secretarial support for bodies established under the European Social Charter, the European Convention for the Prevention of Torture, the Framework Convention for the Protection of National Minorities and for the European Commission against Racism and Intolerance. The Directorate also assists in the implementation of the Council of Europe's inter-governmental programme of activities and assists the Committee of Ministers in the exercise of its functions under the Convention.

(5)   The European Court of Human Rights (ECtHR)[20]

The judges are elected by the Parliamentary Assembly for renewable six-year terms. The maximum age is 70 and there is one judge for each of the Member States. The judges are full time and sit in their individual capacity rather than as

---

12   http://www.coe.int/
13   http://stars.coe.fr/
14   http://www.coe.fr/cm/
15   Article 47 [former Protocol 2(1) and (2)].
16   Article 46(2) [former Article 54].
17   Statute of the Council of Europe, Article 8.
18   Article 15.
19   Article 52 [former Article 57].
20   http://www.echr.coe.int

representatives of their respective States.[21] The first judges were elected in 1959 and the first decision of the ECtHR was in 1961.

1.2.3   Court procedure (admissibility and merits)

Pre-November 1998
Prior to the major changes in procedure introduced by the 11th Protocol, applications were made by Member States, individuals, groups or non-governmental organisations by petitioning the Secretary General of the Council of Europe who forwarded the petition to the European Commission of Human Rights (the Commission) which dealt with the admissibility of the application.[22] If the Commission accepted an application, it had to ascertain the facts and attempt to reach a friendly settlement. If a friendly settlement was reached, the Commission had to draw up a report for the States concerned, the Committee of Ministers and the Secretary General of the Council of Europe. If no friendly settlement was reached, the Commission had to report to the Committee of Ministers stating the facts and the Commission's opinion as to whether there had been a breach of the Convention. Within three months of this, either the Commission or any State involved could bring the case before the ECtHR. If a case was not brought before the ECtHR, the Committee of Ministers decided whether or not there had been a violation.

Post-November 1998
After November 1998, the tasks of the Commission and the ECtHR were effectively merged and are now dealt with by the ECtHR. However, in all but exceptional cases, there will still be a separate hearing as to admissibility.

The ECtHR can deal only with references and applications after all adequate and effective domestic remedies have been exhausted[23] and the complaint must be brought within six months of the final domestic decision.[24] The six-month time-limit is strictly enforced.[25] It is for a State raising as an issue a failure to exhaust a domestic remedy to establish that a domestic remedy, which was certain not only in theory but also in practice, was available and accessible to an applicant.[26]

A Member State may refer an alleged breach to the ECtHR, where a chamber of seven judges decides first upon admissibility and then merits.[27]

Applications to the ECtHR by individuals, groups or non-governmental organisations claiming to be victims of a violation by a Member State[28] are

---

21   Articles 19 to 26.
22   The final meeting of the Commission was at the end of October 1999.
23   In the UK, this will of course now include an application under the HRA 1998.
24   Article 35(1) [former Article 26].
25   Usually a letter rather than a telephone call is required: *Rosemary West v UK* (No 347/28/97).
26   *TW v Malta* (2000) 29 EHRR 185.
27   Articles 33, 29(2) [former Article 24].
28   Article 34 [former Article 25(1)].

commenced by sending a letter to the Registrar of the ECtHR[29] who will issue an application form in suitable cases. A committee of three judges, acting unanimously, could then declare the application inadmissible. Failing such a decision, a chamber of seven judges decides first upon admissibility and then merits.[30] Anonymous applications or those which are substantially the same as a matter already examined before the ECtHR or which has already been submitted to another procedure of international investigation or settlement (eg the UN Human Rights Committee) will not be dealt with.[31] Applications can be declared inadmissible at any stage of the proceedings if they are considered incompatible with the provisions of the Convention or Protocols; or manifestly ill-founded; or an abuse of the right of application.[32] If the application is deemed admissible, the ECtHR will examine the case with the representatives of the parties and can conduct an investigation. The ECtHR should place itself at the disposal of the parties for confidential proceedings with a view to securing a friendly settlement which, if secured, is reported by a decision briefly stating the facts and the solution reached.[33] If there is no friendly settlement, the ECtHR will determine whether or not there has been a violation. In exceptional circumstances, the chamber may, with the permission of the parties, relinquish jurisdiction to the grand chamber of 17 judges.[34] The judgment of the grand chamber is final. A chamber's judgment is final unless, within three months from the date of the judgment, a party requests referral to the grand chamber and a panel of five judges of the grand chamber grants leave.[35] In that case, the grand chamber reconsiders the case and gives a final judgment.

A chamber or grand chamber shall include as an *ex officio* member the judge elected in respect of the Member State concerned in the case.[36] Hearings are in public and documents deposited with the ECtHR Registrar are public unless the ECtHR exceptionally decides otherwise.[37] Reasons must be given for all judgments and admissibility decisions[38] and final judgments must be published. Judgments are by majority and dissenting judgments can be delivered[39] but admissibility decisions by committees must be unanimous.

Rules
A new set of rules governing the working and composition of the ECtHR came into force on 1 November 1998.[40]

---

29   The Registrar, European Court of Human Rights, Council of Europe, F-67075 STRASBOURG CEDEX.
30   Article 29(1).
31   Article 35(2) [former Article 27(1)].
32   Articles 34, 28, 29(1) and 35 [former Article 27(2)].
33   Articles 38 and 39 [former Article 28].
34   Article 30. Instances would include serious questions of interpretation or judgments potentially inconsistent with previous judgments.
35   Articles 42, 43 and 44.
36   Article 27(2) [former Article 43].
37   Article 40.
38   Article 45(1) [former Article 51].
39   Article 45(2).
40   http://www.echr.coe.int/Eng/EDocs/RulesOfCourt.html

Remedies

Convention Member States undertake to abide by the final judgment of the ECtHR[41] and if the internal law of a State allows only for partial reparations, the ECtHR can award just satisfaction to an injured party.[42] The assessment of what an applicant is entitled to by way of just satisfaction is conducted according to the case-law of the ECtHR and not of the national courts.[43] Damages awards have not tended to be high. Interest can be awarded and although the ECtHR will not consider itself bound by national law on the calculation of interest,[44] it will usually adopt the rate applicable in the domestic arena. States are required to abide by the decisions of the ECtHR in any case to which they are parties.

Costs

Costs are in the discretion of the ECtHR. The ECtHR will consider whether costs and expenses were actually and necessarily incurred in order to prevent or obtain redress for the violation. The hourly rate and number of hours of legal work must be reasonable.[45] If an application succeeds in establishing violations of some Articles but not others, the ECtHR will take this into account.

1.2.4   Advisory opinions

The Committee of Ministers can request the grand chamber of the ECtHR to give an advisory opinion on questions arising from the Convention, apart from those relating to the content or scope of the rights or freedoms themselves.[46] This mechanism has never been utilised.

1.2.5   Reporting mechanism

The Secretary General of the Council of Europe can require a Member State to explain the manner in which its internal law ensures the effective implementation of the Convention.[47] This has been done at irregular intervals[48] and, in each case, all Member States were asked to respond but there was no official appraisal of the responses.

1.2.6   Victims and violators

The ECtHR may receive applications from any person, non-governmental organisation or group of individuals claiming to be the victim of a violation by one of the High Contracting Parties of the rights set forth in the Convention or the Protocols thereto.[49] Therefore, complaints *in abstracto* are not in general possible and the ECtHR has held that a law must have been applied to the

---

41   Article 46.
42   Article 41 [former Article 50].
43   *Osman v UK* (2000) 29 EHRR 245.
44   *Bladet Tromsø and Stensaas v Norway* (2000) 29 EHRR 125.
45   *Bladet Tromsø and Stensaas v Norway* (2000) 29 EHRR 125.
46   Articles 31(b), 47, 48, 49 [former Protocol 2].
47   Article 52 [former Article 57].
48   1964 (Articles 2 to 14 and Protocol 1), 1972 (Article 5(5)), 1975 (Articles 8 to 11), 1983 (Children in care), 1988 (Articles 6(1) and 6(3)).
49   Article 34 [former Article 25].

detriment of an applicant in order for the applicant to be a victim. However, under certain conditions, for example where the operation of the law in question is carried out in secret, the ECtHR has held that, in order for the Convention to be effective, an individual may legitimately claim to be a victim of a violation caused by the existence of the legislation.[50] Companies, trade unions, professional associations, religious organisations and political parties can qualify as victims in appropriate cases but State institutions cannot. A violator must be the State or an agent of the State. A State is not responsible for the acts of private persons.

1.2.7 Reservations

The Convention permits reservations to be made upon signature or ratification but requires any reservation to State the specific national law and Convention provision in respect of which the reservation has been made. Reservations are generally narrowly interpreted.[51]

1.2.8 Derogation in time of emergency

Article 15 permits a State to take measures derogating from its obligations under the Convention in time of war or other public emergency threatening the life of the nation.[52] No derogation is permitted from Article 2 (except in respect of deaths resulting from lawful acts of war) or Articles 3, 4(1) and 7.

1.3 THE RIGHTS PROTECTED

1.3.1 Article 2 – right to life

'1. Everyone's right to life shall be protected by law. No one shall be deprived of his life intentionally save in the execution of a sentence of a court following his conviction of a crime for which this penalty is provided by law.

2. Deprivation of life shall not be regarded as inflicted in contravention of this Article when it results from the use of force which is no more than absolutely necessary:

(a)   in defence of any person from unlawful violence;
(b)   in order to effect a lawful arrest or to prevent the escape of a person lawfully detained;
(c)   in action lawfully taken for the purpose of quelling a riot or insurrection.'

The right to life is subject to four exceptions:

(1)   capital punishment (which is in any event prohibited in peacetime by the 6th Protocol);

---

50   *Klass v Germany* (1979–80) 2 EHRR 214.
51   Article 57 [former Article 64]. The UK has made a reservation in respect of Article 2 of Protocol 1 (right to education).
52   The UK derogated from Article 5(3) (prompt production of detainees before a judicial power) in the context of the detention of suspected terrorists connected with Northern Ireland. This derogation was made in 1988 following the ECtHR's judgment in *Brogan v UK* (1988) 11 EHRR 117.

(2) the reasonable use of force in self-defence;
(3) in effecting a lawful arrest or preventing the escape of a person lawfully detained; or
(4) in lawful action taken to quell a riot.

There is no definition as to when life is regarded as beginning and the case-law relating to unborn foetuses has not yet satisfactorily settled the issue.

1.3.2   Article 3 – prohibition of torture[53]

'No one shall be subjected to torture or to inhuman or degrading treatment or punishment.'

Prohibition of torture is not qualified, and a State cannot derogate from it. It is conceivable that certain forms of harassment in the workplace could be argued to be degrading treatment or punishment.

1.3.3   Article 4 – prohibition of slavery and forced labour[54]

'1. No one shall be held in slavery or servitude.

2. No one shall be required to perform forced or compulsory labour.

3. For the purpose of this Article the term "forced or compulsory labour" shall not include:

(a) any work required to be done in the ordinary course of detention imposed according to the provisions of Article 5 of this Convention or during conditional release from such detention;
(b) any service of a military character or, in case of conscientious objectors, in countries where they are recognised, service exacted instead of compulsory military service;
(c) any service exacted in case of an emergency or calamity threatening the life or well-being of the community;
(d) any work or service which forms part of normal civic obligations.'

There is very little case-law under Article 4. In *X, Y, Z, V and W v UK*,[55] an unsuccessful application was based on Article 4(1) claiming that the consent by parents to the enlistment in the armed forces of 15- and 16-year-olds amounted to servitude.

A requirement for trainee lawyers (eg pupil barristers) to undertake *pro bono* work has been held to be capable of being within the definition of 'forced or compulsory labour' although, in the case of *Van der Mussele v Belgium*,[56] such an obligation was held not to amount to a breach. There is a very wide exception for 'any work or service which forms part of normal civic obligations'.

Article 4 is based on the International Labour Organisation Convention No 29 concerning forced and compulsory labour. In 1997, the Committee of Experts to the International Labour Organisation (ILO) expressed the view that

---

53   See **3.6**.
54   See **3.7**.
55   Application No 3435–38/67, (1968) 11 YB 562.
56   (1984) 6 EHRR 163.

prisoners in the UK who work in prisons or workshops in public sector-run prisons, the management of which had been contracted out to private companies, were being 'hired to or placed at the disposal of private individuals, companies or associations' in contravention of ILO Convention No 29. The Committee recommended that this practice should cease or that prisoners receive employment rights (including wage levels) comparable with those earned outside prison. The UK government replied that it believed that none of the existing arrangements for prisoners working in contracted out situations contravened Article 2(2)(c) of the Convention and that prison authorities remained responsible for, and in control of, prisoners at all times. The UK government has undertaken to consider this matter further and, in discussion with the ILO and other interested parties, to try to resolve this issue.[57]

1.3.4   Article 5 – right to liberty and security

'1. Everyone has the right to liberty and security of person. No one shall be deprived of his liberty save in the following cases and in accordance with a procedure prescribed by law:

(a)   the lawful detention of a person after conviction by a competent court;

(b)   the lawful arrest or detention of a person for non-compliance with the lawful order of a court or in order to secure the fulfilment of any obligation prescribed by law;

(c)   the lawful arrest or detention of a person effected for the purpose of bringing him before the competent legal authority on reasonable suspicion of having committed an offence or when it is reasonably considered necessary to prevent his committing an offence or fleeing after having done so;

(d)   the detention of a minor by lawful order for the purpose of educational supervision or his lawful detention for the purpose of bringing him before the competent legal authority;

(e)   the lawful detention of persons for the prevention of the spreading of infectious diseases, of persons of unsound mind, alcoholics or drug addicts or vagrants;

(f)   the lawful arrest or detention of a person to prevent his effecting an unauthorised entry into the country or of a person against whom action is being taken with a view to deportation or extradition.

2. Everyone who is arrested shall be informed promptly, in a language which he understands, of the reasons for his arrest and of any charge against him.

3. Everyone arrested or detained in accordance with the provisions of paragraph 1(c) of this Article shall be brought promptly before a judge or other officer authorised by law to exercise judicial power and shall be entitled to trial within a reasonable time or to release pending trial. Release may be conditioned by guarantees to appear for trial.

4. Everyone who is deprived of his liberty by arrest or detention shall be entitled to take proceedings by which the lawfulness of his detention shall be decided speedily by a court and his release ordered if the detention is not lawful.

---

57   Review of Human Rights Instruments (Amended), see http://www.homeoffice.gov.uk/
hract/amrevrhi.htm

5. Everyone who has been the victim of arrest or detention in contravention of the provisions of this Article shall have an enforceable right to compensation.'

It is difficult to see how Article 5 might have an impact in the employment field other than in areas already covered by the UK laws on false imprisonment.

1.3.5   Article 6 – right to a fair trial[58]

'1. In the determination of his civil rights and obligations or of any criminal charge against him, everyone is entitled to a fair and public hearing within a reasonable time by an independent and impartial tribunal established by law. Judgment shall be pronounced publicly but the press and public may be excluded from all or part of the trial in the interests of morals, public order or national security in a democratic society, where the interests of juveniles or the protection of the private life of the parties so require, or to the extent strictly necessary in the opinion of the court in special circumstances where publicity would prejudice the interests of justice.

2. Everyone charged with a criminal offence shall be presumed innocent until proved guilty according to law.

3. Everyone charged with a criminal offence has the following minimum rights:

(a)   to be informed promptly, in a language which he understands and in detail, of the nature and cause of the accusation against him;
(b)   to have adequate time and facilities for the preparation of his defence;
(c)   to defend himself in person or through legal assistance of his own choosing or, if he has not sufficient means to pay for legal assistance, to be given it free when the interests of justice so require;
(d)   to examine or have examined witnesses against him and to obtain the attendance and examination of witnesses on his behalf under the same conditions as witnesses against him;
(e)   to have the free assistance of an interpreter if he cannot understand or speak the language used in court.'

Rights under an employment contract are 'civil rights',[59] as are rights relating to regulatory bodies. Disputes potentially leading to suspension of employment, disbarment or dismissal fall within the definition of 'civil rights'. Disputes potentially leading to disciplinary action falling short of this do not.[60] Disputes relating to the recruitment, careers (including promotion) and termination of service of civil servants or armed forces personnel have been held to be outside the scope of Article 6(1), although where the State can be compared to an employer who was a party to a contract of employment governed by private law and where the claim in issue relates to a purely or essentially economic right such as the payment of a salary or a pension, Article 6(1) may apply.[61]

The right to a court (and particularly to an appeal) may be subject to limitations permitted by implication provided that such limitations pursue a legitimate aim; are reasonable and proportionate to their aim; and do not

58   See **3.8–3.10**.
59   *Darnell v UK* (1991) 69 DR 306; *Obermeier v Austria* (1991) 13 EHRR 290.
60   *X v UK* (1984) 6 EHRR 583.
61   *Lombardo v Italy* (1996) 21 EHRR 188; *Argento v Italy* (1999) 28 EHRR 719; *Maillard v France* (1999) 27 EHRR 232.

impair the very essence of the right.[62] It has been argued that the right to representation and thereby to legal aid falls under this provision.

It has been successfully argued that the strict application of a procedural time-limit of three days was a violation of Article 6(1).[63] This argument could be employed by applicants or respondents denied an opportunity to put their case to an employment tribunal by the strict imposition of time-limits.

The holding of court proceedings in public is a fundamental principle, but the ECtHR has recognised circumstances in which the press and public may be excluded. The ECtHR has held that hearings before professional disciplinary bodies should be in public.[64]

1.3.6 Article 7 – no punishment without law[65]

'1. No one shall be held guilty of any criminal offence on account of any act or omission which did not constitute a criminal offence under national or international law at the time when it was committed. Nor shall a heavier penalty be imposed than the one that was applicable at the time the criminal offence was committed.

2. This Article shall not prejudice the trial and punishment of any person for any act or omission which, at the time when it was committed, was criminal according to the general principles of law recognised by civilised nations.'

Article 7 is restricted to criminal offences.

1.3.7 Article 8 – right to respect for private and family life[66]

'1. Everyone has the right to respect for his private and family life, his home and his correspondence.

2. There shall be no interference by a public authority with the exercise of this right except such as is in accordance with the law and is necessary in a democratic society in the interests of national security, public safety or the economic well-being of the country, for the prevention of disorder or crime, for the protection of health or morals, or for the protection of the rights and freedoms of others.'

Telephone conversations count as correspondence (*Halford v UK*[67]). There is no decision as yet concerning email or closed-circuit television (CCTV) pictures but they must also be expected to be classified as correspondence.

Transsexuals, and those claiming maternity or paternity leave have tried to argue that Article 8 has been violated. The ECtHR has held that the failure by a State to give legal recognition to transsexuals is not a breach of Article 8.[68]

---

62 *Omar v France* (2000) 29 EHRR 210.
63 *Perez de Rada Cavnilles v Spain* (2000) 29 EHRR 109.
64 *Gautrin v France* (1999) 28 EHRR 196.
65 See **3.11**.
66 See **3.12** and Chapter 5.
67 (1997) 24 EHRR 523.
68 *Sheffield and Horsham v UK* (1999) 27 EHRR 163.

Arguably, many potential points are already covered by present UK employment legislation or EC law provisions. It is important to keep in mind that as a
'living instrument' (see **1.5.7** below) the interpretation of the Convention may
be different in future.

The release without permission of sensitive medical information may well
amount to a violation of Article 8. Storing information about individuals for the
purposes of security vetting may also be regarded as a potential breach of
Article 8.

Article 8 has been held to impose positive obligations on States to protect the
right to private life.

1.3.8   Article 9 – freedom of thought, conscience and religion[69]

> '1. Everyone has the right to freedom of thought, conscience and religion; this
> right includes freedom to change his religion or belief and freedom, either alone
> or in community with others and in public or private, to manifest his religion or
> belief, in worship, teaching, practice and observance.
>
> 2. Freedom to manifest one's religion or beliefs shall be subject only to such
> limitations as are prescribed by law and are necessary in a democratic society in the
> interests of public safety, for the protection of public order, health or morals, or for
> the protection of the rights and freedoms of others.'

Religious groups who are not presently covered by the Race Relations Act 1976,
for example Muslims and Rastafarians, may be able to use this Article to their
advantage.

Employees manifesting their beliefs have not fared well under the Convention.[70] Thus far the Commission and the ECtHR have focused on whether an
employment contract seriously restricts the manifestation of beliefs. If the
contract does not do so, a breach has not been found. For example, a
clergyman in *X v Denmark*[71] was unable to establish a breach by his own church
because the Commission held that he had the right to leave the church and
practise his religion elsewhere.

There is a possible conflict with freedom of expression, for example comments
in the workplace which might be seen as mild by one person could seriously
offend another's religious sensibilities, or serving alcohol at a company's
annual general meeting might make some persons uncomfortable about
attending.

1.3.9   Article 10 – freedom of expression[72]

> '1. Everyone has the right to freedom of expression. This right shall include
> freedom to hold opinions and to receive and impart information and ideas without
> interference by public authority and regardless of frontiers. This Article shall not

---

69   See **3.13**.
70   *X v UK* (1979) 16 DR 101; *Ahmad v UK* (1982) 4 EHRR 126.
71   (1976) 5 DR 157.
72   See **3.14**.

prevent States from requiring the licensing of broadcasting, television or cinema enterprises.

2. The exercise of these freedoms, since it carries with it duties and responsibilities, may be subject to such formalities, conditions, restrictions or penalties are prescribed by law and are necessary in a democratic society, in the interests of national security, territorial integrity or public safety, for the prevention of disorder or crime, for the protection of health or morals, for the protection of the reputation or rights of others, for preventing the disclosure of information received in confidence, or for maintaining the authority and impartiality of the judiciary.'

It is important to emphasise that the right to freedom of expression is far from absolute. National governments have been given considerable leeway by the ECtHR in the definition of what is considered obscene or blasphemous and thereby permitted restriction for the protection of public morals.

The dismissal of a teacher for belonging to the communist party was found to be a breach of Articles 10 and 11 in *Vogt v Germany*.[73] However, some restriction on freedom of expression is inherent in the duties of some employees, such as teachers.[74]

Regulations to restrict the political activities of the local government officers in 'politically restricted posts' were held by a majority of 6:3 not to be violations of Articles 10 or 11.[75]

1.3.10   Article 11 – freedom of assembly and association[76]

'1. Everyone has the right to freedom of peaceful assembly and to freedom of association with others, including the right to form and to join trade unions for the protection of his interests.

2. No restrictions shall be placed on the exercise of these rights other than such as are prescribed by law and are necessary in a democratic society in the interests of national security or public safety, for the prevention of disorder or crime, for the protection of health or morals or for the protection of the rights and freedoms of others. This Article shall not prevent the imposition of lawful restrictions on the exercise of these rights by members of the armed forces, of the police or of the administration of the State.'

Article 11 protects the right to join trade unions and other organisations although not public professional bodies such as the Law Society. It encompasses the right not to join a trade union.[77] It does not expressly protect the right of a trade union to consultation or to conduct collective bargaining or industrial action[78] on employees' behalf. However, in order that a union may effectively protect their interests, members of a trade union have been held to have the right that their union be heard.[79]

---

73   (1996) 21 EHRR 205.
74   *Morissens v Belgium* (1988) 56 DR 127.
75   *Ahmed v UK* (2000) 29 EHRR 1.
76   See Chapter 4.
77   *Young, James and Webster v UK* (1982) 4 EHRR 38.
78   *NATFHE v UK* (1998) 25 EHRR CD 122.
79   *National Union of Belgian Police v Belgium* (1979–80) 1 EHRR 578.

Regulations to restrict the political activities of the local government officers in 'politically restricted posts' were held by a majority of 6:3 not to be a violation of Articles 10 or 11.[80]

'Members ... of the administration of the State' does cover government secret communications workers[81] but is likely to be read narrowly and is unlikely to cover all public officials.

1.3.11   Article 12 – right to marry

'Men and women of marriageable age have the right to marry and to found a family, according to the national laws governing the exercise of this right.'

Legal impediments on the marriage of homosexuals or transsexuals have been found not to violate Article 12.[82] However, the Convention is a living instrument and thus it is possible that this position may change in the future.[83]

1.3.12   Article 13 – right to an effective remedy

'Everyone whose rights and freedoms as set forth in this Convention are violated shall have an effective remedy before a national authority notwithstanding that the violation has been committed by persons acting in an official capacity.'

This right is not incorporated by the HRA 1998.

1.3.13   Article 14 – prohibition of discrimination[84]

'The enjoyment of the rights and freedoms set forth in this Convention shall be secured without discrimination on any ground such as sex, race, colour, language, religion, political or other opinion, national or social origin, association with a national minority, property, birth or other status.'

This is not a general 'anti-discrimination' provision. It merely relates to the rights guaranteed in the Convention (although it does not require a breach of one of those rights). Not every difference in treatment will amount to a violation of Article 14. It must be established that other persons in an analogous or relevantly similar situation enjoy preferential treatment and that there is no reasonable or objective justification for this distinction.[85]

1.3.14   Articles 16 to 18 – exceptions and restrictions

Article 16 – restrictions on political activity of aliens

'Nothing in Articles 10, 11 and 14 shall be regarded as preventing the High Contracting Parties from imposing restrictions on the political activity of aliens.'

---

80   *Ahmed v UK* (2000) 29 EHRR 1; but see *Sibson v UK* (1994) 17 EHRR 193.
81   *Council of Civil Service Unions v UK* (1987) 50 DR 228.
82   *Sheffield and Horsham v UK* (1999) 27 EHRR 163.
83   See also **1.5.7**.
84   See Chapter 5.
85   *Sheffield and Horsham v UK* (1999) 27 EHRR 163.

Article 17 – prohibition of abuse of rights

'Nothing in this Convention may be interpreted as implying for any State, group or person any right to engage in any activity or perform any act aimed at the destruction of any of the rights and freedoms set forth herein or at their limitation to a greater extent than is provided for in the Convention.'

Article 18 – limitation of use of restrictions on rights

'The restrictions permitted under this Convention to the said rights and freedoms shall not be applied for any purpose other than those for which they have been prescribed.'

1.3.15   1st Protocol, Article 1 – right to peaceful enjoyment of possessions

'Every natural or legal person is entitled to the peaceful enjoyment of his possessions. No one shall be deprived of his possessions except in the public interest and subject to the conditions provided for by law and by the general principles of international law.

The preceding provisions shall not, however, in any way impair the right of a State to enforce such laws as it deems necessary to control the use of property in accordance with the general interest or to secure the payment of taxes or other contributions or penalties.'

Possessions can include licences and other economic assets and may extend to the right to bring claims against, for example, an employer.

1.3.16   1st Protocol, Article 2 – right to education (UK reservation)

'No person shall be denied the right to education. In the exercise of any functions which it assumes in relation to education and to teaching, the State shall respect the right of parents to ensure such education and teaching in conformity with their own religious and philosophical convictions.'

The UK has entered a reservation to the effect that the right to education is only accepted 'in so far as it is compatible with the provision of efficient instruction and training, and the avoidance of unreasonable public expenditure'.

1.3.17   1st Protocol, Article 3 – free elections[86]

'The High Contracting Parties undertake to hold free elections at reasonable intervals by secret ballot, under conditions which will ensure the free expression of the people in the choice of the legislature.'

Regulations to restrict the political activities of the local government officers in 'politically restricted posts' were unanimously held not to be a violation of Articles 10 or 11.[87]

---

86   *Ahmed v UK* (2000) 29 EHRR 1, re local government officers and political activities.

87   *Ahmed v UK* (2000) 29 EHRR 1.

1.4   LIMITATIONS AND RESTRICTIONS ON HUMAN RIGHTS

1.4.1   The scope of limitations

Some rights are absolute, for example the prohibition of torture or inhuman and degrading punishment, the prohibition of slavery, the right against retroactive criminal offences, the right to life,[88] the right to non-discrimination in the enjoyment of rights, but most rights can be restricted. However, even in a national emergency there can be no derogation from Articles 2, 3, 4(1), and 7. Limitations are best explored in the context of individual rights, although there are some common features.

The only restrictions allowed are those which are expressly permitted by either the general Articles of the Convention or the limitations contained in individual Articles. There are no inherent limitations. Limitations must be engaged in order to achieve a legitimate aim.

1.4.2   In accordance with the law – Articles 2, 5, 6, 8, 9, 10, 11, 12, 1st Protocol, Article 1

The rule of law requires that the legal basis for any limitation on a Convention right must be identifiable. Statutes, statutory instruments, common law, European law or other published rules are bases for restrictions. Such rules must be accessible and not merely consist of internal guidelines nor be interpreted according to unpublished internal guidelines. They must be sufficiently clear that individuals may be reasonably certain of the consequences of their actions.[89]

1.4.3   Necessary in a democratic society – Articles 8, 9, 10, 11

'Necessary' requires the existence of a pressing social need[90] before a proportionate restriction corresponding to that need can be imposed. The reasons put forward by a public authority for a restriction need to be relevant and sufficient.[91] The principle of 'proportionality' is clearly of great importance in this regard.

---

88   With some exceptions on the right to life.
89   *Sunday Times v UK* (1979–80) 2 EHRR 245.
90   *Handyside v UK* (1979–80) 1 EHRR 737.
91   *Sunday Times v UK* (1979–80) 2 EHRR 245.

1.5   INTERPRETATION[92]

1.5.1   Interpretation of the Convention and Convention rights

The interpretation of the Convention itself is a matter for the ECtHR.[93] The interpretation of Convention rights under s 2 of the HRA 1998 is dealt with in full in Chapter 2.

1.5.2   International law

The ECtHR has frequently relied on international law and the practice and procedure of other international tribunals such as the Permanent Court of International Justice and International Court of Justice, particularly when determining points of jurisdiction, evidence or procedure.[94] International law is directly invoked in Articles 7(1), 15(1) 35(1) [former Article 26] and 1st Protocol, Article 1.

1.5.3   Vienna Convention on the Law of Treaties (1969)[95]

The Vienna Convention came into force on 27 January 1980 and, as it does not have retrospective effect, it is not strictly relevant to the interpretation of the Convention. However, the Vienna Convention codifies customary international law principles and the ECtHR has accepted that it states general principles of international law.[96]

1.5.4   Case-law

There is no doctrine of *stare decisis* as such, but the Strasbourg bodies have generally followed their own decisions.[97] ECtHR judgments have greater authority than Commission decisions.

1.5.5   Purposive construction

Article 31(1) of the Vienna Convention states that a treaty should be 'interpreted in good faith in accordance with the ordinary meaning to be given to the terms of the treaty in their context and in the light of its objects and purposes'.

An approach to interpretation of a treaty which seeks to give effect to its objects and purpose is known as 'teleological'. This permits the ECtHR to seek the interpretation most appropriate to the purpose of the Convention rather than restricting the rights contained within it.[98]

---

92   See Bennion, *Statutory Interpretation* 3rd edn (Butterworths, 1997), pp 523–529.
93   Formerly the Commission and ECtHR.
94   For example, *Belgian Linguistics Case*, Series A, No 5 (1979–80) 1 EHRR 241.
95   Treaty Series No 58 (1980); Cmnd 7964.
96   *Golder v UK* (1979–80) 1 EHRR 524.
97   In *Cossey v UK* (1991) 13 EHRR 622, the ECtHR stated that it usually follows and applies its own precedents as long as this remains in line with present day conditions.
98   See *Soering v UK* (1989) 11 EHRR 439 and *Golder v UK* (1979–80) 1 EHRR 524. See also **2.5.4**.

1.5.6   Effectiveness

This principle ensures that a treaty is interpreted in such a way as to ensure that safeguards are not merely illusory. This has lead to the ECtHR finding that States which are parties to the Convention have a responsibility to promote and protect human rights.[99]

1.5.7   Dynamic interpretation of a living instrument and consensus

The Convention is to be interpreted in the light of present day conditions rather than as an historical document.[100] Reference to changing social attitudes (for example, towards transsexuals) over the half-century of the Convention's life have permitted the ECtHR to allow itself to depart from earlier decisions.

1.5.8   Proportionality

The ECtHR, in interpreting the Convention, is concerned with finding a balance between the needs of the individual and the needs of the wider society, particularly when interpreting the extent of the permitted restrictions on rights.[101] Restrictions on human rights must therefore be proportionate to a legitimate aim and procedural fairness is vital to ensure that the rights of individuals affected by a decision are respected.[102] The burden of proof of proportionality is on the State.

1.5.9   The margin of appreciation

In some areas, recognising the differences between States when it comes to issues such as the protection of public morals or national security, the ECtHR has been willing to bow to national authorities which it sees as the best assessors of policy.[103] The margin of appreciation should not be applicable in the same way to cases brought under the HRA 1998 because the ECtHR has been able to avoid, for example, finding violations of the freedom of expression of allegedly blasphemous artists by stating that national moral standards differ too widely to be centrally defined. However, the discretion to be permitted to public authorities will still remain an important issue under the HRA 1998.[104]

1.5.10   Travaux préparatoires

Although the Council of Europe publishes its own Yearbook, as well as Explanatory Reports on the various Protocols to the Convention, these are of limited use given the interpretation of the Convention as a living instrument, but they have been referred to, particularly in the earlier decisions of the ECtHR.

---

99   See *Artico v Italy* (1981) 3 EHRR 1 and *Golder v UK* (1979–80) 1 EHRR 524.
100   See *Cossey v UK* (1990) 13 EHRR 622.
101   See **1.4**.
102   See *Steel v UK* [1999] 28 EHRR 603, ECtHR.
103   *Handyside v UK* (1979–80) 1 EHRR 737.
104   See **2.6.4**.

1.5.11 Autonomous terms

The ECtHR has determined that some terms in the Convention are to be given meanings independent of those they have in national legal systems.

1.5.12 Positive obligations[105]

Article 13, which is not incorporated into the HRA 1998, requires States which are parties to the Convention to ensure the protection of the rights contained within the Convention. This has enabled the ECtHR to explore the need for States to take positive steps to secure rights, for example, to provide public funding for certain cases or have in place a means by which someone could take legal action to secure their human rights.[106]

1.6 THE COMPARATIVE DIMENSION (THE INTERNATIONAL COMMON LAW OF HUMAN RIGHTS)

1.6.1 The importance of comparative systems in human rights

Historically, human rights tribunals have drawn on decisions in parallel jurisdictions to a greater degree than many other tribunals. This is not a foreign concept to English lawyers, who are well used to citing decisions of higher courts in other Commonwealth countries. Human rights are universal and it is to be expected that the treatment of similar circumstances in the courts of France, South Africa or India may aid English judges in their application of the law. Similarly, the ECtHR has made reference to other Council of Europe instruments; the United Nations (UN) human rights system; other regional systems; and national systems. These references have been made to seek clarification of the Convention by looking at earlier instruments which may have inspired the wording of a particular Article; to interpret the Convention narrowly when it is clear that a right contained in another instrument is deliberately not contained in the Convention; and to ensure that a particular interpretation is in line with other human rights obligations.[107] A familiarity with comparative systems is therefore necessary for an understanding of both the Convention and the HRA 1998.

1.6.2 Council of Europe instruments

The European Convention on the Status of Children Born Out of Wedlock, the European Extradition Convention and European Convention on Trans-frontier Television have all been invoked by the ECtHR or the Commission.

(1) European Social Charter
The UK signed the European Social Charter in 1961 and it came into force in 1965. A revised European Social Charter was promulgated in 1996. The UK has

---

105   *X and Y v The Netherlands* (1986) 8 EHRR 235.
106   *X and Y v The Netherlands* (1986) 8 EHRR 235.
107   For example, the *Kosiek* case, Series A, No 105.

never fully accepted a number of its provisions nor incorporated them into national law. Its remit covers economic and social rights, many of which have a direct bearing on employment issues such as the rights:

- to work;[108]
- to just conditions of work;[109]
- to safe and healthy working conditions;[110]
- to fair remuneration;[111]
- to organise;[112]
- to bargain collectively;[113] and
- to vocational training,[114]

for all, including women;[115] the disabled;[116] and migrant workers.[117]

These 'rights', however, are best regarded as declarations of policy aims rather than substantive and enforceable rights in the sense of Convention rights. For example, in *Young, James and Webster*[118] the majority of the ECtHR held that there was no right to work guaranteed under the Convention but it did stress the individual's right to earn a livelihood.[119] However, in the case of *Airey v Ireland*,[120] the ECtHR rejected a submission that the Convention should not be interpreted so as to promote social and economic rights and pointed out that many of the civil and political rights set out in the Convention have social and economic implications.

(2)   *European Convention on the Prevention of Torture and Inhuman or Degrading Treatment or Punishment*[121]

The UK has signed this treaty, which was promulgated in 1987 and has been in force since 1989. It created a committee with powers to investigate, report and make recommendations. Its impact has been preventative rather than reactive.

(3)   *European Commission Against Racism and Intolerance*[122]

This body was set up in 1994 with the tasks of:

- reviewing Member States' legislation, policies and other measures to combat racism, xenophobia, anti-Semitism and intolerance and their effectiveness;

---

108   Article 1.
109   Article 2.
110   Article 3.
111   Article 4.
112   Article 5.
113   Article 6.
114   Article 10.
115   Article 8.
116   Article 15.
117   Article 19.
118   (1982) 4 EHRR 38.
119   See also *X v Denmark* (1976) 5 DR 157 where the Commission denied the right to work protection under the Convention.
120   (1979–80) 2 EHRR 305.
121   http://www.cpt.coe.int/
122   http://www.ecri.coe.int/

–   proposing further action at local, national and European level;
–   formulating general policy recommendations to Member States; and
–   studying international legal instruments applicable in the matter with a
    view to their reinforcement where appropriate.

1.6.3   UN Human Rights System[123]

A clear evolutionary process can be seen when looking at the rights set out in
the Universal Declaration of Human Rights (1948) (UDHR) and those
protected by the Convention (1950) and the International Covenant on Civil
and Political Rights (1966) (ICCPR). The Preamble to the Convention
includes the following:

> 'Considering the Universal Declaration of Human Rights proclaimed by the
> General Assembly of the United Nations on 10th December 1948;
>
> Considering that this Declaration aims at securing the universal and effective
> recognition and observance of the rights therein declared;
>
> . . .
>
> Being resolved, as the governments of European countries which are like-minded
> and have a common heritage of political traditions, ideals, freedom and the rule of
> law, to take the first steps for the collective enforcement of certain of the rights
> stated in the Universal Declaration.'

Therefore, it is clear that the Convention was not designed to give effect to all of
the rights in the UDHR such as the rights to a nationality,[124] to social security,[125]
to work,[126] to rest,[127] to a reasonable standard of living, including food, clothing,
housing and health care,[128] to education,[129] and to participate in the cultural
life of the community.[130]

The ICCPR has been invoked in a number of ECtHR decisions.[131]

The Commission on Human Rights[132] and UN High Commissioner for Human
Rights[133] provide useful supervisory and reporting functions. However, it is the
mechanism set up under the ICCPR which most closely resembles the
Convention system. The ICCPR entered into force in 1976. The UK currently
derogates from Article 9(3) for similar reasons to the derogation from Article
5(3) of the Convention. The UN Human Rights Committee[134] performs a

---

123   http://www.un.org
124   UDHR, Article 15.
125   UDHR, Article 22.
126   UDHR, Article 23.
127   UDHR, Article 24.
128   UDHR, Article 25.
129   UDHR, Article 26.
130   UDHR, Article 27.
131   For example, *Pretto v Italy* (1984) 6 EHRR 182.
132   By means of the procedures under Resolutions 1503 and 1235, rapporteur's reports on
      particular issues and the Sub-Commission on Prevention of Discrimination and the
      Protection of Minorities.
133   http://www.unhchr.ch/
134   See McGoldrick, *The Human Rights Committee* 2nd edn (Oxford, 1994).

parallel function to that of the ECtHR.[135] It is fair to say that the Human Rights Committee has not had the same success as the ECtHR. The provisions for inter-State complaints (Articles 41 and 42) and individual petitions (optional Protocol) are both optional.

The Convention on the Elimination of All Forms of Discrimination Against Women (1979), the International Convention on the Elimination of All Forms of Racial Discrimination (1966), the Convention Against Torture and Other Cruel, Inhuman or Degrading Treatment or Punishment (1984), and the Convention on the Rights of the Child (1989) all contain provisions which may usefully be invoked in Convention cases.

1.6.4   Other international systems

International Labour Organisation (ILO)
The ILO has promulgated a number of international conventions and produces reports and studies on a number of issues affecting the labour market. In *Van der Musselle*,[136] when the ECtHR had to decide upon the meaning of 'forced or compulsory labour' in Article 4 of the Convention, it turned to ILO Convention No 29, which the ECtHR found to be the inspiration for Article 4.

1.6.5   Other regional systems

(1)   The American Convention on Human Rights
The American Convention on Human Rights (1969) came into force in 1978 under the umbrella of the Organisation of American States. A Commission[137] pre-dates the American Convention, which set up the Inter American Court[138] which was inaugurated in 1979. The American Convention on Human Rights was developed from the American Declaration of the Rights and Duties of Man (1948).

In *X v UK*[139] the Commission invoked the assistance of Article 2 of the American Convention on Human Rights in interpreting Article 2 of the Convention.

(2)   The African Charter on Human and Peoples' Rights
The African Charter on Human and Peoples' Rights (1981) was promulgated by the Organisation of African Unity and entered into force in 1986. While it does not provide the same enforcement mechanisms as the European and American Conventions, it does provide for the establishment of a Commission.

---

135   See Markus G Schmidt 'The Complementarity of the Covenant and the Convention – Recent Developments' in David Harris and Sarah Joseph, *The ICCPR and UK Law* (Clarendon Press, 1995), ch 19.
136   (1984) 6 EHRR 163.
137   http://www.cidh.oas.org/
138   http://corteidh-oea.nu.or.cr/ci/HOME_ING.HTM
139   (1982) 4 EHRR 188.

(3)   The Conference on Security and Co-operation in Europe (CSCE) Process

The Helsinki Final Act of 1975 concluded the Conference on Security and Co-operation in Europe. While not a treaty, it does contain political undertakings and subsequent follow-up conferences have developed diplomatic monitoring procedures and an institutional structure.

1.6.6   Municipal constitutional protection of fundamental rights

Council of Europe members
The Convention has been incorporated into the national legal systems of many Council of Europe members. National constitutions from many countries can be found at http://www.uni-wuerzburg.de/law/.

Commonwealth
The constitutional protection of human rights in many Commonwealth countries is based on the Convention. The *Commonwealth Law Reports* (Constitutional Volume) contains reports of major decisions on such issues. The various Supreme Court and Privy Council decisions reported provide an excellent indication of the way in which a common law jurisdiction will deal with human rights issues.

1.7   THE CONVENTION AND THE LAW OF ENGLAND AND WALES – PAST, PRESENT AND FUTURE

The Convention was largely ignored in the domestic courts until the mid-1970s. Customary international law (but not treaty-based law) is recognised by the domestic courts as an evolving part of the common law without the need for transforming legislation.[140] Many of the principles contained within the Convention may be part of customary international law. However, it is sometimes difficult to show the details of a particular provision of customary international law. A statute passed after the signature of a treaty and dealing with the subject matter of the treaty is construed, if reasonably capable of bearing such a meaning, as consistent with the treaty.[141] However, in English law, a clearly contradictory domestic statute will supersede customary international law, as is usual with common law provisions. In a number of domestic cases over the last two decades the courts have asserted that the Convention contains principles which are already part of the common law.[142]

---

140   *Trendtex v Central Bank of Nigeria* [1977] QB 529; see also *Standard Chartered Bank v International Tin Council* [1987] 1 WLR 641.

141   Lord Diplock in *Garland v British Rail Engineering Ltd* [1983] 2 AC 751.

142   For an excellent full treatment of this topic, see Murray Hunt, *Using Human Rights Law in English Courts* (Hart Publishing, 1998).

1.8   EC LAW

The European Union and the Council of Europe are distinct bodies and the institutions of the EU are not members of the Council of Europe.[143] Article F(2) of the Maastricht Treaty explicitly recognises the Convention.[144]

---

143   ECJ Opinion 2/94 [1996] ECR 1-1759.
144   *Maurissen v Court of Auditors of the European Communities* [1989] ECR 1045, *P v S and Cornwall CC* [1996] ECR I-2143 – particularly AG Tesauro's Opinion.

Chapter 2

THE HUMAN RIGHTS ACT 1998

2.1 THE ACT AND ITS CONTEXT

The Long Title of the HRA 1998 states that it is to give further effect to rights and freedoms guaranteed under the Convention. Before the HRA 1998, the Convention could be considered to resolve ambiguity in a subsequent statute affecting Convention rights[1] and to resolve uncertainties in the common law.[2] The Convention is also of assistance in determining public policy.[3] The Convention would also result in closer scrutiny of discretionary decisions, applying *Wednesbury* principles.[4] Of course, where a provision is passed to align UK law with the Convention, the courts will refer to the Convention in relation to the exercise of any discretion in the provision.[5] However, the Convention could not be used where the domestic law is clear.[6] The position after the HRA 1998 is that the Convention cannot be used where the UK law is clearly intended to be incompatible with the Convention.

The HRA 1998 received Royal Assent on 9 November 1998 and was brought fully into force on 2 October 2000. From that date, rights and freedoms guaranteed under the Convention are available in domestic law. This means that the rights given under the Convention may be relied upon directly in the domestic courts. Employment tribunals will have to construe legislation in a way that is compatible with the Convention rights. Note that by s 7(8) of the HRA 1998 nothing in the Act creates a criminal offence. The HRA 1998 binds the Crown and extends to Northern Ireland.[7]

There will be changes in the form of all legislation as a result of the HRA 1998. By s 19, a Minister of the Crown in charge of a Bill in either House of Parliament must, before the Second Reading of the Bill:

(a) make a statement to the effect that in his or her view the provisions of the Bill are compatible with the Convention rights ('a statement of compatibility'); or

(b) make a statement to the effect that although he or she is unable to make a statement of compatibility, the Government nevertheless wishes the House to proceed with the Bill.

1   *R v Secretary of State for the Home Department, ex parte Brind* [1991] 1 AC 696.
2   *AG v Guardian Newspapers Ltd (No 2)* [1990] 1 AC 109 at p 283 and *Derbyshire CC v Times Newspapers Ltd* [1992] QB 770, aff'd [1993] AC 534.
3   *Blathwayt v Cawley* [1976] AC 397.
4   *R v Ministry of Defence, ex parte Smith* [1996] QB 517, CA, *per* Sir Thomas Bingham MR at p 554.
5   *R v Secretary of State for the Home Department, ex parte Norney* (1995) 7 Admin LR 861.
6   See *R v Staines* [1997] 2 Cr App R 426.
7   HRA 1998, s 22(5) and (6).

The statement must be in writing and be published in such manner as the Minister making it considers appropriate. The form of a statement of compatibility is set out in paragraph 3 of Annexe A to the Guidance for Departments issued to civil servants. The statement will take the form:

> 'In my view the provisions of the ... Bill are compatible with the Convention rights.'

Or:

> 'I am unable to make a statement that in my view the provisions of the ... Bill are compatible with the Convention rights but the Government nevertheless wishes the House to proceed with the Bill.'

2.2   THE INTERPRETATION OF THE HUMAN RIGHTS ACT 1998

A constitutional instrument, such as the HRA 1998, calls for its own principles of interpretation, suitable to its character, so that it is not necessarily appropriate to use all the presumptions that are relevant in private law.[8] The White Paper stated that the HRA 1998 was to be part of a comprehensive programme of constitutional reform. In *Matadeen v Pointu*,[9] the Privy Council stated that the context of a constitution is an attempt:

> 'at a particular moment in history to lay down an enduring scheme of government in accordance with certain moral and political values. Interpretation must take these purposes into account.'[10]

The case of *Fisher* illustrates these principles at work. Section 11 of the Constitution of Bermuda provides:

> '(5) For the purposes of this section, a person shall be deemed to belong to Bermuda if that person – (*a*) possesses Bermudian status – [...] (*c*) is the wife of a person to whom either of the foregoing paragraphs of this subsection applies not living apart from such person [...]; or (*d*) is under the age of 18 years and is the child, stepchild or child adopted in a manner recognised by law of a person to whom any of the foregoing paragraphs of this subsection applies.'

The individual in that case was the Jamaican mother of four illegitimate children all born in Jamaica. She had married a Bermudian in 1972 and the mother and children started residing with the husband in Bermuda in 1975. In 1976 the Minister of Labour and Immigration ordered the children to leave Bermuda. She and her husband sought to quash the order and sought a declaration that the children were to be deemed to belong to Bermuda. The Ministry of Home Affairs appealed to the Privy Council from the Bermuda appeal court against the declaration that the children were so deemed.

The State had argued that ordinary principles of statutory interpretation did not permit the illegitimate children to be deemed to belong. However, the

---

8   *Ministry of Home Affairs v Fisher* [1980] AC 319 at p 329C–E.
9   [1998] 3 WLR 18.
10   [1998] 3 WLR 18 at p 25.

Privy Council expressed the opinion that a constitutional instrument should not necessarily be construed in the manner and according to the rules which applied to Acts of Parliament. This removed the requirement that the presumption that 'child' meant 'legitimate child', applicable to statutes concerning property, succession and citizenship, applied.

The Privy Council further gave the opinion that although the manner of interpretation of a constitutional instrument should give effect to the language used, recognition should also be given to the character and origins of the instrument. In particular, it was relevant in that case that section 11 of the Constitution was one of the sections dealing with the fundamental rights and freedoms of an individual. Section 11(5)(d) was a clear recognition, in that context, of the unity of the family as a group and acceptance that children should not be separated from a group which belonged to Bermuda. Accordingly, 'child' was not to be restricted in its meaning.

The Privy Council stated:

'So far the discussion has been related to Acts of Parliament concerned with specific subjects. Here, however, we are concerned with a Constitution, brought into force certainly by Act of Parliament, the Bermuda Constitution Act 1967 UK, but established by a self-contained document set out in Schedule 2 to the Bermuda Constitution Order 1968 (UK S.I. 1968 No 182). It can be seen that this instrument has certain special characteristics. 1. It is, particularly in Chapter I, drafted in a broad and ample style which lays down principles of width and generality. 2. Chapter I is headed "Protection of Fundamental Rights and Freedoms of the Individual." It is known that this chapter, as similar portions of other constitutional instruments drafted in the post-colonial period, starting with the Constitution of Nigeria, and including the Constitutions of most Caribbean territories, was greatly influenced by the European Convention for the Protection of Human Rights and Fundamental Freedoms (1953) (Cmd. 8969). That Convention was signed and ratified by the UK and applied to dependent territories including Bermuda. It was in turn influenced by the United Nations' Universal Declaration of Human Rights of 1948. These antecedents, and the form of Chapter itself, call for a generous interpretation avoiding what has been called "the austerity of tabulated legalism," suitable to give to individuals the full measure of the fundamental rights and freedoms referred to. 3. Section 11 of the Constitution forms part of Chapter I. It is thus to "have effect for the purpose of affording protection to the aforesaid rights and freedoms" subject only to such limitations contained in it "being limitations designed to ensure that the enjoyment of the said rights and freedoms by any individual does not prejudice ... the public interest."

When therefore it becomes necessary to interpret "the subsequent provisions of" Chapter I – in this case section 11 – the question must inevitably be asked whether the appellants' premise, fundamental to their argument, that these provisions are to be construed in the manner and according to the rules which apply to Acts of Parliament, is sound. In their Lordships' view there are two possible answers to this. The first would be to say that, recognising the status of the Constitution as, in effect, an Act of Parliament, there is room for interpreting it with less rigidity, and greater generosity, than other Acts, such as those which are concerned with property, or succession, or citizenship. On the particular question this would require the court to accept as a starting point the general presumption that "child" means "legitimate child" but to recognise that this presumption may be more easily displaced. The second would be more radical: it would be to treat a constitutional instrument such as this as sui generis, calling for principles of interpretation of its own, suitable to its character as already described, without necessary acceptance of all the presumptions that are relevant to legislation of private law.

It is possible that, as regards the question now for decision, either method would lead to the same result. But their Lordships prefer the second. This is in no way to say that there are no rules of law which should apply to the interpretation of a Constitution. A Constitution is a legal instrument giving rise, amongst other things, to individual rights capable of enforcement in a court of law. Respect must be paid to the language which has been used and to the traditions and usages which have given meaning to that language. It is quite consistent with this, and with the recognition that rules of interpretation may apply, to take as a point of departure for the process of interpretation a recognition of the character and origin of the instrument, and to be guided by the principle of giving full recognition and effect to those fundamental rights and freedoms with a statement of which the Constitution commences. In their Lordships' opinion this must mean approaching the question what is meant by "child" with an open mind. Prima facie, the stated rights and freedoms are those of "every person in Bermuda." This generality underlies the whole of Chapter I which, by contrast with the Bermuda Immigration and Protection Act 1956, contains no reference to legitimacy, or illegitimacy, anywhere in its provisions. When one is considering the permissible limitations upon those rights in the public interest, the right question to ask is whether there is any reason to suppose that in this context, exceptionally, matters of birth, in the particular society of which Bermuda consists, are regarded as relevant.'

The provisions of the HRA 1998, and in particular the Convention rights in Sch 1, are similarly drafted in a broad and ample style which reflects principles of width and generality. The intention of the HRA 1998 was to give further effect to rights under the Convention. These factors call for the generous interpretation suitable to achieve the full measure of the fundamental rights and freedoms referred to in the Act.

2.3   CONVENTION RIGHTS UNDER THE HUMAN RIGHTS ACT 1998

Section 1 defines the rights which are dealt with under the HRA 1998. They are not all of the rights under the Convention. In particular, the right to an effective judicial remedy (Article 13) is not included. 'The Convention Rights' means the rights and fundamental freedoms set out in:

(a) Articles 2 to 12 and 14 of the Convention;
(b) Articles 1 to 3 of the 1st Protocol; and
(c) Articles 1 and 2 of the 6th Protocol,

as read with Articles 16 to 18 of the Convention. Those Articles are to have effect for the purposes of the HRA 1998 subject to any designated derogation or reservation.

The Articles are set out in Sch 1 to the HRA 1998. The Secretary of State may by order make such amendments to the HRA 1998 as he considers appropriate to reflect the effect, in relation to the UK, of a Protocol. Amendment includes repeal.[11] The Secretary of State's power to amend under s 1(4) is therefore subject to scrutiny by the courts on judicial review of the statutory instrument used for the order, on the basis that the instrument does not accord with the purpose (to reflect the effect of a Protocol) for which the power is given to the Secretary of State.[12]

In s 1(4) 'protocol' means a Protocol to the Convention:

(a) which the UK has ratified; or
(b) which the UK has signed with a view to ratification.

Amendments under s 1(4) may be made only once the Protocol concerned is in force in relation to the UK under the Convention. This includes the repeal of a provision.[13]

2.4 DEROGATIONS AND RESERVATIONS

Section 14 of the HRA 1998 deals with derogations. It makes provision for what is referred to as a 'designated derogation'. This means:

(a) the UK's derogation from Article 5(3) of the Convention in relation to certain provisions of the Prevention of Terrorism Acts in respect of Northern Ireland; and
(b) any derogation by the UK from an Article of the Convention, or of any Protocol to the Convention, which is designated for the purposes of the HRA 1998 in an order made by the Secretary of State.

By s 14(3), if a designated derogation is amended or replaced it ceases to be a designated derogation. However, this does not prevent the Secretary of State from exercising the power under subs (1)(b) to make a fresh designation order in respect of the Article concerned. The Secretary of State is required to make such amendments (including by repeal) by order of Sch 3 to the HRA 1998, which currently contains the derogation from Article 5(3), as the Secretary of State considers appropriate to reflect:

(a) any designation order; or
(b) the effect of subs (3), namely that a designated derogation has been amended and therefore ceased to be a designated derogation.

Under s 14, the order may be made in anticipation of the making by the UK of a proposed derogation.

Section 15 of the HRA 1998 makes provision for reservations by means of the same device. A 'designated reservation' means:

---

11   HRA 1998, s 21.
12   *R v Tower Hamlets LBC, ex parte Chetnik Developments Limited* [1988] 2 WLR 654.
13   HRA 1998, s 21.

(a) the UK's reservation to Article 2 of the 1st Protocol to the Convention which accepted the principle in Article 2 (the right to education) only so far as it is compatible with the provision of efficient instruction and training and the avoidance of unreasonable public expenditure; and

(b) any other reservation by the UK to an Article of the Convention, or of any Protocol to the Convention, which is designated for the purposes of the HRA 1998 in an order made by the Secretary of State.

If a designated reservation is withdrawn wholly or in part it ceases to be a designated reservation and the same process must be gone through as with designated derogations.[14]

Section 16 of the HRA 1998 provides that if it has not already been withdrawn by the UK, a designated derogation ceases to have effect for the purposes of the HRA 1998:

(a) in the case of the derogation from Article 5(2) of the Convention, at the end of the period of five years beginning with the date on which s 1(2) came into force;

(b) in the case of any other derogation, at the end of the period of five years beginning with the date on which the order designating it was made.

However, the Secretary of State may at any time before the end of the currency of the derogation from Article 5(2) or an extension of that derogation by order extend it by a further period of five years.[15] Other designated derogations cease to have effect at the end of the period for consideration, unless a resolution has been passed by each House approving the order.[16] However, this does not affect:

(a) anything done in reliance on the order; or

(b) the power to make a fresh order under s 14(1)(b).

The 'period for consideration' means the period of 40 days beginning with the day on which the order was made and in calculating it no account is to be taken of any time during which:

(a) Parliament is dissolved or prorogued; or

(b) both Houses are adjourned for more than four days.

By s 16(7), if a designated derogation is withdrawn by the UK, the Secretary of State must by order make such amendments to the HRA 1998 as the Secretary of State considers are required to reflect that withdrawal. This power to amend includes a power of repeal.[17]

Section 17 of the HRA 1998 makes similar provision for periodic review of designated reservations. The Minister must review the designated reservation to the right to education before the end of the period of five years beginning with the date on which s 1(2) comes into force and if that designation is still in

---

14   See s 15(3)–(5) of HRA 1998.
15   HRA 1998, s 16(2).
16   HRA 1998, s 16(3).
17   HRA 1998, s 21.

force, before the end of the period of five years beginning with the date on which the last report relating to it was laid before Parliament. The Minister must review each of the other designated reservations (if any are made) before the end of the period of five years beginning with the date on which the order designating the reservation first came into force, and if the designation is still in force, before the end of the period of five years beginning with the date on which the last report relating to it was laid before Parliament. Section 17(3) requires the Minister conducting a review under s 17 to prepare a report on the result of the review and lay a copy of it before each House of Parliament.

2.5 INTERPRETATION OF CONVENTION RIGHTS

2.5.1 Decisions and opinions to be taken into account

By s 2(1) of the HRA 1998, a court or tribunal determining a question which has arisen in connection with a Convention right must take into account any:

(a) judgment, decision, declaration or advisory opinion of the ECtHR;
(b) opinion of the Commission given in a report adopted under Article 31 of the Convention;
(c) decision of the Commission in connection with Article 26 or 27(2) of the Convention; or
(d) decision of the Committee of Ministers taken under Article 46 of the Convention,

whenever made or given, so far as, in the opinion of the court or tribunal, it is relevant to the proceedings in which that question has arisen.

Rules are to provide for the manner in which evidence of any judgment, decision, declaration or opinion of which account may have to be taken is to be given in proceedings before any court or tribunal.[18] As the employment tribunals may determine what evidence may be admitted and are not bound by the rules of evidence, the current rules for admission of evidence before them do not strictly need to be amended.

2.5.2 Citation of authorities

The Lord Chancellor's Department Consultation Paper, *Human Rights Act 1998: Rules and Practice Directions,* March 2000 (the 'LCD Consultation Paper') proposed that, in the light of the provisions of s 2(2) of the HRA 1998, rules are not essential and that it would be more appropriate to specify what can be cited as Strasbourg jurisprudence by less formal means such as Practice Directions or guidance. Thus when new law reports are produced, they can be quickly added to the list of permitted citation sources. Courts governed by the Civil Procedure Rules 1998 (CPR 1998) have had the first Practice Direction to Part 39 (hearings) amended to provide for the procedure where a party intends to cite a Strasbourg authority at a hearing. The amendments at para 8 of the Practice

---

18   HRA 1998, s 2(2).

Direction provide that a party must give to the court and any other party a list of the Strasbourg authorities he or she intends to cite and copies of the reports or other sources from which they are to be cited not more than seven days nor less than three days before the hearing. Permission is required to cite from any source other than one of the authorities listed below.

–   Copies of the complete original texts issued by the ECtHR and the Commission, either paper based or from the ECtHR's judgment database (HUDOC), which is available on the Internet.

–   Judgments of the ECtHR (published by Carl Heymanns Verlag KG).

–   Reports, Judgments and Decisions of the ECtHR (published by Carl Heymanns Verlag KG).

–   Decisions of the European Commission of Human Rights (published by Carl Heymanns Verlag KG).

–   Decisions and Reports of the European Commission of Human Rights, volumes 1– 96 (published by Carl Heymanns Verlag KG).

–   European Human Rights Reports (EHRR) (published by Sweet & Maxwell).

–   Human Rights Cases (published by Butterworths).

–   Full texts of Strasbourg authorities taken from the following electronic databases:
    –   Case Law Service (published by Lawtel);
    –   Eurolaw (published by ILI);
    –   JUSTIS (published by Context Electronic Publishers);
    –   Lexis-Nexis; and
    –   Westlaw UK.

Employment tribunals are governed by rules allowing them to regulate their own proceedings. Informal guidance will probably be issued by the tribunals in due course, but it is likely that the sources mentioned above will be acceptable. Practitioners will find UKHRR (Jordans) useful also.

2.5.3   Tools for interpretation

Section 3 of the HRA 1998 requires that, so far as it is possible to do so, primary legislation and subordinate legislation must be read and given effect in a way that is compatible with the Convention rights.[19]

Therefore:

(1) this effectively requires consideration of the construction of any piece of legislation, whenever passed, in the light of the Convention rights; and
(2) so far as it is possible to do so, primary and secondary legislation and subordinate legislation must be given effect to in a way that is compatible with the Convention rights.

---

19   HRA 1998, s 3(1).

Describing the contents of the Convention rights requires practitioners to adopt tools of interpretation that are similar to, but not the same as, those used to interpret EC law.

The requirement that the courts and tribunals must 'read' legislation 'so far as it is possible to do so' in a way that is compatible with Convention rights may have two meanings. The first meaning is that of a literal construction. If the language of the statute is not ambiguous, in the sense of being capable of having two different meanings, it cannot be read in a way that is incompatible with the Convention rights. However, this is not the sense used in the HRA 1998 of 'read' as the term occurs in the context of 'read and given effect'. Thus, the intention is that even where there is no ambiguity in the language used in a statute, it will still be possible to read the legislation so as to be compatible with the Convention rights unless there is a clearly stated indication that a limitation on Convention rights exists in the legislation intended to render the legislation incompatible with the Convention rights. The approach must therefore be:

(1) to see the term being interpreted in the context of the whole legislation of which it forms part; and
(2) to have regard to the purposes of the legislation, and the consequences of the interpretations suggested to the tribunal; and
(3) if the consequence of an interpretation is incompatible with Convention rights, the court must reject that interpretation unless there is such a clear indication that it was the intention of Parliament to legislate incompatibly with the Convention.

Note that the intention behind the legislation was not that courts and tribunals should look only for reasonable interpretations. They are to look at possible interpretations.[20] The White Paper stated the purpose:

'The courts will be required to interpret legislation so as to uphold the Convention rights unless legislation itself is so clearly incompatible with Convention rights that it is impossible to do so'.[21]

Thus it should be possible, using the new interpretive technique, to interpolate words into a statute if necessary in order to render the legislation compatible with Convention rights. The only exception to this rule is where the legislation is clearly intended not to be compatible. Employment lawyers will be familiar with this device in the context of legislation that is implementing European legislation. In *Litster v Forth Dry Dock and Engineering Co Ltd*,[22] the House of Lords interpolated words into an unambiguous provision of secondary legislation, the Transfer of Undertakings (Protection of Employment) Regulations 1981,[23] in order to render them compatible with the purpose of the European Directive which they implement.

If anything, this device may be more far-reaching than the similar interpretive device used in employment cases. The HRA 1998 permits unambiguous

20   See HC Debs, 21 October 1998, cols 421–422, rejecting such an amendment.
21   Paragraph 2.7.
22   [1990] 1 AC 546.
23   SI 1981/1794.

primary legislation to be read and given effect so as to be compatible with Convention rights by the interpolation of words. In the context of EC law this has been rejected as an approach. In *Duke v GEC Reliance*,[24] the House of Lords held that s 2(4) of the European Communities Act 1972 did not empower or oblige a British court to distort the meaning of a British statute in order to enforce against an individual a Community Directive which had no direct effect between individuals. Section 3 of the HRA 1998 reaches further and will require such distortion if it is necessary to give effect to the Convention rights, absent a clear contrary intention in the legislation.

Unlike the requirements of EC law, which apply only when the piece of legislation is implementing EC law, the HRA 1998 applies to all legislation, past and future.

If the meaning of s 3 is ambiguous, there are many Hansard references that may be relied upon in support of the Government's intention in introducing the section.[25]

2.5.4   Teleological interpretation

In addition to the existing canons of interpretation, practitioners will have to be more fully aware of international interpretative tools when considering how a piece of employment legislation is to be interpreted so as to render it compatible with the Convention under s 3. The Vienna Convention on the Law of Treaties, Article 31, requires that the Convention be interpreted:

> 'in good faith in accordance with the ordinary meaning to be given to the terms of the treaty in their context and in the light of its object and purpose.'

Thus, as with EC law, a teleological approach to construction is of prime importance. The effect of this is that Convention rights are not to be construed narrowly. In considering the role of the teleological interpretation of the Convention rights, the most appropriate interpretation will be that which realises the aim and achieves the object of the treaty.[26]

A good example of this approach is the treatment of the conflict between freedom of expression and racist statements.[27]

The object and purpose of the Convention is as an instrument for the protection primarily of individual human beings. This requires that its provisions be interpreted so as to make its safeguards practical and effective.[28] The effect of this adherence is that, where a right has a derogation from it, that derogation must be considered narrowly and from the point of view of the extent to which it removes practical effectiveness from the Convention right as a means of protecting the individual's rights.

---

24   [1988] ICR 339.
25   HC Debs, 3 June 1998, cols 421–442; HL Debs, 18 November 1997, col 535, for example.
26   *Wemhoff v Germany* (1968) Series A, No 7, 1 EHRR 55, para 8.
27   See **3.14.11**.
28   *Loizidou v Turkey* (1995) Series A, No 310; 20 EHRR 99, para 72.

The objects set out in the Preamble are:

- the maintenance of human rights; and
- the further realisation of human rights.

These have been interpreted as including:

- the protection of human rights;[29]
- promoting and maintaining the ideas and values of a democratic society;[30]
- the rule of law.[31]

Rights have been implied into the Convention such as that of the right of access to a court as part of the guarantee of a fair trial under Article 6(1).[32] The ECtHR has stated that the ideas and values of a democratic society are in essence pluralism, tolerance and broadmindedness.[33] Democracy does not require that the views of the majority prevail. A balance must be achieved which ensures the fair and proper treatment of minorities and that avoids any abuse of a dominant position.[34]

2.5.5 Uniformity of terms

Terms under the Convention have to be construed in such a way as to secure uniform application across signatory States, independent of particular legal systems. Thus care must be taken not to transpose the UK meaning of a term to the same term in the Convention if there is evidence that the term has another meaning in other jurisdictions. Such evidence will usually emerge from consideration of the case-law of the ECtHR. It may be that practitioners will be able to adduce evidence of other countries' use of the terms in areas when arguing that the 'living' nature of the Convention requires a fresh scope to be given to the rights involved or when arguing that the meaning of the term in question has a more restricted meaning than that contended by the other party. Such evidence of foreign law would take the form of an expert report. Courts in the UK will be tempted to give the terms of the Convention an independent meaning relative to precedents solely from the UK. Such an approach would be inconsistent with this principle of construction.

Another feature of Convention law is the 'margin of appreciation'. The recognition that terms in the Convention need to have a uniform meaning should not be confused with the doctrine that because different countries have differences in constitutional history, there is an area of discretion left to the State with which the Strasbourg authorities will not interfere. That doctrine has little place in the Convention as incorporated by the HRA 1998. Although the margin of appreciation does not apply, the Convention meaning of a term can be derived from a consideration of previous Strasbourg case-law, or, when

---

29   *Soering v UK* (1989) Series A, No 161; 11 EHRR 439.
30   *Kjeldson v Denmark* (1979–80) 1 EHRR 711.
31   *Golder v UK* (1979–80) 1 EHRR 524.
32   *Golder v UK* (1979–80) 1 EHRR 524.
33   *Handyside v UK* (1979–80) 1 EHRR 737.
34   *Young, James and Webster v UK* (1982) 4 EHRR 38.

arguing that a term of the Convention applies to a new situation, the application of that term of the Convention in other signatory States.

2.5.6   Living instrument

Whilst in the interpretation of EC law reference to the *travaux préparatoires* (see **1.5.10**) will be helpful, such an approach may be misleading in ECtHR law as there is no static construction of the Convention. It must be seen as a 'living instrument which must be interpreted in the light of present-day conditions'. It 'cannot be interpreted solely in accordance with the intentions of [the Convention's] authors as expressed more than 40 years ago'.[35] This means that there is scope, albeit restricted, for development of arguments based on changing social conditions in the UK.

2.5.7   Ensuring effectiveness

One principle that arises out of the teleological approach is that any interpretation placed on the rights must be such as to ensure that the safeguards are 'practical and effective' and not 'theoretical and illusory'.[36] This also gives the court the duty to raise Convention issues even when the parties do not. The principle is the source of the breadth of the concepts of State responsibility and positive obligations.

2.6   DETERMINING THE CONTENT OF A CONVENTION RIGHT

2.6.1   Identifying whether a right has been interfered with

In determining the content of a Convention right, the practitioner should consider:

(1) whether there has been an interference with a right, with regard to the need to construe the Convention broadly in order to give it practical effectiveness (*prima facie*, any interference is unlawful); and
(2) whether the interference is justified by reference to a restriction.

Some rights contain express restrictions (Articles 8(2), 9(2), 10(2) and 11(2)). Such restrictions are strictly and narrowly construed. These are of the same nature, although the interpretation varies slightly between these Articles. There are also express restrictions contained in Article 5(1)(a)–(f) (right to liberty), Article 12 (right to marry), and Article 1 of the 1st Protocol (right to property).

Rights which do not have express restrictions on their face may have implied restrictions. The right to a fair trial contains an implied restriction (Article

---

35   *Loizidou v Turkey* (1995) 20 EHRR 99 at para 71.
36   *Artico v Italy* (1981) 3 EHRR 1.

6(1)), the right to education is also impliedly restricted (Article 2 of the 1st Protocol) as are the rights concerning elections in Article 3 of the 1st Protocol.

Article 16 permits the restriction of political activity by aliens. Any acts aimed at the destruction of Convention rights may be restricted (Article 17). Finally, there are those restrictions contained in a valid derogation.

To be justified, any *prima facie* infringement of human rights must:

(1) be lawful;
(2) be intended to pursue a legitimate purpose;
(3) be 'necessary in a democratic society'; and
(4) not be discriminatory.

2.6.2 'Lawful' or 'prescribed by law'

'Lawful' involves more than formal authorisation. The law must indicate the scope of any such discretion conferred on the competent authorities and the manner of its exercise with sufficient clarity, having regard to the legitimate aim of the measure in question, to give the individual adequate protection against arbitrary interference.[37] Professional bodies' rules, where validly made, may also provide a lawful basis.[38]

To be a legal basis the rule must be published in a form accessible to those likely to be affected by it (see eg *Malone*),[39] although the services of a lawyer may be necessary for access.[40] The criteria for interpretation of a published rule must themselves be published.

To be a legal basis the rule must be certain. The circumstances in which it applies must be reasonably clear so that the application of the rule has a reasonable degree of foreseeability (see eg *Sunday Times*[41] and *Hashman v UK*[42]). Where the law contains a discretion, its limits must be clear and the instructions/practices by which it is administered must be public.[43] Plurality of construction of legislative provision does not in itself result in uncertainty of an undermining degree.[44] However, it is a matter of degree.[45] Development of the common law does not offend this principle provided that the development was reasonably foreseeable.[46] The degree of flexibility permitted will depend on the nature of the right involved and there is no requirement that the subject is notified that the particular law will be aimed at him or her personally.[47]

---

37 *Malone v UK* (1985) 7 EHRR 14, para 68 and see *Padfield v Minister of Agriculture, Fisheries and Food* [1968] AC 997 for the UK administrative law position.
38 *Barthold v Germany* (1985) 7 EHRR 383.
39 *Malone v UK* (1985) 7 EHRR 14.
40 *Sunday Times v UK* (1979–80) 2 EHRR 245.
41 *Sunday Times v UK* (1979–80) 2 EHRR 245.
42 [1999] EHRLR 342.
43 *Silver v UK* (1983) 5 EHRR 347.
44 *Castells v Spain* (1992) 14 EHRR 445.
45 *Rekvenyi v Hungary* (2000) 30 EHRR 519.
46 *S W v UK* (1996) 21 EHRR 363.
47 *Huvig v France* (1990) 12 EHRR 528.

2.6.3   Legitimate objective

The purpose of the State must be sought in good faith and without ulterior motives.

Legitimate objectives have included:

- strengthening international co-operation;[48]
- political neutrality of the police force;[49]
- the need to protect the rights of others to achieve effective political democracy;[50]
- protecting the rights or reputation of others;[51]
- to provide finality and legal certainty and to prevent stale claims from coming to court.[52]

2.6.4   Necessary in a democratic society and the margin of appreciation

The requirement that the act infringing the Convention right be necessary in a democratic society means that the State must prove the existence of a pressing social need which it is trying to meet. A democratic society is characterised by pluralism and tolerance.

State authorities are in a better position than the ECtHR to assess what the interest of the 'democratic society' requires in their particular country. Thus the ECtHR will be reluctant to prescribe this element. This latitude is known as the 'margin of appreciation'. However, it is for the court in each case, to describe the parameters within which the State can act. The importance of the right, the purpose sought to be achieved by the State, and the degree to which practice varies among Convention States are factors which have affected the way in which the ECtHR has approached these parameters, but the UK courts will be able to take a more robust view of these issues, being familiar with what the interest of the 'democratic society' requires in the UK.

The House of Lords has indicated that the margin of appreciation will be not be used by the UK courts. In *R v Director of Public Prosecutions, ex parte Kebilene*,[53] it considered how it might operate. Lord Hope said that in a 'discretionary area of judgment' such as judicial review, the extent of judicial supervision will vary according to such factors as:

(a) the nature of the Convention right in issue;
(b) the importance of that right for the individual; and
(c) the nature of the activities involved in the case.

He said:

---

48   *Waite and Kennedy v Germany* (2000) 30 EHRR 261.
49   *Rekvenyi v Hungary* (2000) 30 EHRR 519.
50   *Vogt v Germany* (1996) 21 EHRR 205.
51   *Jersild v Denmark* (1995) 19 EHRR 1.
52   *Stubbings and Others v UK* (1997) 23 EHRR 213.
53   [1999] 3 WLR 972.

'The doctrine of the "margin of appreciation" is a familiar part of the jurisprudence of the European Court of Human Rights. The European Court has acknowledged that, by reason of their direct and continuous contact with the vital forces of their countries, the national authorities are in principle better placed to evaluate local needs and conditions than an international court: *Buckley v. UK* (1996) 23 E.H.R.R. 101, 129, paras. 74–75. Although this means that, as the European Court explained in *Handyside v. UK* (1976) 1 E.H.R.R. 737, 753, para. 48, "the machinery of protection established by the Convention is subsidiary to the national systems safeguarding human rights," it goes hand in hand with a European supervision. The extent of this supervision will vary according to such factors as the nature of the Convention right in issue, the importance of that right for the individual and the nature of the activities involved in the case.

This doctrine is an integral part of the supervisory jurisdiction which is exercised over state conduct by the international court. By conceding a margin of appreciation to each national system, the court has recognised that the Convention, as a living system, does not need to be applied uniformly by all states but may vary in its application according to local needs and conditions. This technique is not available to the national courts when they are considering Convention issues arising within their own countries. But in the hands of the national courts also the Convention should be seen as an expression of fundamental principles rather than as a set of mere rules. The questions which the courts will have to decide in the application of these principles will involve questions of balance between competing interests and issues of proportionality.

In this area difficult choices may have to be made by the executive or the legislature between the rights of the individual and the needs of society. In some circumstances it will be appropriate for the courts to recognise that there is an area of judgment within which the judiciary will defer, on democratic grounds, to the considered opinion of the elected body or person whose act or decision is said to be incompatible with the Convention. . . . It will be easier for such an area of judgment to be recognised where the Convention itself requires a balance to be struck, much less so where the right is stated in terms which are unqualified. It will be easier for it to be recognised where the issues involve questions of social or economic policy, much less so where the rights are of high constitutional importance or are of a kind where the courts are especially well placed to assess the need for protection.'

2.6.5 Proportionality

A restriction must be 'proportionate to the legitimate aim pursued'.[54] There must be a fair balance between the interests of individuals. There must also be a fair balance between the interests of individuals and those of the wider community. If a measure is restricted in its application and effect, and is attended by safeguards in national law (so that the individual is not subject to arbitrary treatment), it is more likely to be proportionate than not, despite the fact that it infringes the Convention right.[55]

2.6.6 Must not be discriminatory

Article 14 prohibits discrimination in the 'enjoyment of the rights and freedoms set forth in this Convention'. It must be taken into account when

---

54   *Handyside v UK* (1979–80) 1 EHRR 737, para 49.
55   *MS v Sweden* (1999) 28 EHRR 313.

justifying a restriction. A difference in treatment, to avoid being discriminatory, must have reasonable and objective justification.[56] The question will be whether a legitimate aim is sufficient to justify the distinction being made. Restrictions which are reasonable when applied uniformly may be unreasonable if applied in a different way to different groups of people.

2.7 DECLARATION OF INCOMPATIBILITY

2.7.1 The scope of section 3

The requirement under s 3 of the HRA 1998 applies to primary legislation and subordinate legislation whenever enacted, but does not affect the validity, continuing operation or enforcement of any incompatible primary legislation. It also does not affect the validity, continuing operation or enforcement of any incompatible subordinate legislation if (disregarding any possibility of revocation) primary legislation prevents removal of the incompatibility.

Thus it will not be possible, by means of this section, to disapply primary legislation if it is incompatible. The remedy in those circumstances is under s 4 of the HRA 1998 by which if either the Court of Appeal, the House of Lords or the High Court (and see below) is satisfied that the provision is incompatible with a Convention right, it may make a declaration of that incompatibility. This has the consequence that an employment tribunal (which does not have the power to make a declaration of incompatibility) must apply the construction of the statute to which the tribunal would have come without the benefit of the (incompatible) Convention right if it takes the view that a legislative provision is incompatible. Incompatible subordinate legislation may be quashed or disapplied or be subject to a declaration of incompatibility if the primary legislation does not require the incompatibility. A tribunal would be obliged to disapply the provisions of any secondary legislation which was not required by primary legislation to be incompatible.

The court may make a declaration of incompatibility with a specific Convention right if the court is satisfied:

(a) that the provision is incompatible with a Convention right; and
(b) that (disregarding any possibility of revocation) the primary legislation concerned prevents removal of the incompatibility.

It is only the higher courts which have the power to make such a declaration. Section 4(5) of the HRA 1998 stipulates that 'court' means:

(a) the House of Lords;
(b) the Judicial Committee of the Privy Council;
(c) the Courts-Martial Appeal Court;
(d) in Scotland, the High Court of Justiciary sitting otherwise than as a trial court or the Court of Session;

---

56   *Belgian Linguistic Case No 2* (1979–80) 1 EHRR 252, para 10.

(e) in England and Wales or Northern Ireland, the High Court or the Court of Appeal.

A declaration of incompatibility under s 4 does not affect the validity, continuing operation or enforcement of the provision in respect of which it is given. Moreover, it is not binding on the parties to the proceedings in which it is made.[57] Thus the impetus to seek a declaration of incompatibility will be greatest for those parties who are likely to face the same set of circumstances again. For the individual complainant it is not clear that there will be any point in taking a case to the level at which such a declaration can be made, purely for that purpose. Further, the higher court interpreting the legislation would, if it has made a declaration of incompatibility, be unable to interpret the legislation compatibly with the Convention right and would therefore have to determine the construction of the legislation without regard to it. However, it is the first step in the process of ensuring remedial action is taken under s 10 of the HRA 1998.[58] The employment tribunals are themselves public authorities and will act unlawfully if they act incompatibly with the Convention rights. It will be an error of law for a tribunal to fail to have regard to the HRA 1998 in reaching a decision. If the tribunal does have regard to the HRA 1998 but fails to interpret the Convention rights correctly, the decision will contain an error of law in its own right. This will have effect between the parties. When the argument is whether the provision is incompatible or whether it may be interpreted consistently with the Convention, both points will need to be taken. It is only if a declaration of incompatibility is made that no effect is achieved between the parties, and the court on appeal will be obliged to apply the incompatible provision.

By s 21 of the HRA 1998, 'primary legislation' means any:

(a) public general Act;
(b) local and personal Act;
(c) private Act;
(d) Measure of the Church Assembly;
(e) Measure of the General Synod of the Church of England;
(f) Order in Council:
    (i) made in exercise of Her Majesty's Royal Prerogative;
    (ii) made under s 38(1)(a) of the Northern Ireland Constitution Act 1973 or the corresponding provision of the Northern Ireland Act 1998; or
    (iii) amending an Act of a kind mentioned in (a), (b) or (c) above;

and includes an order or other instrument made under primary legislation (otherwise than by the National Assembly for Wales, a member of the Scottish Executive, a Northern Ireland Minister or a Northern Ireland department) to the extent to which it operates to bring one or more provisions of that legislation into force or amends any primary legislation.

Section 21 also provides that 'subordinate legislation' means any:

---

57   HRA 1998, s 4(6).
58   See **6.12**.

(a) Order in Council other than one;
    (i)   made in exercise of Her Majesty's Royal Prerogative;
    (ii) made under s 38(1)(a) of the Northern Ireland Constitution Act 1973 or the corresponding provision of the Northern Ireland Act 1998; or
    (iii) amending an Act of a kind mentioned in the definition of primary legislation;
(b) Act of the Scottish Parliament;
(c) Act of the Parliament of Northern Ireland;
(d) Measure of the Assembly established under s 1 of the Northern Ireland Assembly Act 1973;
(e) Act of the Northern Ireland Assembly;
(f) order, rules, regulations, scheme, warrant, byelaw or other instrument made under primary legislation (except to the extent to which it operates to bring one or more provisions of that legislation into force or amends any primary legislation);
(g) order, rules, regulations, scheme, warrant, byelaw or other instrument made under legislation mentioned in (b), (c), (d) or (e) above or made under an Order in Council applying only to Northern Ireland;
(h) order, rules, regulations, scheme, warrant, byelaw or other instrument made by a member of the Scottish Executive, a Northern Ireland Minister or a Northern Ireland department in exercise of prerogative or other executive functions of Her Majesty which are exercisable by such a person on behalf of Her Majesty.

2.7.2   What are the consequences of incompatibility for the parties?

In *Earl Spencer and Countess Spencer v UK,*[59] the Commission recalled the principle that States are dispensed from answering to an international body for their acts before they have had an opportunity to put matters right through their own legal system. In this regard, the provisions of Article 26 represent an important aspect of the principle that the machinery of protection established by the Convention is subsidiary to the national systems safeguarding human rights.[60] Arguably, a declaration of incompatibility is not a national remedy, as it has no effect on the state of affairs between the parties. Although Parliament may make a remedial order in the light of the incompatibility, a party will not have to wait until that is done before seeking a remedy from the Convention bodies. The focus of attention shifts away from the courts to Parliament once the declaration of incompatibility is made.

Where there is doubt as to whether the legislative provision is compatible with the Convention, consideration should be given to whether the common law is capable of development to reflect the rights of the parties under the Convention. If the scope of the legislation involved does not exclude the application of the common law, it may be possible to argue that a common law cause of action does, or should be developed to, cover the situation.

59   Application No 28851/95 and No 28852/95, (1998) 25 EHRR CD 105.
60   *Akdivar v Turkey* (1997) 23 EHRR 143, 1996, EHRR IV, No 15, p 15, para 65.

2.8 CROWN INTERVENTION

2.8.1 The right of the Crown to intervene

Under s 5 of the HRA 1998, the Crown has a right to intervene in proceedings in which a court is considering whether or not to make a declaration of incompatibility. Rules of court make provision for the notices which the Crown must receive.[61] Such notice may be given at any point in the proceedings.[62] The Crown, if it chooses to be joined, may be joined as a party via:

(a) a Minister of the Crown (or a person nominated by the Minister);
(b) a member of the Scottish Executive;
(c) a Northern Ireland Minister;
(d) a Northern Ireland department.

A person who has been made a party to criminal proceedings (save in Scotland) as the result of a notice under subs 5(2) may, with leave, appeal to the House of Lords against any declaration of incompatibility made in the proceedings.

2.8.2 Rules of court and declarations

The notice will be given under Part 19 of the CPR 1998. The Practice Direction to CPR 1998, Part 19 (Parties and Group Litigation), para 6 is expanded. The practice direction provides that in a human rights case where a court is considering whether or not to make a declaration of incompatibility, the notice given under CPR 1998, r 19.4A is to be sent by the court to the person named in the list published by HM Treasury under s 17 of the Crown Proceedings Act 1947.[63] The notice will be in the form directed by the court but will usually contain the directions given by the court and all statements of case in the claim.[64]

The Minister or other person permitted by the HRA 1998 to be joined as a party must (unless the court orders otherwise) if he or she wishes to be joined, within 21 days of the date of the notice given by the court, give notice of his or her intention to be joined as a party to the court and every other party. Where the Minister has nominated a person to be joined as a party, the notice must be accompanied by the written nomination.[65] The notice will be given in all cases including where the Crown, a Minister or a governmental body is already a party to the proceedings.

The same procedure applies where a claim is made under ss 7(1)(a) and 9(3) of the HRA 1998 in respect of a judicial act.[66] The notice must be given to the

---

61 CPR 1998, r 19.4A and Practice Direction to Part 19, para 6.4(1), Practice Direction to Part 28, para 1.2, Practice Direction to Part 29, para 1.2, Practice Direction to Part 52, para 5.1B.
62 For the first known example of this process see *Wilson v First County Trust* (2000) *The Times*, 6 December, where a Convention issue was raised by the court.
63 Practice Direction to Part 19, para 6.4(1).
64 Practice Direction to Part 19, para 6.4(2).
65 HRA 1998, s 5(2)(a), and see Practice Direction to Part 19, para 6.5.
66 See **6.8**.

appropriate person, who is the Lord Chancellor. The notice should be sent to the Treasury Solicitor on the Lord Chancellor's behalf. The statement of the issues which have led to the court considering making a declaration of incompatibility must give details of the judicial act which is the subject of the claim, and of the court or tribunal that made it. Section 9(4) of the HRA 1998 provides that no award of damages may be made against the Crown as provided for in s9(3) unless the appropriate party is joined in the proceedings. The appropriate person is the Minister responsible for the court concerned or a person or department nominated by the Minister.

2.9   SECTION 9 – CLAIMS UNDER SECTION 7(1)(a) FOR JUDICIAL ACTS

CPR 1998, r 19.4A(3) deals with the procedure for HRA 1998 claims involving a claim in respect of a judicial act.

CPR 1998, r 7.11 provides that a claim under s 7(1)(a) of the HRA 1998 in respect of a judicial act may be brought only in the High Court.

CPR 1998, Part 33 (miscellaneous rules about evidence) provides by r 33.9 that where a claim is:

(a)   for a remedy under s 7 of the HRA 1998 in respect of a judicial act which is alleged to have infringed the claimant's Article 5 Convention rights; and
(b)   based on a finding by a Crown Court,

the court hearing the claim may reconsider the evidence of the alleged infringement and the finding of the Crown Court.

2.10   PUBLIC AUTHORITIES

Section 6 of the HRA 1998 deals with acts of public authorities. A 'public authority' is not defined in the Act. However, s 6(3) includes a court or tribunal, as well as any person certain of whose functions are defined as functions of a public nature.

This section, like all statutory provisions, is to be interpreted to be compatible with the Convention rights in Sch 1. Among other Convention rights which are to be referred to for interpretation purposes is Article 17. This provides for limitation of Convention rights as is permitted in the Convention. Section 2 refers to Articles 16 to 18 as the Convention Articles with which Articles 2 to 11 and the Articles of the Protocols referred to in that section are to be read. A limitation on the rights conferred by the treaty exists in the requirement that the State's responsibility must be engaged in some way by the situation giving rise to the claim of infringement of a Convention right. Note that the situations in which the State's responsibility is engaged will vary for different Articles in the Convention.

The definition of a 'public authority' in s 6 does not include either House of Parliament or a person exercising functions in connection with proceedings in Parliament. The aim of this provision is to preserve parliamentary sovereignty. The judicial committee of the House of Lords is covered as a court. It will be possible to argue before the employment tribunals that a public authority has acted unlawfully if it breaches the Convention rights irrespective of the interpretation placed in normal circumstances on the legislation being considered. This will have effects in unfair dismissal law as it could not be argued that a public authority was acting reasonably in dismissing if in order to do so it acted unlawfully.

Section 6 states:

'(1) It is unlawful for a public authority to act in a way which is incompatible with a Convention right.

(2) Subsection (1) does not apply to an act if –
   (a) as the result of one or more provisions of primary legislation, the authority could not have acted differently; or
   (b) in the case of one or more provisions of, or made under, primary legislation which cannot be read or given effect in a way which is compatible with the Convention rights, the authority was acting so as to give effect to or enforce those provisions.

(3) In this section "public authority" includes –
   (a) a court or tribunal, and
   (b) any person certain of whose functions are functions of a public nature,

but does not include either House of Parliament or a person exercising functions in connection with proceedings in Parliament.

(4) In subsection (3) "Parliament" does not include the House of Lords in its judicial capacity.

(5) In relation to a particular act, a person is not a public authority by virtue only of subsection (3)(b) if the nature of the act is private.'

Subsections 6(1) and (5) require some explanation.

2.11 PUBLIC AUTHORITY – 'ACTING IN THE SHOES OF THE STATE'

2.11.1 The definition of a public authority

Section 6(1) of the HRA 1998 provides that it is unlawful for a public authority to act in a way which is incompatible with a Convention right. If the body is an explicit arm of government all of its acts are acts of the State. A local authority employing or dismissing an employee is engaged in an act of the State. Otherwise, the basic question will be whether the act in question is of a private nature. This contrasts those acts that are purely private with those in which the body undertakes a State function. If the act in question is not part of an act of the State, it will not attract s 6 liability. On the other hand, if the act in dispute is part of a State act, certain of the functions of the body exercising it will be public.

This explains why it is thought that there are two types of public authority:

(1) 'full blooded' public authorities, which are explicit arms of government (local or central). All of their acts are covered;
(2) entities, certain of whose functions are public functions. These entities are covered only in respect of acts which are not of a private nature.

However, s 6 does not provide a definition of 'public authority'. The term will cover courts and tribunals by virtue of s 6(4), but will also cover 'any person certain of whose functions are functions of a public nature'. Section 6(5) specifies that in relation to a particular act, a person is not a public authority by virtue only of the fact that certain of his or her functions are of a public nature if the nature of the act is private. The key question is what constitutes an act of a private nature.

It is submitted that on its true construction s 6 includes any body which can be characterised as carrying out functions of a public nature. Certain bodies will always be public authorities because they are creations of legislation (statute, prerogative, or statutory instrument). All of the actions of such a body embody an act of the State, and undertake a function of the State. This will include local authorities, government bodies (eg the Criminal Injuries Compensation Authority, the Crown Prosecution Service (CPS) and other government departments), regulatory bodies, the Advisory, Conciliation and Arbitration Service (ACAS), and ombudsmen. It will also include bodies such as NHS Trusts, RSPCA, English Heritage, the other executive agencies, and other bodies established by legislation.

If a question arises as to the correct approach to the interpretation of the section, and if an ambiguity can be found in it, the Lord Chancellor's speech of 24 November 1997[67] may be of assistance in determining the Parliamentary intention behind it. He said:

> '[section 6(1)] refers to "public authority" without defining the term. In many cases it will be obvious to the court that they will be dealing with a public authority. In respect of government departments, for example, or police officers, or prison officers, or immigration officers, or local authorities, there can be no doubt that the body in question is a public authority . . . In such cases [the section] applies in respect of all their acts, public and private . . .
> . . . provides further assistance on the meaning of public authority. It provides that "public authority" includes, "any person certain of whose functions are functions of a public nature." That provision was said to include bodies which are not manifestly public bodies, but some of whose functions only are functions of a public nature. It is relevant to cases where the courts are not sure whether they are looking at a public authority in the full blooded [section 6(1)] sense with regard to those bodies which fall into the grey area between public and private. . . .'

The Lord Chancellor went on to give examples of a public authority such as Railtrack when exercising public functions in its role as safety regulator. He

---

67　　HL Debs, vol 583, col 811.

emphasised, however, that it would be acting privately in its role as a property developer. Equally, a private security company exercising public functions relating to the management of a contracted-out prison would be a public authority. However, it would be acting privately when guarding commercial premises. He drew attention to doctors in general practice who take private patients. They are public authorities in relation to their NHS functions but not in relation to those private patients. These are public bodies only if the act in respect of which the challenge is being made is of a public (non-private) nature.

The tribunals and courts will therefore need to look at the functions carried out by a body and ascertain whether any of them are functions of a public nature. If any of them are such functions, the tribunal or court will need to decide if the act about which complaint is made is private in nature. This will require an analysis of that act.

In relation to the definition of a public authority, the Government intended that guidance should be taken from judicial review cases. When s 6 was debated in Parliament, the Home Secretary (Jack Straw) stated:[68]

> 'The most valuable asset that we had to hand was jurisprudence relating to judicial review. It is not easily summarised and could not have been simply written into the Bill, but the concepts are reasonably clear and I think that we can build on them. I am happy to lift the veil on the considerations of the Cabinet Committee and say that we devoted a great deal of time and energy to this issue, as I hope hon. Members would expect us to. We decided that the best approach would be reference to the concept of a public function. After stating that it is "unlawful for a public authority to act incompatibly with a Convention right", clause 6 accordingly provides that a public authority includes a court or a tribunal, and "any person certain of whose functions are functions of a public nature."
>
> The effect of that is to create three categories, the first of which contains organisations which might be termed "obvious" public authorities, all of whose functions are public. The clearest examples are Government Departments, local authorities and the police. There is no argument about that.
>
> The second category contains organisations with a mix of public and private functions. One of the things with which we had to wrestle was the fact that many bodies, especially over the past 20 years, have performed public functions which are private, partly as a result of privatisation and partly as a result of contracting out. I am not going to argue with that – it has happened.
>
> For example, between 1948 and 1993, a public authority – the British Railways Board – was responsible for every aspect of running the railway. Now, Railtrack plc does that, but it also exercises the public function of approving and monitoring the safety cases of train operating companies. Railtrack acts privately in its functions as a commercial property developer. We were anxious . . . that we should not catch the commercial activities of Railtrack – or, for example, of the water companies – which were nothing whatever to do with its exercise of public functions.
>
> Private security firms contract to run prisons: what Group 4, for example, does as a plc contracting with other bodies is nothing whatever to do with the state, but, plainly, where it runs a prison, it may be acting in the shoes of the state. The effect of clause 6(7) is that those organisations, unlike the "obvious" public authorities,

---

68   HC Debs, 17 June 1998, cols 409–410.

will not be liable in respect of their private acts. The third category is organisations with no public functions – accordingly, they fall outside the scope of clause 6.

As with the interpretation of any legislation ... it will be for the courts to determine whether an organisation is a public authority. That will be obvious in some cases, and there will be no need to inquire further; in others, the courts will need to consider whether an organisation has public functions. In doing that, they should, among other things, sensibly look to the jurisprudence which has developed in respect of judicial review.

As the hon. and learned Member for Harborough knows, the courts have said that the Takeover Panel amounts to a public authority for the purposes of judicial review. They have also said, however, that the Jockey Club is not susceptible to judicial review, even though it is established by royal charter and performs functions which would be performed by the state or a state agency in other jurisdictions.

To take a topical example, the courts have said that the Football Association is not such a public body as to be susceptible to judicial review, so they are used to drawing a line, and, up to now, the line which they have drawn has been sensible. The Takeover Panel plainly performs a public function – there can be no argument about that, even though it is a private body – and even though the public enjoy football, it is highly debatable whether the functions of the FA are public functions.

The same is true of the Jockey Club and its functions. The courts have been careful in holding susceptible to judicial review bodies which are not plainly agents of the state. The courts will consider the nature of a body and the activity in question. They might consider whether the activities of a non-statutory body would be the subject of statutory regulation if that body did not exist, which covers the point about the Takeover Panel; whether the Government had provided under-pinning for its activities; and whether it exercised extensive or monopolistic powers.

What I have said is intended to make clear why we have drafted clause 6 in the way that we have, and what effect it is intended to achieve.'

There may be differences in scope of the application of Community law concepts such as 'emanation of the State' and the concept of 'public authority' in the HRA 1998. Nevertheless they have much in common, and in determining whether the responsibility of the State is engaged by the fact that the act was carried out by a particular body as a public authority because it is either on occasion or by necessity carrying out a State function, the following analysis based on the Advocate-General's reasoning in *Foster v British Gas*[69] may be of assistance.

Thus it is submitted that:

– **Principle I**
The concept of a public body must be understood very broadly and all bodies which pursuant to the constitutional structure of a State can exercise any authority over individuals fall within the concept of 'the State'. It is immaterial how that authority is organised and how the various bodies which exercise that authority are related. There is no need for any criterion of delegation or control by other public authorities. It is the

---

69   [1991] ICR 84.

nature of the function that the body is intended to carry out that is determinative.

– **Principle II**

In relation to undertakings which, as such, exercise no authority in the strict sense over individuals, the body may represent 'the State' where it has given itself powers which place it in a position to influence decisively the conduct of persons (whatever their nature, public or private, or their sphere of activity) with regard to the subject matter of the Convention right in question. The manner of the State's influence on the conduct of those persons is irrelevant. It may be *de jure* or *de facto*. This might be because the State has a general or specific power (or is simply able as a matter of fact) to give that body binding directions, whether or not by the exercise of rights as a shareholder, to approve its decisions in advance or suspend or annul them after the fact, to appoint or dismiss (the majority of) its directors, or to interrupt its funding wholly or in part so as to threaten its continued existence.

– **Proviso I**

However, the possibility of exercising controlling influence must stem from something other than a general legislative power.

– **Proviso II**

The State must have the power to exercise influence, in particular in connection with the matter to which the Convention right relates or can relate. Once the State has retained a power to exercise influence over a body with regard to the subject matter of the relevant Convention right, from the point of view of individuals it has brought that person within its sphere of authority.

The principle in *Foster* and other cases is that the State may not benefit from its default in respect of anything that lies within the sphere of responsibility which by its own free choice it has taken upon itself, irrespective of the person through whom that responsibility is exercised. This is the same principle as applies to create State responsibility in respect of the acts of private individuals in the Convention.

Note that s 6(5) of the HRA 1998 takes account of this approach to the characterisation of a body as a public authority. It is submitted that certain bodies will be public bodies by virtue of Principle I, and these are the one that have been referred to as 'full blooded' public authorities. Principle II reflects the interrelationship between s 6(3) and (5).

Thus Principle II is of assistance in determining whether, in a particular situation, the act is a public act such as would engage the responsibility of the State for Convention purposes. Thus in *Costello-Roberts v UK*[70] no State responsibility was engaged in relation to acts which were merely ancillary to acts which did engage the responsibility of the State, namely acts in the education process.

---

70 (1995) 19 EHRR 112.

The test under the HRA 1998 requires analysis of the act about which complaint is made as well as the functions being carried out by the body. The remarks of the Lord Chancellor and Home Secretary indicate that it is only when a body (other than an obvious public authority) is carrying out public functions and a complaint is being made about these functions that it will be regarded as a public authority.

2.11.2 Functions

It appears that the concept of 'function' requires the authority to be undertaking some duty of the State or of a public nature. However, the distinction between public and private functions should not be seen as relating to the basis of the authority's power. Over reliance on judicial review authorities may lead to this error. The mere fact that a body obtains its authority from a contractual arrangement (such as in the case of the security company undertaking prison work) will not prevent it from being a public authority.

The essential distinction, which runs through all the judicial review cases and is of assistance, is between a domestic or private tribunal on the one hand and a body of persons who are under some public duty on the other.[71] In considering whether certain of the entity's functions are public functions, the courts will probably take account of whether the power of the entity in question is genuinely consensual, in the sense that in practice a person can truly decide whether or not to submit to it.[72] They will have regard to whether the functions of the body are such that if it did not exist some form of regulation would have been established which would have been public.[73] The courts will also be interested in whether there is a statutory underpinning to the authority's activities, such as the requirement to provide and maintain local housing in the case of a local authority and its contractors. They will also consider the extent of the powers enjoyed by the body. This is likely to mean more than simply economic power. A body which has statutory rights of access, such as the RSPCA, might therefore be seen as undertaking a function of the State. A private school would be undertaking a public function of education. A mediator, appointed privately by parties to a contract, would also probably be undertaking part of the State's function of the administration of justice.

Public authorities may make use of 'private' mechanisms such as contracts. However, the 'functions' of such authorities remain wholly public (see Principle II at **2.11.1** above). An entity might therefore undertake certain public functions, and use a private mechanism in the course of doing so. Such a distinction is not important in relation to the full-blooded arms of State, such as central and local government, but may be important to the position of contractors for a local authority. If the private mechanisms were means of carrying out the public function they would be considered to be non-private in nature, so that the form and content of a contract could then be considered as an act of a public authority which must be compatible with the Convention

---

71   *R v Panel on Take-overs and Mergers, ex parte Datafin Plc* [1987] QB 815 at 847.
72   *Per* Lloyd LJ at p 846.
73   *R v Advertising Standards Authority, ex parte Insurance Services plc* (1990) 2 Admin LR 77.

rights. If the State function was carried out by employing a person to do it, the contract of employment with that person would constitute such a mechanism.

2.11.3 Entities which carry out certain public functions – public and private acts

Application of Principle II is present in s 6(3)(b) of the HRA 1998 which deals with bodies that mix public and private functions. These would include a 'self-regulatory' body which combines the regulation of its members (public function) with lobbying and public-relations activities on behalf of its members (private function). In those cases, the body is to be regarded as a public authority. However, it is only its acts in connection with the discharge of its public functions that are within the scope of s 6.

If the act in question does not further the public function in any respect, it is likely to be seen as private in nature. However, particularly in the area of employment law, there will be difficult cases. Does the contract of employment of a person working on fulfilling the public function of a contracted-out service constitute an act that is private in nature? Clearly, it furthers the fulfilment of the public function of the public authority and so might be seen as not purely private in nature. On the other hand, the contract of a person who works in a centralised department of that same entity might only peripherally further the fulfilment of the public function. It is not clear whether the dismissal of a person working on such a contract would be an act of a private nature since the contractor is standing in the shoes of government in undertaking the contracted-out work and the employment fulfils the object of undertaking that public function. If the employee was dismissed for incapability or poor performance, that act might be not of a purely private nature as it relates to performance of duties directly furthering a public function.

It is important to remember that the distinction between a public and a private act must be read so as to render these concepts, so far as it is possible to do so, compatible with the Convention rights and so as to give effect to those Convention rights listed in Sch 1 and also to give effect to the constitutional position of the HRA 1998.[74]

Where an act is a means to carry out a public function, it is likely to be a public act. In this respect the ECtHR case-law may be of help. Thus in *Ireland v UK*[75] it was decided that it is no defence to strict liability for its agents to State that the agent acted outside the scope of his powers. In *Lopez-Ostra v Spain*[76] it was held that State responsibility is engaged where a private individual's act has been facilitated by the State or if the State has colluded in it. In addition, mere delegation of obligations to private persons by the State is no defence.[77] Finally, where the State has a positive obligation under the Convention it may be responsible for the acts of private persons.[78]

---

74 See **2.2**.
75 (1979–80) 2 EHRR 25 at para 159.
76 (1995) 20 EHRR 277.
77 *Van der Musselle v Belgium* (1984) 6 EHRR 163.
78 See, for example, *Platform 'Ärtze für das Leben' v Austria* (1991) 13 EHRR 204.

When is the responsibility of the State engaged?

In *Van der Musselle*[79] the ECtHR analysed the issue of whether the State's responsibility is engaged by an act. In that case the obligation to grant free legal assistance arose, in criminal matters, from Article 6(3)(c). In civil matters, it sometimes constitutes one of the means of ensuring a fair trial as required by Article 6(1).[80] This obligation is incumbent on each of the contracting parties.

The State in *Van der Musselle* laid the obligation on advocates. Legislation required the organisation of advocates to require members of the Bar to 'defend indigent persons'. However, the State's solution 'did not relieve the Belgian State of the responsibilities it would have incurred under the Convention had it chosen to operate the system itself'. Moreover, the Government recognised at the hearings that 'the obligation', for pupil advocates, 'to act as defence counsel in cases assigned by the Legal Advice and Defence Office' arose from Article 455 of the Judicial Code. The State conceded that Belgian law, by not making any provision for indemnifying pupil advocates, acknowledged at least implicitly that the latter have to bear the expenses incurred in dealing with the cases in question. In addition, the Belgian Bars, bodies which are associated with the exercise of judicial power, are, without prejudice to the basic principle of independence necessary for the accomplishment of their important function in the community, subject to the requirements of the law. The relevant legislation States their objects and establishes their institutional organs; it endows with legal personality in public law each of the Councils of the 27 local Ordres and the General Council of the National Ordre.

2.11.4   As a result of primary legislation, could not have acted differently

Section 6(2) of the HRA 1998 provides that a public authority will not be acting unlawfully if:

'(a)   as a result of one or more provisions of primary legislation, the authority could not have acted differently; or

(b)   in the case of one or more provisions of, or made under, primary legislation which cannot be read or given effect in a way which is compatible with the Convention rights, the authority was acting so as to give effect to or enforce those provisions.'

This defence will not succeed if there is anything short of necessity. The public authority must have been required to act as it did as a result of one or more provisions of primary legislation. The public authority cannot rely solely on the provisions of secondary legislation. Thus if the primary legislation allows a broad range of matters to be dealt with under secondary legislation, an act which results from the specific statutory instrument is not as a result of primary legislation. However, if the primary legislation requires a statutory instrument to be made and it is made in a particular way, the public authority could argue

---

79   *Van der Musselle v Belgium* (1984) 6 EHRR 163.
80   *Airey v Ireland* (1979) Series A, No 32, EHRR 305.

that it could not have acted differently as a result of the primary legislation. When there is an element of discretion in the secondary legislation the defence will not be available.

Where statutory compulsion is cited as the reason for acting in *prima facie* breach of Convention rights, the court will need to see that it was compulsion and not mere discretionary compliance. The House of Lords in *Hampson v DES*[81] considered s 41(1)(b) of the Race Relations Act 1976, whereby acts done in pursuance of a statutory requirement were rendered lawful. The House held that on its true construction the defence was restricted to acts or requirements specified in the instrument, since any wider construction of the expression would be irreconcilable with the purpose of the Act and would allow the imposition of conditions or requirements capable of racial discrimination without any prior opportunity for Parliamentary scrutiny. Where an act is the exercise of an administrative discretion, it is unlikely to be found that the public authority 'could not have acted differently'. An interesting question is whether, where the occasion of the authority's need to act in the way it did was born of its own negligence, a court would find that it could have acted differently. Necessity in respect of torts is not a good defence if the need to act is brought about by negligence on the part of the defendant. Once that issue is raised, the defendant must show on the whole of the evidence that the necessity arose without negligence on his part.[82] Could the other party challenge the lawfulness of the act of a public authority on the basis that it was only as a result of that authority's negligence that the situation in which the primary legislation required action arose? An attack on an omission giving rise to a situation in which the public authority is required to act by primary legislation could be made by attacking the failure of the public authority to act in such a way as was required by Convention rights.

Finally, the primary legislation alleged to give rise to the necessity must be construed in accordance with the Convention rights by s 3 of the HRA 1998. It is only if, on that construction, it still requires an act incompatible with the Convention that the defence can be raised.

2.11.5 'Act'

'Act' includes 'failure to act'[83] and need not be deliberate.[84] Subordinate legislation which is incompatible with the Convention may not be made by a public authority and incompatible physical actions may not be performed. Since the concept of 'act' includes a failure to act, a public authority may be required to make subordinate legislation needed in order to render UK law compatible with the Convention rights. Most importantly, it is unlawful for a court to make an order or give a judgment that is not compatible with the Convention rights.

---

81   [1990] ICR 511.
82   See *Rigby v Chief Constable of Northamptonshire* [1985] 1 WLR 1242 at p 1253.
83   HRA 1998, s 6(6).
84   HC Debs, vol 314, col 1097.

2.12   PRACTICAL EFFECTS

2.12.1   Public authorities

Now that the HRA 1998 is in force, public authorities, including those private bodies exercising public functions, need to examine their existing systems and standards for compatibility with the Convention rights. They also need to consider future policy taking account of the Convention rights and the Act. Current policy will need to meet the requirements of a fair balance between the individual and society. Restrictions on a Convention right will have to be justifiable and relevant.

A member of staff of a public authority involved in taking decisions on behalf of the entity or implementing policy, or working in a personnel department, will be covered insofar as it is unlawful for a public authority to act (or fail to act) in a way which is incompatible with a Convention right.

Full-blooded public authorities will be acting as such in all their actions including the determination of who is to be appointed to a post, concluding a contract with the appointee, personnel policies, and termination of employment. Interestingly, they would also be acting as such when asked for a reference (although unless the procedure for giving or refusing references was very strict, no Article 6 right would be engaged by refusal to provide a reference).

In the case of private contractors carrying out works for a public authority, and thus fulfilling a public duty of that authority, it suggested that their acts are to be taken to be those of the public authority. If that authority is a full-blooded public authority, State responsibility could not be avoided by reference to the mechanism whereby the State performed its act. Thus any act for which the individual could claim that the public authority was liable will also be a public act by the contractor. Thus if a person was employed by a contractor in order to fulfil a contract for a public authority, the process of contracting, employment and termination would be capable of giving rise to liability under s 6 of the HRA 1998. Contractors would, in such situations, need to have regard to the Convention rights. Where the employee is dismissed because of something done or not done in relation to the fulfilment of the employee's duties on the public authority contract, the contractor would clearly be acting in the shoes of the State (in fulfilling the contract). However, if the reason for dismissal did not relate to the contract (eg if the employee was caught stealing from the employer), it is less clear that the termination has any relationship to the public function.

A public authority may be liable under the HRA 1998 if it adopts measures which are such as to permit a private employer or trade union to abuse its powers in relation to the individual.[85] The scope of the illegality envisaged by the HRA 1998 appears to be broad enough to include the results of a public authority's actions or inaction in this respect. Thus it may be arguable under

---

85   *Cheall v UK* (1986) 8 EHRR 74.

the HRA 1998 that a local authority which fails to regulate matters relating to the employment environment in its location acts unlawfully if the effect of that inaction is to permit the employer to abuse its power towards its employees. Similarly, it will be liable for acts of its staff toward one another unless it adopts measures to ensure enjoyment of Convention rights at work.

2.12.2　Exceptions

By s 6(6) of the HRA 1998 'an act' includes a failure to act but does not include a failure to:

(a)　introduce in, or lay before, Parliament a proposal for legislation; or
(b)　make any primary legislation or remedial order.

The public authority comes under the obligation under s 6 unless the act falls within the exceptions intended to preserve the sovereignty of Parliament.

Section 6(2)(a) of the HRA 1998 provides an exception if primary legislation requires a public authority to act in the particular way it has.[86] Parliament (except the House of Lords in its judicial capacity) is excluded as a result of s 6(3) and (4) and therefore may enact and maintain legislation that infringes the Convention. To further this purpose, s 6(6) prevents a party from forcing incompatible primary legislation to be repealed, or enabling judicial interference with primary legislation. As a result of s 6(2)(b), incompatible primary legislation remains effective and as long as it does there is no obligation on any public authority to ignore it.

2.13　SECTION 7 – PROCEEDINGS FOR BREACH BY A PUBLIC AUTHORITY

2.13.1　Bringing proceedings

A person who claims that a public authority has acted (or proposes to act) in a way which is made unlawful by s 6(1) of the HRA 1998 may:

(a)　bring proceedings against the authority under the HRA 1998 in the appropriate court or tribunal; or
(b)　rely on the Convention right or rights concerned in any legal proceedings,

but only if he or she is (or would be) a victim of the unlawful act.

A free-standing case under s 7(1)(a) of the HRA 1998 should be brought in the following ways:

–　using the existing judicial review procedures;
–　in the county court or in the High Court where a claim for damages is made (unless this is associated with a claim for judicial review). The normal jurisdictional limits will apply.

86　See the discussion of *Hampson v DES* [1990] ICR 511 at **2.11.4.**

By s 22 of the HRA 1998, s 7(1)(b) applies to proceedings brought by or at the instigation of a public authority whenever the act in question took place. Otherwise the subsection does not apply to an act taking place before the section came into force.

It is envisaged that Convention rights may be relied upon in any proceedings in which they are, as a result of the HRA 1998, relevant:

> 'the great majority of cases in which the Convention arguments are raised will fall within the scope of such proceedings. That is because, in most cases, it is likely that the victim of an act made unlawful by s. 6 will have available to him an existing course of action or other means of legal challenge, such as a judicial review.'[87]

Section 7(2) states that the expression 'appropriate court or tribunal' means such court or tribunal as may be determined in accordance with rules of court. 'Proceedings against an authority' include a counter-claim or similar proceedings. Employment tribunals cannot hear stand-alone claims under the Convention. However, applicants will be able to rely on the Convention rights in proceedings under existing legislation to require the tribunal to find the act of the public authority unlawful to the extent that it has an effect on that legislation.

Under s 7(11) of the HRA 1998, the Minister (including the Northern Ireland department concerned) who has power to make rules in relation to a particular tribunal may, to the extent that the Minister considers it necessary to ensure that the tribunal can provide an appropriate remedy in relation to an act (or proposed act) of a public authority which is (or would be) unlawful as a result of s 6(1), by order add to:

(a) the relief or remedies which the tribunal may grant; or
(b) the grounds on which it may grant any of them.

Such an order may contain such incidental, supplemental, consequential or transitional provision as the Minister making it considers appropriate.

2.13.2   Procedure in relation to section 7

A free-standing case under s 7(1)(a) of the HRA 1998 should be brought using either the existing judicial review procedures, or in the county court, or in the High Court where a claim for damages is made (unless this is associated with a claim for judicial review). The normal jurisdictional limits will apply. A free-standing case under s 7(1)(a) may also be brought in the county court or in the High Court following a finding of unlawfulness under s 7(1)(b) in some other court or tribunal which did not have the power to award damages or compensation.

The Practice Direction to CPR 1998, Part 16 provides:

> '16.1 A party who seeks to rely on any provision of or right arising under the Human Rights Act 1998 or seeks a remedy available under that Act—
>
> > (1) must state that fact in his statement of case; and

---

87   HC Debs, vol 314, col 1056.

(2) must in his statement of case—

    (a) give precise details of the Convention right which it is alleged has been infringed and details of the alleged infringement;

    (b) specify the relief sought;

    (c) state if the relief sought includes—

        (i) a declaration of incompatibility in accordance with section 4 of that Act, or

        (ii) damages in respect of a judicial act to which section 9(3) of that Act applies;

    (d) where the relief sought includes a declaration of incompatibility in accordance with section 4 of that Act, give precise details of the legislative provision alleged to be incompatible and details of the alleged incompatibility;

    (e) where the claim is founded on a finding of unlawfulness by another court or tribunal, give details of the finding; and

    (f) where the claim is founded on a judicial act which is alleged to have infringed the Convention right of the party as provided by section 9 of the Human Rights Act 1998, the judicial act complained of and the court or tribunal which is alleged to have made it.

(The practice direction to Part 19 provides for notice to be given and parties joined in the circumstances referred to in (c), (d) and (f)).'

Where the claim is in respect of a judicial act the Lord Chancellor may be joined as a party.[88]

In relation to employment tribunals, two situations may arise.

(1) There is a finding of an unlawful act in circumstances of a finding of breach of employment legislation as a result of reliance of those rights under s 7(1)(b) of the HRA 1998. Here the tribunal will have the power to award compensation for the breach of the employment legislation and s 8(1) will require it to consider how to remedy the breach of Convention rights with reference to the remedies appropriate for the breach of employment legislation that it has found.[89]

(2) As a result of reliance on Convention rights under s 7(1)(b) of the HRA 1998 there is a finding of an unlawful act in circumstances in which no finding of a breach of employment legislation is made. Here the tribunal will have no power to award compensation for the breach of the Convention right, as s 8(1) requires it to act within its powers to award a remedy, and it would have no such power at that stage. The individual's remedy would then be to bring a s 7(1)(a) claim in the courts.

Although s 7(11) of the HRA 1998 allows rules to be made for individual tribunals to ensure that they can provide appropriate relief or remedies in relation to an act of a public authority which is unlawful under s 6(1) of the HRA 1998, no such rules were thought necessary for the employment tribunals. There is no intention at the present time to draft rules under s 7(11).

---

88   HRA 1998, s 9(3)–(5).

89   See **6.16**.

2.13.3   Legal proceedings

In s 7(1)(b) of the HRA 1998, dealing with legal proceedings in which a party may rely on the HRA rights, 'legal proceedings' is defined as including:

(a)   proceedings brought by or at the instigation of a public authority; and
(b)   an appeal against the decision of a court or tribunal.

Thus an appeal against the decision of the employment tribunal to the Employment Appeal Tribunal (EAT) will be included in legal proceedings and will permit appeals to be brought on the basis that the tribunal erred in law in failing, either to consider whether a public authority acted in a way incompatible with Convention rights, or in misconstruing the nature of the Convention rights in such a way as to reach a finding that the act of the public authority was compatible with the Convention right. In addition, where the tribunal fails to interpret legislation so as to render it compatible with Convention rights in cases (whether between individuals or with a respondent public authority) it will commit an error of law that may be appealed. Similarly, if the tribunal does not give effect to the Convention rights by using its powers, it will commit an unlawful act, but also an error of law under s 3 of the HRA 1998. If a distinction is to be drawn between 'reading' a provision and 'giving effect' to that provision, there will be a right of appeal to the EAT from a tribunal in respect of the failure of the tribunal to give effect to the statutory provision in a manner that is compatible with the Convention rights. Section 3 empowers a tribunal to read and give effect to legislation compatibly with Convention rights. It therefore has jurisdiction to give effect to legislative provisions in this way. Section 2 of the Employment Tribunals Act 1996 provides that the tribunal shall exercise the jurisdiction conferred on it by any other Act. Where the tribunal fails to give effect to the Convention rights it therefore acts outside its jurisdiction under the Employment Tribunals Act 1996, as s 3 requires the tribunal, in so far as it is possible to do so, to give effect to those rights when exercising statutory provisions. The EAT is likewise under the obligation to read and give effect to Convention rights when contemplating the scope of the jurisdiction of employment tribunals. Thus Convention rights may be relied on for their interpretive and effective aspects in legal proceedings before the EAT.

2.13.4   Judicial review *locus*

Under s 7(3) of the HRA 1998, special rules are made for persons bringing judicial review proceedings. If the proceedings are brought on an application for judicial review, the applicant is to be taken to have a sufficient interest in relation to the unlawful act only if the applicant is, or would be, a victim of that act. Under s 7(4), if the proceedings are made by way of a petition for judicial review in Scotland, the applicant shall be taken to have title and interest to sue in relation to the unlawful act only if the applicant is, or would be, a victim of that act.[90]

---

90   See **6.13.3–6.13.4**.

2.13.5 Victim

For the purposes of s 7(7) of the HRA 1998, a person is a victim of an unlawful act only if he or she is or would be a victim for the purposes of Article 34 of the Convention if proceedings were brought in the ECtHR in respect of that act.[91]

The word 'victim' in Article 25 of the Convention refers to the person or persons directly affected by the act or omission in issue.[92] It is enough if the person is at risk of being affected. The act need not have been carried out on the victim.[93] The risk of harm can be remote or minimal[94] and can amount to distress at the prospect of having to break the law if engaging in protected activities.[95]

The greater the consequences of the manifestation of the risk, the more remote the risk may be. In cases where the consequence is serious and could cause irreparable harm, a person may be a victim if a violation of the Convention is merely possible.[96] However, where individuals alleged that if returned to Sri Lanka they might suffer torture, they were not victims under the Convention when the claim was made before expulsion orders had been made and where if deportation orders were made there was an appeal available with attendant safeguards.[97] Thus where there are several layers of contingency between the point at which the complaint is made and the manifestation of the risk, even a very great consequence may not be enough to bring the complainant within the concept of 'victim'. A further limitation may be that there must be a reasonable likelihood that action infringing a right under the Convention has been taken against the complainant.[98] The Commission has found that the loss of employment by journalists on closure by the State of the press agency which employed them, did not suffice to permit the journalists to claim to be victims of alleged violations of the Convention in respect of the closure.[99]

The person must be directly affected by the act or omission (so excluding most representative actions: *Lindsay v UK*[100]). The person does not need to show detriment amounting to prejudice.[101] The Convention applies to all persons within the jurisdiction of the State parties including outside their territory if the State exercises authority over them.[102] Thus a person working for a public authority, but working abroad, may be able to satisfy the victim requirement. A public authority cannot bring proceedings under the Convention.[103] Where a

---

91 See **6.2.5–6.2.6**.
92 *Corigliano v Italy* (1983) 5 EHRR 334, judgment of 10 December 1982, Series A, No 57, p 12, para 31.
93 *Campbell & Cosans v UK* (1982) 4 EHRR 293.
94 *Norris v Ireland* (1991) 13 EHRR 186.
95 *Sutherland v UK* [1998] EHRLR 117.
96 *Soering v UK* (1989) 11 EHRR 439 (a prolonged period on death row).
97 *Vijayanathan and Pusparajah v France* (1993) 15 EHRR 62.
98 *Hilton v UK* (1986) 57 DR 108.
99 *MS and PS v Switzerland* Application No 10628/83, (1985) 44 DR 175 at p 190.
100 (1997) 24 EHRR CD 199.
101 *Johnston v Ireland* (1987) 9 EHRR 203.
102 *Reinette v France* (1989) 63 DR 189.
103 *Ayuntamiento de M v Spain* (1991) 68 DR 209.

body is found to be a public body in respect of an unlawful act it may be argued that it cannot claim breach of its Convention rights in respect of that finding. However, it is suggested that bodies which are public authorities in respect of a particular act will probably not be categorised as such in relation to their status before the court or tribunal. In those circumstances they would be able to rely on Convention rights as far as the actions or omissions of the judicial body were concerned.

A person may also be considered a victim in an indirect sense. For example, if the person has suffered an injury and the direct victim of the act cannot bring a complaint. Thus in *Abdulaziz, Cabales & Balkandali*[104] the wives of men refused leave to join their wives in the UK were recognised as victims under the Convention. In addition, where the applicant dies during proceedings the claim can be continued by a spouse or close relative if that person has a direct interest in the outcome.[105] However, in *Ahmed v UK*[106] the Commission found UNISON was not a victim in the context of that case. The Local Government Officers (Political Restrictions) Regulations 1990[107] did not affect any rights which UNISON may have under Article 11 of the Convention, and UNISON's freedom of expression was not limited in any way by the regulations, which were not addressed to trade unions but to local authority employees. The regulations did not refer to limitations on individuals' union activity, but prevented a union's members who occupied politically restricted posts in local government from standing for local elections. To the extent that an individual was affected by the regulations in the exercise of his or her Convention rights, for example in his or her freedom of expression by speaking in public in a union context, that individual was the person affected and not the union.

A trade union may claim to be a victim of alleged violations of its own rights.[108] So a trade union may be able to claim to be the victim of a violation of Article 11 of the Convention where the right to join a trade union is completely removed.[109] The union may also act on behalf of its members if it identifies the members directly affected by the act or omission and provides evidence of its authority to represent them.[110]

The shareholders, managing director of a company and the company itself can be victims of an act or omission which affects the company.[111]

2.13.6   Time-limits for stand alone claims

Under s 7(5) of the HRA 1998, proceedings under s 7(1)(a) must be brought before the end of:

---

104   (1985) 7 EHRR 471.
105   See eg *Loukanov v Bulgaria* (1997) 24 EHRR 121.
106   (1995) 20 EHRR CD 72.
107   SI 1990/851.
108   *National Union of Belgian Police v Belgium* (1979–80) 1 EHRR 578.
109   *Council of Civil Service Unions et al v UK* (1987) 50 DR 228, where the question of the union's standing was not expressly addressed.
110   *Zentralrat Deutscher Sinti und Roma and Rose v Germany* (1997) 23 EHRR CD 209.
111   *Kaplan v UK* (1982) 4 EHRR 64.

(a) the period of one year beginning with the date on which the act complained of took place; or

(b) such longer period as the court or tribunal considers equitable having regard to all the circumstances,

but this is subject to any rule imposing a stricter time-limit in relation to the procedure in question.

Section 7(5) lays down an extendable time-limit. The wording is similar to that under the SDA 1975 and RRA 1976, with the exception that justice is not mentioned. Nevertheless, guidance can be obtained from the way in which those statutes have operated. In particular, it is likely that the courts considering the requirement to consider all the circumstances of the case will construe the reference as being to the circumstances relating to the delay, and not to the circumstances of the substantive case.[112] Power is given to lay down shorter time-limits by applicable rules.[113]

2.14 SAFEGUARD FOR EXISTING HUMAN RIGHTS

Section 11 of the HRA 1998 provides that a person's reliance on a Convention right does not restrict any other right or freedom conferred on him or her by or under any law having effect in any part of the UK. It also does not affect his or her right to make any claim or bring any proceedings which he or she could make or bring apart from ss 7 to 9. This preserves the right to petition the ECtHR.

2.15 FREEDOM OF EXPRESSION

Section 12 of the HRA 1998 makes special provision for cases involving questions of freedom of expression. If a court or tribunal is considering whether to grant any relief that, if granted, might affect the exercise of the Convention right to freedom of expression, the following special provisions apply.

(1) By s 12(2), where the person against whom the application for relief is made ('the respondent') is neither present nor represented, no such relief is to be granted unless the court is satisfied:
   (a) that the applicant has taken all practicable steps to notify the respondent; or
   (b) that there are compelling reasons why the respondent should not be notified.

(2) No such relief is to be granted so as to restrain publication before trial unless the court is satisfied that the applicant is likely to establish that publication should not be allowed.

---

112   See *Hutchison v Westward Television Ltd* [1977] ICR 279.
113   See Chapter 6.

2.16   REMEDIAL ACTION

Section 10 of the HRA 1998 makes provision for the power to take remedial action. One or more of the following conditions have to be satisfied under s 10(1):

(a)   a provision of legislation has been declared under s 4 to be incompatible with a Convention right and, if an appeal lies:
   (i)   all persons who may appeal have stated in writing that they do not intend to do so;
   (ii)   the time for bringing an appeal has expired and no appeal has been brought within that time; or
   (iii) an appeal brought within that time has been determined or abandoned; or
(b)   it appears to a Minister of the Crown or Her Majesty in Council that, having regard to a finding of the ECtHR made after the coming into force of s 10 in proceedings against the UK, a provision of legislation is incompatible with an obligation of the UK arising from the Convention.

If a Minister of the Crown considers that there are compelling reasons for proceeding by way of remedial action, the Minister may make such amendments to the legislation by order as the Minister considers necessary to remove the incompatibility.[114] Amendment includes repeal.[115] In the case of subordinate legislation, if a Minister of the Crown considers the following conditions satisfied, the Minister may by order make such amendments to the primary legislation as he or she considers necessary.[116] Those conditions are:

(a)   that it is necessary to amend the primary legislation under which the subordinate legislation in question was made, in order to enable the incompatibility to be removed; and
(b)   that there are compelling reasons for proceeding under this section.

If the legislation is an Order in Council, the power conferred by subs (2) or (3) is exercisable by Her Majesty in Council.[117]

Remedial action may also be taken where the provision in question is in subordinate legislation and has been quashed, or declared invalid, by reason of incompatibility with a Convention right and the Minister proposes to proceed under para 2(b) of Sch 2 to the HRA 1998. Schedule 2 makes further provision about remedial orders.[118] Paragraph 2(b) of Sch 2 provides that no remedial order may be made unless it is declared in the order that it appears to the person making it that, because of the urgency of the matter, it is necessary to make the order without a draft being approved by Parliament by means of resolution of both Houses.

---

114   HRA 1998, s 10(2).
115   HRA 1998, s 21.
116   HRA 1998, s 10(3).
117   HRA 1998, s 10(6).
118   HRA 1998, s 10(7).

'Legislation' for the purposes of remedial action does not include a Measure of the Church Assembly or of the General Synod of the Church of England. Thus the Government cannot intervene in these measures by means of a remedial order. By para 1(1) of Sch 2, a remedial order may contain such incidental, supplemental, consequential or transitional provision as the person making it considers appropriate. It may also be made so as to have effect from a date earlier than that on which it is made and make provision for the delegation of specific functions. The Minister may make different provision for different cases.

Paragraph 1(2) of Sch 2 provides that the power to contain such incidental, supplemental, consequential or transitional provision as the person making the order considers appropriate includes:

(a) power to amend primary legislation (including primary legislation other than that which contains the incompatible provision); and

(b) power to amend or revoke subordinate legislation (including subordinate legislation other than that which contains the incompatible provision).

The remedial order, by para 1(3) of Sch 2, may be made so as to have the same extent as the legislation which it affects. Finally, no person is to be guilty of an offence solely as a result of the retrospective effect of a remedial order.[119]

Paragraph 2 of Sch 2 provides a procedure to be followed in making remedial order. No remedial order may be made unless:

(a) a draft of the order has been approved by a resolution of each House of Parliament made after the end of the period of 60 days beginning with the day on which the draft was laid; or

(b) it is declared in the order that it appears to the person making it that, because of the urgency of the matter, it is necessary to make the order without a draft being so approved.

Paragraph 3 of Sch 2 makes provisions for a remedial order to be laid before Parliament in draft and requires the following conditions to be satisfied before a draft may be laid before Parliament:

(a) the person proposing to make the order has laid before Parliament a document which contains a draft of the proposed order and the required information; and

(b) the period of 60 days, beginning with the day on which the document required was laid, has ended.

Representations made during the period of 60 days during which the document containing a draft of the proposed order and the required information was before Parliament are to be considered. The draft of the order laid under para 2(a) must be accompanied by a statement containing:

(a) a summary of the representations; and

(b) if, as a result of the representations, the proposed order has been changed, details of the changes.

---

119 HRA 1998, Sch 2, para 1(4).

It is at that stage that the order may be laid before Parliament for resolution within 60 days. However, the Act envisages that there may be occasions when this procedural timetable would be inappropriate due to the urgency of the situation to be addressed. Paragraph 4 of Sch 2 makes provision that if a remedial order ('the original order') is made without being approved in draft, the person making it must lay it before Parliament, accompanied by the required information, after it is made. If representations have been made during the period of 60 days beginning with the day on which the original order was made, the person making it must (after the end of that period) lay before Parliament a statement containing:

(a) a summary of the representations; and
(b) if, as a result of the representations, he or she considers it appropriate to make changes to the original order, details of the changes.

Where such a statement is required, the person making it must:

(a) make a further remedial order replacing the original order; and
(b) lay the replacement order before Parliament.

If, at the end of the period of 120 days beginning with the day on which the original order was made, a resolution has not been passed by each House approving the original or replacement order, the order ceases to have effect (but without that affecting anything previously done under either order or the power to make a fresh remedial order).

For the purposes of Sch 2, 'representations' means representations about a remedial order (or proposed remedial order) made to the person making (or proposing to make) it and includes any relevant Parliamentary report or resolution; and 'required information' means:

(a) an explanation of the incompatibility which the order (or proposed order) seeks to remove, including particulars of the relevant declaration, finding or order; and
(b) a statement of the reasons for proceeding under s 10 and for making an order in those terms.

Schedule 2 makes provision for the computation of time in relation to the passing of remedial orders which are outside the scope of this book.

2.17   FREEDOM OF THOUGHT AND RELIGION

Section 13 of the HRA 1998 provides:

'(1) If a court's determination of any question arising under this Act might affect the exercise by a religious organisation (itself or its members collectively) of the Convention right to freedom of thought, conscience and religion, it must have particular regard to the importance of that right.

(2) In this section "court" includes a tribunal.'

This provision appears to promote freedom of thought over and above the other Convention rights. It is submitted that all s 13 does is to reflect the importance within the Convention of the freedoms under Article 9. It does not mean that the court or tribunal must disregard the rather narrow concept of freedom of thought, conscience and religion in the Convention in favour of a more liberal approach.[120]

2.18 JUDGES OF THE ECtHR

Section 18 of the HRA 1998 makes provision for appointment to the ECtHR but these provisions and provisions on judicial pensions are outside the scope of this book.

---

120 See **3.13** for further discussion.

Chapter 3

USING THE HUMAN RIGHTS ACT 1998 IN THE CONTEXT OF EMPLOYMENT LAW

3.1 INTRODUCTION

This chapter examines some of the potential applications of the Convention rights in employment law. In **3.1**–**3.4** we discuss the impact of Convention rights in general terms, **3.5** gives a checklist and in **3.6** onwards we discuss individual Articles and employment law. Where the state acts as an employer, its actions are governed by the Convention rights.[1] Thus, under the HRA 1998, all acts of a public authority as an employer must be compatible with the rights under the Convention. The State may also be responsible for a failure to take positive measures to protect individuals against interference by other private individuals with a right under the Convention.[2]

Although the ECtHR does not recognise a right to work under the Convention,[3] the right to earn a livelihood is regarded as important.[4]

Dismissal may be the form taken by an interference with a Convention right.[5] Clearly, other detriments, such as suspension or warning,[6] or threatening disciplinary action,[7] may also constitute the act of infringement.

A public authority may also be liable in respect of the fairness of procedures for selecting job applicants. It is arguable that such a process determines the civil rights of unsuccessful applicants who are not thereafter able to insist on being appointed. The successful candidate for appointment thereby gains the option of accepting a contractual relationship with the public authority. However, it is doubtful that the selection process constitutes one by which the civil rights and obligations of the applicant are determined. If it does, the public authority will have to observe the guarantees of Article 6 in its appointment procedures. Convention jurisprudence indicates that other Convention rights may not be applicable to the refusal of the public authority to appoint, because the right of equal access to public service was excluded from the final draft of the Convention.[8]

---

1   *Swedish Engine Drivers Union v Sweden* (1979–80) 1 EHRR 617 at para 37.
2   *Young, James and Webster v UK* (1982) 4 EHRR 38.
3   *X v Denmark* (1975) 3 DR 153.
4   *Young, James and Webster v UK* (1982) 4 EHRR 38.
5   *Vogt v Germany* (1996) 21 EHRR 205 at para 44
6   *B v UK* (1985) 45 DR 41.
7   *Young, James and Webster v UK* (1982) 4 EHRR 38.
8   See *Glassenap v Germany* (1987) 9 EHRR 25 at para 49.

3.2   THE CONTRACT OF EMPLOYMENT

The fact that an individual has entered into a contract with certain restrictions contained in it may not prevent an infringement of a right occurring even when that infringement is foreshadowed in the contract.

However, the consensual nature of a particular contract will be taken into account in assessing whether there has been an infringement. Thus, in *Ahmad v UK*[9] the Commission took account of the fact that the applicant had accepted teaching obligations 'of his own free will' which had an effect on his ability to perform religious observance. On the other hand, in *Van der Musselle*[10] the court did not regard the fact that a lawyer entered the profession voluntarily as preventing a potential breach of the Convention if an individual could only enter the profession on terms that might interfere with a Convention right. Such a contract may form the basis for justification of the infringement. The right to free expression carries with it responsibilities and therefore it may be possible to restrict that right by contract.[11] The court will protect the Convention rights within an employment context, but it must be shown that in the context of the case that there is an Article which is engaged by the facts. However, the following principles should be noted.

(1) Provisions of a contract of employment will be interpreted so as to be compatible with the Convention rights without qualification if they are imposed by statute such as:
  (a) a clause providing for equal pay for equal work;[12]
  (b) an invention created by an employee shall, as between the employee and his or her employer, be taken to belong to the employer if it was made in the normal course of the employee's duties or in the course of duties specifically assigned to the employee;[13]
  (c) where a literary, dramatic, musical or artistic work is created by an employee in the course of employment, the employer is the first owner of any copyright in the work subject to any agreement to the contrary;[14]
  (d) where a design is created by an employee in the course of employment, the employer is the owner of any design right;[15]
  (e) terms and conditions specified by subordinate legislation, for public authority employees.

(2) Provisions of a contract of employment between an individual and a public authority will be void if they are unlawful acts of that public authority.

---

9   (1982) 4 EHRR 126.
10   (1984) 6 EHRR 163.
11   See **3.12.10**.
12   Equal Pay Act 1970, s 1.
13   Patents Act 1977, s 39.
14   Copyright, Designs and Patents Act 1988, s 11.
15   Copyright, Designs and Patents Act 1988, s 207.

(3) Non-contractual policies of an employer may conflict with Articles of the Convention. If the policy itself is in conflict and is the act of a public authority, it will be of no effect, and implementation of it will be an unlawful act.

(4) Individual acts of a public authority which conflict with Convention rights are unlawful acts and may attract a remedy independent of any outcome of the particular case.

(5) Employment contracts are governed by the common law of contract and in particular by the provisions on contracts for services in the Employment Rights Act 1996 (ERA 1996) and other legislation such as the Equal Pay Act 1970, the Disability Discrimination Act 1995 and the Unfair Contract Terms Act 1977. Section 98 of the ERA 1996 provides that a person may be fairly dismissed only on certain specific grounds, which it lists. Most contracts of employment make reference to grievance or disciplinary procedures and these will either form part of the contract or will be a measure by which the employer's behaviour in dismissing the employee is judged by a tribunal.

(6) Suspension may be a contractual right of the employer if express, or may constitute a breach of the contract itself. Absent an express term that suspension may be without pay, suspension will require the employer to pay the employee.

(7) Dismissal will generally ensue from some form of procedure being followed. Save in cases of gross misconduct or other fundamental breach of the contract, the dismissal will be with notice.

Irrespective of the HRA 1998, the provisions of a contract must be interpreted so as to be consistent with the UK's international treaty obligations. Consideration of whether a provision is consistent with Convention rights requires consideration of:

(1) whether the provision (or its actual or potential implementation) engages a Convention right;

(2) if the provision does engage a Convention right, by showing a *prima facie* infringement, it will be consistent with the Convention right if the apparent infringement can be justified by reference to Convention law principles;

(3) justification will almost always require detailed consideration of the facts of Convention cases by reference to the aims and principles of the Convention.

The approach of the courts and tribunals after the HRA 1998 may perhaps start from the approach adopted by Scarman LJ:

> 'it is no longer possible to argue that because the international treaty obligations of the UK do not become law unless enacted by Parliament our courts pay no regard to our international obligations. They pay very serious regard to them: in particular, they will interpret statutory language and apply common law principles, wherever possible, so as to reach a conclusion consistent with our international obligations: see *Salomon v. Customs and Excise Commissioners* [1967] 2 Q.B. 116

(particularly *per* Diplock L.J. at p. 143) and *Post Office v. Estuary Radio Ltd.* [1968] 2 Q.B. 740.'[16]

In *Ahmad v ILEA*, Scarman LJ[17] considered s 30 of the Education Act 1944 (the same words are re-enacted in the School Standards and Framework Act 1998, s 59(4)(b)). This provided that no person could be disqualified from being a teacher in a county or voluntary school by reason of his religious opinions. The section was incorporated into the teacher's contract and he was dismissed for insisting on attending worship during school hours. Scarman LJ construed the contract broadly so that any attendance at any place for religious worship entitled the teacher to adjustments to the school timetable to accommodate his practice.

Where the term is simply part of an agreement between individuals, what is the impact of the Convention rights? It will depend on what the content of the term is and whether the State has a positive duty to protect the Convention right in question. Thus a contract of employment may require confidentiality. Nothing in the Convention militates against confidentiality clauses as such. There will be occasions when the existence of a confidentiality clause will conflict with the right of freedom of expression. Thus a tribunal in a public interest disclosure case will have to consider its own responsibility to protect the right to freedom of expression. At present, the public interest disclosure provisions do not protect a person who suffers a detriment or dismissal not because the employer believes that the individual has made a disclosure, but instead believes that the individual is about to make a disclosure. It may be that the duty to give effect to the Convention rights under s 3 of the HRA 1998 (in giving effect to statutory provisions) requires the provisions of the ERA 1996 dealing with public interest disclosure to be interpreted in such a way (or given effect to in such a way) as protects the individual against such action by the private employer. Another area concerning confidentiality clauses, in which competing interests will have to be balanced by the courts, is that of restrictive covenants relating to disclosure of information. Here there is a conflict between the right of the business owner to protect the goodwill of the owner's enterprise (a right relating to property) and the right of the individual to free expression.

The impact of the contract of employment in relation to particular Articles as they arise is discussed below.

3.3 NON-CONTRACTUAL RELATIONSHIPS BETWEEN EMPLOYER AND EMPLOYEE

The acts of public authorities must be compatible with the Convention rights. Such acts include non-contractual practices and policies. Much of the discussion below centres on Article 6 rights.

---

16 Dissenting judgment of Scarman LJ in *Ahmad v ILEA* [1977] ICR 490.
17 [1977] ICR 490.

3.3.1 Suspension pending disciplinary proceedings

Sometimes an employer will instruct an employee not to have contact with co-workers during a period of suspension for the investigation of misconduct. It is highly unlikely that a suspension which is of short duration would offend against provisions of the Convention. However, once again, no hard-and-fast rule can be laid down. In *Carter v UK*,[18] a firefighter attempted a challenge to such an order. He had been accused of harassment and suspended following investigation pending the outcome of disciplinary proceedings. He was prohibited from entering any fire service premises without prior permission and was requested not to contact or speak to any of his service colleagues. This prohibition together with the request placed restrictions on his social and everyday life. He alleged that the restrictions prevented him from communicating with his friends and that they almost prevented him from communicating with his family. He alleged violation of Article 8 (respect for private life) and Article 10 (the right to receive and impart information).

Respect for private life includes the right to establish and develop relationships with other human beings and a person's private life cannot be limited to an 'inner circle' in which he can live his own personal life as he chooses. The request and requirements were an interference with Article 8. In the particular case, which involved the protection of public safety and preventing disorder and crime, there was a legitimate aim pursued. Proportionality of the restrictions on the applicant's private life was considered. There was controversy surrounding the charges against him that threatened harm to the teamwork of the service. It was noted that he was only a part-time employee, and thus his entire life did not centre on activities at the fire station. The restriction on the applicant was a proportionate response to a pressing social need. It was also within the State's margin of appreciation.

In other circumstances an employer would find it very much more difficult to justify such an instruction, and a public authority would face the prospect (absent justification of the infringement) of an award of damages being made against it, or of proceedings for an injunction to require the authority to permit contact between the suspended employee and work colleagues.

Whether contractual or not, the following acts may be affected by Article 6 of the Convention in the employer–employee relationship. Although they concern private law relations they are 'civil' disputes within the meaning of Article 6, which applies to those disputes which have a decisive impact on the ability of an individual to continue his job or profession:

- suspension;[19]
- dismissal;[20]
- professional suspension/disbarment.[21]

---

18   Admissibility Decision Application No 36417/97 (1999) June 29.
19   *Obermeier v Austria* (1991) 13 EHRR 290.
20   *X v UK* (1984) 6 EHRR 583.
21   *Albert and Le Compte v Belgium* (1983) 5 EHRR 533.

The procedural safeguards required by Article 6 will be required in relation to suspension or dismissal in the following kinds of circumstances. In the *Obermeier* case[22] the applicant had a dispute with his employer concerning paid activities which the employer proposed to withdraw from him. He instituted proceedings in the Labour Court. On the day following the first hearing, his employer, who considered that it was entitled to take this decision at any time without giving reasons, suspended him from his duties. He tried to force the employer to start the disciplinary proceedings. He then challenged the suspension in the courts seeking a declaration and/or specific performance. He alleged suspension was to penalise him for having instituted legal proceedings against the company and was therefore unjustified. The court of first instance dismissed his complaint, but his appeal was upheld as regards the revocation of the suspension. In the meantime the company had decided to dismiss him by 'administrative retirement'. For the purposes of Austrian law he was a disabled person and so his dismissal had to be authorised by the Disabled Persons Board which gave consent because the relationship of trust had been irreparably damaged. He appealed against this decision, alleging inter alia that the Board had failed to hold an inquiry into the case and had obtained only the company's observations. The applicant, before the Labour Court considering his remitted case on suspension, challenged the lawfulness of his dismissal which he alleged had been pronounced before the authorisation from the Disabled Persons Board had become final. However, this claim was rejected by the Labour Court as the proceedings before the Administrative Court (concerning the Disabled Persons Board decision) did not have suspensive effect. The Austrian Supreme Court quashed the decisions of the Labour Court, finding that the company should have waited until the Disabled Persons Board's authorisation had become final. As the applicant's dismissal was invalid, he had an interest in challenging the suspension and the Supreme Court remitted the case to the Labour Court again. The proceedings relating to the suspension, which had commenced in 1983, had still not been determined nine years later. The applicant complained to the Commission that he had been impeded in his access to a court and that a dispute concerning his civil rights had not been determined within a reasonable time (a breach of Article 6). It was not contested before the ECtHR that the dispute relating to his suspension concerned private-law relations between employer and employee. It was a 'civil' dispute for the purposes of Article 6(1). The Article was therefore engaged by the dispute relating to his suspension. A dispute as to dismissal was said to be 'unquestionably also a "civil" matter within the meaning of Article 6'.[23]

3.3.2 Disciplinary hearings

The rights under Article 6 include:

–   the right to an independent and impartial tribunal;
–   the right to disclosure;

---

22   *Obermeier v Austria* (1991) 13 EHRR 290.
23   See also *X v UK* (1984) 6 EHRR 583.

- the right to an adversarial hearing;
- the right to receive reasons; and
- the right to have decisions made within a reasonable period.

Where a public authority conducts disciplinary proceedings with a view to determining whether or not an employee should be dismissed, that process may attract the guarantees of Article 6, and if it does not the courts will look to see whether any right of redress against the actions of the public authority in the tribunals or courts is sufficient to remedy the absence of these procedural safeguards.[24]

3.4   UNFAIR DISMISSAL

3.4.1   The right not to be unfairly dismissed

The right not to be unfairly dismissed is a purely statutory creation. As a result its scope is determined by the ERA 1996. Although s 98 of the ERA 1996 must be construed compatibly with the Convention rights, it will not be possible to use purely procedural guarantees such as that contained in Article 6 to expand its scope. Other Convention rights will affect the application of the concept.

3.4.2   The qualifying period

The qualifying period for unfair dismissal does not prevent access to a court. In *Stedman v UK*,[25] the Commission considered the two-year qualification period (now one year). Employees of two years' standing had access at that time to an industrial tribunal to claim unfair dismissal, and in many cases an employee would have a civil remedy for breach of contract. The applicant had no claim in contract as she was dismissed with notice when she refused to sign a new contract that included a term that she work on Sundays. The Commission noted that the right of access to a court is not an absolute one. The State is allowed a certain margin of appreciation. The Commission considered that restricting access to a tribunal for unfair dismissal for employees of two years' standing pursued the legitimate aim of offering protection to those in established employment who had given a minimum of two years' service to an employer, without burdening the employer to the extent that dismissal within a two-year 'probationary period' was likely to lead to court proceedings. On this basis the court concluded that the restriction of access to a tribunal to employees of two years' standing was not arbitrary and did not impair the very essence of the right under Article 6(1).[26]

3.4.3   Tests applied by the employment tribunal

In an ordinary unfair dismissal claim, the employment tribunal usually has to consider s 98 of the Employment Rights Act 1996 and to apply the following test:

---

24   See **3.8** and **3.4.3** *et seq* for a discussion of the effect of Article 6.
25   (1997) 23 EHRR CD 169.
26   See *Ashingdane v UK* (1985) 7 EHRR 528.

'Where the employer has fulfilled the requirements of subsection (1), the determination of the question whether the dismissal is fair or unfair (having regard to the reason shown by the employer) –

(a)   depends on whether in the circumstances (including the size and adminis-trative resources of the employer's undertaking) the employer acted reasonably or unreasonably in treating it as a sufficient reason for dismissing the employee, and

(b)   shall be determined in accordance with equity and the substantial merits of the case.'[27]

It is important to recall that this provision defines the scope of the civil right to be determined by the tribunal. The question of whether the employer acted reasonably or unreasonably in treating the reason for dismissal as a sufficient reason for dismissing the employee imports a test whereby if the decision falls within a band of reasonable responses it will be treated as sufficient. The effect of this is that the tribunal cannot decide what actually happened, but must look to what the employer believed and decide whether that belief was sufficient in the circumstances. In misconduct cases the Court of Appeal in *Foley v Post Office*[28] reaffirmed the test in *British Homes Stores v Burchell.*[29]

British Home Stores v Burchell states that the tribunal errs in law if it substitutes its own view for that of the employer. Many authorities on unfair dismissal have concluded that the employment tribunal may not decide what it would have done in the circumstances of the case but must decide whether the employer acted reasonably.[30] The variety of responses open to an employer means that if dismissal was within the limits of the range of reasonable responses, the dismissal will be fair.[31]

In *Iceland Frozen Foods Ltd v Jones*[32] the principles were said to be:

'(1)   the starting point should always be the words of s 57(3) [the predecessor of s 98(4) of the Employment Rights Act 1996] themselves;

(2)   in applying the section an [employment tribunal] must consider the reasonableness of the employer's conduct, not simply whether they (the members of the [employment] Tribunal) consider the dismissal to be fair;

(3)   in judging the reasonableness of the employer's conduct an [employment] tribunal must not substitute its decision as to what was the right course to adopt for that of the employer;

(4)   in many (though not all) cases there is a band of reasonable responses to the employee's conduct within which one employer might reasonably take one view and another quite reasonably take another;

(5)   the function of the [employment] tribunal, as an industrial jury, is to determine whether in the particular circumstances of each case the decision to dismiss the employee fell within the band of reasonable responses which a reasonable employer might have adopted. If the dismissal falls within the band the dismissal is fair; if the dismissal falls outside the band it is unfair.'

27   ERA 1996, s 98(4).
28   [2000] ICR 1283.
29   [1980] ICR 303.
30   See *Grundy (Teddington) UK Ltd v Willis* [1976] ICR 323.
31   See *Rolls Royce v Walpole* [1980] IRLR 343.
32   [1982] IRLR 439.

In *Linfood Cash and Carry Ltd v Thomson,*[33] the EAT held that in a misconduct case the tribunal may not interfere because it prefers the evidence of one witness to the incident to that of another. It must conclude that no reasonable employer would accept the evidence of the witness whose evidence of the misconduct it wishes to reject. The tribunal cannot therefore, if it applies this test, decide if misconduct took place, but can only characterise the employer's reaction to the facts which the employer believed (or ought to have believed if it had been acting reasonably).

The tribunal can find a dismissal to be unfair because the process leading up to it was procedurally flawed. In relation to the civil right not to be unfairly dismissed, the tribunal may characterise the dismissal as unreasonable due to such a fault and it therefore has the power to determine all matters of fact and law relevant to that characterisation.

Does the guarantee under Article 6 permit the tribunal to determine whether the applicant committed the act for which he was dismissed? The Court of Appeal in *Foley v Post Office*[34] reaffirmed that tribunals must not substitute their own view for that of the employer in determining whether the dismissal was fair or not. A series of cases, and informed opinion, had criticised the traditional approach to the determination of unfair dismissal. Mummery LJ stated:

'In my judgment, the Employment Tribunals should continue to apply the law enacted in section 98(1), (2) and (4) of the Employment Rights Act 1996 ("the 1996 Act"), giving to those provisions the same interpretation as was placed for many years by this court and the Employment Appeal Tribunal on the equivalent provisions in section 57(1), (2) and (3) of the Employment Protection (Consolidation) Act 1978 ("the 1978 Act")

8. This means that for all practical purposes:

9. (1) "The band or range of reasonable responses" approach to the issue of the reasonableness or unreasonableness of a dismissal, as expounded by Browne-Wilkinson J in *Iceland Frozen Foods Ltd v Jones* [1983] ICR 17 at 24F–25D and as approved and applied by this court (see *Gilham v Kent County Council (No 2)* [1985] ICR 233; *Neale v Hereford & Worcester County Council* [1986] ICR 471; *Campion v Hamworthy Engineering Ltd* [1987] ICR 966; and *Morgan v Electrolux* [1991] ICR 369), remains binding on this court, as well as on the Employment Tribunals and the Employment Appeal Tribunal. The disapproval of that approach in *Hadden* (see p. 1160E–F) on the basis that (a) the expression was a "mantra" which led Employment Tribunals into applying what amounts to a perversity test of reasonableness, instead of the statutory test of reasonableness as it stands, and that (b) it prevented members of Employment Tribunals from approaching the issue of reasonableness by reference to their own judgment of what they would have done had they been the employers, is an unwarranted departure from binding authority.

10. (2) The tripartite approach to (a) the reasons for, and (b) the reasonableness or unreasonableness of, a dismissal for a reason relating to the conduct of the employee, as expounded by Arnold J in *British Home Stores Ltd v Burchell* [1980] ICR 303 at 304 and 308G–H, and as approved and applied by this court in *W Weddel & Co Ltd v Tepper* [1980] ICR 286, remains binding on this court, as well as on

---

33   [1989] ICR 518.
34   [2000] ICR 1283.

Employment Tribunals and the Employment Appeal Tribunal. Any departure from that approach indicated in *Hadden* (for example, by suggesting that reasonable grounds for belief in the employee's misconduct and the carrying out of a reasonable investigation into the matter relate to establishing the reason for dismissal rather than to the reasonableness of the dismissal) is inconsistent with binding authority.

11. Unless and until the statutory provisions are differently interpreted by the House of Lords or are amended by an Act of Parliament, that is the law which should continue to be applied to claims for unfair dismissal. In so holding I am aware that there is a body of informed opinion which is critical of this interpretation of the 1996 Act.'[35]

It appears therefore that the public authority employer contemplating dismissing a person, and the tribunal trying to determine whether that dismissal is unfair, are considering wholly different civil rights. The employer is considering whether to terminate the contract. The tribunal is attempting to characterise the decision of the employer as reasonable or unreasonable. In that determination the key question for the employer ('has this person committed misconduct?') plays little part. In those circumstances, can it be said that the tribunal has power to determine all matters of fact and law relevant to the termination of the contract?

In *C v UK*[36] it had emerged at the tribunal hearing that, when the Council dismissed the applicant, it had been mistaken as to certain facts which further investigation could have clarified. In particular, it appeared that, in an incident which gave rise to a final warning, a signature which was allegedly forged was in fact authentic. The tribunal found, however, that the dismissal was not affected by this mistake, since in relation to the other matter to which the warning related, a false claim for overtime, the final warning was still valid. The tribunal also found the whole evidence before the disciplinary hearing was such that new evidence, concerning the possibility of entry to the school without leaving evidence of a break-in, would not have affected the outcome. The tribunal concluded therefore that the applicant had not been unfairly dismissed.

In common law, employment is a contractual relationship in which dismissal, with due notice, is entirely lawful. It is a well-established principle of law that any conduct by an employee which is in breach of the contract, such as dishonesty, may, depending on its circumstances and gravity, merit dismissal without notice. Under the ERA 1996, a dismissed employee may generally complain to an employment tribunal that his dismissal was 'unfair'. If the tribunal so decides, it may award the employee compensation or, in specified circumstances, order reinstatement or re-engagement. If this order is not complied with, additional compensation may be awarded. The legislation, however, merely provides a remedy for certain dismissals which under the ERA 1996 are 'unfair'; it does not prohibit them.

The Commission in *C v UK* noted that for a dismissal to be fair the employer must show that there was a reason for the dismissal and that this reason was one

---

35   [2000] ICR 1283 at pp 1287–1288.
36   (1987) 54 DR 162.

of those specified in the statute. In a conduct case the reason must be connected with the conduct of the employee. The Commission noted the statutory test, and then noted that the case-law of the UK courts establishes that the question which has to be addressed by the employer when considering dismissal (and by the tribunal when considering whether a dismissal is fair) is not whether the employee is guilty, in terms of the criminal law, but the question of what, given the information available to the employer at the time when it addresses the question and in the circumstances of the case, it is reasonable for the employer to do. It is not sufficient for an employer to rely on an honest belief in the employee's guilt; there must be reasonable grounds and the employer must act reasonably in all the circumstances. An employer must also have sufficient information to enable it reasonably to assume guilt on the part of the employee and must have carried out such investigation as was reasonable. The standard of proof by which these matters are to be determined at a hearing before an employment tribunal is that applicable in a civil case (ie proof on the balance of probabilities). Where the grounds for dismissal are misconduct which might also amount to a criminal offence, such as theft, the employer is not required to have satisfied itself as to the existence of these grounds on the same standard of proof as is required for the proof of guilt in criminal cases (ie proof beyond reasonable doubt). The standard required in unfair dismissal cases is that which has been described as justifying a 'reasonable conclusion of management'. Although the Commission can take any point arising under the Convention, nothing was said in its decision to challenge this approach to the matters open to the tribunal.

C v UK cannot be seen as a ringing endorsement of the proposition that unfair dismissal procedures are adequate to deal with all aspects of the civil rights in issue in the disciplinary proceedings. In that case it would not have mattered whether there was a claim for wrongful dismissal or unfair dismissal being considered. The decision concerning dismissal was determined by the existence of two facts, only one of which was proven to be false. Where a single reason was given for dismissal and was shown to be based on erroneous information, the applicant to the tribunal will want to have the absence of misconduct established. Whether the tribunal can deal with that issue will be a consideration that is to be taken into account in determining whether the tribunal has full jurisdiction to deal with all substantive and legal matters relevant to the civil right.[37] In *Bryan* it was said (at para 45):

> 'Furthermore, in assessing the sufficiency of the review available to Mr Bryan on appeal to the High Court [on a point of law], it is necessary to have regard to matters such as the subject matter of the decision appealed against, the manner in which that decision was arrived at, and the context of the dispute, including the desired and actual grounds of appeal.'

The employee seeking to have the fact of misconduct challenged should bring proceedings for breach of contract in addition to any claim for unfair dismissal. In that context, he or she will be able to argue that the public authority employer must observe the guarantees of Article 6 in the disciplinary processes

---

37   *Bryan v UK* (1996) 21 EHRR 342.

leading up to dismissal. The argument will be that had the Article 6 guarantees been observed it would have been apparent that the misconduct had not been perpetrated by the applicant. If the misconduct was not perpetrated by the applicant, no misconduct entitling termination of the contract would have existed. This finding has consequences in the damages the public authority employer must pay for the breach of contract. They will not be confined to the period during which any fair procedure would have been followed, but will include damages for the consequences of failing to follow that fair procedure.

The tribunal has jurisdiction in relation to breach of contract claims in misconduct cases and can therefore determine the question of whether the misconduct actually occurred so as to permit a summary dismissal of an employee. The tribunal's jurisdiction is over claims for damages for a breach of contract (ETA 1996, s 3). Section 3 of the ETA 1996 must be construed so as to give practical effect to Article 6. A person whose complaint is that his Article 6 rights were not guaranteed in the context of a dismissal which is before the tribunal would otherwise have to seek redress by bringing an action against the public authority employer in the county court under s 7(1)(a) of the HRA 1998. However, all financial aspects of the claim (barring a claim for just satisfaction damages under s 8 of the HRA 1998) could be dealt with by the tribunal. In practice therefore such a person would be prevented from seeking redress for breach of Article 6 by the disproportionate cost of s 7(1)(a) proceedings. One method of ensuring access to a court would be to construe the procedural section conferring jurisdiction in respect of the civil right (breach of contract) as conferring jurisdiction on tribunals to consider whether a breach of contract had occurred because the employer had dismissed a person who had not committed an act of misconduct warranting dismissal at common law. The concept of 'damages for breach of contract' must be construed in accordance with s 8 of the HRA 1998 so as to compensate for the loss of the chance of retaining employment had the employer reached the correct conclusion concerning the misconduct by observing the guarantees of Article 6.

Such an approach would run counter to that in *Janciuk v Winerite*,[38] in which the EAT held that where a contract is terminable on notice, the measure of damages to which the employee was entitled on summary dismissal was the amount which the employer would have been bound to pay had his contract been terminated lawfully. The argument that the employee should have been compensated for the loss of a chance of a favourable outcome in (contractual) disciplinary proceedings was rejected. The EAT reasoned that when, for the purposes of calculating compensation, the court considered what would have been the loss had the contract been performed, the court assumed that the contract breaker would have performed the contract in a way most favourable to himself. The EAT applied *Lavarack v Woods of Colchester*.[39] It would not determine what might have happened had the employer known that it had no right to terminate the contract summarily, and then calculate compensation on a loss of chance basis. It is submitted that in the case of a public authority

---

38   [1998] IRLR 63.
39   [1967] 1 QB 278.

employer failing to reach the correct determination of the civil rights under the contract as a result of a failure to observe Article 6 guarantees in the disciplinary procedure, such a course is not open to the tribunal. The tribunal considering whether a breach of contract had occurred would have to construe that concept so as to give effect to the rights of the employee under the Convention. It is possible to construe the concept of a breach of contract so as to include a failure to observe the procedural guarantees of Article 6. The tribunal would then have to compensate the employee for the lost chance of retaining his job had those guarantees been observed. In *Janciuk* the EAT said that, in cases of bad faith on the part of the employer, the court could analyse the chances of the employee not being dismissed had the procedure been followed. It is submitted that the maximum effect can be given to the Article 6 guarantees if the employer is able to have that issue determined before the tribunal.

It is also not clear that the rule in *Laverack* can be applied to a situation in which the tribunal must, so far as it is possible to do so, give effect to its powers so as to render them compatible with the Convention rights under Article 6. If the public authority employer concedes that it would have operated the contract in the manner most favourable to itself, it could only argue for such consequences as are compatible with the application of the Article 6 guarantees. If the tribunal reached the conclusion that the employer would not have concluded that misconduct had taken place if it had followed the Article 6 guarantees, it could not also reach the conclusion that the employer would have dismissed the employee anyway at the end of the procedure. The employer who had reached such a conclusion and who was acting in good faith would not have dismissed. To limit the damages to the period the disciplinary proceedings would have taken is to ignore this consequence and would be incompatible with the concept of a fair trial. That concept must be taken to include the notion that the decision maker having derived a conclusion from the evidence does not act inconsistently with that conclusion.

A respondent seeking to argue against recovery for breach of Article 6 under the breach of contract jurisdiction of the tribunal could argue that it is not clear that the employee is practically barred from seeking damages in the county court under s 7(1)(a), and that if the proper approach is in fact to determine what would have happened had the employer followed a proper procedure it is not disproportionate to expect the claim for damages to be brought in the county court. In many cases, the sums at issue as a result of this argument would exceed the tribunal's financial jurisdiction over contract claims.

3.4.4 Criminal conduct

An unfair dismissal for conduct amounting to a criminal offence does not amount to a criminal charge within the meaning of Article 6. In the decision of *Krause v Switzerland*,[40] the Head of the Federal Department of Justice and the Police gave a television interview in which he stated that a person, albeit awaiting trial, had committed criminal offences. On the facts of the case the Commission found that the presumption of innocence had not been breached,

---

40   Application No 7986/77, (1978) 13 DR 73.

but affirmed the general principle that Article 6(2), protects everybody against being treated by public officials as being guilty of an offence before this is established according to law by a competent court. Article 6(2), therefore, may be violated by public officials if they declare that somebody is responsible for criminal acts without a court having found so.

In *C v UK*[41] the Commission drew a distinction between civil proceedings and criminal proceedings arising out of the same events. This addresses an issue frequently raised by those who are dismissed for misconduct. They complain that they have been dismissed when they were innocent of an offence. However, by virtue of the different standards of proof normally observed in such proceedings, acquittal at the end of a criminal trial, because the accused has not been shown to be guilty of an offence beyond all reasonable doubt, does not necessarily preclude that same person's civil liability on the balance of probabilities.

Whilst State officials are under an obligation to observe scrupulously the presumption of innocence with regard to pending criminal proceedings, particularly those officials involved in the prosecution, trial or appeal, such an obligation does not generally arise in respect of a person's civil obligations *vis-à-vis* the State, as in that case with a contract of employment in the State public service. Thus, if the assessment by the applicant's employer of the applicant's honesty and fitness for further service is communicated to the applicant only by way of a notice of dismissal and is not publicly communicated, no breach of Article 6 will be found. If the reason for dismissal is made public a breach may arise.

However, an assertion of guilt in the tribunal will not attract Article 6(2) guarantees. Considering whether the employer had acted fairly and reasonably in dismissing does not involve determinations of any criminal charge to which the presumption of innocence would attach. Generally, a tribunal should adjourn pending the outcome of a criminal case arising out of the facts leading to dismissal.

3.4.5　The impact of the Human Rights Act 1998

Scarman LJ in *Ahmad*[42] provides a good example of the way in which unfair dismissal cases will be affected by the HRA 1998. He held, dissenting, that the tribunal had misconstrued the statutory term of the contract by considering the question of reasonableness independently of the proper construction of s 30 of the Education Act 1944, and therefore of the appellant's contractual rights.[43] Under the HRA 1998 the provision of the ERA 1996 relating to unfair dismissal will have to be construed consistently with the requirements of the Convention. Note that the outcome in *Ahmad* may have been correct in terms of the Convention in any event (see 'The effect of the contract on religious freedom' at **3.13.3**).

41　(1987) 54 DR 162.
42　*Ahmad v ILEA* [1977] ICR 490.
43　See *Ahmad v ILEA* [1977] ICR 490 at p 505.

If an employer's actions conflict with the Convention rights usually a tribunal will consider (without its aid) that the employer acted unreasonably in dismissing. However there will be cases, such as *Boychuk v H J Symons Holdings Ltd*,[44] which might now be decided differently in the light of the HRA 1998, and the tribunals in difficult cases, such as those involving sensitive moral issues, may find assistance in determining the question of reasonableness by having regard to the proper interpretation to be given to that concept in the light of the HRA 1998.

In *Boychuk*, an audit clerk whose duties brought her into contact with the public, was dismissed for persistently insisting on wearing a badge bearing the words 'Lesbians Ignite'. The EAT dealt with this by saying that there are limits upon an employer's discretion to dismiss an employee because the employer will not accept the employee's attire, hair, behaviour and the like. The EAT took the view that it is essentially a matter for the discretion of the tribunal. Under the HRA 1998, however, that proposition cannot stand. The evaluative decision of the tribunal will have to take account of the fact that a person's expression of their sexuality is a fundamental aspect of their private life. There will remain a balancing exercise between the employer's decision and the right of free expression/private life, but this will have to take account of whether the decision was proportionate to the right of the individual. It will not be enough to judge the action of the employer simply by reference to what reasonable employers would do in the circumstances without bringing into account the expectation that the reasonable employer would respect the fundamental rights of the individual and act proportionately to those rights. The employment tribunal will also need to recall its positive obligation to ensure respect for the individual's private life even between private parties.

In *Boychuk*, the appellant put forward the proposition that an employer cannot forbid behaviour unless the employer can establish that the behaviour is such that others are offended to such an extent that it affects not merely the conduct of the business within the office itself, but substantially impairs the prospects of success of the business as a going concern. This argument reflects the fact that the employer has a right of control over its property and that this must not be infringed. Clearly, when an employer can show that conduct is having an effect on the business, the tribunal will have to balance the right contended for by the applicant for individual freedoms against the employer's right not to have its possessions unnecessarily controlled by legislation requiring it to sustain losses as a result of honouring the rights of the individual.

In *Boychuk*, the reasoning of the EAT reflected this.

> 'What is necessary in a case of this kind ... is the striking of a balance between the need of the employer to control the business for which he is responsible, in the interests of the business itself – and after all, it is upon its continued prosperity that everybody's interests depend – a balance between that need, on the one hand, and the reasonable freedom of the employee, on the other. How that will be done in different cases will depend very much on the circumstances and the facts.'[45]

---

44 [1977] IRLR 395.
45 [1997] IRLR 395 at para 7.

The EAT in *Boychuk* held that the possibility of offence to customers and the interests of the business would be sufficient. In the light of the HRA 1998 the employer might reasonably dismiss if such damage to the business, but not offence *per se*, were probable rather than theoretical. There would have to be some evidence at least of questioning to see whether the behaviour was having that effect.

If there is nothing to suggest that the employee's freedom of expression is affecting the business there will be no Convention right to balance against the employee's right. The balancing exercise will then be conducted purely by reference to whether the restriction on the employee's right is proportionate to a legitimate aim and established by law.

The Scottish case of *Saunders v Scottish National Camps Association Ltd*[46] would probably now be decided differently. There the applicant was dismissed from his job as a maintenance handyman at a children's camp on discovery of his homosexuality and the fact that he had been involved in a homosexual incident. The incident did not involve children. His dismissal was found to be fair by the tribunal, and the EAT would not disturb this finding as it was a commonly held view (even if it was scientifically untrue) that homosexuals were more likely than heterosexuals to commit acts of child abuse. In the light of the HRA 1998 the tribunal would, it is submitted, need to consider its obligation to ensure respect for private life. Necessarily the tribunal's model of the reasonable employer would act in a way compatible with the applicant's Convention rights, including his right to respect for his private life. In the absence of a risk, interference with that right by dismissing the applicant would probably not be justifiable.

3.5   USING THE HUMAN RIGHTS ACT 1998

3.5.1   Checklist

HRA 1998 interpretations or causes of action will be heavily dependent on the factual content of the case. For example, in the case of a person, certain of whose functions are functions of a public authority, the practitioner will only be able to establish the nature of the act (public or private) by reference to the scope of the Convention rights and the facts of the case. In order to be a public act the employer must be undertaking some function of the State[47] in carrying out the act.

The suggested checklist is therefore:

(1) Act: what is the nature of the act of the employer/employee about which complaint is made?
    (a) Is it a private or public act?
    (b) If public, is it an act that is within the scope of employment legislation or the common law?

---

46   [1980] IRLR 174.
47   See **2.10** *et seq*.

(c) If the act is private, Convention rights do not apply to render it unlawful, however any legislation applicable to the private act must be construed so far as possible, so as to be compatible with the Convention rights. The court or tribunal must also give effect to that legislation so far as possible to give effect to the Convention right identified. Where the situation is covered by the common law, the court remains under an obligation to exercise any of its powers conferred by primary or secondary legislation so far as it is possible to do so in a manner compatible with the Convention rights.

(d) If the act is not within the scope of any existing legislation, after the interpretive exercise is concluded:

    (i) in the case of a public body, a s 7 'stand alone' right may arise;

    (ii) in the case of the private body, no cause of action exists, unless at common law or in equity.

(2) Engaging: on the facts given by the client, identify the Convention right on which the claimant/defendant may be able to rely:

    (a) if there is nothing on the face of the Convention, do any of the rights in the Convention bring into play a positive obligation on the court or tribunal to protect/promote the right in question when giving effect to its statutory powers?

    (b) is there any question of discrimination in the application of the Convention right, thus engaging Article 14?

(3) Victim: if the factual situation is within the scope of one of the Convention rights, is there an interference with the right? Identify the way in which the right is being infringed and attempt to characterise the features of the case which infringe that right in terms of the practical effects of the State's act or omission on the individual.

(4) Justification: if there is an infringement can it be justified? Is there a justification of the act or a justification that would indicate that exercise of the court's powers in a particular way was a construction of the legislation which is compatible with the Convention rights and the duty to give effect to them:

    (a) Does the right permit justification?

    (b) Is the interference identified prescribed by law?

    (c) What objective(s) does the interference identified pursue?

    (d) Is the interference identified necessary in a democratic society?

    (e) Can the court or tribunal give effect to its statutory powers in a way which is compatible with the Convention requirements for the particular situation identified, once the question of justification is considered? The question here is whether the infringement is justified and if not what is the court or tribunal able to do to rectify the situation in terms of its ability to make findings or grant a remedy?

(5) If no interpretation of a statute is possible to render the construction of the statute compatible with the Convention, higher courts may consider making a declaration of incompatibility unless it is possible to give effect to

the statutory provisions so as to render them compatible with the Convention rights.

(6) If a 'stand alone' cause of action under s 7(1)(a) is identified, the venue is the county court or High Court.

The introduction of the HRA 1998 presents problems for the courts and practitioners alike. For the courts there is a danger that they will be overwhelmed by citation of many authorities whose relevance is dubious. On the other hand, the practitioner will be aware that the courts are not currently familiar with the case-law of the Strasbourg authorities to which s 2 enjoins them to have regard. The first shots in the consequent war between bench and bar have already been fired. The courts have stated that it is important that only material necessary and relevant to the facts of the particular case is placed before the court.[48] There has been criticism of the unfocused use of ECtHR arguments. Practitioners should therefore consider whether their hard-won citation is really necessary. It is helpful to remember that the principles of interpretation of the Convention rights are as important as the case-law. The Strasbourg authorities tend to work on a fact-specific basis, thus rendering the value of their case-law difficult to judge, and the danger of deriving a general principle from looking at a particular case that much greater.

3.5.2   Effected items

Practitioners will have to become familiar with scrutinising:

−   an Act;
−   a piece of secondary legislation; or
−   an action or omission of a public authority; or
−   public acts of a person certain of whose functions are of a public nature,

to determine whether they are compatible with the Convention rights. We have referred to these in what follows as 'the effected items' as a convenient shorthand.

The Government has provided a guide to civil servants on the way in which legislation and administrative practice will be affected (*The Human Rights Act 1998: Guidance for Departments*). This, and the core guidance for public authorities published by the Human Rights Unit, may be of assistance in gauging the reach of the Convention rights where a body is identified as a public authority.[49]

The duty to interpret legislative provisions compatibly with the Convention rights means that if there is a possible interpretation that upholds the Convention right, the legislation must be read in that way, even if there are more plausible interpretations. The duty to give effect to the Convention rights in relation to legislative provisions requires the tribunal or court to regard the

---

48   *Williams v Cowell (t/a The Stables)* [2000] 1 WLR 187.
49   Available on www.homeoffice.gov.uk//hract/hramenu.htm and follow links there.

effected items and characterise them as lawful or unlawful having regard to the objects and purposes of the Convention rights. The effect given to, or the interpretation placed on, a legislative provision cannot, in other words, be compatible with the Convention rights if it limits them or prevents achievement of those purposes.[50]

The individual Articles in the context of employment law are considered below.

3.6 ARTICLE 3

3.6.1 Factual indicators of potential application

If the effected item[51] affects a person's physical or mental well-being, Article 3 may be relevant. Consideration should be given to the application of Article 3 in particular in cases of bullying or harassment, or where there is found to be a conspiracy against the individual by the employer. Thus where a woman is made the subject of a prolonged campaign of sexual harassment (see, for example, *Porcelli*[52]), it is possible that a breach of Article 3 has occurred. If the victim is vulnerable (for example mentally ill or personally sensitive) this may lower the threshold at which an act may constitute a breach of Article 3.

The Article prohibits torture and inhuman or degrading treatment or punishment. It aims to give protection from physical and mental ill-treatment of a certain degree of severity, seen in the context of the particular victim's case. The judgment concerning the severity of the treatment depends on all the circumstances of the case, such as the nature and context of the treatment or punishment, the manner and method of its execution, its duration, its physical or mental effects and, in some instances, the sex, age and state of health of the victim.[53] Thus a detailed analysis should be before any tribunal urged to make a finding of breach.

Treatment has been held by the ECtHR to be 'inhuman' because, inter alia, it was premeditated, was applied for hours at a stretch and caused either actual bodily injury or intense physical and mental suffering. Treatment is also 'degrading' if it is such as to arouse in its victims feelings of fear, anguish and inferiority capable of humiliating and debasing them.[54] In order for punishment or treatment associated with it to be 'inhuman' or 'degrading', the suffering or humiliation involved must in any event go beyond that inevitable element of suffering or humiliation connected with a given form of legitimate treatment or punishment. The question whether the purpose of the treatment was to humiliate or debase the victim is a further factor to be taken into account,[55] but the absence of any such purpose cannot conclusively rule out a finding of a violation of Article 3.

---

50   See **2.5.3** *et seq.*
51   See **3.5.2**.
52   *Porcelli v Strathclyde Regional Council* [1986] ICR 564.
53   *Soering v UK* (1989) Series A, No 161, p 39 at para 100.
54   *Ireland v UK* (1979–80) 2 EHRR 25.
55   *Raninen v Finland* (1998) 26 EHRR 563.

To be humiliating, the treatment must be such as to be degrading in the sense of grossly humiliating the victim before others or driving the victim to act against his or her will or conscience.[56]

An employee could seek to rely on the latter aspect, for example, if required to undertake an order, when the order runs against the employee's conscience. However, it is not clear whether the threat of dismissal would be regarded as sufficiently grave to be characterised as 'driving' the person to act against his or her will. In such a case, the tribunal might need to consider how this Article affects its interpretation of the range of reasonable responses should the employer dismiss the employee for refusing to undertake the order on these grounds. It is suggested that the employee would need to have communicated the nature of the objection before the tribunal would need to take account of Article 3. Without such communication it is unlikely that the person would be regarded as a victim for the purposes of the Convention. However, where it was known that the order would run against the employee's conscience, the victim condition may be considered to be satisfied.

3.6.2   Inhuman or degrading treatment and torture

In *V v UK*,[57] the ECtHR observed that Article 3 enshrines one of the most fundamental values of democratic society. It prohibits in absolute terms torture or inhuman or degrading treatment or punishment, irrespective of the victim's conduct.[58] The nature of the conduct of the applicant is, therefore, immaterial to the consideration under Article 3. Where degrading treatment is found, therefore, there would appear to be no scope for a finding that the victim contributed to his own loss arising from it as that would arguably limit the effect of the prohibition.

3.6.3   Bullying and harassment

A public authority which had permitted degrading treatment to continue would act unlawfully, through omission. It would be vicariously liable for the actions of its employees in bullying treatment. An employee who had been the subject of degrading treatment might be able to obtain an injunction to prevent further occurrences of the treatment, or to require the employer to take reasonable steps to prevent such humiliation occurring again. It is submitted that this right would be independent of any right not to be the subject of discrimination. However, the degree of humiliation would have to be severe and public. It is unlikely that an employee would wish to continue working for an employer in those circumstances. Nevertheless, in a large employer which had the capacity to ensure that the parties were not forced to work together, there might be a prospect of effective practical steps being taken so as to render the injunction effective. Note that treatment which is intended to cause suffering can amount to inhuman treatment and punishment, so although the injury caused may appear slight, when factors such as the

---

56   *The Greek Case*, Report of 5 November 1969, (1969) 12 YB 186–510.
57   (2000) 30 EHRR 121.
58   *Chahal v UK* (1996) RJD–V 1831, p 1855 at para 79.

vulnerable situation of the victim and the perpetrator's attitude are taken into account the treatment may reach the requisite level of severity.[59]

The State has positive obligations to secure the rights guaranteed by Article 3 and to prevent breaches of the Article by one private individual against another.[60] Thus the tribunal procedure rules and legislation may need to be interpreted in such a way that a person who has to give humiliating evidence in the course of proceedings is protected from being humiliated. This obligation goes beyond the current statutory requirements relating to private medical matters in disability cases and sexual misconduct allegations. The tribunal would have to regulate the procedure at the hearing in order to prevent humiliation of a witness, and where necessary cross-examination may lead to this result, the representatives of the parties should consider applying in chambers for directions on how the cross-examination is to be dealt with so that the tribunal can achieve the protection of the witness. Although Article 3 creates rights which are absolute and in respect of which it is not possible to derogate, the treatment has to be of sufficient severity for it to constitute a breach. A person giving evidence of a humiliating nature at a tribunal, for example evidence relating to personal hygiene, might have the right not to be identified under this Convention right if the giving of that evidence would expose that person to a great deal of media interest for no good purpose. If the degree of potential humiliation were sufficient the tribunal might be obliged to hear the evidence in chambers and not to identify the person involved in the decision.

In *Waters v Commissioner of Police*,[61] the House of Lords considered that the employer owes a duty of care to the employee to prevent harassment. If the employer knew that acts being done, or which might foreseeably be done, to the employee by fellow employees might cause him physical or mental harm and did nothing to protect him against such acts, the employer might be in breach of his duty of care towards the employee. Lord Hutton noted that:

> 'I consider that a person employed under an ordinary contract of employment can have a valid cause of action in negligence against her employer if the employer fails to protect her against victimisation and harassment which causes physical or psychiatric injury. This duty arises both under the contract of employment and under the common law principles of negligence.'

He referred to the implied term that:

> 'the employer shall render reasonable support to an employee to ensure that the employee can carry out the duties of his job without harassment and disruption by fellow workers.'

This has been held to exist by the EAT in *Wigan Borough Council v Davies*.[62]

The scope of the protection offered against bullying by Article 3 may be slightly broader than the implied term. However, it is likely that the courts will be

---

59   *Tomasi v France* (1993) 15 EHRR 1.
60   *Aksoy v Turkey* (1997) 23 EHRR 553.
61   [2000] 1 WLR 1607.
62   [1979] ICR 411 at p 414.

inclined to find the protection offered by domestic law to be adequate in this area, so that there is no need to have recourse to Article 3.

3.6.4   Protection from harassment

The Protection from Harassment Act 1997 prohibits harassment consisting of a course of conduct (including words) which amounts to harassment of another, and which the harasser knows or ought to know amounts to harassment of the other (s 1). The person whose course of conduct is in question ought to know that it amounts to harassment of another if a reasonable person in possession of the same information would think the course of conduct amounted to harassment of the other. However, this does not apply to a course of conduct if the person who pursued it shows –

(a)   that it was pursued for the purpose of preventing or detecting crime;
(b)   that it was pursued under any enactment or rule of law or to comply with any condition or requirement imposed by any person under any enactment; or
(c)   that in the particular circumstances the pursuit of the course of conduct was reasonable.

Section 3 provides for a civil remedy whereby an actual or apprehended breach of s 1 may be the subject of a claim in civil proceedings by the person who is or may be the victim of the course of conduct in question. Damages may be awarded for (among other things) any anxiety caused by the harassment and any financial loss resulting from the harassment. Breach of an injunction against such behaviour may result in arrest. A person cannot be convicted of an offence under s 1(6) in respect of any conduct which has been punished as a contempt of court. The phrase 'harassing a person' includes alarming the person or causing the person distress (s 7). However, a 'course of conduct' must involve conduct on at least two occasions.

The action is not treated as an action for personal injury for the purposes of the limitation period (see s 6).

The existence of an action for a course of conduct amounting to harassment in the sense given to that term in the Protection from Harassment Act 1997 may be enough for the State to be able to say that it has discharged its positive obligation to protect the individual from that type of degrading treatment. Where there is a single act which is grossly degrading, however, the State may have to provide protection for the individual against breach of Article 3 rights. There is also no warrant for the introduction of a concept of reasonableness into Article 3. The conduct of a person in exposing another to degrading treatment may be entirely proportionate to an aim which is reasonable. That will not alter the character of the treatment: it will remain degrading treatment.

3.7 ARTICLE 4

3.7.1 The scope of Article 4

Article 4 represents the prohibition on forced labour. The concept of forced labour means that the worker performs the work involuntarily. The requirement to do the work must be unjust or oppressive, or the work must involve unavoidable hardship. In *Iversen v Norway*,[63] the applicant had been convicted of an offence when he left his post in the public dental service in a northern district. Norwegian legislation required him to do this service for one year. This was held by the Commission not to amount to forced labour. As well as not fulfilling the conditions set out by the ILO (see **3.7.2** below), the work was 'for a short period, provided favourable remuneration and did not involve any discriminatory, arbitrary or punitive application'. Thus if the labour is for a short period and with favourable remuneration, not involving a diversion from voluntarily undertaken professional work, it is unlikely to constitute a breach of this Article. Further, Article 4(3)(d) provides that work undertaken as part of a person's normal civic obligations is exempt. Having said that, it is not possible for a person to contract himself into bondage.[64]

3.7.2 Forced labour and compulsory labour

A detailed examination of Article 4 was undertaken in *Van der Musselle v Belgium*.[65] Article 4 does not define what is meant by 'forced or compulsory labour' and no guidance on this point is to be found in the various Council of Europe documents relating to the preparatory work of the Convention. The authors of the Convention based themselves, to a large extent, on an earlier treaty of the ILO, Convention No 29 concerning Forced or Compulsory Labour.[66]

States undertook 'to suppress the use of forced or compulsory labour in all its forms within the shortest possible period'.[67] With a view to 'complete suppression' of such labour, States were permitted to have recourse thereto during a 'transitional period', but 'for public purposes only and as an exceptional measure, subject to the conditions and guarantees' laid down in Articles 4 *et seq*.[68] The main aim of the ILO Convention was originally to prevent the exploitation of labour in colonies, which were still numerous at that time.

ILO Convention No 105 of 25 June 1957, which entered into force on 17 January 1959, complemented ILO Convention No 29, by prescribing 'the immediate and complete abolition of forced or compulsory labour' in certain specified cases.

---

63   *Iversen v Norway* (1963) 6 YB 278.
64   See *De Wilde v Belgium* Series A, No 12, (1979–80) 1 EHRR 373.
65   (1984) 6 EHRR 163.
66   Adopted on 28 June 1930, entered into force on 1 May 1932 and modified in 1946.
67   ILO Convention No 29, Article 1(1).
68   ILO Convention No 29, Article 1(2).

Subject to Article 4(3), the Convention lays down a general and absolute prohibition of forced or compulsory labour. The ECtHR in *Van der Musselle* took into account the ILO Conventions and especially ILO Convention No 29, noting the striking similarity between para 3 of Article 4 of the Convention and para 2 of Article 2 of ILO Convention No 29.

Paragraph 1 of Article 2 of ILO Convention No 29 provides that 'for the purposes' of that Convention, the term 'forced or compulsory labour' means 'all work or service which is exacted from any person under the menace of any penalty and for which the said person has not offered himself voluntarily'. In *Van der Musselle*, the ECtHR took this as a starting point for interpretation of Article 4 of the Convention. The ECtHR noted that the Convention is a living instrument to be read 'in the light of the notions currently prevailing in democratic States'.

In construing the phrase 'forced or compulsory' labour, the ECtHR stated that the first of these adjectives brings to mind the idea of physical or mental constraint. 'Compulsory' does not refer just to any form of legal compulsion or obligation. Work to be carried out in pursuance of a freely negotiated contract cannot be regarded as falling within the scope of Article 4 on the sole ground that one of the parties has undertaken with the other to do that work and will be subject to sanctions if he or she does not honour that promise.

What there has to be is work 'exacted ... under the menace of any penalty' and also performed against the will of the person concerned, that is work for which the person 'has not offered himself voluntarily'.

The definition given in Article 2(1) of ILO Convention No 29 means the ECtHR will inquire whether there is in the circumstances of the present case 'the menace of any penalty'.

The prospects must be sufficiently daunting to be capable of constituting 'the menace of [a] penalty', having regard both to the use of the adjective 'any' in the definition and to the standards adopted by the ILO on this point.[69]

Contracts which contain clauses which may or may not be penal may engage Article 4 if their effect is to compel the employee to work for the employer. Training bonds potentially carry this risk. However, it is not enough that a particular contract contain the clause, because the employee has voluntarily undertaken that obligation. What brings the Article into play is an industry-wide practice, such that if a person wants to undertake a profession he or she must agree to one or other of these clauses. Thus the court will ask whether the applicant 'offered himself voluntarily' for the work in question.

3.7.3   Article of limited application

It is suggested that Article 4 will in fact be of limited application in employment law. Article 4 may be relevant when considering whether a contract of employment, although unlawful for some reason, should nevertheless found

---

69   *Abolition of Forced Labour: General Survey by the Committee of Experts on Application of Conventions and Recommendations*, 1979, para 21.

unfair dismissal rights. A person may have been forced to work for the employer on disadvantageous terms and conditions as a result of a threat of a penalty, such as being reported to the immigration service as dismissed in circumstances of high unemployment and of it being alleged that the employee is no longer able to maintain or accommodate himself or herself without recourse to public funds.

3.7.4 Consent

In *Van der Musselle,*[70] the State argued that the avocat had consented in advance to the situation he complained of, so that it ill became him to object to it subsequently. On the eve of embarking on his career, the future professional was said to make 'a kind of prospective assessment': he or she will weigh up the pros and cons, setting the 'advantages' of the profession against the 'drawbacks' it entails. The employer would argue that the drawbacks were 'perfectly foreseeable' by the future professional since he or she was not unaware either of the existence or of the scope of the obligations that he or she would have to bear as regards entering into the relevant clause. In *Van der Musselle,* the obligations to provide free representation were 'limited' in quantity and limited in time. In a training bond case, the employer can also argue that the employee had knowledge of the corresponding advantages: the freedom that the employee would enjoy in acquiring skills which are transferable. It could argue that one of the distinctive features of compulsory labour was therefore lacking and this was sufficient to establish that there had not been a violation of Article 4(2).

However, the ECtHR felt that it could not attach decisive weight to this argument. Mr Van der Musselle had accepted the requirement to provide (during pupillage) his services free of charge and without reimbursement of his expenses, whether he wanted to or not, in order to become an 'avocat'. The ECtHR noted that his consent was determined by the normal conditions of exercise of the profession at the relevant time. What he gave was an acceptance of a legal régime of a general character. The applicant's prior consent, without more, does not therefore warrant the conclusion that the obligations incumbent on him do not constitute compulsory labour for the purposes of Article 4(2) of the Convention. The ECtHR stated that account must be taken of other factors. The ECtHR rejected the view that for there to be forced or compulsory labour, for the purposes of Article 4(2) of the Convention, not only must the labour be performed by the person against his or her will, but either the obligation to carry it out must be 'unjust' or 'oppressive' or its performance must constitute 'an avoidable hardship', in other words be 'needlessly distressing' or 'somewhat harassing'. None of these are necessary elements therefore.

The ECtHR adopted a different approach. It must find that that there is a risk *comparable* to the menace of a penalty, and then determine the relative weight to be attached to the argument regarding the applicant's 'prior consent'. The ECtHR will then have regard to all the circumstances of the case in the light of

---

70   *Van der Musselle v Belgium* (1984) 6 EHRR 163.

the underlying objectives of Article 4 of the Convention in order to determine whether the service required of the employee falls within the prohibition of compulsory labour. This could be so in the case of a service required in order to gain access to a given profession, if the service imposed a burden which was so excessive or disproportionate to the advantages attached to the future exercise of that profession that the service could not be treated as having been voluntarily accepted beforehand; this could apply, for example, in the case of a service unconnected with the profession in question. However, it is arguable that training bonds require performance of a service which is directly connected to the profession in question, namely the exercise of the trainee's skills for the benefit of the employer.

3.7.5 Justification

The structure of Article 4, especially para 3, 'delimits' the content of the right under Article 4. It indicates what 'the term "forced or compulsory labour" shall not include'. The ECtHR used para 3 as an aid to the interpretation of para 2 in *Van der Musselle*. Article 4, para 3 is grounded on the governing ideas of the general interest, social solidarity and what is in the normal or ordinary course of affairs. The final sub-paragraph, namely sub-para (d) which excludes 'any work or service which forms part of normal civic obligations' from the scope of forced or compulsory labour, is of especial significance in cases involving contractual arrangements (see below).

In *Van der Musselle*[71] the court took account of the compensating social status of an avocat. The ECtHR concluded that the burden imposed on the applicant was not disproportionate. According to his own evidence, acting for a particular *pro bono* client accounted for only 17 or 18 hours of his working time. Even if one adds to this the other cases in which he was appointed to act during his pupillage – about 50 in three years, representing, so he said, a total of some 750 hours there remained sufficient time for performance of his paid work (approximately 200 cases).

In an industry-wide training bond case, therefore, the ECtHR will weigh the prejudice by reason of the bonding against the advantages to the employee and consider whether these are excessive. Finally, the ECtHR would have regard to the standards still generally obtaining in the UK and in other democratic societies concerning the practice of bonding. It would also consider whether the notion of 'normal civic obligations' extends to obligations incumbent on a specific category of citizens by reason of the position they occupy, or the functions they are called upon to perform, in the community.

The concept of 'normal civic obligations' does not have as its object contractual relations as such. It is meant to cover obligations held by all citizens of the State. These would include filling in tax documents.[72] In *Gussenbauer v Austria*,[73] a complaint that an obligation in law that lawyers give some of their services *pro bono* was forced labour was held to be admissible. The State argued that it was

---

71   *Van der Musselle v Belgium* (1984) 6 EHRR 163.
72   *W v Austria* (1977) 7 DR 148.
73   (1973) 42 CD 41.

part of the applicant's normal civic obligations. However, the Commission accepted that since the obligation applied only to lawyers it could not be part of normal civic obligations.

3.7.6 Injunctions

The courts have been unwilling to grant injunctions to force employer and employee to continue working together, as the contract is a voluntary arrangement. The effect of a gardening leave clause is not to force them to work together, but simply to maintain the contract without the employer requiring the employee to work. The courts distinguished coercing an employee to work for the employer and restraining an employee from working for any other employer.[74] The nature of that injunction does not exact any work or labour.

3.8 ARTICLE 6

3.8.1 The scope of Article 6

Article 6 guarantees procedural fairness in relation to criminal charges and the determination of civil rights and obligations, with a view to ensuring the fundamental principle of the rule of law. A restrictive interpretation is not appropriate for Article 6.[75] Therefore a broad interpretation is to be given to it so as to achieve its purpose.

If the effected item[76] provides for the making of decisions concerning a person's private rights or lays down procedures for the determination of cases, Article 6 may guarantee a right to a fair trial concerning those rights or within those procedures. The guarantees contained in it must be met by all court proceedings, and public authorities carrying out disciplinary hearings may need to observe the requirements of Article 6.

The approach to whether an Article 6 issue arises is described below.

(1) Characterise the right over which there may be a dispute, establishing whether it has a basis (and if so what) in UK law. Is the right of a public or private nature within the meaning of those terms *in the Convention?*

(2) Determine whether there is a dispute over that right.

(3) Characterise the tribunal or decision maker.

(4) Check to see whether the guarantees in Article 6 have been observed.

(5) If they have not, ascertain whether there is a justification for not observing them.

---

74   See *Evening Standard Co Ltd v Henderson* [1987] ICR 588.
75   *Moerira de Azevedo v Portugal* (1990) 12 EHRR 721.
76   See **3.5.2**.

3.8.2   The content of Article 6

The rights under Article 6 include the right to an independent and impartial tribunal; the right to disclosure; the right to an adversarial hearing; the right to receive reasons; and the right to have decisions made within a reasonable period.

Potentially, these rights affect:

–   suspension;[77]
–   dismissal;[78]
–   professional suspension/striking off a professional register.[79]

Before the Article is engaged, however, there must be a civil right or obligation which is being decided.

3.9   IS THERE A CIVIL RIGHT AND OBLIGATION?

3.9.1   Identifying civil rights and obligations

The key question is whether the proceedings in issue are decisive of relations in civil law.[80] Employment law has been held to give rise to civil rights within the meaning of Article 6.[81] 'Civil rights and obligations' are rights and obligations that exist under private law, although they may arise in a public law context. The distinction between private and public law is not that used in UK law. It has an autonomous meaning in Convention law.[82] Rights arising under a contract may be included but also the refusal to register a doctor with his professional body, to grant a taxi licence, or other professional qualification, or a decision in relation to disciplinary proceedings are covered by the HRA 1998. Cases which illustrate the difference between a private law right, which attracts Article 6, and a public law right, which does not, include *Feldbrugge v The Netherlands*,[83] *Salesi v Italy*,[84] and *Schuler-Zgraggen v Switzerland*.[85]

In broad terms, all rights which are of a pecuniary nature or those having an importance for the individual are civil rights.[86] It is, however, a question of the factors in the case. In *Editions Périscope v France*, the ECtHR held Article 6 applicable to an action whose subject-matter was 'pecuniary' in nature and which was founded on an alleged infringement of rights which were likewise pecuniary rights. Thus where personal, economic or individual characteristics are predominant in a dispute, it has the character of private law, and will be covered by Article 6(1). This means that the balancing exercise, an example of

---

77   *Obermeier v Austria* (1991) 13 EHRR 290.
78   *X v UK* (1984) 6 EHRR 583.
79   *Albert and Le Compte v Belgium* (1983) 5 EHRR 533.
80   *Ringeisen v Austria* (1971) Series A No 13, (1979–80) 1 EHRR 455.
81   *Buchholz v FRG* (1981) 3 EHRR 597.
82   *König v FRG* (1979–80) 2 EHRR 170.
83   (1986) 8 EHRR 425.
84 · Judgment of 26 February 1993, Series A, No 257–E.
85   (1993) 16 EHRR 405.
86   *Editions Périscope v France* (1992) 14 EHRR 597.

which is set out below, may be of little importance in employment cases which relate to pecuniary loss by the claimant. In *X v UK*,[87] the chief executive of a company was served notice by the DTI that he was not a 'fit and proper person' for the post. He had the opportunity to make representations at a hearing by the Secretary of State's civil servants. However, they did not communicate to him the grounds of the allegations against him. The Commission accepted that the decision directly affected his contractual right to occupy the post as chief executive, and so qualified as a 'civil right' for the purposes of Article 6(1).

In *Feldbrugge*,[88] the private-law features (ie the 'personal and economic') nature of certain State benefits, their connection with a contract of employment, the affinities of the scheme with private insurance) led the ECtHR to hold Article 6 was applicable to proceedings relating to benefits under a Health Insurance Act and to the obligation to pay contributions to health insurance.

In the *Schuler-Zgraggen* judgment,[89] the ECtHR stated that 'as a general rule' Article 6(1) applied in the field of social insurance and that State intervention was not sufficient to establish that Article 6(1) was inapplicable. However, the most important consideration was that the applicant had suffered 'an interference with her means of subsistence' and was claiming 'an individual, economic right flowing from specific rules laid down in domestic law'.

It is not sufficient to show that a dispute is 'pecuniary' in nature for it to contain civil rights and obligations as there are 'pecuniary' obligations to the State or its subordinate authorities which, for the purpose of Article 6(1), are to be considered as belonging exclusively to the realm of public law and are accordingly not covered by the notion of 'civil rights and obligations'. Apart from fines imposed by way of 'criminal sanction', this will be the case, in particular, where an obligation derives from tax legislation or is otherwise part of normal civic duties in a democratic society.

In considering whether the right being determined is a public law right, the ECtHR will consider first the character of the legislation governing it.[90] In relation to an insurance obligation, a State may undertake the regulation of the framework of the right and of overseeing its operation. It may specify categories of beneficiaries, define the limits of the protection afforded, lay down the rates of the contributions and the allowances. However, such intervention may not suffice to bring the right within the sphere of public law (and thus out of the scope of Article 6). So the mere fact of State intervention in an area of private law, such as the making of redundancy payments, cannot render the right to a redundancy payment a matter of public law for Convention purposes.

The ECtHR will take the compulsory nature of a right or obligation as an indicator of its public nature. Is the obligation or right derived from an agreement or from the law itself? However, certain rights, which are a result of legal requirements, may be characterised as private rights. For example, rules

---

87   (1998) 25 EHRR CD 88.
88   *Feldbrugge v The Netherlands* (1986) 8 EHRR 425.
89   (1993) 16 EHRR 405.
90   *Feldbrugge v The Netherlands* (1986) 8 EHRR 425.

that make insurance cover compulsory for the performance of certain activities do not prevent the entitlement to benefits, to which this kind of insurance contract gives rise, being a private law right.

A further feature of a situation that may make the right public, and so not engaging Article 6, is the assumption by the State or by public or semi-public institutions of full or partial responsibility for ensuring it.

The features of public law in a situation may be outweighed by the private law features. In *Schouten and Meldrum v The Netherlands*,[91] the ECtHR considered contributions to a social insurance scheme for whose payment the employer is made responsible. It held that, as a rule, these are not of crucial importance to the applicant's livelihood. Although the obligations in issue are certainly 'personal, economic and individual', the same may be said of all 'pecuniary' obligations *vis-à-vis* the State or its subordinate authorities, even those which must be considered to belong exclusively to the realm of public law. It held that factor not to be decisive.

However, the ECtHR went on to hold that a feature of greater import is the link between the social insurance schemes and the contract of employment. The insurance provisions derived directly from statute and not from an express clause in the contract, but were grafted onto the contract and formed one of the constituents of the relationship between employer and employee.[92]

Most employment law situations will give rise to public law rights. However, if in doubt, the following issues can be usefully considered.

–   Whether an administrative decision affects a legal relationship between individuals. If it does, civil rights and obligations are at issue.

–   What is the substance of the alleged civil right (in the above regard) rather than the way in which it is classified in UK law? The ECtHR will look at the contents and effects of the right in preference to the classification.

–   Is the right pecuniary in nature, such as the right to pay?

–   Is the right of crucial importance to the person's livelihood? If so, it is likely to be a private law right for Convention purposes and therefore a civil right.

For a case in which the right was said to be public rather than private, see *McCullough v UK*.[93] There the applicant challenged an exclusion order arguing that by excluding him from entering Great Britain, his Article 6 rights had been violated. He argued that his right to freedom of movement, to seek employment and right to pursue his family life had been denied by the exclusion order which he was unable to challenge by taking proceedings in court. The Commission rejected the claim on the basis that these general rights are not

---

91   (1995) 19 EHRR 432.
92   See *Feldbrugge v The Netherlands* (1986) 8 EHRR 425.
93   (1998) 25 EHRR CD 34.

recognised by the domestic law of the UK. It took the view that the right to freedom of movement in the EU is of a public law nature. Not all matters arising from the right of free movement are likely to be treated in the same way. Thus the EAT has taken the view that certain aspects of the EU right of free movement may found a right in UK private law. In *Bossa v Nordstress*,[94] an Italian national who alleged that he had been refused employment by an employer in the UK on account of his nationality was entitled to bring a claim under the Race Relations Act 1976 despite the fact that the employment in question was 'wholly or mainly outside Great Britain' within the meaning of s 8(1) of the Act. The provisions in the Race Relations Act 1976 excluding claims in respect of employment outside Great Britain were held to be deficient and failed to give supremacy to Article 48 of the Treaty of Rome, which provides for freedom of movement for workers and 'the abolition of any discrimination based on nationality between workers of the Member States'.

3.9.2   Is there a dispute?

There has been some doubt as to whether Article 6 requires that there be a dispute.[95] In *H v France*,[96] the ECtHR found that for Article 6 to apply it was sufficient that the outcome of the proceedings should be 'decisive for private rights and obligations'. A dispute may exist where what is at stake is whether there is a right or not, or the manner of the exercise of a right (if the dispute is of a serious nature, see *Benthem v Netherlands*[97]).

Disciplinary procedures

In *Darnell v UK*,[98] the UK Government argued that Article 6(1) cannot apply to internal disciplinary hearings. The applicant submitted that these proceedings concerned his 'civil rights' since they ended his employment, affected his professional reputation and effectively ended his right to practise as a consultant microbiologist. The Commission stated that the claim or dispute must be 'genuine and of a serious nature' and must involve the determination of 'civil rights and obligations'.

The proceedings concerned the dismissal of the applicant from his contractual employment with the Trent Regional Health Authority, his appeal against this dismissal, and judicial review applications challenging the fairness of the procedure as well as an application to the industrial tribunal challenging the fairness of the dismissal. As to when the 'proceedings' for the purposes of Article 6 began, the applicant submitted that the period should run either from the date on which a formal complaint was made against him or the date on which he was suspended from duty. The Government argued that the starting point should be the date when the Secretary of State confirmed the decision to terminate the applicant's employment.

---

94   [1998] ICR 694.
95   *Moerira de Azevedo v Portugal* (1991) 13 EHRR 721 at para 66.
96   (1990) 12 EHRR 74.
97   (1986) 8 EHRR 1 at para 32.
98   Application No 15058/89 (Commission decision – partly admissible).

The Commission noted that the period before his dismissal concerned the internal inquiry and disciplinary hearing carried out by the applicant's employer. The Commission decided that this period could not be taken into account for the purposes of Article 6(1) of the Convention.

> 'Until the dismissal occurred, there was no "dispute" as to the legality or fairness of that dismissal. The Commission has therefore taken the date of the applicant's appeal as the starting point of the dispute.'

It appears that the Commission decision was predicated upon whether there was a challenge to the legality or fairness of the decision to dismiss in that case. The Commission appears to have distinguished between a challenge to the fairness and legality of the dismissal and the fairness and legality of the disciplinary procedures leading up to that dismissal. However, both are procedures determinative of civil rights.

Thus if a person disputes the legality of a suspension or a disciplinary procedure, a dispute can become crystallised at that point as to that issue and the subsequent procedures for resolution of that conflict may have to observe the Article 6 rights.

In *C v UK*,[99] the Commission also expressed the view that internal professional disciplinary proceedings against persons employed in public service may not attract the guarantees of Article 6(1).

There can also be circumstances in UK law where the legality of a dismissal which has not yet happened can be challenged. Thus if a person is under notice of dismissal, on occasion an injunction can be obtained to maintain the contract of employment. In such proceedings, it could be argued that Article 6 rights had not been observed in the process leading up to termination, for example where a person had disputed the legality of the dismissal during the course of an appeal against the decision to dismiss. The appeal proceedings would have to observe the guarantees of Article 6 unless the failure could be justified (see also Chapter 6).

3.9.3   Does the right have a basis in domestic law?

The right has to be recognised in domestic law. Thus the right of a party to continue to be employed under a contract of employment would constitute a right recognised in domestic law. This is the basis for the grant of injunctions to maintain an employment contract relationship in certain circumstances. However, unless another Article of the Convention requires a right to exist, Article 6 will not force a remedy to be created by the UK courts. A number of UK employment statutes have created statutory rights with limiting definitions excluding people from a right of redress. Casual workers will thus remain outside the ambit of the ERA 1996.[100]

Before the court can say that there is a civil right, there must be at least an argument that the right is recognised under UK law.[101]

---

99   (1987) 54 DR 162.
100   *Carmichael v National Power Plc* [1999] 1 WLR 2042.
101   See *Kerojärvi v Finland* 19 July 1995, Series A, No 322, p 12 at para 32.

The distinction between a civil right and matters which are not rights recognised by UK law can be seen from *Tinnelly v UK*,[102] in which the court distinguished between a section which defines the scope of the substantive right *in limine* and one which provides a respondent with a defence to a complaint.

The scope and contents of statutory rights will therefore be determined by the national law establishing them, unless that formulation contravenes an Article other than Article 6. However, some statutory defences may be challenged under Article 6 if they have the effect of barring an applicant from access to a court. In *Tinnelly* the limitation was effected by service of a certificate raising matters of national security. That had nothing to do with the scope of the right under the legislation involved, but barred an applicant who would otherwise have had a right under the legislation. A casual worker could not claim that Article 6 had been breached by the scope of the term 'employee' in the ERA 1996, as the concept of unfair dismissal is determined solely by statute. The casual worker may claim wrongful dismissal and have access to a court to determine that right, but simply does not have the right to claim unfair dismissal. Concepts which define the scope of a right, such as 'disabled person', 'racial group', 'employee', 'worker', are therefore unlikely to be extended by reference to Article 6.

The Sex Discrimination Act 1975, the Race Relations Act 1976 and the Disability Discrimination Act 1995 all contain similar provisions allowing a person to present a defence that a provision of legislation required them to behave in the way in which they did.

Thus s 41 of the Race Relations Act 1976 provides:

'(1) Nothing in Parts II to IV shall render unlawful any act of discrimination done—
 (a) in pursuance of any enactment or Order in Council; or
 (b) in pursuance of any instrument made under any enactment by a Minister of the Crown; or
 (c) in order to comply with any condition or requirement imposed by a Minister of the Crown (whether before or after the passing of this Act) by virtue of any enactment.
 References in this subsection to an enactment, Order in Council or instrument include an enactment, Order in Council or instrument passed or made after the passing of this Act.

(2) Nothing in Parts II to IV shall render unlawful any act whereby a person discriminates against another on the basis of that other's nationality or place of ordinary residence or the length of time for which he has been present or resident in or outside the United Kingdom or an area within the United Kingdom, if that Act is done—
 (a) in pursuance of any arrangements made (whether before or after the passing of this Act) by or with the approval of, or for the time being approved by, a Minister of the Crown; or
 (b) in order to comply with any condition imposed (whether before or after the passing of this Act) by a Minister of the Crown.'

---

102   (1999) 27 EHRR 249.

The House of Lords in *Hampson v Department of Education and Science*[103] decided that the exemption applied only to acts done in necessary performance of an express obligation contained in an enactment, instrument or Order in Council. The exercise of a power or discretion is not exempt.

If it can be established that the act was in the necessary performance of an express obligation, the HRA 1998 would require this provision to be construed as far as possible to give effect to the applicant's Article 6 rights. There will be an argument whether such a provision limits the scope of the civil rights under the various pieces of anti-discrimination legislation. The structure of the Race Relations Act 1976 is that Part I defines what discrimination is. Part II creates the civil right by stipulating in employment situations that it is unlawful to discriminate. The effect of s 41 is therefore to exclude from the scope of the civil right acts which are done in necessary performance of an express obligation in an enactment.

Article 6 does not in itself guarantee any particular content for (civil) 'rights and obligations' in the substantive law of the contracting States.[104] It is a procedural guarantee of a fair hearing in the determination of whatever substantive rights exist as a matter of national law.[105]

Where a person falls outside the scope of a statute, therefore, there is no right to bring Article 6 into play unless a common law right can be found.[106] However, if the effect of the restriction is to limit what would otherwise be recognised as a right at common law there may be a civil right that would require the application of Article 6.

Where the complaint is that the law allows certain actions to take place, this may not give rise to a dispute concerning a civil right having a basis in national law. Thus in *Gustafsson v Sweden*[107] the applicant's complaint under Article 6(1) was not that he was denied an effective remedy enabling him to submit to a court a claim alleging a failure to comply with domestic law but was essentially directed against the fact that a union's industrial action was lawful under Swedish law. There was therefore no right recognised under Swedish law to attract the application of Article 6(1) of the Convention.

Public funding for tribunals
The Scottish executive decided that public funding should be made available from 15 January 2001 for bringing claims in the employment tribunals. This was decided in response to claims brought using Article 6.[108]

There is a very strong case indeed to be made that proceedings to establish equal pay are too complicated to be evaluated for conditional fee purposes. At

---

103   [1990] ICR 511.
104   *W v UK* (1987) Series A, No 121, pp 32–33 at para 73 and see *H v Belgium* (1988) 10 EHRR 339.
105   *Dyer v UK* (1984) 39 DR 246 at 251. There an application was held to be inadmissible, as there was a statutory immunity from legal action by the applicant soldier.
106   *Powell v UK* (1990) 12 EHRR 355.
107   Application No 15573/89.
108   *The Scotsman* (2000) 20 November.

the same time, there is a clear inequality of arms for the woman seeking to establish her right to equal pay against an employer that has a personnel department or lawyers representing it.

3.9.4   Is the right determined?

The decision must be 'directly decisive' of a person's civil rights for the dispute procedure to attract the guarantees of Article 6. The ECtHR decided in *Ringeisen*[109] that the phrase 'in the determination of his civil rights and obligations' covers 'all proceedings the result of which is decisive for private rights and obligations'. Where the decisive nature of the process is identified, the character 'of the legislation which governs how the matter is to be determined' and of the 'authority' which is invested with jurisdiction in the matter are of little consequence. On the basis of this reasoning, disciplinary procedures which result in a dismissal may be said to determine the employee's civil rights. In *Le Compte*,[110] the question of whether there was a dispute over a civil right was said to amount to whether there were 'two conflicting claims or applications' concerning that right. The word 'dispute' (contestation) should not be construed too technically and should be given a substantive rather than a formal meaning. In *Le Compte*, it was held that there was a dispute where an allegation of misconduct (which was denied) before a professional conduct body was involved. The ECtHR considered that a tenuous connection or remote consequences do not suffice. Article 6(1) civil rights and obligations (ie private law rights) must be the object – or one of the objects – of the dispute. However, in *Le Compte*, this kind of direct relationship between the proceedings existed and the right to continue to exercise the medical profession in relation to suspensions ordered by a professional body was to deprive the applicants temporarily of their rights to practise. That right was directly in issue before the Appeals Council and the Cour de Cassation, which bodies had to examine the applicants' complaints against the decisions affecting them.

References
The effect of a bad reference may be that a prospective employer decides not to give a job to the applicant. However, this is probably not a process which is determinative of the civil rights of the applicant. It cannot be said to be decisive of those rights because there is an element of choice in the prospective employer. The extent to which the process is likely to be thought decisive will rest, it is suggested, on the evidence of the likely effects of the reference given. The concept of whether a decision is determinative of a civil right was given a narrow construction in the pre-HRA 1998 case of *R v Secretary of State for Health, ex parte C*[111] in the light of *Le Compte*. There, a childcare worker sought judicial review of the decision to include his name on the Department of Health's Consultancy Service Index. This lists persons about whom there are concerns about suitability for employment in childcare. The former employer sent to the Secretary of State information about the worker's dismissal following alle-

---

109   *Ringeisen v Austria* (1971) Series A No 13, (1979–80) 1 EHRR 455.
110   *Le Compte v Belgium* (1982) 4 EHRR 1.
111   [1999] 1 FLR 1073, aff'd [2000] 1 FLR 627, CA.

gations of sexual and physical abuse of children in his care. The worker argued that his name should not have been listed as a result of allegations which had not been proved beyond reasonable doubt. Inclusion would jeopardise his future employment prospects. He argued that use of the index was contrary to Article 6(1). However, Richards J dismissed the application on the basis that the index was a scheme enabling prospective employers to obtain references. There was no obligation on the State to conduct a factual investigation into the allegations or to require allegations to be proved to the criminal standard. The State had to ascertain whether the employer acted reasonably in deciding that the allegations were, on a balance of probabilities, true. Given the scheme's purpose, inclusion in the list was not directly determinative of a person's right to work in the chosen area of employment and did not therefore constitute a determination of that person's civil rights under Article 6(1). He said: 'A tenuous connection or remote consequences will not suffice'.[112] The practical effects of such inclusion are, it is submitted, a better guide to whether the decision is determinative than the characterisation of the list as merely a mechanism for prospective employers to obtain references. However, this decision illustrates that practitioners will have to provide evidence to a court or tribunal about the practical effects of a decision (when that effect is not a matter of law) before the court will be willing to infer that the decision is determinative of civil rights.

Bartholomew v London Borough of Hackney[113] considered the duty of care towards the subject of a reference.[114] After being suspended over allegations of financial irregularities and presenting a race discrimination case which was settled on terms including severance and the termination of the disciplinary proceedings, the claimant applied for another job. The prospective employer contacted the defendant for a reference. In the reference provided, the defendant stated that the claimant had taken voluntary severance while suspended for alleged gross misconduct. It also stated that the charges had automatically lapsed on his departure. The job offer was withdrawn and the employee sued the defendant council for damages for negligence. The court held that a reference does not always have to be full and comprehensive, provided it is not inaccurate or misleading.

The significance of choice in the ordinary reference case can be illustrated by asking what the likely outcome would have been had an opportunity been given for the ex-employee to have an input into the reference process. Should the council have contacted the potential subject of the reference and given him a chance to comment on it before sending it? The process of giving a reference may be decisive as to whether a person enters into a contract with another and thus acquires a civil right under that contract, but it is not determinative of any private law right in the sense that a decision to dismiss and thus terminate the rights under the contract is determinative. Is the position different where references are taken up after the contract of employment is entered into? Most

---

112   [1999] 1 FLR 1073 at p 1085C.
113   [1999] IRLR 246.
114   See also *Spring v Guardian Assurance plc* [1994] IRLR 460.

such positions are taken up 'subject to satisfactory references'. In such cases the decision to give an unsatisfactory reference is still not determinative of the rights under the new contract, as the new employer may choose to ignore the content of the reference, and the decision as to whether the reference is satisfactory will be that of the new employer. Where there is an industry-wide minimum standard of acceptability, such as that in *ex parte C*,[115] it is submitted that even if characterised as a reference, the inclusion of persons on such a warning list will in practical terms be decisive of their right to earn a living in that field. However, this is not the case for most references. In such cases there is no need for the public authority employer to provide the Article 6 guarantees to the subject of the reference when providing it for the benefit of the new employer, even though the subject of the reference is owed a duty of care in respect of accuracy.

3.9.5   Disciplinary proceedings before professional bodies

The general principle is that disciplinary proceedings must comply with Article 6 or there must be a right of appeal or of review to a court or tribunal which satisfies the requirements of the Article.[116] Thus in *König v Germany*,[117] the applicant complained about the duration of proceedings which he had instituted before administrative courts after an administrative body had withdrawn his authorisation to run his clinic and then his authorisation to practise medicine. The rights at issue included the right 'to continue his professional activities' as a medical practitioner 'for which he had obtained the necessary authorisations'. These rights were classified as private and so as civil for the purposes of Article 6(1).[118] In the employment context of decisions by professional bodies, regard will be had, among other matters, to the effects the decision has on the person's right to work in his chosen profession.[119]

3.9.6   Right of access to a court

Article 6 will not be breached where the proceedings taken as a whole amount to a fair hearing. Whilst Article 6(1) embodies the 'right to a court' it does not oblige the State to submit disputes over 'civil rights and obligations' to a procedure conducted at each of its stages before 'tribunals' meeting the Article's various requirements. The ECtHR takes into account the demands of flexibility and efficiency as justifying the prior intervention of administrative or professional bodies and of judicial bodies which do not satisfy the requirements in every respect. The legal tradition of many Member States of the Council of Europe supports this approach. However, an appeal body with a further right of appeal on a point of law against its decision to a higher court may need to satisfy the requirements of Article 6. Thus where there is the possibility of appeal to or

115   *R v Secretary of State for Health, ex parte C* [1999] 1 FLR 1073.
116   *Le Compte v Belgium* (1982) 4 EHRR 1.
117   Judgment of 28 June 1978, Series A, No 27, p 8, para 18, and p 28, para 85; and see also *Engel and Others v The Netherlands* Judgment of 8 June 1976, Series A No 22, pp 36–37 at para 87.
118   Paragraphs 88–91 and 93–95.
119   *Le Compte v Belgium* (1982) 4 EHRR 1.

review by a court which has the power to determine all relevant matters of fact and law, a defect in relation to earlier proceedings under Article 6 may in effect be remedied.

Article 6(1) embodies the 'right to a court', of which the right of access, that is, the right to institute proceedings before a court in civil matters, constitutes one aspect. However, this right is not absolute, but may be subject to limitations. These are permitted by implication since the right of access by its very nature calls for regulation by the State. The court must be satisfied that limitations applied to that right do not restrict or reduce the access left to the individual in such a way or to such an extent that the very essence of the right is impaired. A limitation will not be compatible with Article 6(1) if it does not pursue a legitimate aim and if there is not a reasonable relationship of proportionality between the means employed and the aim sought to be achieved.[120]

Decisions taken by an administrative authority will have to be capable of review in a court or tribunal unless the conditions of Article 6 are met by the original decision. This aspect will generally be covered by the right of application to an employment tribunal (or court) unless the defect in the procedure was such as to strike at the essence of the right to a fair hearing.[121]

However, this means that the tribunal must cover questions of fact just as much as law.

> 'For civil cases, just as for criminal charges (see the *Deweer* judgment of 27 February 1980, Series A no. 35, pp. 24–25, par. 48), Article 6 par. 1 (art. 6–1) draws no distinction between questions of fact and questions of law. Both categories of question are equally crucial for the outcome of proceedings relating to "civil rights and obligations". Hence, the "right to a court" (see the above-mentioned *Golder* judgment, p. 18, par. 36) and the right to a judicial determination of the dispute (see the above-mentioned *König* judgment, p. 34, par. 98 in fine) cover questions of fact just as much as questions of law. Yet the Court of Cassation does not have jurisdiction to rectify factual errors or to examine whether the sanction is proportionate to the fault ...'[122]

Does the employment tribunal satisfy this requirement when it considers a claim for unfair dismissal involving an allegation that Article 6 rights have been infringed and that as a result the wrong factual conclusion was reached regarding whether misconduct had taken place? The tribunal has jurisdiction to characterise the dismissal as fair or unfair by judging whether the employer acted reasonably in treating the reason for dismissal as sufficient for dismissal in the circumstances. If the Article 6 guarantees have not been observed it will be unlikely that the dismissal will be fair. However, *Polkey v AE Dayton Services Ltd*[123] indicates that:

> 'Where there is no issue raised by sections 58 to 62 [of the Employment Protection (Consolidation) Act 1978] the subject matter for the tribunal's consideration is the employer's action in treating the reason as a sufficient reason for dismissing the

---

120   *Stubbings and Others v UK* (1997) 23 EHRR 213.
121   See 'Anonymous informants' at **3.9.13** below.
122   *Le Compte v Belgium* (1982) 4 EHRR 1.
123   [1988] ICR 142 at 153.

employee. It is that action and that action only that the tribunal is required to characterise as reasonable or unreasonable. That leaves no scope for the tribunal considering whether, if the employer had acted differently, he might have dismissed the employee. It is what the employer did that is to be judged, not what he might have done. On the other hand, in judging whether what the employer did was reasonable it is right to consider what a reasonable employer would have had in mind at the time he decided to dismiss as the consequence of not consulting or not warning.'

To satisfy the requirements of Article 6, a tribunal must have the power to rectify factual errors. The employment tribunals hearing unfair dismissal cases, relative to the statutory right contained in the ERA 1996, do have powers to rectify factual errors. Where a fact is relevant to the issue of whether the employer acted reasonably or not, the tribunal is entitled to make a finding. Tribunals are empowered to characterise the actions of the employer as either reasonable or unreasonable in accordance with s 98 of the ERA 1996. They are not required to determine the facts outside the question of whether the employer acted reasonably in treating the reason for dismissal as sufficient for dismissal. Thus it is irrelevant that a person did not commit the act of misconduct for which he or she was dismissed. The Article 6 requirements will not generally alter that principle. However, where the failure to observe the guarantees of Article 6 goes to whether the misconduct was committed or not, such as when the employer does not reveal the source of its information so that its motivation/veracity may be challenged, that failure may go to the heart of fairness under Article 6. [124]

In *Golder v UK*,[125] the ECtHR concluded that: '[Article 6(1)] secures to everyone the right to have any claim relating to his civil rights and obligations brought before a court or tribunal'. Therefore it is not applicable merely to proceedings already in progress: it may also be relied on by anyone who considers that an interference with the exercise of one of his or her civil rights is unlawful and complains that he or she has not had the possibility of submitting that claim to a tribunal meeting the requirements of Article 6(1). On the face of it, this would cover a person who had not qualified for unfair dismissal rights, who might seek to rely on Convention rights either to found a claim against a public authority, or to obtain a declaration that the provisions of the ERA 1996 are, in this respect, incompatible with the Convention. [126] If the nature of the civil right not to be unfairly dismissed is determined by national law, a person with less than one year's service does not have the right. If this qualification period is considered to be part of the right, Article 6 will not have any effect. However, if it is regarded as in the nature of a defence, Article 6 may apply. However, although it will not be possible for employees of less than one year's service to claim unfair dismissal, such employees have a HRA 1998, s 7 claim against the employer (if a public authority) and, in certain cases, a contractual claim arising from failure to follow a fair procedure. Employees of private bodies who do not qualify for unfair dismissal rights may use Article 6 to require the court

---

124   See **3.9.13**.
125   Series A, No 18, (1979–80) 1 EHRR 524.
126   However, see **3.9.13**.

to construe their contracts in accordance with the international treaty obligations of the UK so as to imply a term that the principles of natural justice would be observed in the process leading to their dismissal.

A procedure should not prevent access to it. Thus a disciplinary procedure which did not give the employee sufficient time to prepare a case, or allowed evidence to be produced without warning could be incompatible with Article 6. In the case of a public authority body, if considered decisive for the private rights of the parties, the employee may have a s 7 claim.

Will the HRA 1998 right require the extension of public funding to Equal Pay Act 1970 cases, as under the current procedure the expense of mounting such cases can prevent the individual from securing the rights under the law? The existence of *pro bono* representation may result in a finding that Article 6 has not been breached in respect of the provision of public funding. In *McTear v UK*,[127] the applicant complained that the refusal of public funding for her proposed negligence action against Imperial Tobacco Limited, in respect of the illness and subsequent death of her husband as a result of smoking, breached her right of access to court under Article 6. In admissibility proceedings, the ECtHR rejected the complaint because her legal representatives had agreed to represent *pro bono*, and therefore the applicant had not been denied her right of access to the courts. It is submitted that the existence of conditional fee representation would also undermine the argument that there was a practical bar to obtaining representation. However this, in itself, may do nothing to provide access to the tribunals given the nature of the cases and, in particular, the way in which evidence is adduced during the course of proceedings in equal value claims as it is unlikely that a risk assessment carried out at anything other than a very late stage of proceedings would result in a lawyer being willing to take the case on under such an agreement. The mere possibility of such agreements, or *pro bono* representation, will not be enough to provide practical access to the tribunals in such cases. In Scotland, public funding is now available for tribunal cases.

Implied limitations on the right of access to a court

The right of access is not absolute and may be subject to implied limitations. Such limitations must not restrict or reduce the very essence of the right. Limitations will not be compatible with Article 6(1) if they do not pursue a legitimate aim or if there is not a reasonable relationship of proportionality between the means employed and the aim sought to be achieved.[128]

Thus in *Williams v Cowell (t/a The Stables)*[129] the employee complained of racial discrimination having been dismissed for communicating with other Welsh speakers in Welsh rather than English. The employment tribunal sitting in Wales conducted proceedings in Welsh. The employee argued that the EAT should conduct its proceedings in Wales in accordance with the Welsh

---

127   Application No 40291/98, 7 September 1999.
128   *Bellet v France* 4 December 1995, Series A, No 333-B, p 41 and *Ait-Mouhub v France* (2000) 30 EHRR 382.
129   [2000] 1 WLR 187.

Language Act 1993 or, if proceedings were held in London, the language of proceedings should be Welsh. The Court of Appeal dismissed the appeal by him from the refusal of the EAT to agree to either course. It held that the EAT had a discretion as to venue which the Court of Appeal had no grounds to overturn. The EAT had not acted contrary to the Convention as the employee could understand and speak English. Clearly the procedure, in that case, had not prevented access to the tribunal.

One area in which this principle might be thought to have impact is in relation to interim orders of the tribunal continuing employment in certain cases (for example s 6 or s 12 of the ERA 1999). The time-limit allowed for bringing an application for such an order is very limited. However, it is likely that the courts would find that the time-limit is proportionate to the aim of the legislation, so the introduction of the Convention rights will not alter the period within which the claim must be lodged. It would be more difficult for the courts to accept that the limitation period in s 128 of the ERA 1996 could be justified where relief was claimed by a person who had sought to be represented by a fellow employee, and therefore may well not have had access to professional advice instantly. In *MP v Spain*,[130] there was a three-day time-limit for lodging an appeal. The applicants used registered post to send the appeal but it was received outside the three-day period and the court rejected it. The Commission held that this was an unrealistic time-limit that denied the applicants their Article 6 rights. The disparity in principles of extension of time-limits between unfair dismissal and discrimination claims is examined later.[131]

3.9.7   Equality of arms

Equality of arms has been said to be one of the essential and inherent elements of a fair trial.[132] Although the CPR 1998 do not apply to tribunals, the question of how to achieve a fair trial with disparate representation was dealt with by the High Court in *Maltez v Lewis*.[133] The requirement of the CPR 1998 that a party who could afford less experienced representation than the opponent could achieve equality of arms by that party's representatives being given more time to carry out work than the other party's reflects the principle of equality of arms. Similarly, a larger legal firm could be required to prepare bundles for the court. However, there is no power to prevent a party from instructing the legal representative of his or her choice. If there is an imbalance it can be dealt with in other ways. The employment tribunals will also have to take account of the special context of costs in which they operate. Thus in considering whether to make an order in the case, the tribunal would need to bear in mind that the work the company is required to do will result in costs which cannot be recovered and, given the amounts of money involved in most unfair dismissal claims, may represent an unfair procedure for a company with a valid defence to the whole claim. The company cannot be forced away from the tribunal

---

130   Application No 28090/95, 21 October 1997.
131   See **3.10.4**.
132   *X v Germany* (1963) 6 YB 520.
133   (1999) 96 (21) LSG 39.

judgment simply by costs. The individual circumstances of each applicant and respondent will need to be fully considered by the tribunal in deciding on any interlocutory step in the proceedings, as the applicant's right to a fair trial must be weighed against the irrecoverable nature of the costs incurred by the step.

Where a job evaluation study is conducted after a dispute has arisen concerning equal pay, it is arguable that the requirement of equality of arms means that the person raising the dispute on equal pay should have input into it, otherwise the right to a fair trial will not be observed. Thus in *Montovanelli v France*[134] it was said that it would not be met if the applicant is not involved in the preparation of the court expert report, and the defendants to proceedings are.

The practice adopted by the EAT of showing the parties the comments of the chair of the employment tribunal is consistent with the requirements of disclosure under Article 6. Equality of arms requires that each party be given a reasonable opportunity to present his or her case under conditions which do not place the party at a substantial disadvantage. The actions of a Swiss court in sending its comments to the appellate court which did not show them to the complainant struck at the important factor of litigants' confidence in the workings of justice. This requires them to know that they have had the opportunity to express their views on every document in the file.[135] The rule relating to the *ex parte* grant of witness orders by the tribunal may need to be reviewed and/or justified in the light of these principles.

3.9.8   Delay

Article 6 may also be breached where the public authority fails to organise its system so as to avoid delays in the determinative process. Delay in disciplinary hearings may raise an issue under Article 6. The UK courts have previously taken the view that they have jurisdiction to entertain an application for judicial review based on a prolonged adjournment of disciplinary proceedings by a professional body.[136] In that case, the ECtHR would not intervene although disciplinary proceedings had begun in July 1990, were then adjourned until October and further adjourned until March 1991. Post-HRA 1998, the court will look more closely at the effect on the guarantees in Article 6 of such a delay. In *Stamoulakatos v Greece (No 2)*[137] the applicant lodged an appeal against the refusal to grant him a pension in May 1988. There were adjournments and the final hearing was held in October 1995 but the decision had still not been issued by the time he lodged his application to the ECtHR. This was a breach of the requirement under Article 6 that decisions are made within a reasonable time. A public authority decision-maker might therefore act unlawfully should he fail to make a decision after a prolonged period. However, where delays are not attributable to the State it will not give rise to a claim under Article 6.[138]

---

134   RJD 1997-II 32.
135   *Niederost Huber v Switzerland* (1998) 25 EHRR 709.
136   *R v UK Central Council for Nursing, Midwifery and Health Visiting, ex parte Thompson* [1991] COD 275.
137   [1998] HRCD 113.
138   *Proszak v Poland* (2000) 30 EHRR 328.

The reasonableness of the time taken in proceedings is assessed in the light of the circumstances of the case. Thus where an applicant's condition called for exceptional diligence (he had contracted HIV), despite the fact that there were a number of cases to be dealt with, a delay of six years was unreasonable.[139] This principle may be significant in relation to cases concerning persons dying from progressive illnesses generally and, in particular, in disability discrimination cases. Some cases require exceptional diligence, for example where the right of access to a child is at stake.[140] The court will consider matters such as the nature of the interests at stake for the applicant and the serious and irreversible consequences that the action has on other Convention rights as requiring the authorities to act with exceptional diligence.

3.9.9 The requirement for reasons for a decision

Although Article 6 obliges courts to give reasons for their decisions, it cannot be understood as requiring a detailed answer to every argument.[141] The practice of some employment tribunals not to give any meaningful reasons for their interlocutory decisions may be susceptible of challenge under this requirement. It is in any event inconsistent with the decision in *Independent Research Services Limited v Catterall.*[142] Reasons should be given in interlocutory cases as well as final decisions. These reasons, although not needing to be lengthy, must provide enough information for the parties to know why the case has been determined as it has.

Public authorities reaching a decision on a civil right will need to take account of the requirement to provide reasons for their decisions. Such an infringement may be justified by reference to proportionality in many cases, but where the matter affects the rights under the Convention the duty may be more difficult to ignore. Where a person is dismissed there is already a right to written reasons for dismissal.[143] However, this right is limited to persons with qualifying service. A public authority employer will have to be able to justify not giving reasons for dismissal in all cases, regardless of length of service.

3.9.10 Independent tribunal established by law

The right of access is to a hearing before an independent tribunal established by law.[144] In *Le Compte*,[145] the ECtHR took the view that for civil cases Article 6(1) draws no distinction between questions of fact and questions of law. Both categories of question are equally crucial for the outcome of proceedings relating to 'civil rights and obligations'. Therefore the 'right to a court' and the right to a judicial determination of the dispute cover questions of fact just as much as questions of law. If the higher court does not have jurisdiction to rectify factual errors or to examine whether the sanction is proportionate to the

---

139   *Pailot v France* [1998] HRCD 451.
140   *Paulsen-Medalen and Svensson v Sweden* (1998) 26 EHRR 260.
141   *Van der Hurk v The Netherlands* (1994) Series A, No 288, p 20.
142   [1993] ICR 1.
143   Section 92 of ERA 1996.
144   *Belilos v Switzerland* (1988) 10 EHRR 466 at 500–502.
145   *Le Compte v Belgium* (1982) 4 EHRR 1.

fault, Article 6(1) may not be satisfied unless its requirements are met by the lower tribunal itself.[146]

The fact that a body exercises judicial functions does not suffice to make it a tribunal. To be an independent tribunal the body must satisfy the following requirements:

– independence of the executive and of the parties to the case;
– the duration of its members' term of office must be sufficient;
– guarantees must be afforded by its procedure.[147]

The court will look at the duration of the term of office of a person who sits on the body. The longer the term, the more likely the person will be independent. Where members of the body have interests very close to those of one of the parties to the proceedings, the impartiality of the body will be called into question, but if half the membership are independent there is an assurance of impartiality. The court will also look at the method of election of the members to detect bias. The court will assume the personal impartiality of members of the body until there is proof to the contrary.

In the Scottish criminal case of *Gibbs v Ruxton*,[148] the defendant argued that a warrant issued for his arrest after he failed to attend an intermediate hearing was issued by a temporary sheriff whose appointment by the Secretary of State was *ultra vires*. As the appointing statute's provision limited the appointment of temporary sheriffs to temporary emergencies, and Parliament must be presumed to have legislated in conformity with the Convention, temporary appointments could not be made on a long-term basis without identifying particular needs on a particular occasion. The Scottish High Court rejected his arguments, holding that in order to avoid delay in the administration of justice, the appointing section had to be construed broadly to cover what was expedient.

However, the Court agreed that it could be argued that the Secretary of State would have been acting *ultra vires* if he had chosen to make use of the appointing section to replace permanent sheriffs with temporary sheriffs as a matter of policy and without regard to the particular circumstances in which temporary sheriffs were used. On the question of construction of the appointing section, the Convention supported the lawfulness of long-term appointments rather than on a case-by-case basis, thus providing security of tenure.

In *Smith v Secretary of State for Trade and Industry*,[149] a sole director and controlling shareholder of an insolvent company applied for a redundancy payment from the Secretary of State, under ERA 1996, s 166. The EAT granted permission to appeal because employment tribunals were linked to the Secretary of State.

---

146 See *County Properties Limited v The Scottish Ministers* 2000 GWD 26–1007.
147 *Neumeister v Austria (No 1)* (1968) Series A No 8, (1979–80) 1 EHRR 91, *De Wilde, Ooms and Versyp v Belgium (No 1)* (1971) Series A No 12, (1979–80) 1 EHRR 373, *Ringeisen v Austria (No 1)* (1971) Series A No 13, (1979–80) 1 EHRR 455.
148 2000 GWD 1–15.
149 [2000] ICR 69.

The director had the right under Article 6 to have his case determined by 'an independent and impartial tribunal'. The director was bankrupt and the Official Receiver, acting as his trustee in bankruptcy, was an officer of the DTI's Insolvency Service. Although the HRA 1998 was not yet in force, the proceedings might well have been ongoing at the time of implementation, so that this was an appropriate case in which to grant leave to appeal in order that the matter might be considered further.

An illustration of how the Commission approaches the issue of independence and its effects can be found in *Stefan v UK*.[150] The applicant's registration as a GP was suspended after the GMC found unfitness to practise. Two of the 13 members of the GMC are non-medical. She applied to the Privy Council in respect of this decision but the review was rejected. Before the Commission she complained of breach of Article 6. She argued that the GMC was investigator, prosecutor and adjudicator in the proceedings. She claimed that it was not substantively or in appearance independent or impartial. Further, she claimed that the Privy Council review was not sufficiently broad to satisfy Article 6(1).

The Commission noted the lack of safeguards in GMC committee. There was no term of appointment established. The adjudications were not always independent of the GMC policy. The legal assessor had no role in the determination. The Privy Council review, however, remedied these defects thus fulfilling Article 6(1).

The concepts of impartiality and independence were considered in *Findlay v UK*.[151] In order to establish whether a tribunal can be considered as 'independent', regard must be had, inter alia, to the manner of appointment of its members and their term of office, the existence of guarantees against outside pressures and the question whether the body presents an appearance of independence.[152]

As to the question of 'impartiality', there are two aspects to this requirement. First, the tribunal must be subjectively free of personal prejudice or bias. Secondly, it must also be impartial from an objective viewpoint, that is, it must offer sufficient guarantees to exclude any legitimate doubt in this respect.[153]

If the body is established by legislation it will clearly be established by law. The body must have judicial functions, fair procedures, and be capable of taking binding decisions.[154] Even if there are procedures available to the tribunal, if it does not follow them it will cease to be acting as a body established by law.[155] This raises the spectre of tribunals and courts being found to have acted unlawfully under s 9 of the HRA 1998 where they fail to observe their own rules of procedure. However, the effect is mitigated as damages will only be awarded where the court or tribunal has acted in bad faith.[156]

---

150   (1998) 25 EHRR CD 130.
151   (1997) 24 EHRR 221.
152   *Bryan v UK* 22 November 1995, Series A at No 335–A, p 15 at para 37.
153   *Pullar v UK* (1996) 22 EHRR 391.
154   *Benthem v The Netherlands* (1986) 8 EHRR 1.
155   *Rossi v France* (1989) 63 DR 105.
156   See **6.9**.

3.9.11   Public hearing

Matters of professional secrecy or protection of the private life of the complainants or of third parties may justify a private hearing. The parties to the dispute, absent such matters, are entitled to have the proceedings conducted in public. Parties can waive this right of their own free will, whether expressly or tacitly. [157] Even if a later appeal is conducted in public that may not remedy the defect if the higher body cannot deal with all matters (factual or in law) concerning 'civil rights and obligations'.

3.9.12   Civil servants – public officials

Article 6 guarantees do not extend to disputes relating to the recruitment, employment and dismissal of public officials. [158] However, the public servant may rely on the Article where purely, or essentially, economic issues are at stake. [159] If the individual is simply employed by the public authority but is not technically a civil servant and if the individual has a contract or if the terms and conditions of employment provide access to the ordinary courts for the determination of any dispute, Article 6 may apply.

In *Lombardo v Italy*, [160] the dispute was essentially about an obligation on the State to pay a pension to a civil servant in accordance with legislation. The State was not using its discretionary powers and could therefore be compared to an employer who is a party to a contract of employment governed by private law. Therefore the right to receive this pension if certain conditions were met was to be regarded as a 'civil right' within the meaning of the Article. A decision to send a civil servant on leave whilst a dispute was being considered was essentially related to his career. [161] In *Maillard v France*, [162] the applicant lodged a complaint about the assessment of his service in the navy during 1983 and applied to have his career retrospectively reassessed. This complaint was ultimately upheld but not until March 1996. He complained that this breached his right to a trial in reasonable time as required by Article 6.

The ECtHR held that the disputes in question were primarily concerned with his career, and that in any case disputes concerning the recruitment, careers and termination of service of civil servants were as a general rule outside the scope of Article 6(1).

On the other hand, in *Couez v France* [163] the ECtHR held that the claim relating to entitlements to sick leave as a result of injury at work was considered to be distinct. The outcome was bound to have a decisive effect on the applicant's economic rights because if the administrative court quashed the authorities' refusal to regard the applicant's sick leave as having been due to a work-related

---

157   *Deweer v Belgium* (1979–80) 2 EHRR 439 at para 49.
158   *Neigel v France* (2000) 30 EHRR 310 and *Balfour v UK* [1997] EHRLR 665 (Commission admissibility decision).
159   *De Santa v Italy* (1997) 2 September, unreported.
160   Series A, No 249-B (1996) 21 EHRR 188.
161   *Huber v France* (1998) 26 EHRR 457.
162   (1999) 27 EHRR 232.
163   [1998] HRCD 810.

accident, the rules on civil servants injured in the execution of their duty would have applied to the applicant and he would also not have been sent on compulsory unpaid leave of absence.

The recognition by a competent authority would have enabled the applicant to receive his salary until fit to return to work. Thus the Article will apply to public officials in employment disputes where the outcome of the dispute is bound to have a decisive effect on the applicant's economic rights.

Although internal professional disciplinary proceedings against a person employed in public service may not attract the guarantees of the Article, if a contract of employment (in the civil service) allows access to civil courts to determine the respective civil liabilities of the parties, the proceedings before the courts may usually be said to determine civil rights and obligations within the meaning of the Article.

3.9.13 Anonymous informants

When a public authority reaches a conclusion about the guilt or innocence of a person in a misconduct case, a question will arise as to whether it is entitled to maintain the anonymity of the witness in proceedings to which Article 6 guarantees apply. It may be that Article 6(1) requires the identity of the witness to be revealed. In criminal cases the ECtHR has held that written reports by anonymous witnesses are insufficient to guarantee a fair trial as there is no opportunity to challenge the evidence.[164] For the public authority conducting disciplinary proceedings against an employee, the question will have to be whether the proceedings against the employee can be fair if there is no opportunity for the employee to challenge the motivation and background of the witness. Thus if there is independent corroborating evidence, which may be challenged by the employee, the public authority employer may be able to justify not revealing the identity of the informant. However, if that evidence is successfully challenged, the public authority may act unlawfully where it reaches the decision on the sole basis of the informant's evidence. For the employee, it can be argued that if he or she knows the identity of the informant it may be possible for the employee to question that person's credibility as a result of background information. Most public authorities will need to proceed cautiously. When the facts of the case are such that the informant's Convention rights might be breached, there may be some justification for retaining anonymity. It should be retained, however, only if it is absolutely necessary, and if it is still possible for the employee to have a fair hearing.

The employment tribunal has to deal with two questions in this context:

(1) Should it make a finding that Article 6 was breached?

(2) Was the dismissal reasonable?

These may seem to be two distinct questions, but they are linked in the following way. When a case of misconduct is based on anonymous information, the tribunal will need to consider:

---

164 *Kostovski v The Netherlands* 12 EHRR 434.

–   If the employer is a public authority, did it act lawfully in retaining the anonymity of the informant?
–   Can the proceedings before the tribunal be regarded as fair if that anonymity is preserved or relied upon?

It is arguable that if the public authority did not act lawfully in reaching its decision it cannot have acted reasonably, and that, since the decision of the employer is based on the procedure it adopts, if that procedure was unlawful because it was in breach of s 6 of the HRA 1998, the decision to dismiss cannot be characterised as reasonable. Note that the link between the dismissal and the unlawfulness is much closer than, for example, the characterisation of a dismissal as an act of less favourable treatment under the Disability Discrimination Act 1995 and the characterisation of that dismissal as unfair.[165] If a finding of unlawfulness under s 6 were made in respect of the procedure, it would indicate that the public authority employer had been unable to justify the infringement as lawful, proportionate and necessary in pursuit of a legitimate aim. It would not be possible for a tribunal to find such a dismissal was reasonable, as the tribunal is obliged to construe the concept of reasonableness in unfair dismissal so as to give effect to it in a way which is compatible with the Convention's aims.

The guidelines in *Linfood Cash & Carry v Thomson*[166] may not result in an employer giving the employee a fair trial in determining his civil rights. The guidelines are as follows.

(a)   The evidence must be reduced to writing (for example, a statement) and made available to the accused employee.

(b)   There should be particulars of:

(i)   dates, times and places of incidents;
(ii)   the conditions of, and opportunities for, observation where relevant;
(iii) circumstantial evidence such as why the witness was alerted or can remember matters;
(iv)   whether the informant knows the accused or bears him or her a grudge.

(c)   The employer should investigate these particulars and should seek corroboration.

(d)   The employer should enquire as to the character of the informant.

(e)   If the informant does not wish to attend the disciplinary hearing the chairman of the hearing should interview the informant and assess the credibility and weight to be attached to his or her evidence.

(f)   If matters arise during the course of the disciplinary hearing that should be put to the informant, the disciplinary hearing should be adjourned for this to take place.

---

165   See *Kenrick v Heinz* [2000] IRLR 144.
166   [1989] IRLR 235.

In the case of a public authority, the problem with these guidelines is that where a private grudge exists, it may be known to very few persons. Although investigations may go some way to reveal whether such a grudge exists without the employee having to know the identity of the informant, the employee may be the only person who knows the reason why the informant would want to lie about his or her activities. The question for the tribunal in an ordinary case is simply whether the employer has acted reasonably in adopting this procedure, and so the fact that the employer has taken reasonable steps to establish whether the informant knows and bears a grudge towards the employee may suffice. However, the public authority employer must provide justification for not allowing the employee the chance to cross-examine the witness with a knowledge of the witness's identity and background. That justification would require the public authority to show a lawful basis, necessity and proportionality.

There might be a justification for refusing to disclose where the Convention rights of the informant may be in issue. Where there would be a risk of humiliating or degrading treatment of the informant as a result of disclosure, the public authority would have a duty to prevent infringement of that right. Similarly, where information had been disclosed in circumstances giving rise to a duty of confidentiality, the public authority would have a lawful basis for its refusal. However, in such cases there would have to be some factual basis showing that the refusal was proportionate to the aim sought (preservation of confidences), and which outweighed the right of the employee to a fair trial.

In discrimination cases involving an allegation of misconduct by the applicant, it is suggested that it is more difficult for the employer to refuse to accord the applicant a fair hearing by refusing to reveal the identity of an informant against him or her.

For the tribunal the question in an unfair dismissal claim will be whether the employer acted reasonably in treating the reason for dismissal as sufficient for dismissal in all the circumstances. It may be that it would not be necessary for it to examine the identity of the informant of misconduct in those circumstances. The question of whether it was reasonable for the employer to believe the informant's account can be judged on the *Thomson* basis.[167] However, where the applicant was denied a fair trial at the internal disciplinary hearing because he or she did not have the opportunity to cross-examine the witness with a knowledge of who was informing against him or her, that is a defect that the tribunal proceedings cannot remedy if it were to apply the *Thomson* guidelines rigidly. The tribunal does not have the opportunity to determine whether the misconduct took place and therefore does not have the power to determine all relevant matters of fact so as to be able to guarantee a fair trial. The defect is also one which takes away the very essence of the right to a fair trial. Where there is no proportionate justification for maintaining anonymity the tribunal would have to find that the public authority employer had breached s 6 of the HRA 1998. If the applicant did not receive a fair trial from the employer, the

---

167   *Linfood Cash & Carry v Thomson* [1989] IRLR 235.

dismissal is likely to be unfair, as a reasonable public authority would act lawfully.

Note that the civil right being determined by the public authority employer and that being determined by the tribunal proceedings for unfair dismissal are different. The public authority employer is determining the private law rights under the contract (for example whether it is to be terminated). However, the tribunal may be called on to judge whether the misconduct occurred for the purposes of determining whether there has been a breach of contract in a case of summary dismissal for that misconduct. In those circumstances the tribunal would have to permit cross-examination of the informant. The tribunal would find it more difficult to justify permitting the informant to remain anonymous in such employment tribunal proceedings. In an unfair dismissal claim, the applicant can argue that the identity of the informant should be disclosed as it is relevant to the question of whether the employer acted reasonably or not. The quality of the investigation of the information surrounding the informant will go to the question of whether it was reasonable for the employer to treat the misconduct it believed to have occurred as a sufficient reason for dismissal. For example, the investigation by the employer of the informant's motive might be affected by the identity of the persons to whom the employer spoke. The applicant would not be able to level proper criticism at the employer's investigation unless he or she knew not only the persons to whom the employer spoke, but also the identity of the person about whom the employer spoke.

The employer would have to be able to show that there was a lawful basis for refusing to impart the identity of the informant during the tribunal proceedings. In most situations, any risk of breaches of other Convention rights will have receded by the time the case is heard, but there might be justification in refusing to permit the disclosure of the informant's identity where there is some evidence that the applicant might contact him or her at home without permission, thus infringing the informant's right to a private life. However, in other cases the heat may not have gone out of the situation, and the informant may be just as much at risk when the case is heard as when the disciplinary hearing was being held.

3.9.14   The approach of the UK courts to issues in Article 6

Will a public authority act unlawfully if it does not conduct disciplinary proceedings in accordance with the Convention? Generally, it is submitted that it will not. The employee will still have access to the courts or tribunals in respect of the employer's procedure. The courts or tribunals will have the power to deal with all matters of fact and law relating to the disciplinary matter as it relates to the contractual obligations between the parties. Section 6 of the HRA 1998 creates a statutory tort in respect of the breaches of the Convention by the public authority. What is the situation of a worker with no access to the tribunal and who is subject to a non-contractual procedure? The first question for the courts, in a case in which the contractual obligations do not give rise to rights covering the procedure adopted to determine the civil rights of the parties, will be whether there is a dispute as to a civil right of the parties where the employee alleges that he or she was not given a fair hearing in that process. Clearly, subject to the public service exception, a disciplinary procedure which may result in dismissal is determinative of the rights under the contract (continuation or termination). Where the disciplinary procedure is non-contractual there is no breach of contract claim if the employer adopts an unfair procedure in the terms of Article 6. There is no general obligation on the employer to act fairly and reasonably implied in contracts of employment. [168] The case of *McClory* may illustrate a possible exception. There, three employees were suspended after having been involved in a fight. The suspension was for a period of about six months. Their contract permitted them to be suspended with or without pay, but during the suspension they did not receive the overtime payments that they would otherwise have received. They brought proceedings for damages for the overtime payments. The court was prepared to imply a term that the employers would exercise their right to suspend only on reasonable grounds and would continue the suspension for as long only as there were reasonable grounds for doing so. However, the argument for an implied term that the rules of natural justice applied between the employer and the employee was rejected.

In certain cases, the requirements of Article 6 will affect the contractual relationship so that the rules of natural justice will in effect be implied. Thus, if the employee cannot have his or her claim for breach of those rules determined by a tribunal, he or she will have recourse to the courts. The courts will have to consider whether, by its acts, the public authority failed to observe the principles of Article 6 in determining the employee's civil right to continued employment. Thus, even if there is no implied term incorporating the rules of natural justice in a contract claim against the public authority, the employee will be able to argue that, as he or she has no redress elsewhere for the breach of Article 6, the court can find that the employer has acted unlawfully in the determination of the employee's civil rights, and may award damages for this, even if no breach of contract were to be found.

However, there is a further step which might be contemplated. It might seem attractive to employees to seek to extend Article 6 protection to relationships between employees and private employers. The argument would run as follows: all contracts of employment contain a term that the employer will not act in such a way as to undermine the relationship of trust and confidence that should exist between employer and employee. [169] In failing to observe the requirements of Article 6 the employer is in breach of that term in dealing with the process leading to the termination of the contract.

However, in the author's opinion this argument cannot succeed. The most that could be expected by way of implication from the existence of an implied term of trust and confidence is that the employer would act in good faith and fairly. In the author's opinion, the full guarantees of Article 6 would not result from

---

168   *Western Excavating (ECC) Ltd v Sharp* [1978] IRLR 27, [1978] ICR 221, CA and cf *McClory v Post Office* [1992] ICR 758.
169   *Western Excavating (ECC) Ltd v Sharp* [1978] IRLR 27, [1978] ICR 221, CA.

those duties, provided that the court could say that the employer had acted fairly and in good faith in such a way that was unlikely to undermine the relationship of trust and confidence. The self-employed would have to rely on the scope of that implied term, as would the employee who has less than one year's service.

3.10   EMPLOYMENT TRIBUNAL PROCEEDINGS IN THE LIGHT OF THE HUMAN RIGHTS ACT 1998

3.10.1   Introduction

Most of the procedures used by the employment tribunal will pass the test of Article 6. Thus the power to strike out proceedings is likely to be permissible as a proportionate limitation on the rights under Article 6.[170] There it was stressed that procedural bars such as dismissal for want of prosecution served to protect defendants from the prolonged uncertainty surrounding the threat of legal action with the resulting prejudice this might entail for them.

3.10.2   Immunity from suit

The first question must be whether immunity is granted expressly or as a matter of substance. Many pieces of employment legislation state that they will not apply to certain organisations. Although expressed as exclusions from an Act, such limitations confer immunity in respect of the rights under the Act to those organisations. In *Osman v UK*,[171] the ECtHR considered the immunity conferred by public policy in respect of negligence by the police in the investigation of crime. The ECtHR held that the existence of such immunity did not result in there being no civil rights to which Article 6 could attach. The policy rule did not *automatically* doom to failure such a civil action from the outset but in principle allowed domestic courts to make a considered assessment on a case-by-case basis.[172] The ECtHR went on to consider whether the policy rule was a disproportionate interference with their right of access to justice under Article 6. The proximity test was rigid enough to reduce considerably the number of such claims against the police which could proceed to trial.[173] The ECtHR considered that the refusal of the UK courts to examine such claims on their merits (normally applying a blanket exclusion) was a denial of the right to a fair trial.

Any substantive exclusion in respect of a particular organisation imported by a statute will in substance be the grant of immunity from suit. Thus, where the effect of removing organisations such as the police, or the army from the effect of a statute, is to grant complete immunity in respect of the prohibited acts under a statute, there will be a question whether Article 6 is breached.

---

170   See in relation to want of prosecution in libel *FG v UK* Application No 39552/98, (1999) 20 April unreported (admissibility decision).
171   (2000) 29 EHRR 245.
172   *Hill v Chief Constable of West Yorkshire* [1989] AC 53.
173   *Caparo Industries Plc v Dickman* [1990] 2 AC 605.

A different principle may apply in respect of State immunity. In *Waite and Kennedy v Germany*,[174] the applicants sought to proceed in a contractual dispute with the European Space Agency (ESA). Under the ESA Convention the organisation had immunity. The applicants complained of denial of access to a court for a determination of the dispute with the ESA. The ECtHR found the immunity to be in pursuit of a legitimate objective of strengthening international co-operation. The ECtHR considered whether the immunity was proportionate. It found that the ESA Convention provided for modes of dispute settlement in private law claims. It was within the margin of appreciation for the national court to give effect to the immunity and proportionality could not used to compel an international organisation to submit itself to national litigation in relation to employment conditions. The principles of State immunity in the employment context will also probably withstand a challenge by Article 6.

3.10.3 Pre-hearing reviews and deposits

The tribunal rule which requires an applicant to pay a deposit before proceeding with a claim will probably not offend Article 6. The court will consider whether the sum required is disproportionate.[175] However, in tribunal cases the deposit is a small one. In *Ait Mouhub*, the applicant had no resources at all and the deposit he was required to pay before continuing proceedings was substantial. Any new rules in the tribunals will have to ensure a due proportion is kept between the deposit required in respect of the sum in issue and the means of the applicant.[176]

3.10.4 Principle of limitation in unfair dismissal etc

The limitation period of three months in respect of unfair dismissal applications has an exception where it was not reasonably practicable for the applicant to lodge the claim in time under s 111 of the ERA 1996. In *Perez de Rada Cavanilles v Spain*,[177] the applicant was out of time for lodging an application for the enforcement of a settlement in a planning dispute. The court held that a period of three days for the arrival of a postal application was disproportionately restrictive. Therefore there had been a violation of her 'civil rights' under Article 6(1). Given the increase in the amount of the compensatory element in unfair dismissal claims to £50,000, the question arises whether the three-month limitation period is a similar disproportionate restriction on the exercise of the right of recourse to the tribunals. Further, given the meaning attached to 'reasonably practicable' in the case-law, a question arises whether that interpretation places a disproportionate restriction on access to the tribunal itself.[178]

---

174   (2000) 30 EHRR 261.
175   *Ait-Mouhub v France* (2000) 30 EHRR 382.
176   See DTI Press Release of 27 November 2000.
177   (2000) 29 EHRR 109.
178   See *Shultz v Esso Petroleum Co Ltd* [1999] ICR 1202.

There is also a disparity in the limitation period extension mechanism used in cases relating to detrimental treatment in employment ('reasonably practicable') [179] and that used in discrimination cases ('just and equitable'). The requirements of 'just and equitable' extension are easier to meet than those of 'reasonably practicable'. Both rights engage fundamental principles (non-discrimination, private life, right to associate) and both apply to less favourable treatment in employment. It may be difficult to justify the restrictive limitation extension mechanism applied to detriment claims. Given that only disabled persons within the meaning of the Disability Discrimination Act 1995 may bring a claim for disability discrimination, and hence benefit from the 'just and equitable' extension principles, it would be open to a non-disabled person who is barred from bringing a claim relating to action short of dismissal to argue that by virtue of his or her status (non-disabled), he or she is treated less favourably with regard to access to a court than a disabled person. The disparity in mechanisms could possibly be justified by reference to the legitimate aim pursued in disability discrimination cases, and as being proportionate to the issues that the two different types of case raise.

Although the effect of a limitation period is to prevent a claimant having a hearing, this does not infringe Article 6(1), provided the limitation period is proportionate. A very short limitation period might infringe the Article. Thus the seven-day period for holding an interim hearing in certain dismissal claims may present a disproportionately short period, given that the right is for a person to retain his or her job. This will have an impact also under Article 8 as a person's private life may encompass the relationships from which the person is being barred by dismissal.

3.10.5   Limitation and claims for personal injury in discrimination cases

The Court of Appeal in *Sherriff v Klyne Tugs*[180] ruled that a person seeking a remedy for discrimination can claim damages for personal injury caused by that discrimination. The consequence of this is that a later personal injury action arising out of the same facts cannot be brought as it could have been raised in the discrimination claim. The effect of this ruling is that the period during which a person claiming damages for personal injury on account of race, sex or disability is reduced to three months as opposed to three years. The access to the courts of such persons in respect of their personal injury is therefore severely restricted. The ruling results in discrimination in respect of access to the courts (Articles 6 and 14). It is also clearly disproportionate to the issues involved.

3.10.6   Disclosure

The tribunal and other public authorities will act unlawfully if they fail to ensure disclosure of relevant documents in a case provided that this has a

---

179   See, for example, trade union acts short of dismissal, ss 146 and 147 of the TULR(C)A 1992.
180   [1999] ICR 1170.

decisive effect on the fairness of the procedure or if it prevents access to the court.[181] Although this principle seems broad, it is subject to qualifications which suggest that the principles used in the employment tribunals to decide issues of disclosure provide adequate safeguards for that right. *McGinley* concerned members of the armed forces who had been in the vicinity of nuclear bomb tests. They had developed ill health and claimed war pensions. The State refused to grant disclosure of documents which the applicants claimed would show the causal connection between their proximity to the tests and subsequent ill health. The Commission held that although such refusal, without good cause, could constitute a breach of Article 6, it was necessary to establish that such documents existed. Also, in an application to the Pensions Appeals Tribunal the applicants could seek discovery of the documents. The same principle will be arguable in respect of other forms of disclosure, such as replies to questionnaires, further particulars, answers to written questions. Information may not be withheld from the applicants which might assist them accessing the court.[182] However, there is nothing to prevent a claim being issued in the tribunals on the basis of incomplete information. It is possible to seek disclosure after the originating application is issued.

There is no procedure in the tribunals for pre-action disclosure. In a redundancy situation an employee may wish to establish that his dismissal was unfair by reason of unfair selection. The scoring system may have been applied unreasonably. Can the employee use this principle against a public authority in order to obtain pre-action disclosure of relative scoring?

The starting point must be the view expressed in *British Aerospace v Green* by Millett LJ:[183]

> 'A party raises an issue by making an allegation which is disputed. Counsel's submission that the applicants cannot select sample cases without further discovery is an admission that they are seeking discovery in order to find out what allegations they can make.'

The principle in *McGinley*[184] would appear to run counter to this proposition. Provided that the documents can be shown to exist and may serve to found a cause of action, in showing that the application of the scoring system was unreasonable, a fair procedure may require that they be disclosed. In *Eaton Ltd v King*,[185] the Scottish EAT stated that it was sufficient for the employer to have set up a good system for selection and to have administered it fairly. Whether a selection was administered fairly, however, may depend on the comparative scores of the pool for selection. By refusing disclosure of the comparative scores of the pool, therefore, the applicant may be deprived of the opportunity to show that no reasonable employer would have applied the redundancy selection criteria in the way in which they were actually applied.

---

181 *McGinley and Egan v UK* (1999) 27 EHRR 1.
182 See *McColm v UK* Application No 41197/98, 29 June 1999.
183 [1995] ICR 1006 at 1019.
184 *McGinley and Egan v UK* (1999) 27 EHRR 1.
185 [1995] IRLR 75.

Another way in which the question of disclosure may arise in the context of the HRA 1998 is where one right, private life (Article 8), conflicts with the right to a fair trial. Disclosure of confidential documents may be such an area. In *General Mediterranean Holdings SA v Patel*,[186] it was submitted that a necessary concomitant of the right to a fair trial under Article 6 was the right to consult a lawyer secure in the knowledge that what is said will not be revealed without consent, unless there is reasonable cause to believe that the communication involves abuse by the client of the purpose for which the protection exists. In relation to Article 8, it was argued that the right to respect for a person's private and family life, home and correspondence, includes the right to respect for communications between the client and his or her lawyer, and that no interference should be permitted under Article 8(2) unless again there is reasonable cause to believe that the purpose for which the right exists is being abused.[187]

Where material sought is claimed to be privileged, the tribunal will still have to conduct a balancing exercise between the right of the individual claiming privilege and that of the person claiming disclosure. Privilege cannot be an absolute defence in these circumstances. In *Silver*, the ECtHR was of the view[188] that it was permissible to open a letter from a lawyer to a prisoner when the prison authorities had reasonable cause to believe it contained an illicit enclosure which the normal means of detection had failed to disclose.

Toulson J in *General Mediterranean*[189] was considering an application for disclosure of privileged documents in a wasted costs application. He said:

> 'Article 6 gives every person a right to a fair trial, but I do not accept that it follows as a general proposition that this gives a right to interfere with another person's right to legal confidentiality. If that were generally so, the right to legal confidentiality recognised by the court would be useless, since its very purpose is to enable a person to communicate with his lawyer secure in the knowledge that such communications cannot be used without his consent to further another person's cause. In the absence of a general right under article 6 to make use of another person's confidential communications with his lawyer, I do not see how solicitors have a particular right to do so under that article for the purpose of defending a wasted costs application.'

It may be argued that this is to adopt too inflexible an approach, and that in principle the proper solution in such cases would be to treat a person's right under Article 8 to confidentiality in respect of communications with his lawyer as subject to a qualification of the kind proposed by Toohey J in *Carter v Northmore Hale Davy and Leake*.[190] Toohey J himself recognised that his proposal presented problems, even looking at the matter only in the context of a criminal trial.

> 'I have already cited the passage in *R. v Derby Magistrates' Court, Ex parte B.* [1996] A.C. 487, 511–512, in which Lord Nicholls considered the matter also in the

---

186   [2000] 1 WLR 272.
187   *Silver v UK* (1983) 5 EHRR 347, *Campbell v UK* (1993) 15 EHRR 137 and *Niemietz v Germany* (1993) 16 EHRR 97.
188   *Silver v UK* (1983) 5 EHRR 347 at para 46.
189   *General Mediterranean Holdings SA v Patel* [2000] 1 WLR 272.
190   (1995) 183 CLR 121.

context of other types of claim and concluded that there was no principled way by which judges could

"ascribe an appropriate weight, on each side of the scale, to the diverse multitude of various claims, civil and criminal, and other interests of the client on the one hand and the person seeking disclosure on the other hand."

I do not accept the submission that the approach of the House of Lords in that case was in violation of article 6, or that the Convention requires a balancing exercise in individual cases of the kind which the House of Lords considered and rejected as a matter of English law.'

However, although the balancing exercise will almost always result in protection of privileged material, under the HRA 1998 the tribunal or court should conduct such an exercise. The balance will favour only the party seeking disclosure where there is reasonable cause to believe that the party against whom disclosure is sought and his or her legal adviser have in some way colluded.

In criminal cases, the ECtHR has been clear that, absent collusion between lawyer and client, such privileged communication is protected by Article 6(3)(c).[191] In civil proceedings, the right to an adversarial hearing has been held to require full disclosure of matters laid before the court, otherwise the parties would not be able to comment on all the evidence adduced.[192]

The court stated in *McMichael v UK*:[193]

'as a matter of general principle the right to a fair – adversarial – trial "means the opportunity to have knowledge of and comment on the observations filed or evidence adduced by the other party" (see the *Ruiz-Mateos v Spain* judgment of 23 June 1993, Series A no. 262, p. 25, para. 63). In the context of the present case, the lack of disclosure of such vital documents as social reports is capable of affecting the ability of participating parents not only to influence the outcome of the children's hearing in question but also to assess their prospects of making an appeal to the Sheriff Court.'

The extent to which it will be possible for the public authority to rely on the rights of individual employees whose records it holds in order to resist disclosure is reduced by the principles surrounding confidentiality of information on disclosure. Generally, rights of confidentiality have been held to be subject to a qualification that the confidant may be required to disclose confidential information in the course of litigation if it is necessary for the fair disposal of the case.[194]

---

191   *S v Switzerland* (1992) 14 EHRR 670.
192   *McMichael v UK* (1995) 20 EHRR 205.
193   (1995) 20 EHRR 205.
194   *D v The National Society for the Prevention of Cruelty to Children* [1978] AC 171, *Science Research Council v Nassé* [1980] AC 1028 and *British Steel Corporation v Granada Television Limited* [1981] AC 1096.

3.10.7   Combination of applications

In certain cases, the employment tribunal can combine originating applications. By rule 18 of the Rules of Procedure,[195] if it appears to an employment tribunal that:

(a) a common question of law or fact arises in some or all the originating applications; or

(b) the relief claimed in some or all of those originating applications is in respect of or arises out of the same set of facts; or

(c) for any other reason it is desirable to make an order under rule 18,

the tribunal may order that some or all of the originating applications be considered together.

Thus in the case of two applicants dismissed for misconduct, one of whom only is facing criminal trial, the tribunal may be considering whether their cases should be combined. Before the tribunal makes an order combining proceedings it must ensure that each of the parties concerned has been given an opportunity at a hearing (or at least the tribunal must send a notice giving opportunity) to show cause why such an order should not be made. The result of this rule may be that the two cases can be heard at the same time. When the criminal trial of one applicant would substantially delay the hearing in relation to another applicant, it may be that it is not possible to justify the substantial delay that would occur, as cases must come to trial within a reasonable time. If the effect of combination is an unreasonable delay for the applicant whose circumstances do not require a delay, Article 6 may have been breached. Some guidance may be obtained from the criminal case of *Hentrich v France*[196] in respect of substantial delay resulting from consolidation of cases.

3.10.8   The ability of the tribunal to regulate its own procedures: unlawfully obtained evidence.

Rule 9(1) of the Rules of Procedure[197] provides that:

> 'The tribunal shall, so far as it appears to it appropriate, seek to avoid formality in its proceedings and shall not be bound by any enactment or rule of law relating to the admissibility of evidence in proceedings before the courts of law. The tribunal shall make such enquiries of persons appearing before it and witnesses as it considers appropriate and shall otherwise conduct the hearing in such manner as it considers most appropriate for the clarification of the issues before it and generally to the just handling of the proceedings.'

When evidence has been obtained in breach of the right to respect for private life (see **3.12.7**), the public authority party seeking to bring that evidence

---

195   The Rules of Procedure are contained in Sch 1 to the Employment Tribunals
       (Constitution and Rules of Procedure) Regulations 1993, SI 1993/2687.

196   (1994) 18 EHRR 440.

197   See footnote 195 above.

before the tribunal may have committed an unlawful act under s 6 of the HRA 1998, and there may be a question of whether reliance on that evidence by the tribunal would itself constitute an infringement of Article 8 by the tribunal. The tribunal has a positive obligation to protect the right to respect for private life. The act of the public authority employer obtaining the evidence and the act of the tribunal in admitting the evidence are susceptible to justification where the infringement of Article 8 has a lawful basis (at the least). In the case of the tribunal, there must be a question as to whether rule 9 of the procedure rules provides a sufficiently clear and precise basis for a party to know when consideration of evidence obtained unlawfully will be permitted, as it is not possible for a party to know, even with legal advice, whether the tribunal will admit a particular piece of evidence, however obtained. The power to make such enquiries as it considers appropriate must be construed in the light of s 3 of the HRA 1998 so as to give practical effect to the right of privacy.

However, the EAT has provided some guidelines for the application of rule 9 in *Aberdeen Steakhouses Group Plc v Ibrahim.*[198] Whilst this does not provide guidance on whether illegally obtained evidence should be admitted, the power to regulate procedure must be exercised judicially. It may be that this provides a sufficiently clear basis for parties to know when evidence obtained illegally may be admitted. The tribunal will have to conduct a balancing exercise in determining whether the illegality outweighs the probative value. In *Morley's of Brixton v Minott,*[199] the EAT held that the tribunal could not exclude from its consideration evidence in the form of a confession to the employer, which had been obtained in contravention of the Judges' Rules. The EAT pointed out that in the context of unfair dismissal claims, the tribunal was concerned not with the guilt or innocence of the employee, but the state of mind of the employer. On that basis there was no justifiable basis to exclude the confession. However, where the evidence is obtained in breach of a Convention right, the positive obligation on the tribunal to protect that right by not permitting the evidence to be adduced must be considered. The tribunal will be bound to consider this argument whether the employer is a public authority or a private body, as the positive obligation is the tribunal's.

If rule 9(1) is considered to be sufficiently clear and precise the tribunal will be able to rely on the legitimate aim of the administration of justice in deciding to rely on the evidence. The only other question for the tribunal is whether the admission of the evidence obtained in breach of Article 8 is necessary in a democratic society. It is likely that the tribunal's ability to rely on such evidence for the purpose of administration of speedy, efficient and informal justice will be regarded as proportional in most cases. However, when the evidence has been obtained after a gross breach of Article 8 the tribunal may have to consider whether its probative value outweighs that infringement.

In relation to the public authority employer seeking to produce such evidence, it is arguable that the existence of a discretion in the employment tribunal to

198   [1988] ICR 550.
199   [1982] ICR 444.

admit the evidence will not stand as an appropriate procedural safeguard for the right to privacy.

Thus evidence obtained as a result of a search which has no legal basis will need to be treated with caution. In most employment situations such evidence will have been obtained unlawfully because there is no clear and precise legal basis permitting the employer to obtain evidence by means of a search. A tribunal confronted with a public authority employer that has conducted a search or surveillance in breach of Article 8 will have to consider whether any right reserved to conduct such searches or surveillance by the contract of employment is sufficiently clear and precise to provide the required lawful basis. Where the tribunal finds that the evidence was unlawfully obtained, it may make a finding that s 6 of the HRA 1998 has been breached by the public authority employer.

When is there a sufficiently clear and precise legal basis? This will be a question determined on the analysis of the particular circumstances of the case. In *Funke v France*,[200] customs officers made a search and seized documents at the applicant's house in order to obtain particulars of overseas assets held by the applicant and his wife. Although the search and seizures did not result in any criminal proceedings under the relevant financial dealings regulations, they did lead to parallel proceedings for disclosure of documents and for interim orders. As a result of these disclosure proceedings, the applicant was convicted and fined by the Strasbourg police court for failing to provide the customs authorities with statements of his overseas bank accounts. The applicant complained that the search and seizures effected at his home infringed Article 8. The ECtHR found an infringement of the right to a fair trial and a breach of Article 8. The search and seizures made at the applicant's house interfered with his right to respect for his private life, his home and his correspondence, as secured in Article 8(1). The interferences had a legitimate aim since they were in the interest of the economic well-being of the country. The exceptions provided for in Article 8(2) are to be interpreted narrowly, and the need for them in a given case must be convincingly established. The relevant legislation and practice must afford adequate and effective safeguards against abuse. The interferences here were a violation of Article 8 because the customs authorities possessed very wide powers when undertaking searches and seizures; in the absence of any requirement of a judicial warrant, the restrictions and conditions provided for in law were insufficient for the interferences with the applicant's right to have been strictly proportionate to that legitimate aim pursued. The customs authorities never lodged a complaint against the applicant alleging an offence against the relevant financial dealings regulation. Although there were some restrictions on the powers, amounting to a certain degree of control, these were too lax and full of loopholes. There were therefore no adequate procedural safeguards.

Considered purely as an issue under Article 6, the ECtHR has generally left it to the contracting States to create and maintain rules concerning admissibility of evidence. Under Article 6, the concern is whether the proceedings, taken as a

---

200   (1993) 16 EHRR 297.

whole, were fair.[201] Article 6 of the Convention does not result in a blanket exclusion of unlawfully obtained evidence.

In *Schenk v Switzerland*,[202] the applicant had been convicted of incitement to murder his wife. Part of the evidence heard against him was a tape recording of a telephone conversation with him, which had been recorded without his knowledge. He claimed that the use of the recording contravened Article 6(1). He also alleged that the recording violated the right to respect for private life, which included the right to confidentiality of telephone conversations. The ECtHR held that the use of the recording in evidence did not deprive Schenk of a fair trial. The ECtHR took the Article 6 and Article 8 issues together and did not feel it necessary to consider the case under Article 8.

Unlawfully obtained evidence, such as an unauthorised recording of a telephone conversation, might be admissible in court proceedings where the court relied on a set of additional corroborating evidential elements in order to determine the guilt of an accused. Article 6 did not lay down any rules on the admissibility of evidence, as this was primarily a matter for domestic law. The ECtHR had to ascertain whether the trial as a whole was fair.

Schenk had been aware of the lawfulness of the recording and had been able to challenge its authenticity before the courts. He had obtained an investigation of and could have examined the persons allegedly involved in the making of the recording. The ECtHR also attached weight to the fact that the recording was not the only evidence on which the conviction was based.

It should be noted that, in that case, there was other evidence supporting the finding of guilt. In particular, there was no abuse of power by the State authority because the tape had been made by private person and given to the police. Where the public authority has used a private investigation team, however, it would remain the State's act as they would be acting on its behalf in making the tape.

3.10.9 Private life and surveillance

There are limits on the notion of a private life that may be relevant to surveillance by video. For example, where the activity of the subject of the video evidence is undertaken in public view, he or she may have no reasonable expectation of privacy.[203] Thus where an individual is followed from his or her house to his or her place of undeclared work, there is nothing unlawful either in UK or Convention law. However, if in order to make the video the other party committed an unlawful act, such as trespass, it may infringe the right to respect for private life. Even when the party making the video committed an unlawful act, infringing the right to respect for private life, the tribunal will need to consider whether that right is outweighed by the right to a fair trial. Generally,

---

201   See *Miailhe v France (No 2)* (1997) 23 EHRR 491.
202   (1991) 13 EHRR 242.
203   See *Friedl v Austria* (1996) 21 EHRR 83.

it is likely that the tribunal will consider that the right to a fair trial will be more important. However, the nature of the infringement will need to be taken into account. By parity of reasoning, a secret tape recording of a conversation taking place in a public venue would not engage the right of respect for privacy in its subject. Where one party makes a tape recording during a meeting without the knowledge of the other party, it may be that this does infringe the right to respect for the private life of the other. However, the element of privacy would be lacking, it is suggested, if the meeting was being minuted with the intention that the minutes would be available to the parties to the conversation.

3.10.10   Public interest immunity

In *Balfour v FCO,*[204] a member of the diplomatic service complained of unfair dismissal. He sought discovery of particular documents from the Foreign and Commonwealth Office, which was subject to a certificate of public interest immunity. This was refused on the ground that the employment tribunal had no power to go behind the certificates issued on the ground of national security (the documents concerned the security and intelligence services). The Court of Appeal held that the tribunal had an obligation to be vigilant to ensure that a claim of public interest immunity was raised only in appropriate circumstances and with appropriate particularity. However, once a certificate of a Minister of State demonstrated that the disclosure of documentary evidence posed an actual or potential risk to national security, the court should not exercise its right to inspect that evidence. The tribunal was constrained by the terms of the certificates. The importance of the case to the applicant did not matter.

Section 41 of and Sch 8 to the Employment Relations Act 1999 make provision for cases involving national security by replacing s 193 of the ERA 1996. In essence, if it is shown that an action complained of (for example, action short of dismissal or unfair dismissal) was taken for the purpose of safeguarding national security, the employment tribunal shall dismiss the complaint. Under tribunal rules made pursuant to Sch 8, a Minister will have power:

(a)   to direct a tribunal to sit in private for all or part of particular Crown employment proceedings;
(b)   to direct a tribunal to exclude the applicant from all or part of particular Crown employment proceedings;
(c)   to direct a tribunal to exclude the applicant's representatives from all or part of particular Crown employment proceedings;
(d)   to direct a tribunal to take steps to conceal the identity of a particular witness in particular Crown employment proceedings;
(e)   to direct a tribunal to take steps to keep secret all or part of the reasons for its decision in particular Crown employment proceedings.

Where the applicant is excluded from proceedings, the rules will permit another person to be appointed to represent the applicant's interests in the proceedings. The publication and registration of reasons for the tribunal's decision may be restricted. An excluded person may be permitted to make a

---

204   [1994] ICR 277.

statement to the tribunal before the commencement of the proceedings, or the part of the proceedings, from which that person is excluded.

Section 10A of the Employment Tribunals Act 1996 provides that procedure regulations may enable an employment tribunal to sit in private for the purpose of hearing evidence from any person which in the opinion of the tribunal is likely to consist of:

(a) information which that person could not disclose without contravening a prohibition imposed by or by virtue of any enactment;

(b) information which has been communicated to him or her in confidence or which he or she has otherwise obtained in consequence of the confidence reposed in him or her by another person; or

(c) information the disclosure of which would, for reasons other than its effect on negotiations with respect to any of the matters mentioned in s 178(2) of the Trade Union and Labour Relations (Consolidation) Act 1992, cause substantial injury to any undertaking of his or hers or in which he or she works.

In Crown employment, the 'undertaking' which might be injured is the national interest. Section 10B creates an offence of infringing the restriction of publicity in cases involving national security. Former provisions relating to national security are repealed or qualified so as to correspond with this new style of dealing with national security cases. Thus the certification procedure in s 69(2) of the Race Relations Act 1976 is qualified and the certification process in the Disability Discrimination Act 1995 is repealed.

When a submission is made to the employment tribunal that certain evidence should be excluded as a result of a public interest immunity argument, the tribunal should probably not conduct a hearing in the absence of the interested parties. There should be, as between the parties, equality of arms.[205] The rules made pursuant to the provisions relating to national security cases will have to ensure that the applicant's right to a fair trial in these circumstances is minimally infringed.

It is suggested that merely showing that the action was taken for the purposes of safeguarding national security will not be enough. The State will have to show that the action was necessary and proportionate to that purpose before dismissal of the claim would not infringe the applicant's right to a fair trial.

3.10.11 The quality of representation

If the procedural guarantees of Article 6(1) reflect the principles set out later in the Article, the tribunal may need to consider whether there would be a breach of s 6 of the HRA 1998 arising from the tribunal permitting manifestly ineffective representation by a party's representative to prejudice the party's right to a fair trial. Where the lack of effective representation is manifest and is brought to the attention of the tribunal, it may need to consider whether to grant an adjournment or to take other action in order to safeguard the right of

---

205 See, in the context of criminal law, *Rowe & Davis v UK* (2000) 30 EHRR 1.

the disadvantaged party to a fair trial. It would need to be obvious to the tribunal that the representative was representing at a lower level than the tribunal would normally expect of that kind of representative.[206]

The Convention is intended to guarantee not rights that are theoretical or illusory but rights that are practical and effective. This is particularly so in relation to representation in view of the prominent place held in a democratic society by the right to a fair trial.[207]

However, the State does not undertake to represent parties in tribunal proceedings, as there is no provision made for public funding. Anyone can represent another before employment tribunals. Where public funding is available, the State undertakes the administration of justice by funding representation. That representation is limited to solicitors and barristers.[208] Thus, for example, where a representative repeatedly ignores tribunal orders, despite instructions, and the party is faced with showing cause why his or her originating application or notice of appearance should not be struck out, the quality of the representation that the party has had during the proceedings will be relevant. The applicant, for example, cannot obtain any declaration of his or her employment rights in negligence proceedings against the representative. If the quality of representation is so poor that the right to a fair trial is infringed, the tribunal will have to consider whether that infringement (represented by the decision to strike out on the basis of non-compliance) is justified. Where a fair trial is still possible, it is suggested that striking out will not be the most appropriate course.[209] Where the ineffectiveness of representation becomes apparent at the hearing of the case, the tribunal will need to ask itself whether by not attempting to ensure that the party's case is properly heard, despite the poor representation, it omits to perform a s 6 duty as it fails to guarantee a fair trial to that party. Thus if the representation is preventing a fair trial, the tribunal may have to adjourn the hearing so that the defect can be remedied, possibly ordering costs against the representative's client, as that is a matter that can be remedied by negligence proceedings.

3.10.12   Disclosing links/bias

The right to an impartial tribunal is breached if there is a 'legitimate doubt' about impartiality.[210]

3.10.13   Medical disclosure and financial information

Where disclosure is sought from an applicant relating to personal information, such as medical or financial matters, the tribunal will have to consider whether disclosure infringes the subject's right to respect for his or her private life and

---

206   See *Kamasinski v Austria* (1991) 13 EHRR 36.
207   *Artico v Italy* (1981) 3 EHRR 1 and *Airey v Ireland* (1979–80) 2 EHRR 305.
208   See by analogy *Van der Musselle v Belgium* (1984) 6 EHRR 163.
209   See *National Grid v Virdee* [1992] IRLR 555.
210   *Hauschildt v Denmark* (1990) 12 EHRR 266 at para 46 and see *Smith v Secretary of State for Trade and Industry* [2000] ICR 69, and *Director-General of Fair Trading v The Proprietary Association of Great Britain* (Court of Appeal, 21 December 2000).

correspondence. The tribunal will have to ask whether the disclosure sought is necessary in a democratic society for protection of the rights of others. So the tribunal will balance the rights of the person seeking disclosure (to a fair trial) against the right of the other party (to respect for private life). However, when an individual is seeking disclosure from a public authority (for example financial information) that body will not be able to rely on Article 8 rights. The principal question will remain how relevant and necessary the documents are for a fair determination of the issues between the parties.

Although financial information is covered by the right to a private life, in most cases before the employment tribunals the applicant will need to be able to show his or her loss. The balance of competing interests will generally favour the respondent obtaining disclosure of the applicant's financial affairs in detail.

3.10.14   Interlocutory stages of tribunal proceedings

Article 6 may have less serious impact on the interlocutory stages of tribunal proceedings. The requirement of a public hearing, for example, does not necessarily apply to interlocutory hearings.[211] One aspect of a fair hearing is the availability of a reasoned decision.[212] However, it is not clear that these reasons must be recorded in some particular form. Thus it might be adequate that the representatives of the party have the opportunity to make a note. In the tribunals, and increasingly in other courts, certain interlocutory decisions may be dealt with by correspondence. In these circumstances, proper reasons should be given for interlocutory decisions. It is unlikely, however, that this requirement will go beyond what the employment tribunal already requires in respect of interlocutory decisions.[213]

3.10.15   Adjournments

In the early life of the tribunals there were many cases which emphasised the duty of the tribunal to raise and investigate matters such as loss with unrepresented applicants,[214] or to ensure that every assistance should be given to the unrepresented party.[215] In the latter case, the policy basis was said by the EAT to be:

> 'that the whole spirit of this legislation, stemming back to the initial days when the industrial tribunals were first created, that the proceedings should be as informal as possible. The little man, or the little woman, trying to put a case of grievance, should be given every assistance so that his or her case will have been put and properly considered'.

Employment tribunals frequently have persons representing themselves before them. Article 6 includes the right to equality of arms. When an adjournment is

---

211   *X v UK* (1970) 30 CD 70. Cf in relation to merits hearings of arbitration of small claims *Scarth v UK* (1998) 26 EHRR CD 154.
212   *Van de Hurk v The Netherlands* (1994) 18 EHRR 481 at para 61.
213   See *Independent Research Services Limited v Catterall* [1993] ICR 1.
214   See *Smith Kline French v Coates* [1977] IRLR 220.
215   *Mortimer v Reading Windings* [1977] ICR 511.

sought by an unrepresented party, and the tribunal considers that there are complicated legal arguments involved in the case, the right to a fair trial may require the tribunal to adjourn proceedings. This is particularly so where the other party is represented by a lawyer. The employment tribunal's rules on costs where an adjournment has been caused probably will not represent a practical denial of the right to a fair trial of the party seeking the adjournment. It will be a question of balancing the right of the person seeking the adjournment against the other party's right to a fair trial which includes the right not to be subjected to unnecessary delay in the determination of civil rights or obligations.

3.11   ARTICLES 6(2) AND 7: CRIMINAL CHARGES

Disciplinary proceedings as such cannot be characterised as 'criminal' although in certain specific cases the proceedings may be criminal. The ECtHR gave a restrictive meaning to the expression.[216] The ECtHR must ascertain:

–   whether the provision(s) defining the offence charged belong to criminal law, disciplinary law or both concurrently;
–   the nature of the offence, which is a factor of greater importance;
–   the degree of severity of the penalty that the person concerned risks incurring. There belong to the 'criminal' sphere deprivations of liberty liable to be imposed as a punishment, except those which by their nature, duration or manner of execution cannot be appreciably detrimental.

These principles were applied by the ECtHR in *Campbell and Fell v UK*[217] and the ECtHR went on to say:

> 'The court considers that these factors, whilst not of themselves sufficient to lead to the conclusion that the offences with which the applicant was charged have to be regarded as 'criminal' for Convention purposes, do give them a certain colouring which does not entirely coincide with that of a purely disciplinary matter.'

Article 6 requires that a law (including the common law) which imposes a criminal offence or penalty be sufficiently clearly drafted or defined so that a person can reasonably be able to foresee that a certain act would be an offence. There are a number of employment related areas which this might affect, such as obligations under health and safety legislation and sanctions for failure to comply with tribunal orders. Generally, these are already sufficiently clearly drafted to comply with Article 6.

In addition in *Saunders v United Kingdom*[218] the applicant was required to provide evidence in relation to suspected fraudulent share dealings to DTI inspectors and these were used against him in subsequent criminal proceedings. He claimed that he had been deprived of a fair trial generally, and that his right to be presumed innocent under Article 6(2) had been breached. The

---

216   *Engel v The Netherlands (No 1)* (1979–80) 1 EHRR 647.
217   (1985) 7 EHRR 165.
218   (1997) 23 EHRR 313.

ECtHR rejected the Government's argument that this was a legitimate restriction on the right against self-incrimination.

Article 7 requires that there be no retrospective criminal offences created. Where an offence relates to an activity protected by the Convention, particularly under Articles 8 to 11, the offence and decision to prosecute must be justified as legitimate, necessary and proportionate.

3.12   ARTICLE 8

3.12.1   The scope of Article 8

Article 8 is perhaps the most fecund of the Convention rights. If the effected item affects a person's private or family life the provisions of Article 8 may be relevant. It provides that everyone has the right to *respect* for his or her private and family life, home and correspondence. Therefore, it does not establish an absolute right to private or family life. In an employment context, interception of correspondence, telephone tapping and searches (at home or at work) will be covered. Access to information about a person's identity is also covered, but also a person's right to have and to express an identity. The individual has the right to express his or her sexuality under this provision. In a health and safety context, the Article supports the right to be free from severe environmental pollution such as severe pollution from a workplace full of cigarette smoke.

The Article covers the collection and use of information concerning an individual. It will therefore have impact on the extent to which an employer during the course of an investigation into an employee acts reasonably in dismissing an individual when relying on something in that person's life outside work. The right to have and form social relationships and the protection of a person's reputation are also covered by the Article. This means that an effected item[219] must respect the right of the person to social relationships at work, so that a rule against office affairs (for example) might run counter to it.[220]

An effected item may lawfully interfere with these rights if it is in accordance with the law and is necessary in a democratic society in the interests of national security, public safety, the economic well-being of the country, for the prevention of disorder or crime, for the protection of health or morals, or for the protection of the rights and freedoms of others.

The State has an obligation under Article 8 to take steps to provide the rights and privileges guaranteed by the Article and to protect people against the activities of other private individuals that prevent the effective enjoyment of these rights. In the context of unfair dismissal decisions, this may be relevant

---

219   See **3.5.2**.
220   See *X v Iceland* (1976) 5 DR 86.

where tribunals are considering absence from work dismissals, where the absences are accounted for by family needs. The tribunals may on certain facts have to interpret the legislation in such a way as to protect those rights by finding that an employer who dismissed for these reasons dismissed unfairly. The mutual enjoyment by parent and child of each other's company constitutes a fundamental element of family life.

Searches of an individual's home or person may constitute an infringement of this right. Article 8 creates a positive obligation. The State must take action to show that Article 8 rights are protected effectively. Potentially, the Article requires the adoption of measures designed to secure respect for private life even as between individuals.[221] This positive obligation on States has implications for the development of common law rights of privacy before the courts (see below). Clearly, the right to respect for family and private life will have a major impact on sex discrimination cases (see Chapter 5).

3.12.2   Family life

The ECtHR has in *Rees v UK*[222] and *Cossey v UK*[223] confined the application of Article 12 of the Convention to the traditional marriage between persons of opposite biological sex. Article 12 refers to the right 'to marry and to found a family' and in that context it is easy to understand that the word 'family' may be restricted in its scope. Article 8 provides the right 'to respect for his private and family life'. In this context the Commission has held that a stable homosexual relationship between two men does not fall within the scope of the right to respect for family life, but that such a relationship may be a matter affecting private life: *S v UK*.[224] Some protection for such a relationship is thus recognised in the human rights jurisprudence. Moreover, in the developing jurisprudence of the ECtHR it is recognised that family life is not confined to families based on marriage but may encompass other *de facto* relationships such as that in *X, Y and Z v UK*[225] where X had by gender reassignment surgery come to live as a man with Y, who was a woman, and her child, Z, who had been born through AID treatment. In *Salgueiro da Silva Mouta v Portugal*,[226] a homosexual man claimed that an award of custody of his daughter to her mother was an unjustified interference with his right to respect for family life, and also with his right to respect for his private life since he was required in respect of his right of access to his daughter to conceal from her his homosexuality. His claim was held admissible.

3.12.3   Private life

The notion of private life indicates an inner circle where the individual can live without State interference.[227] The principle of 'private life' under Article 8(1)

---

221   *X & Y v Netherlands* (1986) 8 EHRR 235.
222   (1987) 9 EHRR 562.
223   (1991) 13 EHRR 622.
224   (1986) 47 DR 274.
225   (1997) 24 EHRR 143.
226   Application No 33290/96, 1 December 1998 (unpublished).
227   *Niemietz v Germany* (1993) 16 EHRR 97.

was in *Niemietz* extended to business premises including a professional person's offices, and the right to preserve the confidentiality of communications with clients was considered to be part of the right to privacy. The right also covers the right to develop one's own personality and to create and maintain relationships with others. It protects the right to occupy an existing home without interference and to enjoy its comforts. It offers protection from harassment by others.[228] The right also protects against noise nuisance.[229] The provisions of Article 8 will cover business premises as well as residential premises.[230] When a search is carried out of residential or business premises, it will need to be justified under Article 8(2). In *Halford v UK*,[231] the right was held to prohibit unregulated telephone tapping.

The right to a private life extends to corporate bodies. One area in which a company's right to privacy may be infringed is in relation to disclosure of documents in tribunal and court cases where a balance must be struck between the right to a fair trial and the right to privacy. It is submitted that it will only be in cases in which the nature of the documents discloses personally private information about employees that the right to privacy would outweigh the ordinary considerations relating to the right to a fair trial.

3.12.4   A right to privacy

Confidences

In the UK there has been no law of privacy.[232] Instead, the right to a private life is protected by, amongst other remedies, the torts of harassment, trespass to the person, and the remedy of breach of confidence. Breach of confidence requires that:

(a) the information itself must have 'the necessary quality of confidence about it';

(b) the information 'must have been imparted in circumstances importing an obligation of confidence'; and

(c) there must have been an 'unauthorised use of that information to the detriment of the party communicating it'.[233]

Thus it has been said that 'there is, however, no law against taking a photograph' and that therefore mere taking of a photograph of a person's land cannot turn an act which is not a trespass into the plaintiff's air space into one that is a trespass,[234] although harassment by constant aerial surveillance might amount to actionable nuisance. However, in cases dealing with publication in breach of confidence, an action for account of profits has been considered an adequate remedy for breach.[235]

---

228   *Whiteside v UK* (1994) 76 DR 80.
229   *Arrondale v UK* (1982) 26 DR 5.
230   *Niemietz v Germany* (1993) 16 EHRR 97.
231   [1997] IRLR 471.
232   *Kaye v Robertson* [1991] FSR 62 *per* Glidewell LJ at p 66.
233   *Coco v AN Clark Engineers Ltd* [1969] RPC 41 at p 47.
234   *Bernstein v Skyviews Ltd* [1978] 1 QB 479.
235   *Earl Spencer and Countess Spencer v UK* (1998) 25 EHRR CD 105.

The 'Spycatcher case'[236] related to the publication by newspapers of extracts from a book entitled 'Spycatcher' in which the author purported to recount his service in MI5. The duty of confidence is broad enough:

> 'not merely to embrace those cases where a third party receives information from a person who is under a duty of confidence in respect of it, knowing that it has been disclosed by that person in breach of his duty of confidence, but also to include certain situations ... where an obviously confidential document, such as a private diary, is dropped in a public place, and is then picked up by a passer-by.'

An order for an account of profits was made against *The Sunday Times* in relation to its previous publication of extracts of the book.[237]

The case of *Hellewell v the Chief Constable of Derbyshire*[238] related to photographs taken of a man while he was in police custody which local shopkeepers had asked the police to supply for use by their security staff to reduce shoplifting. The applicant was unsuccessful in his application for an injunction to prevent the circulation of his photograph, the court finding that the Chief Constable would be bound to succeed in the main action in establishing a 'public interest' defence. Laws J stated as follows:

> 'If someone with a telephoto lens were to take from a distance with no authority a picture of another engaged in some private act, the subsequent disclosure of the photograph would, in my judgment, as surely amount to a breach of confidence as if he had found or stolen a letter or diary in which the act was recounted and proceeded to publish it. In such a case, the law should protect what might reasonably be called a right of privacy, although the name accorded to the cause of action would be breach of confidence.'

In the case of *Michael Barrymore v News Group Newspapers Limited*,[239] the second defendant had released information as regards his relationship with the plaintiff (including letters exchanged between them) to the first defendant, the latter foreseeing a series of press Articles on the matter. The High Court granted an injunction to restrain further publications of this information in the newspaper. The law on preservation of confidences protected his privacy.

In *Earl Spencer and Countess Spencer v the UK*[240] the Commission held that the UK law on publishing confidences constituted a domestic remedy which had not been shown to be ineffective and therefore should have been exhausted before recourse to Convention law. Where the court or tribunal is considering whether there has been an infringement of the right to private life by means of

---

236 *Attorney-General v Guardian Newspapers (No 2)* [1990] AC 109.
237 See also *Shelley Films Ltd v Rex Features Ltd* [1994] EMLR 134 where the defendant photographic agency had bought and supplied to a newspaper a photograph taken without authorisation on the set of a film which was in closed and secret production. In fixing the agency with the requisite knowledge, the High Court referred to a defendant coming into possession of information in circumstances where he 'ought as a reasonable person to know' that the plaintiff intended the information to be kept confidential.
238 [1995] 1 WLR 804 at p 805.
239 [1997] FSR 600.
240 Application No 28851/95 and No 28852/95, (1998) 25 EHRR CD 105.

surveillance, the principles relating to the law on confidences should be taken into account.

The Commission in *Spencer* stated:

> 'the remedy of breach of confidence (against the newspapers and their sources) was available to the applicants and that the applicants have not demonstrated that it was insufficient or ineffective in the circumstances of their cases. It considers that, insofar as relevant doubts remain concerning the financial awards to be made following a finding of a breach of confidence, they are not such as to warrant a conclusion that the breach of confidence action is ineffective or insufficient but rather a conclusion that the matter should be put to the domestic courts for consideration in order to allow those courts, through the common law system in the UK, the opportunity to develop existing rights by way of interpretation.'

Thus where a person has divulged information in confidence to a work colleague and that person breaks that confidence the victim may have a remedy against a public authority in the following respects:

(a) to restrain the further broadcasting of the information;
(b) as a breach of contract (the personnel office divulged the information);
(b) a breach of his or her right to respect for private life where the common law remedies relating to breach of confidences do not protect the right to respect for his or her private life; and
(d) where the information is stored data under the Data Protection Act 1998.

3.12.5 Harassment at work

Harassment at work may constitute actionable discrimination on the ground of race or sex or for a reason relating to disability. However, there may be situations in which the employee cannot use the anti-discrimination legislation. One example is where the victim is subjected to intrusive unpleasant behaviour as a result of a personality clash. The public authority will need to have taken steps to prevent workers engaging in this kind of behaviour in the course of their employment, as the public authority has a positive obligation to ensure respect for private life between individuals.

The law of tort provides for actions claiming damages in respect of trespass to the person (false imprisonment, battery or assault), trespass to land or to goods. There are also dicta suggesting an action may lie in tortious interference with the highway.[241] The tort of nuisance provides remedies where there is undue interference with the use and enjoyment of land.

In the case of *Khorasandjian v Bush*,[242] the Court of Appeal held, by a majority, that where the defendant (an ex-boyfriend) was pestering the plaintiff, inter alia, by repeated telephone calls, such conduct amounted to private actionable nuisance in that it interfered with the ordinary and reasonable use of property, and that the county court had power to grant an injunction in this context.

An action may also be brought in tort in respect of conduct which is calculated to impair the plaintiff's health whether physical or mental and having that

---

241 *Thomas v National Union of Mineworkers* [1986] Ch 20.
242 [1993] QB 727.

effect.[243] In this last case, in which the plaintiff complained of being the victim of a campaign of harassment from a former male friend, the Court of Appeal granted an interlocutory injunction prohibiting the defendant from 'assaulting, molesting or otherwise interfering with the plaintiff by doing acts calculated to cause her harm'. In the case of *Khorasandjian v Bush*,[244] the Court of Appeal also appears to have considered that the grant of an interlocutory injunction was justified under this line of authority. While it did not appear in that case that the plaintiff was as yet suffering from any physical or psychiatric illness, there was an obvious risk that the cumulative effect of the campaign of harassment would cause such illness. Consequently, the courts were entitled to look at the defendant's conduct as a whole and to restrain his acts of harassment on a *quia timet* basis. The majority of the court thus approved an injunction by the county court judge restraining the defendant from harassing or molesting the plaintiff. The dissenting judge considered that the injunction should have been restricted to 'acts calculated to do the (plaintiff) harm'.

The Protection from Harassment Act 1997 creates a tort of harassment (as well as a criminal offence). Section 3 permits a claim for damages and for an injunction to be sought. Harassment is not specifically defined by the 1997 Act. However, s 7 provides that there must be a course of conduct causing alarm or distress to a person. 'Conduct' includes words and 'a course of conduct' is defined as conduct on two or more occasions. However, conduct falling short of this standard may infringe the victim's right to respect for his or her private life. There may still need to be recourse to the common law in such cases. There, the court's duty to ensure that the exercise of its powers give effect to the Convention rights may require it to consider the degree of interference with a person's rights under Article 8 as a more important factor. The tort of trespass to the person in *Wilkinson v Downton*[245] is certainly too stringent to afford adequate protection for Article 8 rights and the same may be said for the provisions of the Protection from Harassment Act 1997.

Thus in *Powell v Boldaz*,[246] a parent whose child died of a rare disease brought a claim for damages which was struck out as disclosing no cause of action. The proceedings related to psychiatric injuries that he allegedly suffered as a result of a GP's falsification of medical records pertaining to the child's death. He argued for trespass to the person in accordance with *Wilkinson v Downton*.[247]

The Court of Appeal dismissed his appeal against the order to strike out the pleading. They said that the injuries suffered by him did not constitute a form of the tort of trespass to the person in accordance with *Wilkinson v Downton*. This would involve:

(i) a statement;
(ii) known to be false made; and

---

243 *Wilkinson v Downton* [1897] 2 QB 57; *Janvier v Sweeney* [1919] 2 KB 316; *Burnett v George* [1992] 1 FLR 525.
244 [1993] QB 727.
245 [1897] 2 QB 57.
246 [1998] Lloyd's Rep Med 116.
247 [1897] 2 QB 57.

(iii) with the intention of causing the subsequent injury.

The Court of Appeal held that the intention to injure the claimant could not be imputed to the defendant as he did not have the necessary degree of foresight to appreciate the consequences of his actions. The requirements of intention, knowledge and injury to health protect only a narrow category of situations in which a person's right to privacy under Article 8 is protected.

If the infringement is constituted by a campaign against a person's lifestyle in a work situation, Article 8 protects a person who does not wish to resign the post (in which case a constructive dismissal claim might be available), but who cannot claim under any of the discrimination legislation or the Protection from Harassment Act 1997. Since Article 8 covers the right to express one's identity and to foster relationships at work, its purpose is not limited to those situations in which a risk to the person's health is identified or where there is injurious alarm or distress. The purpose of the Article is, in part, to protect the dignity of the person whose private life is in issue. Such a person may be able to claim against a public authority under s 7(1)(a) of the HRA 1998.

3.12.6 Correspondence

Correspondence includes letters, telephone calls, faxes and e-mails. In *X v Germany*,[248] the Commission held that respect for correspondence did not require a fully functioning postal service. In *Halford v UK*,[249] an assistant chief constable who had brought discrimination proceedings against her employers successfully claimed that the interception of her private telephone conversations on an internal network at work interfered with her right to private life. In *Petra v Romania*,[250] national law allowed prison governors to retain letters or other documents considered to be unsuited to the process of rehabilitating a prisoner. The governor intercepted a prisoner's letters. The prisoner claimed that this violated his right to privacy of correspondence.

3.12.7 Searching and surveillance

Although the tribunals have a discretion to regulate their own procedures, and the rules of evidence do not apply to them, they are obliged to construe that discretion so as to give effect to the tribunals' positive obligation under Article 8. Thus where an employer seeks to introduce into evidence covert surveillance there may be two consequences. First, if the employer is a public authority the act of conducting covert surveillance may be unlawful and actionable. The tribunal may make a finding to that effect. Secondly, the tribunal's discretion may be exercised so as to exclude the evidence which was unlawfully obtained. Such infringements may be susceptible to justification.

One source of justification may be the contract, if it acknowledges the right of the employer to maintain surveillance of the employee in certain specified circumstances (for example, during normal working hours, or whilst absent

---

248 (1979) 17 DR 227.
249 (1997) 24 EHRR 523.
250 (1998) 5 BHRC 497.

through sickness). If the employee has agreed in advance that in certain specified situations surveillance (which otherwise would interfere with respect for private life) may take place, the question of whether the employee's rights under Article 8 have been infringed will arise, but will take the form of whether the interference in that right and the manner in which the surveillance was carried out was disproportionate to the aim of the agreement. It would be advisable for the employer to include in the contract reference to the objective of the surveillance. Thus if telephone calls may be intercepted, the contract should point this out and the objective for which this step may be taken. In the case of a public authority employer, the employer would have to be able to list one of the reasons in Article 8(2). Thus surveillance whilst a person is absent through sickness might be necessary to prevent fraud on the employer. A private employer might feel it necessary to include a reference to such justification. The court or tribunal would, however, need to be convinced that any infringement of privacy was necessary in a democratic society.

Similarly, there would have to be a very clear mandate for the employer to be able to search either the employee or his or her home before an infringement of Article 8 could be avoided. It may be that in highly sensitive industries, after an express agreement to the effect that searches may be carried out in specified situations, the infringement could be justified.

Of course, not all searches are carried out in those circumstances, and the need for a search will often arise in the case of an ex-employee who is suspected to be retaining company documents. The use of a search order under CPR 1998, r 25.1(h) may be necessary. These civil searches have been held to be justified in pursuit of protecting the rights of others and under the exception relating to the economic well being of the country.[251]

In *McLeod v UK*,[252] the police used common law and statutory powers to enter private premises to prevent a breach of the peace. This was held to be an adequate legal basis ('in accordance with the law') and conducted to prevent crime (a legitimate aim). The way in which the search was carried out had, however, been a disproportionate act. The police did not find out whether the subject was at home, nor whether their warrant to search allowed the ex-husband authority to enter. Although the aim was a legitimate one, the action was a breach of Article 8. Thus even if the public authority employer has a legal basis for a search, and good reason to conduct it in pursuit of a lawful aim, the manner in which it is performed may result in a breach.

The English common law provides no remedy against interception of communications, since it 'places no general constraints upon invasions of privacy as such'.[253] However, in *Halford v UK*,[254] the ECtHR held that Article 8 could apply to telephone calls made from business premises as well as from the home and Ms Halford would have a reasonable expectation of privacy in

251   *Chappel v UK* (1990) 12 EHRR 1.
252   (1998) 5 BHRC 364.
253   Mr Justice Sedley in *R v Broadcasting Complaints Commission, ex parte Barclay*, 4 October 1996 [1997] COD 57.
254   (1997) 24 EHRR 523.

relation to such calls, as she had not been warned that they might be intercepted.

Interception of communications

The Telecommunications (Lawful Business Practice) (Interception of Communications) Regulations 2000[255] came into force on 24 October 2000 (the 'Lawful Business Practice Regulations 2000'). They are made under the Regulation of Investigatory Powers Act 2000 (RIPA 2000), s 4. RIPA 2000 creates a civil liability by s 1(3). This provides that any interception of a communication which is carried out at any place in the UK by, or with the express or implied consent of, a person having the right to control the operation or the use of a private telecommunication system is actionable by the sender or recipient, or intended recipient, of the communication. On a private telecommunications network, the sender, recipient or intended recipient may bring an action under this subsection. So where an employee believes that his or her employer has unlawfully intercepted a telephone conversation with a third party, either the employee or the third party may sue the employer. The following conditions must be fulfilled. The interception must be without lawful authority and must be either:

(a) an interception of that communication in the course of its transmission by means of that private system; or

(b) an interception of that communication in the course of its transmission, by means of a public telecommunication system, to or from apparatus comprised in that private telecommunication system.

The creation of a civil liability means that the proper forum for actions is the court as a breach of statutory duty.

Section 1(5) of RIPA 2000 stipulates that conduct has lawful authority if, and only if:

(a) it is authorised by or under s 3 or s 4 of RIPA 2000;

(b) it takes place in accordance with an interception warrant; or

(c) it is in exercise, in relation to any stored communication, of any statutory power that is exercised (apart from s 1 of RIPA 2000) for the purpose of obtaining information or of taking possession of any document or other property,

and conduct (whether or not prohibited by s 1) which has lawful authority for the purposes of s 1 is also taken to be lawful for all other purposes.

The significance of this definition of lawful conduct is that it is supposed to provide a lawful basis for interference with the right to privacy. Thus a tribunal considering whether evidence has been lawfully gathered in this manner would have to conclude that it was so gathered. A detailed exposition of RIPA 2000 is outside the scope of this book. However, s 2 contains the definitions of 'postal service' and a number of other key concepts. Thus it defines a 'private telecommunication system' as any telecommunication system which, without

---

255   SI 2000/2699.

itself being a public telecommunication system, is a system in relation to which the following conditions are satisfied:

(a) it is attached, directly or indirectly and whether or not for the purposes of the communication in question, to a public telecommunication system; and

(b) there is apparatus comprised in the system which is both located in the UK and used (with or without other apparatus) for making the attachment to the public telecommunication system.

A 'telecommunications service' is any service that consists in the provision of access to, and of facilities for making use of, any telecommunication system (whether or not one provided by the person providing the service). Finally, a 'telecommunication system' is any system (including the apparatus comprised in it) which exists (whether wholly or partly in the UK or elsewhere) for the purpose of facilitating the transmission of communications by any means involving the use of electrical or electro-magnetic energy.

Section 2(2) provides that a person intercepts a communication in the course of its transmission by means of a telecommunication system if, and only if, he:

(a) so modifies or interferes with the system, or its operation;

(b) so monitors transmissions made by means of the system; or

(c) so monitors transmissions made by wireless telegraphy to or from apparatus comprised in the system,

as to make some or all of the contents of the communication available, while being transmitted, to a person other than the sender or intended recipient of the communication. Accessible storage is included in the concept of transmission. So while data is accessibly stored, it is treated as if it were in the course of transmission.

Certain conduct is authorised without an interception warrant. Section 3(1) of RIPA 2000 provides that conduct consisting in the interception of a communication is authorised if the communication is one which, or one which that person has reasonable grounds for believing, is a communication sent by a person who has consented to the interception and the intended recipient of which has also consented. The interception of a communciation is also authorised if the communication is one sent by, or intended for, a person who has consented to the interception or where surveillance by means of that interception has been authorised under Part II of RIPA 2000. Where all parties to the communication consent to the interception therefore, no question of unlawful interception arises under RIPA 2000. There will be a substantive question of whether a general consent would suffice. Must the consent be given to the interception of the particular communication or can a general consent, for example given in a contract, authorise the interception? The Lawful Business Practice Regulations 2000 give some guidance on these issues.

Clearly, where conduct falls under s 1(6) a person with the right to control a private network may intercept their own network without committing an offence under RIPA 2000. However, where the controller of a private network intercepts communications on the network he may still be exposed to civil liability if he has permitted private communications to be sent over that medium. Thus where a public authority employer has permitted private e-mails to be sent between members of staff on his network, he may be in breach of their right to privacy as a result of this practice regardless of a technical reservation of a right to monitor.

Section 4 provides that the interception of a communication in the course of its transmission by means of a telecommunication system is authorised if it falls within regulations. These are to detail the situations in relation to which further conditions are required to be satisfied before conduct may be treated as authorised by virtue of s 4 of RIPA 2000. The regulations may also authorise any conduct as appears to him to constitute a legitimate practice reasonably required for the purpose, in connection with the carrying on of business, of monitoring or keeping a record of:

(a) communications by means of which transactions are entered into in the course of that business; or
(b) other communications relating to that business or taking place in the course of its being carried on.

However, these regulatory powers do not authorise the interception of any communication except in the course of its transmission using apparatus or services provided by or to the person carrying on the business for use wholly or partly in connection with that business (s 4(3)).

References to a business include references to any activities of a government department, of any public authority or of any person or office holder on whom functions are conferred by or under any enactment (s 4(7)). There are a number of statutory exceptions created by the other subsections of s 4. The Lawful Business Practice Regulations 2000 echo that definition of 'business' as including the activities of a government department, of any public authority or of any person or office holder on whom functions are conferred by or under any enactment (reg 2).

The Regulations use the concept of a communication that is relevant to a business. This is a reference to one of the following:

(a) a communication:
    (i) by means of which a transaction is entered into in the course of that business; or
    (ii) which otherwise relates to that business; or
(b) a communication which otherwise takes place in the course of the carrying on of that business.

By reg 3 of the Lawful Business Practice Regulations 2000, conduct is authorised, if it consists of interception of a communication, in the course of its transmission by means of a telecommunications system, which is effected by or with the express or implied consent of the system controller for certain purposes. The 'system controller' means, in relation to a particular telecommunication system, a person with a right to control its operation or use. The employer will generally be such a person in relation to most telecommunication systems at work.

Under reg 3(1), the purposes that, with implied or express consent, authorise interception conduct are:

'(a)   monitoring or keeping a record of communications:
    (i)   in order to –
       (aa)   establish the existence of facts, or
       (bb)   ascertain compliance with regulatory or self-regulatory practices or procedures which are –
          applicable to the system controller in the carrying on of his business, or
          applicable to another person in the carrying on of his business where that person is supervised by the system controller in respect of those practices or procedures, or
       (cc)   ascertain or demonstrate the standards which are achieved or ought to be achieved by persons using the system in the course of their duties, or
    (ii)   in the interests of national security, or
    (iii)   for the purpose of preventing or detecting crime, or
    (iv)   for the purpose of investigating or detecting the unauthorised use of that or any other telecommunication system, or
    (v)   where that is undertaken –
       (aa)   in order to secure, or
       (bb)   as an inherent part of,
       the effective operation of the system (including any monitoring or keeping of a record which would be authorised by s 3(3) of the Act if the conditions in paras (a) and (b) thereof were satisfied); or
 (b)   monitoring communications for the purpose of determining whether they are communications relevant to the system controller's business which fall within reg 2(b)(i) above; or
 (c)   monitoring communications made to a confidential voice-telephony counselling or support service which is free of charge (other than the cost, if any, of making a telephone call) and operated in such a way that users may remain anonymous if they so choose.'

However, under reg 3(2), this conduct is authorised only if:

'(a)   the interception in question is effected solely for the purpose of monitoring or (where appropriate) keeping a record of communications relevant to the system controller's business;
 (b)   the telecommunication system in question is provided for use wholly or partly in connection with that business;
 (c)   the system controller has made all reasonable efforts to inform every person who may use the telecommunication system in question that communications transmitted by means thereof may be intercepted; and
 (d)   in a case –
    (i)   concerning national security, the person by or on whose behalf the interception is effected is a person specified in s 6(2)(a) to (i) of the Act;
    (ii)   concerned with monitoring communications for the purpose of determining whether they are relevant to the controller's business, the communication is one which is intended to be received (whether or not it has been actually received) by a person using the telecommunication system in question.'

Interceptions are authorised only if the controller of the telecommunciations system on which they are effected has made all reasonable efforts to inform potential users that interceptions may be made. The Regulations do not authorise interceptions to which the persons making and receiving the communications have consented as these are not prohibited by the Act.

By reg 2(c), the term 'regulatory or self-regulatory practices or procedures' means practices or procedures:

'(i) compliance with which is required or recommended by, under or by virtue of –
  (aa) any provision of the law of a Member State or other State within the European Economic Area; or
  (bb) any standard or code of practice published by or on behalf of a body established in a Member State or other State within the European Economic Area which includes amongst its objectives the publication of standards or codes of practice for the conduct of business; or
(ii) which are otherwise applied for the purpose of ensuring compliance with anything so required or recommended.'

Monitoring or recording communications is authorised only to the extent that Article 5 of Directive 97/66/EC of the European Parliament and of the Council of 15 December 1997 concerning the processing of personal data and the protection of privacy in the telecommunications sector so permits.

3.12.8 Data on the individual

Individual protection

Article 8 protects the individual from having private information disclosed to third parties. The ECtHR held that this includes the unnecessary disclosure of confidential medical information in legal proceedings in *Z v Finland*.[256] In disability cases, medical information concerning an applicant may therefore be restricted to that which is necessary for the determination of the questions in issue between the parties. Public authority employers face a dilemma in cases where the employee is seeking information about other employees. In *TV v Finland*,[257] the Commission held the disclosure of the fact that a prisoner was HIV positive to prison staff directly involved in his custody and who themselves were subject to obligations of confidentiality was justified as being necessary for the protection of rights of others.

Where information is passed on between authorities an infringement of the right to privacy may also take place unless it has been authorised by the subject. In *MS v Sweden*,[258] the applicant had sustained a back injury and objected to disclosure of medical records, which contained confidential information, to the Social Insurance Office for the purpose of assessing her compensation claim. The ECtHR recognised that the object of disclosure was a proper one: to enable the Office to determine whether the conditions for granting compen-

---

256 (1998) 25 EHRR 371.
257 Application No 21780/93, 76A DR 140.
258 (1997) 3 BHRC 248.

sation had been met. It also recognised the 'fundamental importance' of protecting personal data, guaranteed by Article 8 of the Convention. What it then did was to 'examine whether, in the light of the case as a whole, the reasons adduced to justify the interference were relevant and sufficient and whether the measure was proportionate to the legitimate aim pursued'. The ECtHR noted that the information was 'communicated by one public institution to another in the context of an assessment of whether she satisfied the legal conditions for obtaining a benefit which she herself had requested'. It was a condition of national law that the Social Security Office had requested the information. The Office was under a duty to treat it as confidential. Accordingly:

> 'the court considers that there were relevant and sufficient reasons for the communication of the applicant's medical records by the clinic to the office and that the measure was not disproportionate to the legitimate aim pursued. Accordingly, it concludes that there has been no violation of the applicant's right to respect for her private life, as guaranteed by Article 8 of the Convention.'[259]

In the UK the issue of access by the State to data about the individual was considered recently in *Woolgar v Chief Constable of Sussex Police.*[260] The claimant was a registered nurse and matron of a nursing home. She was arrested after a patient died in her care. She was interviewed by the police under caution. The police informed the claimant and the local health authority's registration and inspection unit (RIU) that there was insufficient evidence to charge her with any criminal offence. The RIU, which was concerned with other allegations against her, referred the matter to the United Kingdom Central Council, which contacted the police for relevant information. The police sought the plaintiff's authority to disclose a transcript of the interview to the regulatory body but she refused her consent. The Court of Appeal upheld the refusal of an injunction restraining disclosure. It stated that the public interest in securing the flow of information to the police for criminal proceedings required that information given in confidence would not be used for some collateral purpose. However, this interest had to be balanced against the countervailing public interest in protecting public health and safety. This permitted the police to disclose to a regulatory body operating in that field such confidential information as the police reasonably believed was relevant to an inquiry by that body. Such information could be disclosed only on the basis that in other respects confidentiality would be maintained. Where the police were minded to disclose such material, they should, unless it was impracticable or undesirable, inform the person affected in time for that person, if so advised, to seek the court's assistance. If the police refused disclosure, the regulatory body could make an application to the court.

Individual access
In *Gaskin v UK,*[261] the ECtHR ruled that the refusal to allow access to case records based solely on the refusal of the compiler of that record to consent to

---

259   (1997) 3 BHRC 248, p 257 at para 44.
260   [2000] 1 WLR 25.
261   [1990] 1 FLR 167.

the disclosure of the record requires a system whereby an independent authority can determine whether such a refusal is reasonably made. Otherwise such refusal constitutes a breach of the obligations imposed by Article 8 of the Convention. In *Gaskin*, the DHSS issued a circular setting out the principles governing disclosure of social service case records giving the policy that, subject to certain safeguards, they should be available to the subject of the records. One exception was that information derived from a third party in confidence could not be disclosed without the third party's consent. The refusal to disclose the case records constituted a breach of Article 8 of the Convention but not Article 10.

The ECtHR held that there was a positive obligation arising out of Article 8 to disclose the case notes which related to the individual's private or family life. The records were the only record of his formative years. However, the confidentiality of the file assisted the effective operation of the childcare system (a legitimate aim). The consent requirement was appropriate as a precondition of disclosure but some independent authority should decide whether access is to be granted where a contributor withholds consent.

The Data Protection Act 1998 provides in s 7 for the rights of the subject of data to have access to it on satisfaction of certain conditions. It also provides that an individual is entitled:

(a) to be informed by any data controller whether personal data of which that individual is the data subject are being processed by or on behalf of that data controller;
(b) if that is the case, to be given by the data controller a description of:
    (i) the personal data of which that individual is the data subject;
    (ii) the purposes for which they are being or are to be processed; and
    (iii) the recipients or classes of recipients to whom they are or may be disclosed;
(c) to have communicated to the individual in an intelligible form:
    (i) the information constituting any personal data of which that individual is the data subject; and
    (ii) any information available to the data controller as to the source of those data; and
(d) where the processing by automatic means of personal data of which that individual is the data subject for the purpose of evaluating matters relating to the individual such as, for example, performance at work, creditworthiness, reliability or conduct, has constituted or is likely to constitute the sole basis for any decision significantly affecting the individual, to be informed by the data controller of the logic involved in that decision-taking.

Section 7(2) of the Data Protection Act 1998 provides that a data controller is not obliged to supply any such information unless the data controller has received:

(a) a request in writing; and
(b) except in prescribed cases, such fee (not exceeding the prescribed maximum) as the data controller may require.

The data controller must also be supplied with such information as the data controller may reasonably require in order to satisfy himself or herself as to the identity of the person making the request and to locate the information which that person seeks. Where a data controller cannot comply with the request without disclosing information relating to another individual who can be identified from that information, the data controller is not obliged to comply with the request unless:

(a) the other individual has consented to the disclosure of the information to the person making the request; or

(b) it is reasonable in all the circumstances to comply with the request without the consent of the other individual.

The question of whether it is reasonable in all the circumstances will include consideration of the right to respect of the private life of the data subject. Information relating to another individual includes a reference to information identifying that individual as the source of the information sought by the request. The data controller is not excused from communicating so much of the information sought by the request as can be communicated without disclosing the identity of the other individual concerned, whether by the omission of names or other identifying particulars or otherwise. In deciding whether it is reasonable in all the circumstances to comply with the request without the consent of the other individual concerned, regard shall be had, in particular, to:

(a) any duty of confidentiality owed to the other individual;

(b) any steps taken by the data controller with a view to seeking the consent of the other individual;

(c) whether the other individual is capable of giving consent; and

(d) any express refusal of consent by the other individual.

The duty of confidentiality will, it is submitted, have to be construed so as to be compatible with the right to respect for the private life of the data subject under Article 8. The individual making the request, in prescribed cases, may specify that the request be limited to personal data of any prescribed description. If a court is satisfied on the application of any person who has made a request that the data controller has failed to comply with the request, the court may order the data controller to comply with the request. Broadly speaking, the data controller must observe certain principles. Personal data must be processed fairly and lawfully and, in particular, may not be processed unless:

(a) at least one of the conditions relating to all personal data processing is met; and

(b) in the case of sensitive personal data, at least one of the additional conditions is met.

The principles of data processing are as follows. [262]

---

262   Data Protection Act 1998, Sch 1.

(a) It can be obtained for only one or more specified and lawful purposes, and may not be further processed in any manner incompatible with that purpose.

(b) It must be adequate, relevant and not excessive in relation to the purpose for which it is processed.

(c) It must be accurate and, where necessary, kept up to date.

(d) Data processed for any purpose may not be kept for longer than is necessary for that purpose.

(e) It must be processed in accordance with the rights of data subjects under the Data Protection Act 1998 (DPA 1998).

(f) Technical and organisational measures must be taken against unauthorised or unlawful processing of personal data and against accidental loss or destruction of, or damage to, personal data.

(g) It must not be transferred to a country or territory outside the European Economic Area unless that country or territory ensures an adequate level of protection for the rights and freedoms of data subjects in relation to the processing of personal data.

The preconditions for data processing are as follows.

(1) The data subject has given consent to the processing. In the case of sensitive personal data the consent must be explicit.

(2) The processing is necessary:

    (a) for the performance of a contract to which the data subject is a party; or

    (b) for the taking of steps at the request of the data subject with a view to entering into a contract.

(3) The processing is necessary for compliance with any legal obligation to which the data controller is subject, other than an obligation imposed by contract.

(4) The processing is necessary in order to protect the vital interests of the data subject.

(5) The processing is necessary:

    (a) for the administration of justice;

    (b) for the exercise of any functions conferred on any person by or under any enactment;

    (c) for the exercise of any functions of the Crown, a Minister of the Crown or a government department; or

    (d) for the exercise of any other functions of a public nature exercised in the public interest by any person.

(6) The processing is necessary for the purposes of legitimate interests pursued by the data controller or by the third party or parties to whom the data are disclosed, except where the processing is unwarranted in any

particular case by reason of prejudice to the rights and freedoms or legitimate interests of the data subject.

Where the data is sensitive personal data, the processing must be necessary for the purposes of exercising or performing any right or obligation which is conferred or imposed by law on the data controller in connection with employment. Further, the processing must be necessary:

(1) in order to protect the vital interests of the data subject or another person, in a case where:

    (a) consent cannot be given by or on behalf of the data subject; or

    (b) the data controller cannot reasonably be expected to obtain the consent of the data subject; or

(2) in order to protect the vital interests of another person, in a case where consent by or on behalf of the data subject has been unreasonably withheld.

Processing of sensitive personal data is permitted in the following situations.

(1) It is carried out in the course of its legitimate activities by any body or association which:

    (a) is not established or conducted for profit; and

    (b) exists for political, philosophical, religious or trade-union purposes;

and is carried out with appropriate safeguards for the rights and freedoms of data subjects. It must relate only to individuals who either are members of the body or association or have regular contact with it in connection with its purposes, and must not involve disclosure of the personal data to a third party without the consent of the data subject. However, if the personal data has been made public as a result of steps deliberately taken by the data subject it may be processed. Processing of sensitive personal data may take place if:

    (a) it is necessary for the purpose of, or in connection with, any legal proceedings (including prospective legal proceedings);

    (b) it is necessary for the purpose of obtaining legal advice; or

    (c) it is otherwise necessary for the purposes of establishing, exercising or defending legal rights.

(2) It is carried out:

    (a) for the administration of justice;

    (b) for the exercise of any functions conferred on any person by or under an enactment; or

    (c) for the exercise of any functions of the Crown, a Minister of the Crown or a government department.

(3) For medical purposes. 'Medical purposes' means the purposes of preventative medicine, medical diagnosis, medical research, the provision of care and treatment and the management of healthcare services. The processing must be undertaken by:

    (a) a health professional; or

(b) a person who in the circumstances owes a duty of confidentiality which is equivalent to that which would arise if that person were a health professional.

(4) For the purposes of equal opportunities monitoring, if it is sensitive personal data consisting of information as to racial or ethnic origin and the processing is carried out with appropriate safeguards for the rights and freedoms of data subjects.

The details of the DPA 1998 are not within the scope of this work, but the scheme is designed to ensure that courts have regard to the purposes of retaining and disclosing personal data. The courts will therefore need to conduct the kind of balancing exercise that the Convention envisages when determining whether a disclosure or refusal to disclose was unlawful within the DPA 1998.

One area in which access to data may be relevant in an employment context is where the employee wishes to know what information is on his or her personnel file.

3.12.9 Unfair dismissal

How will Article 8 impact on unfair dismissal cases in general? The facts of an unfair dismissal may reveal an issue concerning the private life of the applicant or employer. The positive obligation on the State to create the conditions in which respect for private life is promoted requires the tribunal to look at the reason for dismissal put forward by the employer. Some conduct cases may relate to matters restricting the employee's right to a private or family life. The duty of the tribunal in applying s 98 of the ERA 1996 is to achieve a result which is compatible with the Convention right. That right is to respect for family and private life, and therefore there is a great deal of flexibility in relation to what constitutes respect for that right. If the reason given by the employer is inconsistent with respect for private or family life, the requirement to construe the ERA 1996 compatibly with Article 8 and the duty to give effect to Article 8 would, it is submitted, require the tribunal to conclude that the employer had failed to show a potentially fair reason relating to conduct in such a case.

Some dismissals are effected due to personality clashes. An example is *Stanbury v Overmass & Chapple*,[263] where a full-time working director stopped working for the respondent owing to a clash of personalities, which resulted in him not being re-elected to the board of directors. The reason for the dismissal was held not to be misconduct but 'some other substantial reason' justifying his dismissal. Where the personality clash involves elements of infringement of the private life of the employee (or employer), the tribunal will have to ensure that its consideration of equity and the substantial merits of the case gives effect to the need for respect for family life. An example of a case in which the effective duty of the employer to ensure respect for family life can be seen from the facts in *Treganowan v Robert Knee & Co Ltd.*[264] The personality clash, leading to a tense

---

263 [1976] ITR 7.
264 [1975] ICR 405.

atmosphere in the office, arose from a difference of opinion as to the merits of the permissive society. The other employees disapproved of the applicant's way of life and could not accept her as senior to them in the office. The prime cause of the trouble was not so much Miss Treganowan's way of life as the fact that she persisted in introducing it into the office by continually talking about her association. She was (it was said) insensitive to the atmosphere. She already had an illegitimate child and now she was boasting of her association with a boy almost half her age. The other young girls objected to this attitude and the National Industrial Relations Court held that the employer could not reasonably have dismissed them because of the atmosphere in the office.

The tribunal held that the dismissal was for 'some other substantial reason' and that the dismissal was fair. The National Industrial Relations Court upheld the tribunal's decision. However, if considering the same facts following the HRA 1998 the tribunal would have to consider whether the employer's behaviour in dismissing was reasonable having regard to equity and the substantial merits (and whilst respecting the private life of the applicant). It may be that an employer which does not encourage its employees to be tolerant of each other's private lives could not be said to have been acting reasonably in dismissing as it had failed to take reasonable steps to ensure respect for the private life of the employee.[265]

The tribunals are likely to see the balancing process as an aspect of considering whether the employer has shown that the working relationship is irremediable as a result of the clash.[266] An employer will not generally be held to have acted reasonably in this sort of situation if all steps short of dismissal have not been investigated in order to seek to effect an improvement in the relationship between the members of staff.

In any event, the tribunal will have to consider whether, having regard to the requirement to ensure respect for private life on the facts of the case, the employer's action can be justified in terms of having a basis in the contract or other legal basis, meeting a legitimate objective, and was necessary and proportionate. Given that tolerance is one of the fundamental values of a democratic society, the employer would probably have to show that, although attempts had been made to ensure respect for the applicant's family life, the applicant's behaviour was such as to overstep the proper bounds for tolerance, so that dismissal was the only option.

Another area in which Article 8 may have some impact is constructive dismissal situations in which the reason for resignation is a personality clash. If the employer has taken no reasonable steps to prevent one employee from bullying another in such a way as infringes the other's right to form relationships and express his or her personality, tribunals may be obliged to construe the HRA 1998 as giving effect to Article 8 by finding the resignation was in response to the employer's failure to prevent that personality clash. The contract of

---

265   See also *Gorfin v Distressed Gentlefolk's Aid Association* [1973] IRLR 290.
266   *Turner v Vestric Ltd* [1981] IRLR 23, [1980] ICR 528, EAT.

employment has an implied term that the employer shall not act in such a way as is likely to undermine the relationship of mutual trust and confidence. In the context of the the ERA 1996, the concept of a breach of contract entitling the employee to terminate the contract must be interpreted so as to give effect to the Convention right to respect for private or family life.

The requirement on tribunals to consider equity and the substantial merits of the case in determining whether the employer acted reasonably in dismissing will require them to give effect to those concepts, so far as it is possible to do so, so as to render them compatible with Article 8. Thus in considering a case where the right to respect for private or family life is in issue, the tribunal will have to look at whether the dismissal was meeting a legitimate objective and was necessary and proportionate. In the light of this effect, cases such as *Boychuk*[267] and *Saunders*[268] may need to be reconsidered.

3.12.10   Justification

Justification of an interference with private or family life requires there to be a basis in law. This means:

(1)   a specific legal rule authorising the interference;

(2)   adequate access to that law;[269]

(3)   such precision and clarity in the formulation of the law that the individual can foresee when the law might be applied;[270]

(4)   the restriction on respect for private and family life or phone or correspondence can only be justified if it is aimed at protecting one of the interests listed in Article 8(2). These are:

    (a)   national security;
    (b)   public safety;
    (c)   the economic well-being of the country;
    (d)   the prevention of disorder or crime;
    (e)   the protection of health or morals; and
    (f)   the protection of the rights and freedoms of others.

This list is exhaustive and the interest listed in each case is to be narrowly construed;

(5)   finally, justification can succeed only if the restriction is necessary in a democratic society. This means that there must be a pressing social need for the restriction and the restriction must be proportional to the gain or responding to the pressing social need. It must not go further than is necessary bearing in mind that objective.

For example, Swiss law gives legal professional privilege to information which comes directly from a relationship characterised as lawyer–client. This does not

---

267   *Boychuk v HJ Symons Holdings Ltd* [1977] IRLR 395. See **3.4.5**.
268   *Saunders v Scottish National Camps Association Ltd* [1980] IRLR 174. See **3.4.5**.
269   *Sunday Times v UK* (1979–80) 2 EHRR 245.
270   *Malone v UK* (1985) 7 EHRR 14.

include information not specifically connected with the lawyer's work on instructions from a party to proceedings. The ECtHR rejected the State's argument for justification of an infringement of Article 8, taking the view that the distinction was insufficiently clear. It did not have the precision required so that individuals could predict their liability. Thus it was not 'in accordance with the law'.[271] In *Petra*,[272] the ECtHR held that the State could not rely on the exceptions to the right to private life contained in Article 8(2). The prison governor's power did not satisfy the requirement of accessibility and the law did not indicate with reasonable clarity the scope and manner of exercise of the discretion conferred on the governor.

For an effected item to be 'necessary in a democratic society', it must respond to a 'pressing social need'.[273] An example of a measure being found not to be necessary in a democratic society is *Lambert v France*.[274] There the interception of telephone calls which led to applicant's arrest for drug dealing infringed the right to respect for private life. The calls did not involve the applicant as a participant. They were between other people. The ECtHR considered if the measure was justified by the aim of prevention of crime (see above) and whether it was 'necessary in a democratic society'. The French courts had rejected the applicant's action concerning the interception stating that as he was not a party to the calls he had no standing in the case. However, the ECtHR stated that this could lead to a situation in which anyone who had a conversation on someone else's telephone would lose legal protection and therefore rejected the alleged justification.

An interesting question is whether a complete ban on the use of communications systems at work for personal information would be itself an infringement of the right to privacy, or whether it could justify the use of monitoring of employees' communications. It is unlikely that an employer would be able successfully to enforce such a ban. Such a ban might constitute a restriction on the right of individuals to develop and maintain relationships at work. Many employers make it a matter of misconduct for employees to use the telephone for personal calls. Such a rule could be justified as proportionate to the legitimate aim of protecting the employer's possessions, namely the value of the business's assets or for the prevention of crime. Such rules are usually introduced following misuse of the business telephone for personal calls.

3.13   ARTICLE 9

3.13.1   The scope of Article 9

If the effected item affects the right of a religious organisation to freedom of thought, conscience or religion, Article 9 may need to be considered. It provides that everyone has the right to freedom of thought, conscience and

271   *Kopp v Switzerland* (1999) 27 EHRR 91.
272   *Petra v Romania* (1998) 5 BHRC 497. See **3.12.6**.
273   *Sunday Times v UK* (1979–80) 2 EHRR 245. See **3.5.2**.
274   (2000) 30 EHRR 346.

religion. This includes the freedom to change one's religion or belief, and the freedom either alone or with others to manifest that religion or belief in worship, teaching, practice and observance. There are restrictions on the right to manifest religion or belief (see **1.3.8**).

It is only the freedom to manifest one's religion or belief that is subject to the limitations in Article 9(2). This provides that freedom to manifest one's religion or belief shall be subject only to such limitations as are prescribed by law and are necessary in a democratic society in the interests of public safety, for the protection of public order, health or morals, or for the protection of the rights and freedoms of others.

Against a public authority, a person who suffers a detriment or is dismissed as a result of his or her religious beliefs can claim, under s 7 of the HRA 1998, a remedy for the unlawful action of the public authority. This claim will be brought in the county court (see **6.2**). In all contexts, if the public authority can be shown to have acted in breach of Article 9, it will have acted unlawfully. The unlawful nature of that act can be relied upon by the applicant.

The concepts of the freedom of thought, conscience and religion are very broad indeed, but do not extend beyond the sphere of private, personal beliefs. In *Vereniging Rechtswinkels Utrecht v The Netherlands*,[275] it was held that it did not cover purely idealistic or political goals such as those held by the prisoners' support group. The ECtHR distinguishes between conduct that directly expresses religion or belief and conduct that is simply motivated by it. Only the former is protected and includes trying to convert a neighbour[276] or eating kosher food.[277] Atheists and agnostics may also claim the protection of this right.[278]

However, practices such as distributing leaflets or advertising a religious artefact will not be considered manifestations of religion or belief. Thus, in *C v UK*,[279] non-payment by Quakers of taxes used for defence purposes was found not to be a manifestation of religion or belief.[280]

In the case of *Chapell v UK*,[281] it was considered that individuals or the church body or an association with religious or philosophical objectives could exercise the right of freedom of religion or thought. In the case of non-individuals, establishing that activities amount to a manifestation may be more difficult.

Section 13 of the HRA 1998 requires a court to have particular regard to the importance of the Article 9 right, if its determination of any question arising under the Act might affect the exercise of that right by a religious organisation (either itself or its members collectively). The ECtHR has recognised the need for religious beliefs to be given special regard in determining a case involving competing Convention rights, but has not accorded an automatic precedence

---

275   (1986) 46 DR 200.
276   *Kokkinakis v Greece* (1994) 17 EHRR 397.
277   *DS & ES v UK* (1990) 65 DR 245.
278   *Kokkinakis v Greece* (1994) 17 EHRR 397.
279   (1983) 37 DR 142.
280   See also *Arrowsmith v UK* (1978) 19 DR 5.
281   (1987) 53 DR 241.

to it. Note that for the purposes of religious freedoms an unincorporated association can be a 'victim'.[282]

If a court's (or tribunal's) determination of any question arising under the HRA 1998 might affect the exercise by a religious organisation (itself or its members collectively) of the Convention right to freedom of thought, conscience and religion, it must have particular regard to the importance of that right (s 13(1) and (2)). This section was inserted to meet concerns of certain religious groups that the Act might lead to interference with matters of doctrine, for example by requiring churches to marry homosexual couples.

The concept of 'any question arising under this Act' includes the interpretation of existing legislation in the light of the HRA 1998. One interesting question in the area of unfair dismissal cases is the extent to which the employer which is a religious organisation or member of a religious organisation may pray in aid the moral code of that religion or organisation to suggest that a decision which would otherwise be considered unreasonable is, in fact, reasonable. Tribunals may be required to apply a test of reasonableness, which is not simply a consideration of what the reasonable employer would do, but of what the reasonable employer, who holds the beliefs of the party claiming the right to freedom of religion or that party's conscience, would do.

The section requires tribunals to have particular regard to the freedom of thought. In *Wingrove v UK*,[283] it was suggested that Article 9 should be taken into account but does not supersede other rights under the Convention. It is open to the tribunal to conclude its balancing of competing rights such as the right to free expression in favour of that other right. However, Strasbourg authorities emphasise the democratic importance of an open forum of beliefs and opinions.[284] The right does not oblige a State to provide protection to demonstrators. Thus in *Plattform 'Ärzte für das Leben'*,[285] Article 9 was held not to require the State to protect demonstrations by doctors to manifest their opposition to legalised abortion. Prison authorities were not obliged to provide special literature for a practitioner of a religion usually not practised in the State.[286] Churches may be prevented from advertising their products. Such adverts are a manifestation of a desire to market goods for profit and do not bear the hallmark of being the manifestation of a belief in practice.[287]

Article 9 does not impose a positive obligation on the State to make blasphemy a criminal offence. If there are blasphemy laws there is no duty on public authorities to bring proceedings against publishers of works which offend the sensitivities of any individual or group.[288] However, in *Otto-Preminger-Institut v Austria*[289] the ECtHR held that there is a positive obligation to ensure peaceful

---

282   See **6.2.6** and *Christians Against Racism and Fascism v UK* (1980) 21 DR 138 and *Hautanemi v Sweden* (1996) 22 EHRR CD 155.
283   (1997) 24 EHRR 1.
284   *Kokkinakis v Greece* (1994) 17 EHRR 397.
285   (1991) 13 EHRR 204.
286   *X v Austria* (1965) 8 YB 174, 184.
287   *Pastor X and the Church of Scientology v Sweden* (1979) 22 YB 244.
288   *Choudhury v UK* Application No 17439/90 (Dec) 5 March 1991.
289   (1995) 19 EHRR 34.

enjoyment of the rights under Article 9 for those holding the belief, so the State may be obliged to control the activities of those who seek to prevent those who practise a religion from being able to do so.

Where a contract restricts freedom of religious expression or thought etc, the ECtHR would only be likely to find that there had been a breach where such freedom was wholly excluded by the contract or severely restricted.

3.13.2   Working on a religious day

The dismissal of a shop worker is automatically unfair if the reason (or, if there is more than one reason, the principal reason) for the dismissal was:[290]

(1) that the shop worker refused, or proposed to refuse, to do shop work on Sunday or on a particular Sunday (protected shop worker or betting worker); or
(2) that the shop worker gave, or proposed to give, an opting-out notice to the employer (any shop worker or betting worker).

Section 105(4) of the ERA 1996 provides similar protection in redundancy situations. In *Williams v ASDA Stores Ltd,*[291] the EAT held that an employee had failed to show that he had been dismissed for asserting his statutory right under these provisions. It was held that the actual reason for dismissal was the breach of contract in refusing to work on Sunday when the contract required him to do so. A contractual agreement may provide a lawful basis for the dismissal of such a person.

A worker who claims to have suffered a detriment, in these circumstances, has the right to complain to an employment tribunal.[292]

It will be noted that there are no provisions in the the ERA 1996 to protect applicants for employment (as against existing employees) who object to Sunday working against discrimination at the recruitment stage. An attempt to introduce such provisions into the Sunday Trading Bill was defeated at Committee stage in the House of Commons.[293] The provisions of the the ERA 1996 dealing with Sunday trading will be regarded as adequate protection for those who object to working on a Sunday.

3.13.3   Unfair dismissal

An employer who dismisses an employee for manifesting his or her religious belief will probably be held to be acting unreasonably. Alternatively, in considering whether the action of the employer was reasonable in relation to conduct which is a manifestation of religious belief, the tribunal will have to apply the test of equity and the substantial merits of the case by taking into account the right to freedom of religious expression represented by Article 9.

---

290   ERA 1996, s 101.
291   EAT/306/96.
292   See ss 45 and 48 of the ERA 1996.
293   See HC Debs vol 237, cols 304–321, 9 February 1994. Such provisions may also fall foul of Article 14 taken with Article 9.

By the same token, an employer who dismisses an employee because of the employee's infringement of the employer's right to freedom of religion could pray in aid Article 9 and require it to be taken into account in determining equity and the substantial merits of the case. Certain Commission cases suggest that unless the applicant can show that he or she was pressured to change his or her religious views or prevented from manifesting his or her religion or belief a breach will have occurred.

The effect of the contract on religious freedom

In *Ahmad v UK*,[294] the applicant was a Muslim who complained that he had to leave his job because his contract of employment did not permit time off on Friday for religious observance, and his employer would not permit him the time off. There was no interference with his Article 9 right. The Commission decided that when exercising this right, an individual may need to take account of his professional position and/or his contractual position. The obligations of his contract were accepted 'of his own free will'. When applying for the post, and for six years after taking it up, he had not stated that he might need this time for prayers at the mosque. The Commission regarded it as significant, in this context, that he could have resigned on discovering the conflict between his religion and his work. The Commission decision appears to suggest that it is only arbitrary interference with the right that will be considered as an interference with the right. There was evidence from the State of the needs of its education system on which the interference could be shown not to be arbitrary. The significance of the ability of the individual to preserve his religious freedom by resignation was also stressed in *Konttinen v Finland.*[295] In that case, the Commission drew the distinction between the applicant being dismissed because of religious convictions and being dismissed for failing to observe his contractual duties (hours of work). His refusal to work the contractual hours was not protected by the Convention right, despite being a product of his religious persuasion. The employee was employed by Finnish State Railways. He was dismissed for failing to respect his working hours on the basis that to work after sunset on a Friday was forbidden by the Seventh-Day Adventist Church, of which he was a member. The Commission held that the applicant had failed to show that he was pressured to change his religious views or prevented from manifesting his religion or belief.

In *Stedman v UK*,[296] the applicant was held to have been dismissed for failing to agree to work certain hours rather than for her religious belief as such and was free to resign and did resign from her employment. The Commission considered that, had the applicant been employed by the State and been dismissed in similar circumstances, such dismissal would not have amounted to an interference with her rights under Article 9(1). *A fortiori*, the UK could not be expected to have legislation that would protect employees against such dismissals by private employers. In the absence of the dismissal itself constituting an interference with the applicant's rights under Article 9, the fact that the

---

294   (1982) 4 EHRR 126.
295   (1996) 87 DR 68.
296   (1997) 23 EHRR CD 168.

applicant was not able to claim unfair dismissal before an industrial tribunal (as she lacked the relevant period of continuous employment), could not, of itself, constitute a breach of Article 9 of the Convention.

Where the tribunal has jurisdiction and is considering the factual merits of the claim, however, the actions of the employer may be inspected to see whether they constitute pressure to change religious views or another infringement of the right to religion. Thus actions leading up to dismissal or resignation may constitute an infringement of the Article, even if there is no threat of dismissal supporting the act. The employee of the public authority could then bring a county court action based on that finding.

In the *Church of X v UK,* [297] members of the Church of Scientology were refused extensions of work permits and leave to remain as students. The Commission decided this did not amount to an interference with Article 9. Article 9 did not arise because these refusals did not directly prevent the members of the church from attending the college of the church in the UK.

The fact that the Convention is a living instrument permits the ECtHR to look at the practical realities of the labour market in determining whether (as in the above series of cases) a person's ostensible consent can be regarded as the exercise of a free choice, or whether (as in *Van der Musselle*[298]) that choice is conditioned by the requirements of a profession or trade. In order to recognise the purpose of the Convention in giving effect to the rights, it is suggested that the courts should consider whether the fact that the applicant or incumbent of a position is required by his or her religion to observe certain practices means that the applicant's position in the labour market in relation to a whole sector of employment is disadvantaged. Where a practice such as Sunday working becomes prevalent in the retail sector, for example, the court should consider whether the applicant (with his or her skills and qualifications) is substantially disadvantaged in relation to his or her ability to earn a living. If the skills of the individual suit him or her primarily to working in that sector, so that it would be difficult for that individual to obtain employment in a situation which did not require Sunday working, there appears to be no reason why the reasoning adopted in *Van der Musselle* should not be adopted in relation to the right to exercise freedom of religion in the employment context.

3.13.4 Justification

The provisions of Article 9(2) provide an exhaustive list of restrictions. These are:

(1) public safety;
(2) public order;
(3) health or morals; or
(4) the rights and freedoms of others.

---

297 (1969) 12 YB 306.
298 *Van der Musselle v Belgium* (1984) 6 EHRR 163: see **3.7**.

There can be no justification by reference to interests of national security.

Examples of justification

An orthodox Sikh applied for a job in a chocolate factory, but refused to shave his beard off. A tribunal held that the requirement of no beards was justifiable, even though moustaches and sideburns were allowed. There was no viable alternative and the justification was based on expert evidence about hygiene. The EAT and the Court of Appeal saw no point of law on which an appeal could succeed. The Court of Appeal considered his complaint that the rule infringed his right to freedom or religion under Article 9. Lord Denning MR remarked that Article 9 was not law in this country. He held that the courts should nevertheless pay regard to it. He did note that there were exceptions on grounds of, inter alia, public health. [299]

In *Iskcon v UK*, [300] the Commission held that planning restrictions imposed in respect of the use of a manor as a religious centre by a Krishna society were justified. The Commission considered the weight to be given in planning enforcement proceedings to the applicant's right to freedom of religion. The Commission noted that the planning inquiry gave detailed consideration to the special circumstances of the case. The Commission did not consider that Article 9 of the Convention can be used to circumvent existing planning legislation, provided that in the proceedings under that legislation, adequate weight is given to freedom of religion. In contending that inadequate weight was given to freedom of religion, the applicants argued that this was demonstrated by statements in letters sent by Ministers and an official of the Department of the Environment to the effect that in the decision on the applicant's appeal 'the religious aspects of the Society's activities at Bhak-tivedanta Manor were not relevant'. This statement was interpreted by the Commission, not as suggesting that the religious importance of the Manor to the applicants was not fully taken into account and weighed against the general planning considerations, but rather as making clear that the refusal of planning permission was based on proper planning grounds and not on any objections to the religious aspects of the activities of the applicants.

3.13.5   Article 9 and Article 14

An applicant who is claiming infringement of his right to religion may also be the subject of discrimination in relation to his other Convention rights under Article 14 (see **3.15**). The case of *Ahmad*[301] was taken to the Commission in *X v UK*,[302] where it was found that there was no infringement of the right to religion. However, this was before the advent of the Sunday trading legislation, which clearly places Christian employees in a better position with regard to access to the courts for breaches of their right to religion than other faiths. Given the fact that the right to religious objections to working on particular days of the week have been given recognition in relation (in effect) to one

---

299   *Panesar v Nestle Co Ltd* [1980] IRLR 60; on appeal [1980] IRLR 64, CA.
300   (1994) 76A DR 90.
301   *Ahmad v UK* (1982) 4 EHRR 126. See **3.13.3**.
302   (1981) 22 DR 27.

religion, the other religions whose observance may require worship on a particular day of the week may be able to argue for parity in respect of those days. Alternatively, the Sunday trading provisions may have to be declared incompatible because of their Christian bias.

3.14 ARTICLE 10

3.14.1 The scope of Article 10

Article 10 of the Convention provides for the following rights.

(1) Everyone has the right to freedom of expression, including:

    (a) freedom to hold opinions without interference by public authority and regardless of frontiers; and

    (b) to receive information without interference by public authority and regardless of frontiers; and

    (c) to impart information without interference by public authority and regardless of frontiers; and

    (d) to receive ideas without interference by public authority and regardless of frontiers; and

    (e) to impart ideas without interference by public authority and regardless of frontiers.

(2) States may require the licensing of broadcasting, television or cinema enterprises.

Article 10(2) provides that, because these freedoms carry with them duties and responsibilities, the exercise of these freedoms may be subject to such:

(1) formalities;

(2) conditions;

(3) restrictions; or

(4) penalties

    as are:

    (a) prescribed by law; and

    (b) are necessary in a democratic society;

        (i)   in the interests of national security;

        (ii)   in the interests of territorial integrity;

        (iii) in the interests of public safety;

        (iv)   for the prevention of disorder or crime;

        (v)   for the protection of health or morals;

        (vi)   for the protection of the reputation of others;

        (vii) for the protection of the rights of others;

        (viii) for preventing the disclosure of information received in confidence; or

        (ix)   for maintaining the authority and impartiality of the judiciary.

The right includes the right to hold opinions. This will not assist persons found to have made racist or other discriminatory statements (see below). The term 'expression' covers all types of action intended to express an idea or to convey information.[303] Thus it includes pictures, images or words with that intention.

In the context of Article 10, which makes reference to the responsibilities attaching to the right of freedom of expression, it is possible for a person to contract to limit the right to freedom of expression.[304] However, the State may, even in such circumstances, retain responsibility for protecting the right to freedom of expression, and cannot rely on the 'contracting out' as between two private parties. Thus if it does not provide a remedy for a dismissal based on the exercise of free expression it may be liable unless it can justify the absence of protection in the particular case.[305] The State may have to protect the individual from being compelled to restrict that right if the restriction strikes at the very heart of free expression.

If an act of a public authority has one of these legitimate aims, the interference with the individual's freedom of expression must be 'prescribed by law'. The measure constituting the law must be sufficiently precise to enable the citizen to regulate his or her conduct. The practice of issuing orders binding over people for behaviour which does not amount to a criminal offence, but is considered unacceptable, is not sufficiently precise to provide the basis for justification. Thus where such orders acted as a limitation on the applicants' right to protest against hunting with hounds the orders could not be justified as an infringement of that right of expression.[306]

Article 10 guarantees the right to 'receive information', but not to create access to it if it is not already available.[307]

By s 12 of the HRA 1998, in cases involving public interest disclosure, the right of freedom of expression by the applicant will have to be taken into account, as the matters in issue will relate to that freedom, and the grant or refusal of relief will affect free expression. Thus the provisions of the ERA 1996 dealing with the preconditions under which disclosure can be made to bodies other than the employer will have to be construed so as to give effect to the right of the applicant to impart information.[308] If there is a confidentiality clause in the contract of employment, its significance will have to be weighed against the right of free expression. The tribunal will have to look at the aim of the confidentiality clause, and whether the confidentiality required is necessary in a democratic society. The tribunal will need to look at whether the confidentiality clause was proportionate (at the time it was entered into by the parties) to the infringement of the applicant's right of free expression. In the case of a private employer, when attempting to give effect to the Convention rights of the parties, the tribunal will have to consider also the right of the employer to confidentiality. However, s 12 requires the tribunal to have particular regard to

303   *Stevens v UK* (1986) 46 DR 245.
304   *Vereniging Rechtswinkels Utrecht v The Netherlands* (1986) 46 DR 200.
305   *Rommelfanger v FRG* (1989) 62 DR 151.
306   *Hashman and Harrup v UK* (2000) 30 EHRR 241.
307   *Leander v Sweden* (1987) 9 EHRR 433.
308   ERA 1996, Part IVA.

the right of free expression, and therefore the weight to be attached to such confidentiality clauses in determining whether it was reasonable to make the disclosure the applicant made must be slight.

Public authorities in the full-blooded sense will not be able to enter into valid confidentiality clauses which unnecessarily infringe the right of freedom of expression. Such clauses would be void, unless they had a basis in law and a legitimate aim which was proportionate to the interference with freedom of expression represented by the clause.

Note that Article 10 creates a positive obligation on the State to take steps to protect the individual. The High Court has an obligation to exercise its powers, so far as it is possible to do so, so as to give effect to the Convention rights. There is as yet no right of action in the employment tribunals for persons who suffer a detriment as a result of their right to freedom of expression being infringed. However, the following implications of Article 10 can be identified.

(a) A right not to be unfairly dismissed for the expression of opinion (or other exercise of the rights under Article 10) unless that dismissal can be justified as necessary in a democratic society.

(b) A right not to suffer a detriment where the detriment is suffered as a result of freedom of expression. In those cases the employer would have to be able to show that the detriment was justified under Article 10(2).

(c) Where the employer is a public authority, the right to require the tribunal to declare an act by the employer unlawful by reference to Article 10, and to rely on the implications for the employee's domestic right of that illegality.

(d) Where the case concerns discrimination, the tribunal would have to interpret the HRA 1998 and give it effect in so far as it is possible to do so in a way which is compatible with the right of free expression.

3.14.2   Section 12 of the Human Rights Act 1998

Section 12 of the HRA 1998 requires a court or tribunal to give special consideration to freedom of expression. Freedom of expression includes the right to 'impart information and ideas without interference by public authority', subject to limitations 'prescribed by law' and 'necessary in a democratic society'. Whenever freedom of expression is in issue, regardless of the formal description of the issue, s 12 must be considered.

Note that the expression 'the respondent' is defined in this section. It means the person against whom the application for relief is made. This expression in turn means any relief which, if granted, might affect the exercise of the Convention right to freedom of expression. Therefore, where a party to tribunal proceedings asks the tribunal to impose a restricted reporting order, those persons whose freedom of expression will be restricted by the order will constitute the respondents.

3.14.3   Restricted reporting orders

The effect of a restricted reporting order under the Employment Tribunals Act 1996 (ETA 1996), s 11(2) is that if any identifying matter is published or included in a relevant programme in contravention of a restricted reporting order:

(a) in the case of publication in a newspaper or periodical, any proprietor, any editor and any publisher of the newspaper or periodical;

(b) in the case of publication in any other form, the person publishing the matter; and

(c) in the case of matter included in a relevant programme:

   (i)   any body corporate engaged in providing the service in which the programme is included; and

   (ii) any person having functions in relation to the programme corresponding to those of an editor of a newspaper;

is guilty of an offence and liable on summary conviction to a fine not exceeding level 5 on the standard scale. A 'restricted reporting order' means an order:

(a) made in exercise of a power conferred by regulations made by virtue of s 11; and

(b) prohibiting the publication in Great Britain of identifying matter in a written publication available to the public or its inclusion in a relevant programme for reception in Great Britain.

The restricted reporting order is not made against any individual, but clearly affects all newspapers and journalists. If the expression 'against whom the application for relief is made' is construed so as to give effect to rights under Article 10, it may be possible to argue that *prima facie* the news agencies should be notified of the intention to make the application. Any journalist present in the tribunal would have *locus standi* to make representations based on Article 10 to the effect that the restriction order restricts the journalist's right of free expression.

Thus tribunals when deciding whether to make a restricted reporting order may have to consider this section. Article 10 has been considered in relation to restricted reporting orders. In *R v London (North) Industrial Tribunal, ex parte Associated Newspapers Ltd*,[309] it was argued that the law does not permit a tribunal to make a blanket ban prohibiting the identification of all parties to, or witnesses in, a case in which allegations of sexual misconduct are made when some of the parties or witnesses are not affected by, or making an allegation of, sexual misconduct. It was argued that although the words 'affected by' are not defined in the ETA 1996 or the Employment Tribunals (Constitution and Rules of Procedure) Regulations 1993, SI 1993/2687, they must, in accordance with general principles of construction and the overriding need to safeguard freedom of expression, be construed narrowly for three reasons:

---

309   [1998] ICR 1212.

(i)   because of the fundamental constitutional principle that there should be
      public reporting of judicial proceedings;[310]
(ii) because Article 10 of the Convention should be taken into account in
      statutory interpretation whenever there is an ambiguity;[311].
(iii) because the mischief at which these provisions were aimed shows that a
      narrow construction is appropriate.

The court accepted the applicant's submission that any interpretation should
pay regard to the principle of the importance of the public and contempor-
aneous reporting of court and tribunal hearings. That is part of the normal
principle of the construction of statutes that a provision which enables
interference to take place with basic constitutional rights should be narrowly
construed. The court stated that freedom of the press to report fully and
contemporaneously should be constrained only where and to the extent clearly
necessary. This supports a narrow interpretation of the words in s 11 of the ETA
1996, rather than a wide one. The court stated that it is difficult to see that
Article 10 of the Convention adds significantly to this, given that the principle is
so firmly embedded in the English common law. Under the HRA 1998, it would
appear that there is somewhat greater scope for arguing that a restricted
reporting order should not be made at all. However, this will never be a
knock-down argument, as the right to respect for private life would probably
prevail in most situations in which a restricted reporting order could currently
be made. The tribunal rules relating to restricted reporting orders would have
to be interpreted in a way rendering them compatible with this right.

Where the tribunal is minded to make a restricted reporting order of its own
motion, its obligation to construe its power to do so compatibly with the
Convention rights will require it to take account of the interests of freedom of
expression. Although there is no application in such cases, it is submitted that
the principles in s 12 of the HRA 1998 will apply.

The provisions were introduced during the passage of the HRA 1998 through
Parliament. Concern was expressed as to the possibility of a right to privacy
arising out of Article 8 of the Convention. The HRA 1998 seeks to balance these
competing factors. 'Gagging' orders in defamation cases, sought and without
notice shortly before publication, are covered by s 12(2) and constitute what
the HRA 1998 is aiming at. The tribunal may have to notify the press agency or
those reporters present at the tribunal that an application is being made or an
order is being considered. As the requirement under s 12(2) goes to the
jurisdiction of the tribunal to apply s 11 of the ETA 1996, failure to comply with
this is not a mere procedural irregularity.

Section 12(3) of the HRA 1998 concerns interlocutory injunctions in defamation cases. The courts will require an applicant to show not only a serious
question to be tried but that on balance his claim is likely to succeed. Without
proof that the applicant is 'likely' to succeed at trial, no injunction can be
granted as a result of s 12(3). The further implications of the relationship

---

310   See *Attorney-General v Leveller Magazine Limited* [1979] AC 440, [1979] 1 All ER 745 and *R v
      Felixstowe Justices, ex parte Leigh* [1987] 1 All ER 551, [1987] 2 WLR 380.
311   See *Derbyshire County Council v Times Newspapers* [1992] 1 QB 770.

between justification of defamatory statements, interlocutory injunctions and the common law are outside the scope of this book.

By s 12(4) of the HRA 1998, the court must have particular regard to the importance of the Convention right to freedom of expression. The tribunal must first establish whether any remedy it might grant might affect the exercise of the right to freedom of expression. Section 12(4) provides in particular that if the proceedings relate to material which appears to the court, to be journalistic, literary or artistic material (or to conduct connected with such material), the court or tribunal must have particular regard to:

(a) the extent to which:
    (i) the material has, or is about to, become available to the public; or
    (ii) it is, or would be, in the public interest for the material to be published; and
(b) any relevant privacy code.

Section 12(4) applies only to cases relating to 'journalistic, literary or artistic material'. It is not clear when a case would relate to material of this nature. One issue which the tribunal will have to consider is the extent to which the substance of the claim must relate to such material or whether it is sufficient for the contents of an important part of the evidence to be of that nature. For example, if a person had been dismissed for distributing literature, of which the employer did not approve, at the workplace and he or she claimed that this literature was of a journalistic nature, it is arguable that a claim for unfair dismissal would relate to conduct connected with that material. A tribunal would be obliged to consider the extent to which its decision affects Article 10 rights of its own motion. The mere assertion that the material is of this nature is sufficient to bring the section into consideration. There may be a difficult issue in the case of a person claiming under the public interest disclosure provisions of Part IVA of the ERA 1996 that he or she has been dismissed by reason of making a qualifying disclosure. The material disclosed could be of journalistic merit, and the conduct in disclosing will clearly relate to that material. Section 12 therefore permits a tribunal to apply a restricted reporting order even where the order would limit a party's freedom of expression if that free expression would infringe, for example, the right of an individual to respect for his or her private life. Section 12 does not elevate Article 10 in the hierarchy of Convention rights. It is suggested that it simply reflects the Convention approach to the importance of free expression.

In general terms, all that the tribunal is required to do is to have particular regard to the importance of the right of freedom of expression, so it may take a view as to the content of the material itself. The register of applications before the employment tribunals must contain a summary of each ground of the claim so that a party inspecting it can identify the basis of the grounds. Regulation 9 of the Employment Tribunals (Constitution and Rules of Procedure) Regulations 1993, SI 1993/2687 and Sch 1, rule 10(5) place those grounds in the public domain.[312]

312　*R v Secretary of C.O.E.T. (England and Wales), ex parte Public Concern at Work* [2000] IRLR 658.

Although in most cases a tribunal will not be directly concerned with the extent to which the journalistic material has become available to the public, it will be a relevant consideration when considering the extent of a restricted reporting order. In cases concerning confidential information, the fact that information has already been made public is a relevant factor.[313]

Courts, when considering whether to issue an injunction to restrain publication of what is said to be confidential information by a former employee, will have to have particular regard to the form in which it is to be published if this information can genuinely said to be journalistic etc material. The courts in this context will also be concerned with the 'public interest' defence to injunctive proceedings.[314]

The term 'privacy code' is undefined. By s 12(5) of the HRA 1998, 'relief' includes any remedy or order (other than in criminal proceedings), and 'court' includes tribunals.

3.14.4 Public interest disclosure

One further effect that s 12 of the HRA 1998 may have is on the scope of the provisions of the Public Interest Disclosure Act 1998. Section 47B of the ERA 1996 provides that a worker has the right not to be subjected to any detriment by any act, or any deliberate failure to act, by his or her employer done on the ground that the worker has made a protected disclosure. Section 103A of the ERA 1996 provides that 'an employee who is dismissed shall be regarded for the purposes of this Part as unfairly dismissed if the reason (or, if more than one, the principal reason) for the dismissal is that the employee made a protected disclosure'.

This does not deal with the position of a person who is dismissed because the employer believes that he or she is about to make what would constitute a protected disclosure. It is submitted that a person who is dismissed or subjected to a detriment not because the employer believes that he or she has made such a disclosure but because the employer believes he or she is about to make such a disclosure has the right to have his or her freedom to impart information protected. However, this is an area where, simply by comparing other statutory protection against victimisation, a court might conclude that it was the intention of Parliament not to protect freedom of expression for a person who has not yet made a disclosure. The tribunal will have to determine whether there is an interpretation of these provisions that gives effect to the Convention right to the freedom to impart information.

By s 43C of the ERA 1996, the disclosure must be made in good faith to the employer, or if the worker reasonably believes that the relevant failure relates solely or mainly to:

(a) the conduct of a person other than the employer; or

---

313   See *Attorney-General v Guardian Newspapers Ltd (No 2)* [1990] 1 AC 109.
314   *Price Waterhouse v BCCI* [1992] BCLC 583.

(b) any other matter for which a person other than the employer has legal responsibility,

to that other person.

The test for whether the worker has a 'reasonable belief' is subjective. Section 43B(1) of the ERA 1996 provides that a qualifying disclosure is one which 'in the reasonable belief of the worker making the disclosure tends to show' one or more of a set of six matters. All disclosures, whether they are made internally or externally, and even in extremely serious cases, must satisfy this test in order to be a qualifying disclosure. A disclosure is categorised as a 'qualifying disclosure' if, in the reasonable belief of the worker making the disclosure, the information being disclosed tends to show one of the following:

(a) a criminal offence;
(b) a failure to comply with a legal obligation;
(c) a miscarriage of justice;
(d) the endangering of an individual's health and safety;
(e) environmental damage; or
(f) concealment of information relating to any of the above.

A qualifying disclosure to someone other than the wrongdoer, legal adviser or regulator is made if:

(a) the worker makes the disclosure in good faith;
(b) he or she reasonably believes that the information disclosed, and any allegation contained in it, are substantially true;
(c) he or she does not make the disclosure for purposes of personal gain, and,

in all the circumstances of the case, it is reasonable for the worker to make the disclosure.

One of the following conditions must be met:

(a) that, at the time he or she makes the disclosure, the worker reasonably believes that he or she will be subjected to a detriment by the employer if he or she makes a disclosure to the employer or prescribed person;
(b) if there is no regulatory or supervisory body (prescribed in the Public Interest Disclosure (Prescribed Persons) Order 1999, SI 1999/1549) to whom the disclosure in relation to the relevant failure can be made, the worker reasonably believes that it is likely that evidence relating to the relevant failure will be concealed or destroyed if the worker makes a disclosure to the employer; or
(c) the worker must previously have made a disclosure of substantially the same information:
    (i)   to the employer; or
    (ii) to a prescribed outside body.

In determining whether it is reasonable for the worker to make the disclosure, regard shall be had, in particular, to:

(a) the identity of the person to whom the disclosure is made;
(b) the seriousness of the relevant failure;
(c) whether the relevant failure is continuing or is likely to occur in the future;

(d) whether the disclosure is made in breach of a duty of confidentiality owed by the employer to any other person;

(e) in a case of previous disclosure to the employer or prescribed outside body, any action which the employer or the person to whom the previous disclosure was made has taken or might reasonably be expected to have taken as a result of the previous disclosure; and

(f) in a case of previous disclosure to the employer, whether in making the disclosure to the employer the worker complied with any procedure whose use by the worker was authorised by the employer.

The tribunal in seeking to determine the significance of the confidentiality clause will have to attach little weight to it in order to give effect to the applicant's right of freedom to impart information. Section 12 of the HRA 1998 requires the tribunal to have special regard to that right. If the confidentiality clause arises in a case of a public authority, the act of contracting may be an unlawful infringement of the right of the applicant to impart information. Subject to the issues of justification, the tribunal would have to disapply the confidentiality clause altogether in those circumstances. Section 43J of the ERA 1996 makes void any provision in an agreement that purports to preclude a worker from making a protected disclosure.

3.14.5 Duties of confidentiality

Domestic law recognises that an obligation of confidence can exist by means of an express or implied term in a contract but exists independently of any contract on the basis of an independent equitable principle of confidence.[315] Detriment to the confider is a necessary element, but this may be nominal. Where the confider seeks to restrain the breach of confidence, the detriment to the confider is clear. In cases where there may be no financial detriment to the confider, there may still be a breach of confidence if the breach of confidence involves no more than an invasion of personal privacy.[316] Any profits made should be accounted for to the victim of the breach. The UK law is that it is a sufficient detriment to the confider that information given in confidence is to be disclosed to persons whom the confider would prefer not to know of it, even though the disclosure would not be harmful to the confider in any positive way.

The public authority cannot pray in aid Convention rights as it will not satisfy the victim requirement. The position of the State is regarded as being special in UK law. In some instances, disclosure of confidential information entrusted to a servant of the Crown may result in a financial loss to the public. In other instances, such disclosure may tend to harm the public interest by impeding the efficient attainment of proper governmental ends, and the revelation of defence or intelligence secrets falls into that category.

The State must be in a position to show that the disclosure is likely to damage or has damaged the public interest. In *Attorney-General v Guardian Newspapers (No 2)*,[317] the Crown argued that where the original disclosure has been made by

---

315 *Saltman Engineering Co Ltd v Campbell Engineering Co Ltd* (1948) 65 RPC 203.
316 See, for example, *Duchess of Argyll v Duke of Argyll* [1967] Ch 302.
317 [1998] 3 WLR 776.

a Crown servant in breach of his or her obligation of confidence, any person to whose knowledge the information comes and who is aware of the breach comes under an equitable duty binding his or her conscience not to communicate the information to anyone else, irrespective of the circumstances under which the knowledge was acquired. This argument was rejected.

> 'The general rule is that anyone is entitled to communicate anything he pleases to anyone else, by speech or in writing or in any other way. That rule is limited by the law of defamation and other restrictions similar to these mentioned in Article 10 of the Convention for the Protection of Human Rights and Fundamental Freedoms (1953) (Cmd. 8969). All those restrictions are imposed in the light of considerations of public interest such as to countervail the public interest in freedom of expression. A communication about some aspect of government activity which does no harm to the interests of the nation cannot, even where the original disclosure has been made in breach of confidence, be restrained on the ground of a nebulous equitable duty of conscience serving no useful practical purpose.'

Thus in domestic law the courts have to carry out a balancing exercise between the competing interests of the employer and the public. Depending on a variety of factors, such as the type of information disclosed, the identity of the recipient and the motive for disclosure, the courts would decide whether the disclosure of confidential information amounted to a breach of contract.[318] However, there is no confidence as to the disclosure of iniquity.[319]

3.14.6   Asserting a statutory right

A dismissal will be automatically unfair if the principal reason for the dismissal is that the employee either brought proceedings against the employer to enforce a relevant statutory right, or, alternatively, alleged that the employer had infringed such a right.[320] The 'relevant statutory rights' are:

−   all rights under the ERA 1996;
−   the right to require the employer to cease deductions of union dues or the political fund contribution;[321]
−   the right not to have action short of dismissal taken on union-related grounds;[322]
−   the right to time off for union duties and activities;[323]
−   the right to enforce the entitlement to the national minimum wage.[324]

If the claim is made in good faith, the employee is protected.[325] By s 104(3) of the ERA 1996 the employee need not have specified what the right was, provided it was reasonably clear to the employee what the right was. Article 10 will require the tribunals to interpret these provisions compatibly with the Convention. It is arguable, therefore, that it is not open to the tribunal to find

---

318   See, for example, *British Steel Corporation v Granada Television Ltd* [1981] AC 1097.
319   *Gartside v Outram* (1856) 26 LJ Ch 113 at p 114 *per* Page Wood V-C.
320   ERA 1996, s 104.
321   Trade Union and Labour Relations (Consolidation) Act 1992, ss 68 and 86.
322   Trade Union and Labour Relations (Consolidation) Act 1992, s 146.
323   Trade Union and Labour Relations (Consolidation) Act 1992, s 170.
324   National Minimum Wage Act 1998, s 25.
325   ERA 1996, s 104(2).

that a dismissal was for the 'outrageous' manner in which the right was asserted, or because the employee's conduct necessary for the assertion of the statutory right to the employer breached some provision of the employee's contract.

3.14.7 Justification

Article 10 is a qualified right to freedom of expression. Restrictions on this Article must be prescribed by law and necessary in a democratic society:

- in the interests of national security, territorial integrity or public safety;
- for the prevention of disorder or crime;
- for the protection of health or morals;
- for the protection of the reputation or rights of others;
- for preventing the disclosure of information received in confidence; or
- for maintaining the authority and impartiality of the judiciary.

These Article 10(2) restrictions are to be interpreted narrowly and the necessity for any restrictions must be convincingly established.[326]

Freedom of expression constitutes one of the essential foundations of a democratic society. Subject to Article 10(2), it is applicable not only to 'information' or 'ideas' that are favourably received or regarded as inoffensive or as a matter of indifference, but also to those that offend, shock or disturb. It is in that context that the justifications available for infringements of the right to free expression must be considered.

The adjective 'necessary,' within the meaning of Article 10(2), implies the existence of a 'pressing social need'. In *Grigoriades v Greece*,[327] prosecution for intemperate remarks in the course of disclosing information concerning army life was not 'necessary in a democratic society'. Although the contracting States do have a certain margin of appreciation in assessing whether such a need exists, the ECtHR may give the final ruling on whether a 'restriction' is reconcilable with freedom of expression as protected by Article 10. The ECtHR will look at the interference complained of in the light of the case as a whole and determine whether it was 'proportionate to the legitimate aim pursued' and whether the reasons adduced to justify it are 'relevant and sufficient'.

Sometimes an employer suspends an employee and at the same time forbids the employee to have contact with fellow workers. In the case of a public authority this may represent an unlawful infringement of the right to freedom to impart information, as well as being potentially an interference with the right to a private life. In *Carter v UK*,[328] which was a decision concerning admissibility, the applicant was a fireman, suspended (following a disciplinary hearing) pending the outcome of the hearing. He was prohibited from entering fire service premises without obtaining prior permission and was asked not to contact any of his colleagues. He argued this restricted his social and everyday life and prevented him from communicating with his friends and complained that it constituted a breach of Article 8 and Article 10. The ECtHR,

---

326 *Vogt v Germany* (1996) 21 EHRR 205.
327 (1999) 27 EHRR 464.
328 Application No 36417/97, 29 June 1999.

ruling on admissibility, noted the paramount importance of ensuring internal cohesion and professionalism in the running of a vital public service capable of responding rapidly to the urgency of the demands placed on it. The case had been controversial and divisive for the workplace and threatened harm to the teamwork of the fire service. He was a part-time employee, and thus his life did not centre on work activities. The ECtHR held that the condition imposed was a proportionate response to a pressing social need and one which was well within the margin of appreciation. Thus the public authority employer will have to be able to point to these kinds of considerations before it can justify a requirement that a suspended employee must not speak to colleagues.

Private employers will also need to be aware of this principle in the context of suspensions which form part of a disciplinary procedure potentially leading to dismissal. The employment tribunal considering the fairness of the dismissal must characterise the action of the employer as reasonable or unreasonable, having regard to equity and the substantial merits of the case. In conducting its statutory function it will have to interpret its powers so as to give effect to the Convention rights, and will have to construe s 98 of the ERA 1996 so far as possible so as to render it compatible with the Convention right. Therefore, the private employer may have to justify a decision that the employee must not contact other employees. The tribunal will otherwise have to give effect to the Convention right by finding the conduct of the employer leading up to the dismissal to be unreasonable. Clearly, the ability to contact colleagues may also form the foundation of a defence to a misconduct charge, and so may be viewed as essential to the requirements of Article 10 as the information received and given may be of fundamental importance to the applicant.

A position may attract restrictions on political activities. In *Ahmed v UK*,[329] the applicants held politically restricted local government posts. This meant that they were unable to stand for electoral office. They challenged the Local Government Officers (Political Restrictions) Regulations 1990, SI 1990/851, and claimed, having exhausted domestic remedies, that the regulations denied their right to freedom of expression under Article 10. However, the restriction on their freedom of expression could be justified on account of the need to protect the rights of others to effective political democracy, as councillors must be able to carry out their electoral mandate without encountering political opposition from their advisers. The aim was therefore legitimate. The regulations were clear and their effects foreseeable. The infringement was therefore justified. In *Vogt*,[330] the applicant's suspension from teaching in a State school was in pursuit of a legitimate aim. She was involved in the Communist Party. Restricting her freedom of expression could be justified on account of the need to protect the rights of others to effective political democracy. However, Germany failed to establish convincingly (which was said to be the standard) that it was necessary to limit the applicant's freedom of expression. Where an effected item goes beyond what is necessary in a democratic society it will not be upheld. Thus in *Barthold v Germany*,[331] restraint

329   (2000) 29 EHRR 1.
330   *Vogt v Germany* (1996) 21 EHRR 205.
331   (1985) 7 EHRR 383.

of publication of an article by a vet about the absence of night services (as it breached unfair competition laws) was not upheld for this reason.[332]

3.14.8   National security

The 'Spycatcher' case sheds light on the approach of the UK courts to the issue of justification by national security. The author of a book on the activities of the British Secret Service was restrained by injunction from disseminating the information. The House of Lords held that the Attorney-General had the right to apply for a restraining injunction because of the protection of an important public interest, namely, the maintenance so far as possible of the secrecy of the British Security Service. Discharging the temporary injunctions would unjustly deprive the Attorney-General irrevocably of the opportunity of having that case fairly adjudicated upon at the trial. Lord Templeman stated that it was the duty of the House in its judicial capacity to prevent harm to the Security Service by the widespread dissemination of uncorroborated allegations against it, and to preserve the right and duty of the court to uphold within the jurisdiction the secrecy of the Security Service when necessary and to ensure that the object and intent of orders made by the court were not flouted. Continuing the injunctions was necessary in the public interest in order to maintain the efficiency of the Security Service upon which the safety of the realm was dependent.[333] Lord Brandon said:

> 'The public right to freedom of expression cannot, even in a democratic country such as the UK, be absolute. It is necessarily subject to certain exceptions, of which the protection of national security is one. This is expressly recognised in Article 10(2) of the Convention for the Protection of Human Rights and Fundamental Freedoms, to which the UK has adhered ...'[334]

Lord Templeman noted that in *The Sunday Times v UK*,[335] the ECtHR pointed out that the House of Lords in applying domestic law had balanced the public interest in freedom of expression and the public interest in the due of administration of justice. But the ECtHR:[336]

> 'is faced not with a choice between two conflicting principles, but with a principle of freedom of expression that is subject to a number of exceptions which must be narrowly interpreted. It is not sufficient that the interference involved belongs to that class of exceptions listed in article 10(2) which has been invoked; neither is it sufficient that the interference was imposed because its subject matter fell within a particular category or was caught by a legal rule formulated in general or absolute terms: the court has to be satisfied that the interference was necessary having regard to the facts and circumstances prevailing in the specific case before it.'

Lord Templeman went on to ask whether the interference with freedom of expression constituted by the injunctions was necessary in a democratic society in the interests of national security, for protecting the reputation or rights of others, for preventing the disclosure of information received in confidence or

---

332   See also *Jacubowski v Germany* (1995) 19 EHRR 64.
333   *Attorney-General v Guardian* [1987] 1 WLR 1248.
334   *Attorney-General v Guardian* [1987] 1 WLR 1248 at p 1288.
335   (1979–80) 2 EHRR 245.
336   (1979–80) 2 EHRR 245, p 281 at para 65.

for maintaining the authority and impartiality of the judiciary having regard to the facts and circumstances prevailing at the time and in the light of the events which had happened. He concluded there that all of these justifications were available.

In *Hadjianastassiou v Greece*,[337] a serving officer was sentenced for having disclosed military information of minor importance, concerning a secret arms project. However, the information was classified as a military secret. The aim of the restriction (national security) was legitimate. The ECtHR took account of the 'special conditions' attaching to military life, and the obligation of discretion imposed on its personnel, and found the infringement justified as it did not exceed the limits of the margin of appreciation of the courts trying the case in Greece. In *Brind v UK*,[338] the Commission rejected the complaint concerning the ban on broadcasting the voices of members of proscribed terrorist organisations in the UK. The Commission accepted that the ban was proportionate to the aim of combatting terrorism. A prohibition on publication must not continue after the subject matter is in the public domain in any event. By that stage, a ban is not proportionate, as it serves no purpose.[339] This reflects the approach of domestic law. The 1987 decision of the House of Lords in the Spycatcher case went before the ECtHR.[340] The UK argued that the restraint of publication was a legitimate measure in the interests both of national security and of maintaining confidence in the judiciary. The ECtHR agreed that these were legitimate under Article 10(2) but the injunctions, from the date that the information entered the public domain when they were published in the USA, constituted a disproportionate interference. Thus when the Spycatcher case returned to House of Lords the book had been published worldwide and although the House of Lords held that a duty of confidence could arise in contract or in equity and a confidant who acquired information in circumstances importing such a duty should be precluded from disclosing it to others, the worldwide disclosure had rendered the injunction no longer justified.[341]

3.14.9   Interests of justice

The prevention of publication of information concerning court cases, on the basis that it might put pressure on parties to litigation, or might prejudge the issues, may go further than is necessary in a democratic society for maintaining the authority of the judiciary.[342] Most contempt of court measures are justified, particularly if they are compatible with the purpose of Article 6.[343]

In the context of journalistic sources, s 10 of the Contempt of Court Act 1981 provides protection to the relationship of journalist and source. However,

---

337   (1993) 16 EHRR 219.
338   Application No 18714/91, 9 May 1994, 77 DR 42.
339   See *Vereniging Weekblad 'Bluf' v The Netherlands* (1995) 20 EHRR 189.
340   *Sunday Times Limited v UK (No 2)* (1991) 14 EHRR 229.
341   *Attorney-General v Guardian Newspapers (No 2)* [1988] 3 WLR 777.
342   *Sunday Times v UK* (1979–80) 2 EHRR 245.
343   See *Worm v Austria* (1998) 3 BHRC 180.

where disclosure is sought, and the court is of the view that the interests of justice require disclosure, an Article 10(2) defence may be available. In *X v Morgan-Grampian*,[344] information had been leaked. The employer sought disclosure of the source since the source had stolen the document. However, the ECtHR held that the fine the journalist received when he continued to refuse to disclose amounted to an unjustifiable breach of Article 10. The 'interests of justice' was a legitimate aim relating to the 'rights of others' and the injunction provided sufficient protection to the company to satisfy those interests, and so was proportionate. However, the effect of the contempt order was to stifle the freedom of the press.[345] In *Camelot v Centaur Communications Ltd*,[346] the employer of an employee who disclosed confidential information to a journalist obtained an order which required the newspaper to whom the journalist had passed the information to disclose his source. The employers wanted to know the name of their disloyal employee. The Court of Appeal considered the application of s 10 of the Contempt of Court Act 1981 noting that it was passed in order that domestic law might reflect Article 10 of the Convention. The newspaper offered to destroy the offending documents, but this was not enough. The company complained that the source employee had stolen documents from the company and that the source was at a high level within the organisation or had access to those who were working at that high level. An internal enquiry had not been able to identify the person responsible. The court noted that the company conducted its affairs under a media spotlight and had a very substantial interest in protecting its integrity.

In an ordinary case, the employer can require the return of the documents on the basis that they are its own property or because of a breach of confidence or pursuant to the principle in *Norwich Pharmacal Company v Customs and Excise Commissioners*.[347] Although the order sought by the company was not in terms an order requiring disclosure of the source of information, it is clear that disclosure or facilitation of disclosure of that source would be the effect of the order. In these circumstances, s 10 of the Contempt of Court Act 1981 would be applicable where the press is involved. Whilst, after the HRA 1998, the court will have to consider whether Article 10 would protect the source employee in a broader range of circumstances, it is unlikely that Article 10 would protect identification of a source where documents have been stolen from the employer and the recipient is not the press.

The State is obliged to ensure that any restrictions on Article 10 rights are clear and accessible. In *Open Door Counselling and Dublin Well Woman v Ireland*,[348] a tort under the Irish Constitution aimed at the protection of health and morals failed the test of certainty because the non-directional pregnancy counsellors could not have foreseen that they were committing it. It was not therefore 'prescribed by law'.

---

344   [1991] 1 AC 1.
345   *Goodwin v UK* (1996) 22 EHRR 123.
346   [1998] IRLR 80.
347   [1974] AC 133.
348   (1993) 15 EHRR 244.

3.14.10   Reputation and rights of others

The issue when this defence to infringement of free expression is raised will be whether the sanction or restraint imposed is proportionate.[349] Where a measure is aimed at protecting religious sensibilities, the 'rights of others' defence may be available.[350] In *Mark Tintern v Germany*,[351] the 'rights of others' defence was available when injunctions issued were under competition regulations which prevented a magazine from publishing articles making critical comments about a competing company.

3.14.11   Racist language

Provisions relating to the prohibition of racial discrimination and the prevention of propaganda of racist views and ideas are to be found in a number of international instruments, for example the United Nations Charter 1945 (para 2 of the Preamble; Article 1, para 3; Article 13, para 1(b), 55(c) and 76(c)), the Universal Declaration of Human Rights 1948 (Articles 1, 2 and 7) and the International Covenant on Civil and Political Rights 1966 (Article 2, para 1; Article 20, para 2; and Article 26). The most directly relevant treaty is the International Convention on the Elimination of All Forms of Racial Discrimination 1965 ('the UN Convention'), which has been ratified by a large majority of the contracting States to the Convention. Is an individual respondent entitled to claim the protection against infringement of his right to freedom of expression, which consists in racial abuse? The ECtHR has rejected the idea that racist statements are protected by Article 10. The reasoning is that, although a restriction on the right of a person to make such statements is an infringement of their right to freedom of expression, it is likely that a restriction in respect of such statements is 'necessary in a democratic society'. The ECtHR will consider in particular whether the means employed to achieve the legitimate aim of the State of protecting the rights or reputation of others are disproportionate to that aim. The ECtHR can draw a distinction between the reporting of racist statements[352] and the making of racist statements.[353]

A person has a right not to be subjected to humiliating or degrading treatment, and also not to have his or her reputation smeared by racist abuse. The balance between these rights is clearly in favour of the protection of the victim rather than the discriminator's exercise of freedom of expression. Article 17 prevents a person from deriving from the Convention a right to engage in activities aimed at the destruction of any of the rights and freedoms set forth in the Convention. One of the basic ideas of the Convention, as expressed in its preamble, is justice and peace. The Race Relations Act 1976 was introduced to make 'fresh provision with respect to discrimination on racial grounds and

---

349   See *Oberschlick v Austria* (1995) 19 EHRR 389, but see *Prager and Oberschlick v Austria* (1996) 21 EHRR 1: protection of the reputation of the judiciary.
350   *Otto Preminger Institut v Austria* (1995) 19 EHRR 34.
351   (1990) 12 EHRR 161.
352   *Jersild v Denmark* (1995) 19 EHRR 1.
353   See, for example, *Hennicke v Germany* Application No 34889/97.

relations between people of different racial groups', and was therefore aimed at promoting the aims of the Convention. It is submitted that a person whose racist comments are destructive of this aim, or which infringe the rights of another to a private life or not to have his or her reputation damaged, cannot derive protection from Article 10.

Even if the discriminator can claim that Article 10 has been infringed, the aims of legislating for compensation for discrimination are legitimate, and the means adopted are proportionate to that aim.

For an example of a failed Article 17 defence, consider *Lehideux and Isorni v France.*[354] In *Lehideux and Isorni v France,* an advertisement appeared in *Le Monde* supporting Marshal Pétain who was convicted of collaboration in 1945. The writers were convicted of publicly defending the crimes of collaboration. The applicants claimed this breached their rights under Article 10. France argued that the advert infringed the very spirit of the Convention and the essential values of democracy, and therefore claimed that the applicants were barred from relying on Article 10. The ECtHR rejected this as nothing in the advertisement was directed against the Convention's underlying values. It celebrated a man, and did not promote a policy. The convictions were held to be a disproportionate interference with Article 10.

3.15 ARTICLE 14

3.15.1 Introduction

Article 14 affords protection against discrimination. This means treating differently, without an objective and reasonable justification, persons in 'relevantly' similar situations. However, it is only discrimination in the application of the rights secured under the Convention by the other Articles that is protected. It is not a right not to suffer discrimination. Therefore, the applicant must be able to point to the engagement of another right under the Convention. It is not necessary to establish a violation of another Article. However, if the claim comes within the ambit of another protected right, the applicant can succeed on discrimination alone. This is the case even if the primary violation has not been established, or the State's action has been found to be justified.[355]

If the effected item[356] discriminates against people in an area involving other Convention rights, it may be incompatible with Article 14. This provides for people to enjoy the protection of the Convention rights without discrimination on any ground such as sex, race, colour, language, religion, political or other opinion, national or social origin, association with a national minority, property, birth or other status. 'Other status' has been interpreted widely to include sexual orientation, marital status, illegitimacy, status as a trade union,

---

354   (2000) 30 EHRR 665.
355   *Belgian Linguistic Case* (1979–80) 1 EHRR 241.
356   See **3.5.2**.

military status and conscientious objection. It is clearly a catch all. For further commentary see Chapter 5.

The ECtHR when considering whether an effected item breaches this Convention right will consider among other things whether there was an objective and reasonable justification for treating different categories of people in a different way, and whether any differential treatment was proportionate to the aim pursued. Different types of discrimination have been treated as differing in seriousness. Discrimination on the grounds of sex, race or illegitimacy is harder to justify than other areas of discrimination.

For a claim of violation of Article 14 to succeed, it has to be established, inter alia, that the situation of the alleged victim can be considered similar to that of persons who have been better treated.[357] Further, a difference of treatment is discriminatory if it 'has no objective and reasonable justification', that is if it does not pursue a 'legitimate aim' or if there is no 'reasonable relationship of proportionality between the means employed and the aim sought to be realised'.[358]

3.15.2 Religious discrimination

The ERA 1996 does not protect applicants for employment who object to Sunday working on religious grounds against discrimination at the recruitment stage. This may be an area in which the provisions of the statute would have to be found to be incompatible with Convention rights, as when an amendment was sought to the Sunday Trading Bill it was defeated.[359] However, the following argument is theoretically available. First, members of a racial group have access to the tribunals in respect of discrimination in relation to applications for employment on racial grounds. Secondly, under Article 14 this social group receives better access to the system of justice (Article 6) than does the applicant from the group of religious objectors to Sunday working and the absence of a religious discrimination provision means that the freedom of religious people to observe Sunday as a religious day is curtailed. The State would have to be able to point to justification by reference to a legitimate aim which was necessary in a democratic society.

A second argument is available to other religious groups whose observance requires worship on another day of the week. The protection offered in relation to Sunday favours Christian religious beliefs. Those of other religious persuasions whose observance entails rest on another day of the week are thereby at a disadvantage in relation to their right to manifest their freedom of religion. Such groups are not necessarily protected by race relations legislation, and certainly the protection offered by those means would in many cases be inadequate.

Against a public employer the employee may have a stand-alone claim for discrimination in relation to applications for employment on the basis that the

---

357   *Fredin v Sweden* 18 February 1991, Series A, No 192, p 19 at para 60.
358   *Gaygusuz v Austria* (1997) 23 EHRR 364.
359   HC Debs, vol 237, cols 304–321, 9 February 1994.

employer would be in breach of Articles 9 and 14 in refusing employment on the basis that the applicant would not work a particular day of the week due to religious observance. The common law will not necessarily be capable of development towards a tort of religious discrimination, especially in relation to the recruitment stage of a contract of employment.

If the duty to give effect to Convention rights permits the court or tribunal to interpolate words into a piece of legislation, the provisions of the ERA 1996 relating to Sunday trading may have to be given effect in a way that covers other religious days.

3.16   ARTICLE 1 OF THE 1st PROTOCOL

3.16.1   Introduction

If the effected item[360] affects a person's possessions or ability to carry on a trade or profession, Article 1 of the 1st Protocol, which aims to ensure that a person's (including a company's) possessions are not unfairly interfered with, may be relevant. The term 'possessions' will cover anything of economic value. It will include goods, shares, rights under contracts (including leases and licences), land, rights to run a business, goodwill and damages or other sums awarded by a court or tribunal. However, it covers only existing possessions and existing legal rights. Thus it would cover the right to receive benefits under a pension scheme.

There are three questions to be asked:

(1) Whether any issue arises under Article 1 of the 1st Protocol?
   (a) Is any property or possession involved?
   (b) Does the act or omission amount either to a deprivation of that property or to a control of use of that property?
   (c) If neither, does it interfere with peaceful enjoyment of possessions?

(2) If there is deprivation:
   (a) is it in the public interest?
   (b) if so, has a fair balance been struck between that interest and the individual's interests or does it represent an excessive burden on the individual?

(3) If there is control:
   (a) does it have a legitimate aim?
   (b) is it proportionate?

Article 1 of the 1st Protocol guarantees the right to property and comprises three distinct rules.[361] The first rule is of a general nature, laying down the principle of peaceful enjoyment of property. The second rule covers deprivation of possessions and subjects it to certain conditions. The third rule recognises that the contracting States are entitled, amongst other things, to

---

360 See **3.5.2**.
361 *Sporrong and Lönnroth v Sweden* 23 September 1982, Series A, No 52 p 24 at para 61.

control the use of property in accordance with the general interest or to secure the payment of taxes or other contributions or penalties.

3.16.2   Possessions and property

The following have been held to be possessions under Article 1 of the 1st Protocol.

–   The values of the assets owned by the applicants.

–   Goodwill may be an element in the valuation of a professional practice.[362] On the other hand, future income itself is only a 'possession' once it has been earned, or an enforceable claim to it exists.[363]

–   In the case of *Pressos Compania Naviera SA and Others v Belgium*,[364] the ECtHR accepted that, in the circumstances of that case, a claim in tort was a possession within the meaning of Article 1 of the 1st Protocol, even before it had been determined by the courts.

–   A sum of money the applicant must pay under the Swedish Profit-sharing Tax Act and the supplementary pension scheme.[365]

–   Shares.[366]

Thus 'possessions' may be either 'existing possessions'[367] or valuable assets, including claims, in respect of which the applicant can argue that he or she has at least a 'legitimate expectation' that they will realise.[368]

By contrast, the hope of recognition of the survival of a former property right which has not been susceptible of effective exercise for a long period,[369] or a conditional claim which has lapsed as a result of the non-fulfilment of the condition,[370] are not to be considered as 'possessions' within the meaning of Article 1 of the 1st Protocol.

3.16.3   Deprivation or control of use

The measure complained of must amount to either a formal or to a *de facto* expropriation of the property.[371] Where there was no transfer of the applicant's property nor was he deprived of his right to use, let or sell it, and he was not even deprived of a part of his income from the property, but only prevented from negotiating a new rent by which his income would have increased, there was no expropriation of his property. The measure was therefore categorised as

---

362   Application No 10438/83, *Batelaan and Huiges v The Netherlands*, Dec (1984) 41 DR 170.
363   Application No 10426/83, *Pudas v Sweden*, Dec (1984) 40 DR 234.
364   20 November 1995, Series A, No 332, p 21 at para 31.
365   *SS IAB v Sweden* Commission Decision No 11189/84.
366   *SS IAB v Sweden* Commission Decision No 11189/84.
367   *Van der Musselle v Belgium* 23 November 1983, Series A, No 70, p 23 at para 48.
368   *Pine Valley Developments Ltd and Others v Ireland* 29 November 1991, Series A, No 222, p 23 at para 51, ECtHR, and *Pressos Compania Naviera SA and Others v Belgium* above.
369   *Pelzter v Germany* Application No 35223/97 and Nos 7655–7657/76, Dec (1977) 12 DR 111.
370   *Napoles Pacheco v Belgium* Application No 7775/77, Dec 5 October 1978 (1978) 15 DR 143.
371   See, for example, *G v Austria* Application No 00012484/86.

a control of the use of property which fell to be considered under the second paragraph of Article 1.[372] It is possible that there may be a *de facto* expropriation of possessions even without any formal alienation, on the ground that property has become wholly unusable.[373] However, loss of a restaurant after refusal of a licence was considered to be a result of control of use of property rather than expropriation.[374]

In *Pinnacle Meat Processors Company and Others v UK*,[375] the applicants were engaged in the business of deboning cattle heads, and the loss of business resulted from restrictions imposed on the use of specified bovine material. The Commission assessed the loss of business suffered by the applicants as a control of use rather than as a deprivation of possessions due to the extent of the effect of the measure resulting in that loss of business. In assessing this the court will look at the extent to which the business has a legitimate expectation of being able to continue without control or deprivation of property. Thus the extent to which the business is already regulated will be a factor.

3.16.4   Peaceful enjoyment

Article 1 of the 1st Protocol covers, among other things, the right to peaceful enjoyment of possessions. Thus a company could rely on it (for interpretive purposes) if the actions of the employee were such as to interfere with its right of peaceful enjoyment of its legal rights or physical property by affecting their financial value. The question of whether peaceful enjoyment has been infringed arises only if no question of deprivation or control arises. Only such interferences as have an effect on the financial value of possessions or property give rise to a question of whether the peaceful enjoyment of them has been infringed.[376] Restrictions in private law define property rights and rights to possessions rather than interfering with them.[377]

3.16.5   Justification

Any effected item[378] that interferes with property rights must strike a fair balance between the demands of the community or society and the requirements of the need to protect the individual's fundamental rights. In considering this balance, one of the things that the ECtHR will consider is if, and in what circumstances, compensation is payable. There is a sliding scale of acceptability between the situations in which a person can be deprived of property without compensation. Where no compensation is available, it is only in exceptional circumstances that the State may lawfully interfere with the right to property. The ECtHR cases show that there is considerable scope as to what constitutes an acceptable level of compensation. Any interference with these rights must be under a law which permits the interference and that law must be sufficiently

---

372   See also *Mellacher and Others v Austria* (1990) 12 EHRR 391.
373   *Papamichalopoulos v Greece* 24 June 1993, Series A, No 260-B, p 70 at paras 43–5.
374   *Tre Traktörer AB v Sweden* 7 July 1989, Series A, No 159.
375   Application No 33298/96, Dec 21 October 1998.
376   *Rayner v UK* (1986) 47 DR 5.
377   *X v UK* (1978) 14 DR 234.
378   See **3.5.2**.

certain and accessible. The State is not permitted arbitrarily to interfere with these rights and, if it does, there must be procedural safeguards which will generally have to comply with Article 6.

Justification of a measure can be that it is in the general interest. The court must respect the legislature's judgment as to what is in the general interest unless that judgment is manifestly without reasonable foundation.[379]

The aim of Article 1 of the 1st Protocol is to achieve a fair balance between the demands of the general interest of the community and the requirements of the protection of the individual's fundamental rights. There must therefore be a reasonable relationship of proportionality between the means employed and the aim pursued.[380]

The court will consider whether, taken overall, the applicants can be said to have suffered an 'individual and excessive burden'[381] in relation to the control or deprivation of their property.

In *Ian Edgar (Liverpool) Limited v UK,*[382] this was a factor in ruling the complaint inadmissible. Even assuming that the 1997 handgun control legislation had an appreciable adverse impact on the company's goodwill, to which Article 1 of the 1st Protocol applied, the Commission took into account that the applicant company had at all times had to operate within a framework of control of the trade in firearms, which has existed in the UK since 1920 and which has become progressively more restrictive. In these circumstances, the ECtHR agreed with the UK Government that the applicant company had no legitimate expectation that it would be able to continue to trade in any particular type of firearm, including handguns.[383] It also took account of the fact that handguns formerly accounted for only 30 per cent of its trade, so that it appeared that a substantial part of its trade was not affected by the prohibition on handguns.

As regards deprivation of possessions, there is normally an inherent right to compensation.[384] There is normally no inherent right to compensation in cases of control of property.[385]

3.16.6   Injunctions

The court's power to grant an injunction will also have to be interpreted in accordance with this Convention right. The principles surrounding the grant of an interim or final injunction in employment cases will be affected by the HRA 1998. The Supreme Court Act 1981, s 37(1) provides:

---

379   *Mellacher and Others v Austria* (1990) 12 EHRR 391, para 45 and *James v UK* Series A, No 98 (1986) 8 EHRR 123.
380   *Air Canada v UK* judgment of 5 May 1995, Series A, No 316-A, p 15.
381   *James v UK* 21 February 1986, Series A, No 98, p 34.
382   Application No 37683/97.
383   *Fredin v Sweden* 22 January 1991, Series A, No 192, pp 17–18 at para 54.
384   *James v UK* 21 February 1986, Series A, No 98, p 36 at para 54 and *Lithgow v UK* 8 July 1986, Series A, No 102, p 51 at para 122.
385   *Banér v Sweden* Commission Decision No 11763/85 (1989) 60 DR 128 at p 142.

'The High Court may by order (whether interlocutory or final) grant an injunction or appoint a receiver in all cases in which it appears to the court to be just and convenient to do so.'

The County Courts Act 1984, s 38, provides in so far as relevant:

'(1)   Subject to what follows, in any proceedings in a county court the court may make any order which could be made by the High Court if the proceedings were in the High Court.

(2)   Any order made by a county court may be:
(a)   absolute or conditional;
(b)   final or interlocutory.'

Thus the question of when it appears to the court to be just and convenient must be answered by reference to the requirement that the court must read this provision so as to give effect to the Convention rights. The employer can therefore argue for the grant of an injunction to enforce a restraint of trade clause on the basis that not to grant the injunction would interfere with its property rights by means of a control which does not satisfy the provisions of Article 1 of the 1st Protocol.

In *South Carolina Insurance Co v Assurantie Maatschappij 'De Zeven Provincien' NV*,[386] the House of Lords held that the court has discretion to grant injunctions in only two situations:

(1)   where a party has invaded or threatened to invade a legal or equitable right of another party;
(2)   where a party has behaved or threatened to behave in an unconscionable manner.

Covenants in restraint of trade will be valid only if they are reasonable, for example, in the scope of the activities covered, geographical area, and period of time. In *Office Overload Ltd v Gunn*,[387] the defendant was the branch manager of the claimant's employment agency in Croydon. In his contract of employment he covenanted not to work for or set up a competing business in the Croydon area for one year after ceasing to work for the claimant. After giving notice the defendant immediately started competing. The claimant applied for an interim injunction. Given that to be valid a covenant has to be for a limited period of time, refusal of interim relief will usually deprive a claimant of the benefit of the covenant. The court therefore said that such covenants are in a special category and that if they are *prima facie* valid and there is an infringement the courts will grant an injunction.

A covenant will be *prima facie* valid if:

(a)   all the facts are before the court; and
(b)   the covenant is reasonable in ambit, area and duration.

The question of whether or not to grant an interim injunction will depend on whether it is just and convenient to do so. Where there was a real issue as to

---

386   [1987] AC 24.
387   [1977] FSR 39.

whether dismissal was a repudiatory breach of the contract and there was doubt as to whether the terms of the covenant were too wide, the *American Cyanamid*[388] guidelines were applied.[389] The court has a discretion to grant or refuse an injunction, but that discretion must be operated so as to be consistent with the Convention right to property. Whether a covenant is in unreasonable restraint of trade will depend on the nature of the right being protected by the employer. Thus in circumstances where there is doubt as to whether the covenant is unreasonable because it is too wide, emphasis can be laid on the effect of the actions of the employee on the value of the economically valuable possessions of the employer so as to insist that if the court were not to grant the injunction it would in effect be controlling the employer's use of its property or interfering with its peaceful enjoyment of its property by permitting the employee to compete without restraint. The court would then have to conduct the balancing exercise, asking whether application of s 36 of the Supreme Court Act 1981 had a legitimate aim in this context, and if so whether that legitimate aim placed undue burdens on the employer if the injunction were not granted. It would be possible to construe the section's phrase 'just and convenient' so as to give effect to the Convention right under Article 1 of the 1st Protocol by granting the injunction even where there is doubt as to whether, ultimately, the clause is unreasonably wide. If the clause were obviously unreasonable, the balancing exercise would result in refusal of the injunction because the burden of control would not be excessive. However, where there was an arguable case either way, the requirement to construe the Supreme Court Act 1981 so far as possible so as to give effect to the Convention right would favour the employer.

See also injunctions under Article 4 at **3.7.6**.

Injunctions to restrain breach of confidence are decided in accordance with *American Cyanamid* guidelines.[390]

3.17   THE POWERS OF THE COURT

3.17.1   High Court Powers and the Human Rights Act 1998

Section 19 of the Supreme Court Act 1981 establishes the jurisdiction of the High Court.

'(1)   The High Court shall be a superior court of record.

(2)   Subject to the provisions of this Act, there shall be exercisable by the High Court –

(a)   all such jurisdiction (whether civil or criminal) as is conferred on it by this or any other Act; and

---

388   [1975] AC 396.
389   *Lawrence David Ltd v Ashton* [1991] 1 All ER 385.
390   *Lock International plc v Beswick* [1989] 1 WLR 1268.

(b) all such other jurisdiction (whether civil or criminal) as was exercisable by it immediately before the commencement of this Act (including jurisdiction conferred on a judge of the High Court by any statutory provision).

(3) Any jurisdiction of the High Court shall be exercised only by a single judge of that court, except in so far as it is –
   (a) by or by virtue of rules of court or any other statutory provision required to be exercised by a divisional court; or
   (b) by rules of court made exercisable by a master, registrar or other officer of the court, or by any other person.

(4) The specific mention elsewhere in this Act of any jurisdiction covered by subsection (2) shall not derogate from the generality of that subsection.'

The section appears to provide a statutory basis for the court's jurisdiction. Section 151 of the Supreme Court Act 1981 defines 'jurisdiction'. Jurisdiction includes powers. Section 19 of the Supreme Court Act 1981 can be read as conferring the powers that the court can lawfully exercise. To be read so as to give effect to the Convention rights, s 19 must mean that if the court purports to exercise its powers in a way which does not, so far as possible, give effect to those powers in a way which is compatible with the Convention rights, it acts unlawfully. Any exercise of the powers of the High Court, therefore, which is not compatible with the Convention rights is unlawful.

The duty under s 3 of the HRA 1998 is that so far as it is possible to do so, primary and subordinate legislation must be read and given effect in a way which is compatible with the Convention rights.

Note that s 6(2) of the HRA 1998 makes it clear that 'read' and 'given effect' are two separate activities under the Act. Section 6(2) provides that it is not unlawful for a public authority to act in a way which is incompatible with the Convention rights if:

'in the case of one or more provisions of, or made under, primary legislation which cannot be read *or* given effect in a way which is compatible with the Convention rights, the authority was acting so as to give effect to or enforce those provisions' (emphasis added).

Thus, where one instance of the exercise of any of the court's powers conflicts with a Convention right, but another does not, the power must be exercised so as to give effect to the Convention right. This proposition will apply whether the parties before it are private employers or public authorities. The High Court, as a public body, cannot interpret its powers in such a way as to limit the Convention rights to a greater extent than is provided for in the Convention (Article 17, and s 2 of the HRA 1998), without acting unlawfully.

3.17.2 Positive obligations and the powers of the court/tribunal

The Convention case-law has developed a doctrine that a public authority (ie the State) has a positive obligation to take steps or adopt measures to protect the Convention rights of individuals. Article 1 of the Convention requires

States to secure Convention rights to everyone within the UK's jurisdiction. These rights are to be practical and effective and not theoretical and illusory (see **2.5.7**). In Convention law the State is obliged to provide effective remedies for acts which are arguably infringements of Convention rights. [391] This was the source of a positive obligation to provide effective policing to enable freedom of assembly in *Platform Ärzte für das Leben v Austria.* [392] Article 8 was also said to require positive measures to secure respect for private and family life between individuals.

The implementation of this obligation must have regard to the fair balance that has to be struck between the competing interests of the individual and the community as whole.

Arising from the requirements of effectiveness and practicality, the High Court has a positive duty to establish a legal framework in the common law and equity which provides effective protection for the Convention rights of individuals, and by the same token to prevent breaches of the Convention.

Employment practitioners will be familiar with the case of *De Souza v Automobile Association.* [393] The applicant attempted to take the matter to the ECtHR. [394] The Commission dismissed her application as manifestly unfounded. The applicant complained of racial discrimination during her employment with a private company. This complaint was rejected by various employment and appellate tribunals. The applicant overheard a conversation in which she was insultingly referred to as a 'wog', but the tribunals did not consider that this, along with her other allegations, to have occasioned her any significant detriment in her work.

She alleged breaches of Articles 3, 4, 6(1) and 14 of the Convention. In rejecting her complaint of racial discrimination, the Commission said:

> 'The Commission notes that the applicant's complaints under Articles 3, 4 and 14 (Art. 3, 4, 14) of the Convention concern principally her private employer, which complaints the Commission is unable to examine by virtue of its competence ratione personæ. However, English domestic law has provided protection from racial discrimination and abusive conditions of employment under the Race Relations Act 1976 and substantial employment protection legislation. Enforcement of this protection for employees is ensured by specialised courts, namely Industrial Tribunals and Employment Appeal Tribunals, followed by the other normal channels of appeal to the Court of Appeal and the House of Lords. In this respect the British Government has taken positive steps to protect persons within its jurisdiction from possible degrading treatment through discrimination, and from forced labour.'

The reasoning of the Commission demonstrates the ECtHR's approach to positive obligations. The ECtHR will not find a positive obligation unless it finds that the domestic law does not positively protect the right in question, which should be protected under the Convention.

---

391   Article 13.
392   (1991) 13 EHRR 204.
393   [1986] ICR 514.
394   *De Souza v UK* Application No 12237/86.

It is only when the High Court is considering a case where the Convention would require a result different to that achieved under the law that the obligation arises on the court to exercise its powers to give effect to the Convention right in issue. The difficult question that will have to be answered is the extent to which the High Court can maintain that the existing provisions of tort or contract adequately protect the Convention right concerned (and see *Earl Spencer and Countess Spencer v UK*[395]).

Exercise of the court's discretionary powers will require the court to look at any impact this might have on Convention rights. If the exercise of the power infringes the Convention right, it will have to consider whether that infringement is justified by reference to the Convention law on the point.

3.17.3   Civil Procedure Rules 1998 and Human Rights Act 1998

One feature of the Civil Procedure Rules 1998 (CPR 1998), SI 1998/3132, is active case management. The court is given a duty actively to manage cases.[396] The court is empowered (and obliged) to decide promptly which of the issues in a case need full investigation and trial. It may therefore dispose summarily of the others,[397] including by striking out a statement of case in whole or in part[398] or by giving summary judgment[399] if the claimant or defendant has no reasonable prospect of success. The CPR 1998 allows for exercise of these powers on the court's own initiative, without hearing the parties or allowing an opportunity to make representations.[400] The order must include a statement of the right of the parties to make an application to have the order set aside, varied or stayed. It is unlikely therefore that the power would violate Article 6 of the Convention.

The policy aim of the CPR 1998 is, in part, that justice should be dispensed without delay. The CPR 1998 provide sanctions for parties who have failed to comply with time-limits imposed for carrying out steps.[401] Although Article 6(1) provides a guarantee for a hearing of the merits of the claim, it also requires that hearing to take place within a reasonable time. Where a party seeking an extension is responsible for a delay which is prejudicing the opposing party, the latter may rely on Article 6 for the proposition that the extension should not be granted. The court, or tribunal, would have to balance the competing interests, but it is not clear whether the kind of delay that would bring Article 6 into play would be the same as the kind of delay that operated under the previous rules of court. It is submitted that Article 6 will simply be a factor in considering delay, subject always to the caveat that if a public authority

---

395   (1998) 25 EHRR CD 105.
396   CPR 1998, r 1.4 and Part 26.
397   CPR 1998, r 1.4(2)(c).
398   CPR 1998, r 3.4.
399   CPR 1998, Part 24.
400   CPR 1998, r 3.3(4).
401   CPR 1998, r 3.4(2).

is responsible for the delay it may be liable for the consequences of the delay as an unlawful act.

3.17.4 The devolution legislation

Schedule 8 to the Government of Wales Act 1998 contains provisions dealing with devolution issues arising out of that Act. Schedule 10 to the Northern Ireland Act 1998 contains provisions dealing with devolution issues arising out of the Northern Ireland Act 1998. Finally, Sch 6 to the Scotland Act 1998 contains provisions dealing with devolution issues arising out of the Scotland Act 1998.

A devolution issue will involve a question whether a devolved body has acted or proposes to act within its powers (which includes not acting incompatibly with Convention rights and Community law) or has failed to comply with a duty imposed on it.

Chapter 4

COLLECTIVE RIGHTS

4.1 INTRODUCTION

Trade unions were first legalised in Britain in 1871. Their aim was to increase the power of workers by replacing individual negotiation of contracts with collective bargaining between employers and employees. For a century thereafter, trade unions grew in size and importance, so that during the 1970s 60 per cent of workers were members of trade unions and nearly 80 per cent of workers were employed on terms which had been fixed by collective bargaining.

After 1979, however, trade union membership in Great Britain fell for 18 consecutive years. At the end of 1997, there were 233 listed trade unions, with a total membership of 7.8 million workers; membership was 40 per cent lower than the peak level reached in 1979. In more recent years, between 1989 and 1998, the proportion of all employees who were union members fell from 39 per cent in 1989 to 30 per cent in 1998. The decline in membership was particularly pronounced among male employees, manual employees and those in production industries – all areas where membership has traditionally been highest. By contrast, union membership density fell less slowly among female employees, those working in part-time jobs, and non-manual employees.

In 1998, an estimated 8 million employees, or 35 per cent of all employees, were covered by collective bargaining over pay. Employees working in the public sector and larger workplaces were much more likely to say that they were covered by collective agreement. 10.1 million employees worked in organisations where trade unions were recognised.[1]

There are many reasons for the decline in trade union membership in recent years. These include: the dramatic shrinkage in heavy industry, coal mining, steel working and in the docks and shipbuilding; the internationalisation of trade and business; and changed social and political attitudes to trade unions and membership.

Importantly, also, legislative changes have affected nearly every sphere of trade union activity. During the period of Conservative Government from 1979–1997 consecutive Acts affected numerous changes: much industrial action was outlawed; the right to recognition was abolished; unions were exposed to liability in tort; the closed shop was effectively outlawed; secret postal ballots were made obligatory for industrial action, elections for members of a union's national executive and for the maintenance of political funds; individual union

---

1   Source: *Labour Market Trends, July 1999, Government Statistical Service.*

members were given the right to avoid their contractual obligations to their fellow members and the right to join any union of their choice (undermining the TUC's Bridlington Agreement) and every member was required to sign an individual consent form every three years to renew their union dues.

At the same time, however, EC law resulted in legislation being passed to require management consultation with trade unions/workers' representatives on collective redundancies, transfer of undertakings, and health and safety measures.

More recently, the Labour Government elected in 1997 has promoted a different, more even, balance between the interests of unions and employers. One of the first acts of the Labour Government was to permit employees at Government Communications Headquarters to rejoin free trade unions. European measures which have been implemented have included the Working Time Directive (Directive 93/104/EC), the European Works Council Directive (Directive 94/45/EC) and the Parental Leave Directive (Directive 94/34/EC). The national minimum wage has been introduced, along with the Employment Relations Act 1999, giving trade unions the right to demand recognition by employers when voted for by a majority of their workforce.

Most significant, for the purpose of this book, is the bringing into force of the HRA 1998. It implements, at a national level, the right of association and of peaceful assembly.

4.2   NATURE OF TRADE UNIONS

4.2.1   UK law

For the purposes of UK law, a trade union is defined by s 1 of the Trade Union and Labour Relations (Consolidation) Act 1992 (TULR(C)A 1992). In summary, a trade union is an organisation consisting wholly or mainly of workers, whose principal purposes include the regulation of relations between workers and employers. It is also an organisation consisting of constituent or affiliated organisations with the same principal purposes.

A trade union is treated by law as having a private and a public personality. At English common law, it is an unincorporated association. Nevertheless, while s 10(1) of the TULR(C)A 1992 enacts (and confirms) that a trade union is not a body corporate, s 10(2) and Part I of the TULR(C)A 1992 attribute to trade unions five characteristics of a body corporate:

(1) a trade union can make a contract;[2]
(2) a trade union can sue or be sued in its own name;[3]
(3) a trade union may be prosecuted in its collective name for any offence alleged to have been committed by it or on its behalf;[4]

---

2   TULR(C)A 1992, s 10(1)(a).
3   TULR(C)A 1992, s 10(1)(b).
4   TULR(C)A 1992, s 10(1)(c).

(4) the property of a trade union is held by trustees on trust for the union (not its members);[5]

(5) judgments, orders or awards made in proceedings brought against a trade union are enforceable against any property held on trust for it to the same extent and in the same manner as if it were a body corporate.[6]

4.2.2 Convention for the Protection of Human Rights and Fundamental Freedoms

Article 11(1) of the Convention provides that:

'Everyone has the right to freedom of peaceful assembly and to freedom of association with others, including the right to form and join trade unions for the protection of his interests.'

However, the freedom of association guaranteed is not unconditional. Article 11(2) provides that the right can be curtailed where this is:

'... necessary in a democratic society in the interests of national security or public safety, for the prevention of disorder or crime, for the protection of health or morals or for the protection of rights and freedoms of others.'

Article 11(2) goes on to exclude members of the armed forces, the police and civil service from the guaranteed right. See further **4.5.2**.

The rights guaranteed by Article 11 are linked to the rights of freedom of thought, conscience and religion under Article 9 and the right to freedom of expression under Article 10. Article 11 has its historical roots in Articles 20 and 23(4) of the Universal Declaration of Human Rights (UDHR). Article 20 of the UDHR guarantees the rights of peaceful assembly and association, while Article 23(4) is identical to Article 11(2). Articles 21 and 22 of the International Covenant on Civil and Political Rights are also similar to Article 11 of the Convention.

The jurisprudence of the ECtHR and interpretation of the Convention is informed by these and other international instruments. Both the Commission and the ECtHR, when considering trade union rights and freedoms, have taken notice of State ratifications of ILO Conventions No 87 (concerning the freedom of association and protection of the right to organise) and No 98 (concerning the application of the principles of the right to organise and to bargain collectively). The rights of trade unions to draw up their own rules, to administer their own affairs and to establish and join trade union federations are recognised in Articles 3 and 5 of ILO Convention No 87. Article 11 is generally interpreted to guarantee freedom of trade unions within these spheres. The Strasbourg organs have also taken notice of Article 6 of the European Social Charter, which affirms the voluntary nature of collective bargaining and collective agreements.

---

5   TULR(C)A 1992, s 12(1).
6   TULR(C)A 1992, s 12(2).

4.3　TRADE UNION MEMBERSHIP

Membership of trade unions, at common law, is governed by contractual rights and obligations between the members inter se. However, since statute has enacted that a trade union can make a contract and sue or be sued in its own name, these contractual rights and obligations are enforced by and against the union rather than by and against all the members. The particular rights and obligations are typically drawn up by the union members and set out in the union constitution or rule book. A member of a union is a person who has been defined as a member by the rule book. Once the member has entered into a contract of association with the union, the member has the rights which have been conferred upon him or her by its rules.

The union's rule book will usually set out conditions of entry to the union, the powers of discipline and expulsion and a right to resign. It will also normally State the name and head office of the union, set out the principal purposes of the union, describe its structure and officers, State its authority to call official industrial action, provide rules for the appointment of trustees and management of the union's property, funds, benefits, pension schemes and political fund, provide rules for elections and ballots, contain standing orders for the conduct of meetings and allow for the alteration of the rules themselves and for the dissolution of the union.

Part I of TULR(C)A 1992 sets statutory limits to the freedom of unions to contract with members in these areas. Furthermore, the union's rules must not unlawfully discriminate on the grounds of race, sex, disability or EC nationality.[7]

Most unions are obliged by statute to supply a copy of their rule book to any person on request, either free of charge or on payment of a reasonable sum.[8]

Membership of trade unions is lawful. Section 11 of the TULR(C)A 1992 enacts that a trade union is a lawful organisation. At common law, some or all trade unions would be unlawful by reason of restraint of trade; by joining, each member fettered his or her right to decide for himself or herself upon what terms the member would sell his labour.

All trade unions now have a statutory obligation to present their membership statistics to the Certification Officer of Trade Unions and Employers' Associations. The latest statistics on trade union membership are recorded and analysed annually in *Labour Market Trends*, a Government Statistical Service publication.

7　Sex Discrimination Act 1975, ss 12, 48, 49; Sex Discrimination Act 1986, s 6; Race Relations Act 1976, ss 11, 38; Disability Discrimination Act 1995, ss 13–15; EC Regulations 1612/68 and 312/76.

8　TULR(C)A 1992, s 27.

4.4 INDIVIDUAL'S RIGHT TO BE A MEMBER

4.4.1 Existing UK law

Under existing UK employment law, freedom of association exists, in the sense of a right not to be subjected to various detriments on the grounds of membership/non-membership of a trade union.

The protection guaranteed by UK law is threefold. It is unlawful for an employer to:

(1) refuse a person employment;
(2) dismiss an existing employee;
(3) victimise an employee by taking action short of dismissal against the employee,

on the grounds that the employee is, or is not, a member of a trade union, or is a union activist, or has refused to pay money to charity in lieu of union dues.

(1) Refusal of employment

It is already unlawful to refuse a person employment because that person is, or is not, a member of a trade union.[9] Employment in this context means employment under a contract of service or apprenticeship only.[10] However, ss 144 and 145 of the TULR(C)A 1992 also prohibit refusal to deal with suppliers or prospective suppliers of goods and services on trade union grounds, so self-employed persons are also protected.

A person will be taken to have been refused employment if, having sought employment with a person, that person:

– refuses or deliberately omits to entertain and process the application or enquiry;
– causes the applicant to withdraw or cease to pursue the application or enquiry;
– refuses or deliberately omits to offer the applicant employment of that description;
– makes an offer of such employment the terms of which are such as no reasonable-employer who wished to fill the post would offer and which is not accepted;
– makes an offer of such employment but withdraws it or causes the applicant not to accept it.[11]

Further, an offer of employment may be deemed a refusal of employment where the offer contains an objectionable condition and the applicant declines the offer because of the objectionable condition.[12] Employment agencies are liable in the same way as employers.[13]

---

9   TULR(C)A 1992, s 137.
10 TULR(C)A 1992, s 143.
11 TULR(C)A 1992, s 137(5).
12 TULR(C)A 1992, s 137(6).
13 TULR(C)A 1992, ss 138 and 141.

Certain employments are excluded from protection, see **4.5.1** below.

The wording of the TULR(C)A 1992 outlaws refusal of employment because of trade union membership or non-membership and not because of trade union activities. However, in *Harrison v Kent County Council*[14] the Employment Appeal Tribunal (EAT) held that s 137 did give a remedy to a person refused a job on account of his union activity. The EAT held that it was a fallacy to assume that because s137 does not mention union activities, it gives no remedy to a person refused a job on account of union activity, 'in this context a divorce of the *fact* of membership and the *incidents* of membership is illusory'. There are contrary *obiter dicta* in some of the speeches of the House of Lords in *Associated Newspapers Ltd v Wilson, Associated British Ports v Palmer*[15] but the *Harrison* case remains the only authority directly in point.

Under s 137(3) of the TULR(C)A 1992, where an advertisement for a job is published which indicates that the job is only open to union members, or non-union members, as the case may be, a person who does not satisfy the condition and who seeks and is refused the relevant job, shall be conclusively presumed to have been refused employment for that reason.

A person who has been refused employment unlawfully under s 137 has a right of complaint to an employment tribunal within three months of the date of the conduct complained of.[16] Where a tribunal finds a complaint under s 137 or s 138 well founded, it must make a declaration to that effect. It may also award compensation, which 'shall be assessed on the same basis as damages for breach of statutory duty and may include compensation for injury to feelings'.[17] It may also make a recommendation that the respondent within a specified period of time take action to obviate the effect of the unlawful discrimination upon the complainant.[18]

(2) Unfair dismissal on the grounds of union activities

It is automatically unfair to dismiss an employee because the employee is, or is not, a trade union member, or has taken part in union activities at an appropriate time.[19] It is also automatically unfair to dismiss an employee on the grounds that the employee proposes to join or leave a trade union, or to take part in the activities of an independent trade union at an appropriate time. Section 152(3) of the TULR(C)A 1992 states that if the reason for the dismissal was that the employee refused to pay money (for example to charity) in place of union dues, that is to be treated as a dismissal on the grounds of non-membership of a trade union.

References to a union include references to a branch or section of a union.[20] 'At an appropriate time' means a time outside the employee's working hours or a

---

14   [1995] ICR 434, EAT.
15   [1995] IRLR 258, [1995] ICR 406.
16   TULR(C)A 1992, s 139.
17   TULR(C)A 1992, s 140(1) and (2).
18   TULR(C)A 1992, s 140(1)(b).
19   TULR(C)A 1992, s 152.
20   TULR(C)A 1992, s 152(4).

time within working hours when the employer has agreed that the employee can take part in union activities.[21]

In redundancy situations, it is automatically unfair to select an employee for redundancy on the same union grounds.[22] It is unfair to dismiss an employee for belonging to any trade union or for belonging to a particular trade union.[23]

It is also automatically unfair to dismiss an employee because the employee will not make payments in lieu of membership dues or because the employee will not agree to corresponding deductions from pay.[24]

The two-year qualifying period[25] and the upper age limit of 65[26] do not apply to dismissals on trade union grounds.[27] Contracting out is generally forbidden, but there were exceptions in ss 197 and 110 of the ERA 1996.

Certain employments are excluded from protection, see further **4.5.1** below.

What constitutes 'activities of an independent trade union'? It has been said that these words should not be interpreted too restrictively, *Dixon and Shaw v West Ella Developments Ltd*.[28] Accordingly, an employee is protected when engaged in union-organised activities and when acting as an individual union member. Protection covers an individual consulting a union representative, or complaining to a union representative about unsafe working conditions. An official of a trade union is protected when carrying out official functions at an appropriate time.

A 'predisposition' or assumed predisposition to take part in union activities, based on past union activities in previous employment, will be an unfair reason for dismissal under s 152 of the TULR(C)A 1992.[29]

Section 238A of the TULR(C)A 1992[30] extends protection against dismissal to those taking part in lawfully organised industrial action. It will be automatically unfair to dismiss such employees in specified circumstances from 24 April 2000.

With regard to dismissal for failure to belong to a union, where the employer is forced to dismiss by threat or use of industrial action either the employer or the employee can apply to the employment tribunal to have the union joined as a party to proceedings for unfair dismissal.[31] The employment tribunal can order the trade union to pay the whole or part of any compensation awarded to the complainant.[32]

---

21   TULR(C)A 1992, s 153(2).
22   TULR(C)A 1992, s 153.
23   *Ridgway and Fairbrother v National Coal Board* [1987] IRLR 80, [1987] ICR 641, CA.
24   TULR(C)A 1992, s 152(3).
25   ERA 1996, s 108.
26   ERA 1996, s 109.
27   TULR(C)A 1992, s 154.
28   [1978] IRLR 151, [1978] ICR 856, EAT.
29   *Fitzpatrick v British Railways Board* [1991] IRLR 376, [1992] ICR 221, CA; *Port of London Authority v Payne* [1992] IRLR 447, EAT.
30   Inserted by s 15 of and Sch 5 to the Employment Relations Act 1999.
31   TULR(C)A 1992, s 160(1).
32   TULR(C)A 1992, s 160(3).

Where an employee is dismissed on union grounds, the employee may apply to the employment tribunal for interim relief.[33] This must be done within seven days of the effective date of termination.[34] Otherwise, the time-limit for presenting a complaint to the employment tribunal arising out of dismissal on union grounds, is the normal three-month time-limit. If the applicant seeks compensation, the basic award is subject to a statutory minimum.[35] If the employee seeks reinstatement or re-engagement but is not reinstated or reengaged, the employee can seek an additional award.[36]

(3) Victimisation on the grounds of union activities
Section 146(1) of the TULR(C)A 1992 provides:

> '(1) An employee has the right not to have action short of dismissal taken against him as an individual by his employer for the purpose of –
>
> (a)   preventing or deterring him from being or seeking to become a member of an independent trade union, or penalising him for doing so,
>
> (b)   preventing or deterring him from taking part in the activities of an independent trade union at an appropriate time, or penalising him for doing so, or
>
> (c)   compelling him to be or become a member of any trade union or of a particular trade union or of one of a number of particular trade unions.'

On the other hand, it is permissible for an employer to offer inducements to employees who agree to switch from a system of collective bargaining to individual contracts, and to withhold such benefits to those who decline such a change.[37]

It should be noted that the purpose of the employer's action is relevant under s 146, whereas it is not under the provisions relating to unfair dismissal for union activities.

Some employments are excluded from protection, see **4.5.1** below.

If an employee is subjected to detrimental treatment under s 146 he may complain to an employment tribunal within three months of the date of the (last) act of victimisation. If the tribunal finds the complaint well-founded, it must make a declaration to that effect and may award compensation.[38] The compensation may include pecuniary loss and injury to reputation and feelings.[39] Where the employee is victimised by the employer by reason of the threat of industrial action, the employer cannot rely on the industrial pressure to defend the employee's complaint. Nevertheless, the employer can apply to have the union joined as a party to the proceedings and the employment

---

33   TULR(C)A 1992, s 161.
34   TULR(C)A 1992, s 161(2).
35   TULR(C)A 1992, s 156.
36   ERA 1996, s 117, as amended.
37   TULR(C)A 1992, s 148(3)–(5).
38   TULR(C)A 1992, s 149.
39   *Cleveland Ambulance NHS Trust v Blane* [1997] IRLR 332, EAT.

tribunal can again order the trade union to pay the whole or part of any compensation awarded to the complainant.[40]

4.4.2 Convention for the Protection of Human Rights and Fundamental Freedoms

The right of the individual to belong to a trade union under the Convention is contained in Article 11. Article 11(1) provides that:

'Everyone has the right to freedom of peaceful assembly and to freedom of association with others, including the right to form and join trade unions for the protection of his interests.'

There are a number of limitations to this right. Article 11(2) provides that the right can be curtailed where:

'necessary in a democratic society in the interests of national security or public safety, for the prevention of disorder or crime, for the protection of health or morals or for the protection of rights and freedoms of others.'

The Article also excludes members of the armed forces, the police and civil service from the guaranteed right. See further **4.5.2** below.

The ECtHR has also held that professional associations, established by law and requiring membership of all practising professionals, are not trade unions or 'associations' within the meaning of Article 11(1). See, for example, *Le Compte, Van Leuven and De Meyer v Belgium*[41] and *A v Spain*.[42] Thus, the legal requirement that all medical doctors be members of the British Medical Association does not offend against Article 11(1). Nevertheless, in accordance with the general right to trade union membership, the ECtHR in *Le Compte* insisted that a State requirement for professionals to belong to professional associations does not abrogate the private right of those professionals to establish other associations for the promotion of their interests.

The right to freedom of association is further limited in that the Convention does not create rights which are enforceable by individuals *inter se*. The remedy for infringement of a Convention right is a complaint by an individual against the State (as legislator or employer), that the State has failed to protect the Convention right. Article 11, therefore, guarantees general legislative protection against discrimination on the grounds of trade union membership. States must allow individuals to form such trade unions as they please. States are not allowed, for example, to establish single trade unions with compulsory membership.

As in existing British law, there is a corresponding right for employees not to belong to a trade union, or other association. It is true that the wording of the Convention states a freedom of association, but not a freedom *not* to associate.

---

40   TULR(C)A 1992, s 150.
41   (1982) 4 EHRR 1.
42   Application No 13750/88, (1990) 66 DR 188.

The ECtHR, however, has declared that the Convention has a life of its own and does guarantee a limited freedom not to associate.[43]

What, then, is the content of the right to trade union membership? The meaning of 'freedom of association' for trade union members, was considered by the Commission in its decision on *X v Ireland*.[44] The Commission, referring to ILO Convention No 87, held that freedom of association concerns an unobstructed membership. It considered that intimidation of an employee to make the employee relinquish his or her function within a trade union might therefore be an encroachment on that freedom. The Convention therefore, in a less detailed way than existing UK law, contains a right not to be victimised on the grounds of union activities. By analogy and extension, the Convention also contains rights not to be dismissed or refused employment solely for belonging to a trade union.

The scope of the activities and aims of trade unions guaranteed by the Convention was considered by the ECtHR in *Union of Belgian Police*.[45] The ECtHR looked at the words 'for the protection of his interests' in Article 11 and said:

> 'These words, clearly denoting purpose, show that the Convention safeguards freedom to protect the occupational interests of trade union members by trade union action, the conduct and development of which the State must both permit and make possible ... What the Convention requires is that under national law trade unions should be enabled, in conditions not at variance with Article 11, to strive for the protection of their members' interests.'

However, Article 11 is not designed to provide detailed and comprehensive trade union law, and the ECtHR has not been prepared to rewrite national trade union law on the limited basis of Article 11.

In *Swedish Engine Drivers Union v Sweden*,[46] the ECtHR noted that Article 11 is phrased in very general terms and 'does not secure any particular treatment of trade unions or their members'. The complaint of the Swedish Engine Drivers Union was that the body which negotiated conditions of service for State employees refused to negotiate with the applicant union. The ECtHR decided that, since the union could engage in other types of activities on behalf of its members, Article 11 was not breached. While, in the *Swedish Engine Drivers* case, the ECtHR acknowledged that Article 11 demanded that States protected rights that are 'indispensable for the effective enjoyment of trade union freedom', the ECtHR has taken a very restrictive view of what these 'indispensable' rights were. In that case and in *Schmidt and Dahlstrom*[47] the ECtHR indicated that Article 11 does not confer the right to trade union recognition nor to have collective agreements concluded with a particular trade union, nor

---

43   See *Sigurjonsson v Iceland* (1993) Series A No 264, 16 EHRR 462 (Judgment 30 June 1993) ECtHR.
44   Application No 4125/69, (1971) 14 YB 198 at 222.
45   Series A No 19, (1980) 1 EHRR 578 (Judgment 17 October 1975) ECtHR.
46   Series A No 20, (1980) 1 EHRR 617 (Judgment 6 February 1976) ECtHR at para 20 of its judgment.
47   Series A No 21, (1980) 1 EHRR 632 (Judgment 6 February 1976) ECtHR.

the right to strike. Member States have a free choice of means for securing trade union interests.

4.4.3 Effect of the Human Rights Act 1998

While s 6 of the HRA 1998 obliges the courts to develop the common law in a way which is compatible with the Convention, it is unlikely that the incorporation of Article 11 in English employment law will provide much more detailed protection of the right to trade union membership than already exists for employees under the TULR(C)A 1992 and the ERA 1996.

As with the ECtHR, this has been the approach of the British courts in interpreting Article 11 before the incorporation of the Convention into British law. In *UKAPE v ACAS*,[48] Lord Scarman, agreeing with Lord Denning's observations in the same case in the Court of Appeal said:[49]

> 'I agree with Lord Denning MR that article 11 of the convention and the common law recognise and protect the right of association, which in the present context includes the right to join a trade union. But it does not follow from the existence of the right that every trade union which can show it has members employed by a particular company or in a particular industry has the right of recognition for the purposes of collective bargaining. I would be surprised if either the convention or the common law could be interpreted as compelling so chaotic a conclusion. If the common law is to be so understood (and I do not accept that it is), Parliament has averted the mischief by statute. And, if it be a possible interpretation of the European Convention, I shall not adopt it unless and until the European Court of Human Rights declares that it is correct.'

Of course, when bringing a claim to an employment tribunal, an employee of a public authority could, in his or her ET1 form, add breach of Article 11 as a cause of action to other claims for dismissal/victimisation/refusal of employment brought on the same facts. Article 11 binds the State as employer, whether its relations with its employees are governed by public or private law.[50]

It is unlikely that there will be separate recovery of compensation for breach of Article 11. In deciding whether to make an award of compensation, the employment tribunal will have to have regard to the restrictive principles applied by the ECtHR itself under Article 41, s 8(4) of the HRA 1998. In any event, s 8(3) of the HRA 1998 provides that no award of compensation will be made unless it is 'necessary in order to afford just satisfaction to the person in whose favour it is made'. There may be a few situations in which employment tribunals will consider that the detailed provisions for compensation set out in the relevant sections of TULR(C)A 1992 (see **4.4.1** above) do not provide an adequate monetary remedy for an aggrieved employee. See further, 'Remedies' at **6.4**, and see **6.17.2**, below.

The HRA 1998 may also extend protection against victimisation to a greater class of workers than is already covered by the TULR(C)A 1992 and the ERA 1996.

---

48   [1980] ICR 201, HL.
49   [1980] ICR 201, HL at p 214F–H.
50   *Swedish Engine Drivers' Union v Sweden* (1979–80) 1 EHRR 617 at 627, para 37.

Self-employed persons are already protected from refusal to deal with them as suppliers of goods and services on trade union grounds by ss 144 and 145 of the TULR(C)A 1992. However, there is no equivalent protection against victimisation. Protection from victimisation on trade union grounds under s 146 extends only to an 'employee', defined in s 295 of the TULR(C)A 1992 as 'an individual who has entered into or works under . . . a contract of employment'. Nevertheless, the HRA 1998 provides that it is unlawful for a public authority to act in a way which is incompatible with a Convention right.

Thus, if the public authority were to act in a way which obstructed or penalised a self-employed person's trade union membership, that person could have a free-standing action in the county court for breach of Convention rights.[51] In determining what was/was not a breach of Article 11 in this context, it is likely that the county court would be guided by the acts prohibited in s 146(1) of the TULR(C)A 1992.

4.5   EXCEPTIONS TO THE RIGHT TO MEMBERSHIP

4.5.1   Existing UK law

Protection from refusal of employment on the grounds of trade union membership does not extend to persons seeking employment:

–   in the police service;[52]
–   in the armed services;[53]
–   in Crown employment where national security needs to be safeguarded;[54]
–   overseas, or as certain types of fisherman and mariner.[55]

Protection from unfair dismissal and 'action short of dismissal' on the grounds of union activities does not extend to employment in the police force;[56] overseas employment which began before 25 October 1999;[57] Crown employment where national security needs to be safeguarded;[58] or as certain types of fisherman and mariner.[59]

Regarding national security, protection is excluded under the ERA 1996 and TULR(C)A 1992 if there is in force a 'certificate issued by or on behalf of a Minister of the Crown certifying that employment of a particular description specified in the certificate, or the employment, of a particular person . . . is . . . required to be excepted' from those provisions 'for the purpose of safeguarding national security'.[60] The existence of such a certificate is conclusive

51   See *X v Ireland* (1971) 14 YB 198 at 222.
52   TULR(C)A 1992, s 280.
53   TULR(C)A 1992, s 274(1).
54   TULR(C)A 1992, ss 273 and 275.
55   TULR(C)A 1992, ss 284, 285(1), (2).
56   ERA 1996, s 200; TULR(C)A 1992, s 280.
57   ERA 1996, s 196 (repealed by ERA 1999, s 32(3)); TULR(C)A 1992, s 285(1).
58   ERA 1996, s 193; TULR(C)A 1992, ss 273 and 275.
59   ERA 1996, ss 196(2), 199; TULR(C)A 1992, ss 284, 285(2).
60   TULR(C)A 1992, s 275 and ERA 1996, s 193.

proof of exemption of the employment from the protection of the relevant Acts and the courts do not have any power under these Acts to scrutinise the validity of the certificate.

Contracting out

Any provision in an agreement (whether a contract of employment or not) which purports to preclude a person from bringing proceedings before an employment tribunal under the provisions of the TULR(C)A 1992 is void.[61] Any provision in an agreement which seeks to exclude or limit the scope of any provision of the TULR(C)A 1992 is similarly void.

Therefore, there can be no contracting out of the right to complain to an employment tribunal of refusal of access to employment on the ground of trade union membership or of 'action short of dismissal'.

However, a complaint of unfair dismissal is brought under the provision of the ERA 1996. Contracting out is generally forbidden thereunder.[62] Previously, an individual who was employed under a fixed term of at least one year could, nevertheless, agree in writing to exclude the right to complain of unfair dismissal on non-renewal of the fixed term. A claim for unfair dismissal was then excluded if the dismissal consisted of the expiry of that term without it being renewed.[63] This provision was repealed by s 18 of the Employment Relations Act 1999, which came into force on 25 October 1999.

4.5.2 Convention for the Protection of Human Rights and Fundamental Freedoms

By Article 11(2) of the Convention it is provided:

> 'No restrictions shall be placed on the exercise of these rights other than such as are prescribed by law and are necessary in a democratic society in the interests of national security or public safety, for the prevention of disorder or crime, for the protection of health or morals or for the protection of rights and freedoms of others. This article shall not prevent the imposition of lawful restrictions on these rights by members of the armed forces, of the police or of the administration of the State.'

It is well settled that a government's activities as employer are susceptible to scrutiny under Article 11.[64]

The Commission has considered restrictions on the exercise of trade union rights in English law in *Council of Civil Service Unions v UK*.[65] The British Government had ceased to allow civil servants working at GCHQ telecommunications interception station to belong at a trade union. The Commission ruled

---

61   TULR(C)A 1992, s 288.
62   ERA 1996, s 203.
63   ERA 1996, s 197(1).
64   *Schmidt and Dahlstrom v Sweden* (1976) 1 EHRR 632.
65   Application No 11603/85, (1987) 50 DR 28.

that the petition was inadmissible on the grounds that workers at GCHQ were members of the administration of the State and the restriction on union membership was lawful under the second sentence of Article 11(2).

The Commission considered that to be 'lawful' any restrictions permitted by Article 11(2) had to be imposed in accordance with national law and could not be arbitrary. With regard to arbitrariness, the Commission decided that the restriction on membership at GCHQ was not arbitrary, accepting the UK Government's assessment (which was strongly contested by the unions) that GCHQ was vulnerable to industrial action at any moment and the guarantees offered by unions against such action were not adequate.

'Restrictions' were considered by the Commission as encompassing a complete ban on the exercise of the rights in Article 11.

The Commission has been prepared to scrutinise whether employees are indeed 'members of the administration of the State'. In *Vogt v Germany*,[66] the Commission said that German school teachers were not members of the administration of the State. The ECtHR in *Vogt v Germany*[67] said that the same part of Article 11(2) 'should be interpreted narrowly in the light of the post held by the official concerned', but did not decide the point. On the substantive issue of freedom of expression, the ECtHR considered that the State could impose a duty of discretion on civil servants, but that the right of freedom of expression still applied to them. The State would nevertheless have to establish that any interference with the right was, indeed, prescribed by law, made in pursuance of a legitimate aim, and 'necessary in a democratic society'.

4.5.3   Impact of the Human Rights Act 1998

As the ECtHR has done in *Vogt v Germany*, domestic courts should examine restrictions on the rights of employees to determine whether such employees are, indeed, 'members ... of the administration of the State'. If they are not, restrictions authorised by Article 11(2) will not be permitted to apply to their employment.

Clearly, the Commission decision in *Council of Civil Service Unions v UK*[68] does not indicate that Article 11 offers significant additional protection to employees who are 'members ... of the administration of the State'. At most, the Commission's view was that Article 11 allows some limited examination of the reasons for restrictions on the rights to membership – so that these are not imposed 'arbitrarily'. This goes slightly further than existing English law, which considers that the existence of a certificate from a relevant Minister is conclusive of the exclusion of trade union membership rights.

In this context, however, it is salient to note that national courts, considering similar restrictions, will not be able to apply the doctrine of 'margin of appreciation'.[69] A supra-national court must permit some difference of

---

66   1993 COM Rep at para 88.
67   (1996) 21 EHRR 205.
68   (1987) Application No 11603/85, (1987) 50 DR 28.
69   See *R v Director of Public Prosecutions, ex parte Kebilene* [1999] 3 WLR 972 and **2.6.4**.

approach among differing States. National courts, by contrast, are seized of claims arising only in their own jurisdiction. They must, therefore, decide whether the relevant interference is 'proportionate'. Proportionality requires that the interference by the State corresponds to a pressing social need and is proportionate to the legitimate aim pursued.[70] EC law will be informative in this area.

Contracting out

Convention rights can be waived, but only if done unequivocally.[71] If an employee has signed a contract containing terms excluding Convention rights – for example, a confidentiality clause limiting freedom of speech – the signing of the contract alone is not enough to exclude the rights.[72] The employee must have been made specifically aware of the waiver of the Convention rights. Prior to the repeal of ss 197(1) and (2) of the ERA 1996, it was normal practice for employees to sign separate waivers in respect of exclusion of rights to claim unfair dismissal.

Good practice would dictate that separate waivers should be signed in respect of Convention rights.

4.6 RIGHTS TO NON-MEMBERSHIP

4.6.1 Existing UK law

The rights described in **4.4.1** apply equally to non-union members. Hence a worker has the right not to be refused employment, not to be unfairly dismissed and not to be subjected to victimisation on the ground that he or she is not a member of an independent trade union.[73]

These sections effectively outlaw the closed shop in English law – both the pre-entry closed shop, in which a worker cannot apply for a job unless he or she is a union member, and the post-entry closed shop, in which a worker would be required to join a union within a stated period after having taken up the job.

4.6.2 Convention for the Protection of Human Rights and Fundamental Freedoms

Article 11 of the Convention mirrors Article 23(4) of the Universal Declaration on Human Rights and Fundamental Freedoms, which guarantees the right to form and join trade unions.

However, Article 23(2) of the Universal Declaration, which provides that 'No one may be compelled to an association', has no corresponding provision in the Convention.

---

70   *Olson v Sweden* (1988) Series A No 130.
71   *Deweer v Belgium* (1980) Series A No 35, 2 EHRR 439, para 49; *Pfeiffer and Plankl v Austria* (1992) Series A No 227, 14 EHRR 692 at para 37.
72   See *Rommelfanger v FRG* (1989) 62 DR 151.
73   TULR(C)A 1992, ss 137, 138, 146 and 152.

Nevertheless, 'negative freedom of association' – the right not to belong – has been said by the Commission to be a necessary corollary of the explicit right to belong in Article 11(1). In *X v Belgium*,[74] the Commission stated: 'the very concept of freedom of association with others also implies freedom not to associate with others or not to join unions'.

As mentioned above, in *Sigurjonsson v Iceland*[75] the ECtHR reasoned that if a person is to be free to join, then it must follow that he or she cannot be compelled to join a trade union under Article 11.

The closed shop
The question of an individual's right to non-membership arises most obviously in the context of the closed shop.

In the unlikely event that any future UK government were minded to abolish British anti-closed shop legislation, the ECtHR has held some previous British post-entry closed shop arrangements to be in breach of Article 11 .

Young, James and Webster v UK[76] concerned an agreement between British Rail and the NUR, ASLEF and TSSA railway unions under which British Rail could fairly dismiss any employee who refused to join a union, unless the tenets of the employee's religion prohibited trade union membership.

Both the Commission and the ECtHR avoided making a blanket pronouncement on the compatibility of the closed shop system with Article 11. Six of the 18 judges of the ECtHR in *Young, James and Webster* considered that a freedom to join a trade union implied a corresponding freedom not to have to join. Nine others simply said that a freedom to join implied at least a limited freedom not to have to join. Three of the judges, in dissenting opinions, considered that, while Article 11 guaranteed freedom to join a trade union, 'negative freedom of association' had been deliberately excluded from the Convention, and was not logically required by it. As the applicants were not prevented from joining a trade union, they did not come within the Convention's protection.

The majority of the ECtHR, however, held that the Article had been violated on the facts of the case. The particular closed shop did strike at the rights guaranteed under Article 11, as compulsory membership had been introduced after the workers were already into employment and these workers had strong objections to union membership. Furthermore, the consequence of not joining a union was a very harsh one, that is, dismissal. In practice, also, the applicants had a very limited number of unions from which to choose membership and could not form their own trade union.

> 'Assuming that Article 11 does not guarantee the negative aspect of that freedom on the same footing as the positive aspect, compulsion to join a particular trade union may not always be contrary to the convention.

---

74   Application No 4072/69, (1970) 13 YB 708 at 718.
75   (1993) Series A No 264 16 EHRR 462, ECtHR (Judgment 30 June 1993).
76   [1981] IRLR 408.

However, a threat of dismissal involving loss of likelihood is a most serious form of compulsion and, in the present instance, it was directed against the persons engaged by British Rail before the introduction of any obligation to join a particular trade union. In the court's opinion, such a form of compulsion, in the circumstances of the case, strikes at the very substance of the freedom guaranteed by article 11. For this reason alone there has been an interference with that freedom as regards each of the three applicants.'[77]

The ECtHR adopted a similar approach to the case of *Sigurjonsson v Iceland*.[78] In that case, the ECtHR found that a requirement in law that a taxi licence holder be a member of an association of taxi drivers was in violation of Article 11. The ECtHR was most troubled by the fact that the applicant could not earn a living as a taxi driver if he were not a member of the association. Furthermore, the applicant had at all times objected to becoming an association member and had held a licence at a time when membership was not required. His objections were based on strongly held beliefs.

The ECtHR rejected the government's justification argument under Article 11(2). It found the reasons put forward justifying compulsory membership, namely that the arrangement facilitated administration of the taxi service in the public interest, were 'relevant but not sufficient'. The government could demonstrate expediency but not pressing social need.[79]

Young, James and Webster and *Sigurjonsson* must be contrasted with *Sibson v UK*.[80] The employee, S, had been a member of the Transport and General Workers Union (TGWU). Following allegations as to his good faith relating to the handling of union funds, he resigned from the TGWU and joined another union. He was shunned by some of his fellow employees and the employees voted for a closed shop agreement. They threatened strike action if S were not employed elsewhere or did not rejoin the TGWU. The employer claimed that it was contractually entitled to move S to another depot. S refused and resigned, claiming he had been constructively dismissed. In the Court of Appeal, it was decided that the employer was entitled to transfer S by virtue of the terms of his employment contract. Thus, he had not been constructively dismissed. Before the ECtHR, S argued that the fact that he had been required either to rejoin the TGWU or move to another depot was contrary to his rights under Article 11. He claimed that UK law provided no meaningful remedy for a person like himself.

The ECtHR distinguished S's case from its previous decision on UK closed shops in *Young, James & Webster*. S did not object to rejoining the TGWU because of personal convictions regarding trade union membership – he would have rejoined if he had received an apology. Likewise, he was not faced with the prospect of dismissal – his employer offered him a transfer which was within the terms of his contract of employment. Consequently, S was 'not subjected to a form of treatment striking at the very substance of the freedom of association guaranteed by Article 11'.

---

77 *Young, James and Webster v UK* [1981] IRLR 408, p 417 at paras 85–87.
78 Series A No 264 at paras 36, 37 (1993).
79 Series A No 264 at para 41 (1993).
80 Series A No 258–A (1993).

4.6.3   Impact of the Human Rights Act 1998

In summary, closed shops are likely to be incompatible with the Convention, and therefore with the HRA 1998 where:

(1) the employee objects to union membership on principle (freedom of conscience is separately guaranteed by Article 9 of the Convention);

(2) the employee faces losing his or her livelihood if he or she does not join the relevant union.

Again, any HRA 1998 claim based on Article 11, arising out of a closed shop arrangement, additional to an application to an employment tribunal under TULR(C)A 1992, would be available only to an employee of a public authority. Again, also, it is unlikely that there will be any separate recovery of compensation for breach of Article 11. See **4.4.3**, above, and further, 'Remedies' at **6.4**, and **6.17.2** below.

As stated in **4.4.3**, the HRA 1998 may, additionally, extend protection against victimisation to a greater class of workers than is already covered by the TULR(C)A 1992 and the ERA 1996. By the same reasoning, if the public authority were to act in a way which obstructed or penalised a self-employed person's *lack of* trade union membership, that person could have a free-standing action in the county court for breach of Convention rights.

Further, as noted above, the definition of association does not extend to a professional organisation established by the government and governed by public law. In general, these professional organisations are established not only to protect the interests of their members but also related public interests. In *Le Compte, Van Leuven and De Meyere v Belgium*,[81] the ECtHR decided that compulsion to register with a professional institution called the 'Ordre des médicins' did not violate rights under Article 11. The 'Ordre' was a public law institution, set up by legislation to take measures in the public interest. Furthermore, and conclusively, although doctors were required to join the 'Ordre', there was nothing to prevent them setting up their own professional organisations. Several of these did, in fact, exist. The right to non-membership of a trade union under Article 11, therefore, did not include a right not to belong to such a professional body. The Commission has also upheld the principle of compulsory membership in various other organisations, such as university student organisations in Sweden, and Veterinary Surgeons' Council in Germany.

Domestic courts would apply the same reasoning. The advent of the HRA 1998 will not, therefore, allow British doctors, for example, to claim a right not to belong to the British Medical Association.

---

81   Series A No 43 at paras 64–65 (1981).

4.7 RIGHT TO ADMISSION AND REFUSAL OF ADMISSION

4.7.1 Existing UK law

An individual's right to admission to a trade union is, under present UK law, governed primarily by statute. Section 174 of the TULR(C)A 1992 provides that an individual has the right not to be excluded or expelled from membership of a trade union save on limited specified grounds. These are as follows.

(1) The applicant does not satisfy, or no longer satisfies an enforceable membership requirement contained in the rules of the union.[82] The rules may require the member to practise a particular trade to be eligible to join, or may require the member to have achieved a particular rank or expertise within that trade or profession.[83]

(2) The applicant does not qualify for membership of a local union because the applicant does not work in the area of that union.

(3) The union is a union of employees of one particular employer or group of employers (a staff association) and the applicant is not employed by that employer or those employers.[84] In this context, s 177(1)(c) provides, 'employment' includes 'any relationship whereby an individual personally does work or performs services for another person'.

(4) The applicant's exclusion or expulsion is attributable entirely to his own conduct.[85] Certain types of conduct are not permissible reasons for refusal of membership on this ground. Section 174(4) states that these excluded reasons are:
   (a) being or having been: a member of another trade union; employed by a particular employer or at a particular place; a member of a political party;
   (b) conduct for which a member may not be disciplined by a trade union under s 65 of the TULR(C)A 1992 (failing to participate in industrial action, taking legal action against the union etc).

An individual who claims that he or she has been excluded or expelled from a trade union in contravention of s 174 may complain to an employment tribunal.[86] The complaint must be presented within six months beginning with the date of exclusion or expulsion.[87] If the complaint is upheld, the tribunal must make a declaration to that effect.[88] If the trade union then permits the applicant to become a member, the applicant can return to the employment tribunal and seek compensation.[89] If the trade union continues to refuse

---

82   TULR(C)A 1992, s 174(2)(a).
83   TULR(C)A 1992, s 174(3).
84   TULR(C)A 1992, s 174(2)(c).
85   TULR(C)A 1992, s 174(2)(d).
86   TULR(C)A 1992, s 174(5).
87   TULR(C)A 1992, s 175(1).
88   TULR(C)A 1992, s 176(1).
89   TULR(C)A 1992, s 176(2).

admission to the applicant, in spite of the tribunal's declaration, the applicant must seek compensation from the EAT.

4.7.2   Convention for the Protection of Human Rights and Fundamental Freedoms

Under the Convention, an association has no general obligation to admit or continue the membership of an individual.[90]

Nevertheless, in *Cheall*, the Commission made the point that the right of a trade union to choose its members is not absolute. Matters of admission to membership and expulsion are for union rules and there is no general right of an individual not to be admitted nor to be expelled, but for the right to join a union to be effective, the State must protect the individual against any abuse of a dominant position by trade unions.

Such abuse might occur, for example, where exclusion or expulsions were not wholly in accordance with union rules or where the results were wholly arbitrary or where the consequences of expulsion or exclusion resulted in exceptional hardship such as job loss because of a closed shop.

4.7.3   Impact of the Human Rights Act 1998

As a result of *Cheall v UK*,[91] where a union expelled or refused to admit a member, and there were any of the following features present:

(1)   the expulsion/non-admission was not in accordance with union rules;
(2)   the expulsion/non-admission was arbitrary;
(3)   the consequence of expulsion or exclusion were that the member lost his or her employment or otherwise suffered exceptional hardship,

the expulsion could offend against Convention standards.

The member would not, however, have a free-standing cause of action under the HRA 1998 against the trade union. In employment tribunal proceedings, the expelled member might argue on the facts of the particular case, for a broad interpretation of ss 64–67 and ss 174–178 of the TULR(C)A 1992. The member might argue that expulsion where any of the *Cheall* features were present would be in breach of the HRA 1998, even if it did not offend against the strict wording of the sections. For example, a member might argue that, although the trade union could establish one of the specified grounds in s 174 of the TULR(C)A 1992, other members had not been expelled in the same circumstances. The expulsion was thus arbitrary and not in accordance with a human rights construction of TULR(C)A 1992.

4.7.4   Refusal of membership and the right not to associate

From an entirely different perspective it might be argued that the provisions of the TULR(C)A 1992 dealing with refusal of admission/expulsion from a trade

---

90   *Cheall v UK* Application No 10550/83, (1986) 8 EHRR 74.
91   Application No 10550/83, (1986) 8 EHRR 74.

union infringe the right of the majority of members of a trade union not to associate with a particular member. It could be argued before an employment tribunal that the grounds in ss 64–67 and ss 174–178 of the TULR(C)A 1992, upon which the majority's right not to associate are overridden, are too broad. Those sections of the TULR(C)A 1992 should be interpreted narrowly, so as to be limited to grounds where the features set out in *Cheall*[92] (see **4.7.3**) were, in fact, present.

4.8 DISCIPLINE AND EXPULSION

4.8.1 Existing UK law

As stated in **4.7.1**, an individual's right not to be excluded or expelled from a trade union is governed by s 174 of the TULR(C)A 1992.

General powers of discipline are governed by the union's rule book. A power to discipline or expel must be expressly set out in the union's rules as courts will not imply such powers, save in exceptional circumstances.[93]

Unions are required to act according to the rules of natural justice. Thus, a member facing discipline has the right to be heard by an unbiased tribunal,[94] the right to be given notice of any charges of misconduct made against him or her,[95] and the right to answer such charges at a fair hearing.[96] Unions are not, however, susceptible to judicial review, being private rather than public bodies. Rather, the rules of natural justice are implied into their contract of association.

While union discipline is governed by the union rules, s 63 of the TULR(C)A 1992 gives a statutory right not to be denied access to the courts, with certain qualifications to that right.

An individual also has the right not to be 'unjustifiably disciplined' under s 64 of the TULR(C)A 1992. 'Discipline' is widely defined in s 64(2), as a determination that a member be expelled, or should pay a sum to the union, or a determination that a sum tendered in respect of an obligation to pay subscriptions or other sums to the union be treated as unpaid, or a determination that the member be deprived of some or all benefits, or another union is encouraged not to accept the individual into membership, or a determination that the member 'should be subjected to some other detriment'.

---

92   *Cheall v UK* Application No 10550/83, (1986) 8 EHRR 74; see **4.7.3**.
93   *Dawkins v Antrobus* (1881) 17 ChD 615, CA.
94   *Taylor v National Union of Seamen* [1967] 1 All ER 767.
95   *Annamunthodo v Oilfield Workers' Trade Union* [1961] AC 945, [1961] 3 All ER 621, PC.
96   *Burn v National Amalgamated Labourers' Union* [1920] 2 Ch 364.

4.8.2　Convention for the Protection of Human Rights and Fundamental Freedoms

The rights of trade unions to draw up their own rules, to administer their own affairs and to establish and join trade union federations are recognised in Articles 3 and 5 of ILO Convention No 87. Article 11 is generally interpreted to guarantee freedom of trade unions within these spheres.

As noted above at **4.7.2**, the Commission considered the rights of trade unions to draw up their own rules and to administer their own affairs in *Cheall v UK*.[97] In general, 'trade union decisions in these domains must not be subject to restrictions and control by the State ... [and] As a corollary, such decisions must be regarded as private activity for which, in principle, the State cannot be responsible under the Convention'. The conditions in which the State might need to step into trade union matters, where, for example, a trade union had acted in abuse of its position, or arbitrarily, are considered at **4.7.2**.

4.8.3　Impact of the Human Rights Act 1998

As with refusal of membership/expulsion, the member would not, however, have a free-standing cause of action under the HRA 1998 against the trade union where it had acted arbitrarily. The remedy would be complaint against the State. Alternatively, the member or the trade union could argue for broad or narrow interpretations of ss 64–67 of the TULR(C)A 1992, to prohibit or allow disciplinary action where any of the features listed in *Cheall*[98] were present.[99]

4.9　ROLE OF THE STATE REGARDING MEMBERSHIP RIGHTS

Under existing law, as a signatory to the Convention, the UK Government is bound to give effect to the Convention in implementing legislation. Under the HRA 1998, of course, the UK Government is specifically bound to give effect to the HRA 1998 and courts, when interpreting that legislation, must do so as to give effect to Convention rights.

The ECtHR has addressed the duties of States regarding employment legislation. In the Commission's report on the *Schmidt and Dahlstrom* case,[100] it said,

> 'It follows that freedom of association and the right to form and join trade unions are concepts which apply also in the relationship between trade unions and employers. In other words, the State might be bound to suppress certain measures taken by employers against unions and their members.'

97　Application No 10550/83, (1986) 8 EHRR 74.
98　*Cheall v UK* Application No 10550/83, (1985) 8 EHRR 74.
99　See further, **4.7.3**.
100　*Schmidt and Dahlstrom v Sweden* Series A No 21 at para 33 (1976). See further, **4.7.3**.

In *Young, James and Webster*,[101] the Court held that the British Government could be liable for the violation of Article 11 since it was the domestic law in force at the relevant time which made lawful the treatment of which the applicants complained.

4.10 RECOGNITION AND BARGAINING

4.10.1 Introduction

As stated above, in 1998, 10.1 million employees worked in organisations where trade unions were recognised. Overall, the number of employees working in such organisations fell by 340,000 since the category was first included in the Labour Force Survey in 1993, a reduction of 4.5 per cent in the period. Of the 10.1 million employees in workplaces with union recognition, almost 8 million were covered by collective bargaining; this equates to 35 per cent of all employees. In the private sector, only 7 per cent of companies with fewer than 25 employees use collective bargaining for wage negotiation, compared with 31 per cent of establishments with more than 25 employees. The difference in establishment size has a much less dramatic impact on the public sector, where 61 per cent of small workplaces and 78 per cent of larger ones are covered by collective bargaining.

4.10.2 Existing UK law

Under Sch 1, Part I to the TULR(C)A 1992, an independent trade union, or trade unions, which are unable to agree terms for their recognition with a relevant employer are able to make an application to the Central Arbitration Committee (CAC) for an order that it be recognised. After a ballot of the workforce is held and the ballot shows that a majority of those voting and 40 per cent of the workforce support trade union recognition, the CAC must then declare recognition. Firms with fewer than 20 employees are excluded from the scheme.

There is a specific procedure for determining the collective bargaining structures if a union has voluntary recognition from an employer but the method of bargaining is not agreed or honoured. Again, the procedure applies only to employers with at least 21 employees.

Once a union is recognised, statute confers the following rights upon it: the right for its members and officials to time off work for union activities; the right to information from the employer for the purpose of collective bargaining; rights to consultation on collective redundancies;[102] rights to information and consultation on transfer of undertakings;[103] rights to information and consul-

---

101   Series A No 44 at para 52 (1981), [1981] IRLR 408.
102   TULR(C)A 1992, ss 168, 181 and 188, respectively.
103   SI 1981/1794.

tation under the Health and Safety at Work etc Act 1974[104] and rights to information and consultation on occupational pension schemes.[105]

4.10.3   Convention for the Protection of Human Rights and Fundamental Freedoms

In terms of the content of a right to form and join trade unions, the Strasbourg organs have adopted a rather restrictive, literal approach. So long as trade unions may be formed and their memberships recognised, States conform with the requirements of Article 11. Neither the Commission nor the ECtHR have accepted arguments seeking to promote the effectiveness of trade unions in protecting their members' interests. Trade unions may themselves sometimes count as victims in the context of the violations of Article 11.[106]

The extent to which Article 11 obliges States to engage with trade unions was considered in *National Union of Belgian Police v Belgium.*[107] The union complained that the Belgian Government had refused to recognise it as a representative union, when only such unions were recognised for collective bargaining purposes. The ECtHR rejected the argument that the right to be consulted was a necessary condition of effective trade union activity. The ECtHR did decide, however, that the words in the Article, 'for the protection of his interests', did require that trade unions have a right to be heard on matters of union concern. The ECtHR unanimously decided that there had been no breach of the Convention in that case. Although the National Union of Belgian Police had no right to be consulted, its freedom to make representation to the government and to present claims were sufficient manifestations of the right to be heard.

Similar arguments were considered in *Swedish Engine Drivers' Union v Sweden.*[108] Again, the ECtHR concluded that Article 11 did not require a State to enter into collective agreements with unions, but repeated its view that 'members of a trade union have a right, in order to protect their interests, that the trade union should be heard'.[109] National law must enable trade unions 'to strive for the protection of their members' interests'. In the *Swedish Engine Drivers* case, such rights to protect their interests did exist and there was no breach of Article 11.

Thus, there is no State-guaranteed right to conclude collective agreements. To provide such a right would be a more extensive obligation than the contracting States had undertaken under Article 6(2) of the European Social Charter.[110] Article 6(2) provided:

> 'To promote, where necessary and appropriate, machinery for voluntary negotiations between employers and employers' associations and workers' organisations,

---

104   SI 1977/500 and SI 1992/2051.
105   Pension Schemes Act 1993, s 11(5) and SI 1996/1172.
106   *Schmidt and Dahlstrom v Sweden* (1979–80) 1 EHRR 632.
107   Series A No 19 (Judgment 22 October 1975), (1979–80) 1 EHRR 578.
108   Series A No 20 (Judgment 6 February 1976), (1979–80) 1 EHRR 617.
109   Series A No 20 at para 40.
110   Series A No 20 (1976) at p 15.

with a view to the regulation of terms and conditions of employment by means of collective agreements.'

The converse is also true; as there is no right to enter into collective bargaining, there is no equivalent right to refuse to enter into a collective agreement. In *Gustafsson v Sweden*,[111] Mr G owned a youth hostel and restaurant. In the relevant industry, the employers' association and the trade union had concluded collective agreements on pay and conditions. Neither Mr G nor his staff were members of the employers' organisation or union, respectively, and were not bound by the collective agreement. The union took lawful secondary action, causing financial loss to Mr G and the Swedish Government declined to intervene, on the basis that it was a dispute between private parties. Mr G argued to the ECtHR that his freedom not to associate was being violated by his being forced to join the employers' organisation. The ECtHR rejected his application. Whereas, under Article 11, there is an implied right to refuse to join a trade union, there is no implied right not to participate in a collective agreement.

Under UK law prior to the implementation of the Employment Relations Act 1999, there was no statutory right to recognition. Indeed, under British law, the House of Lords held that even the Convention-guaranteed right to union representation did not exist. In *Associated Newspapers Limited v Wilson; Associated British Ports v Palmer*,[112] the employers offered their employees personal contracts in substitution for collective agreements and denied pay rises to those employees who declined to sign them. The House of Lords held that there was no discrimination against those who refused to do so. Under s 146 of the TULR(C)A 1992, the right not to have 'action' short of dismissal taken on the grounds of union membership, did not include 'omissions' short of dismissal. The House of Lords made it clear that there was no right to union representation in British law.[113]

There was thus an apparent conflict between British law and the Convention, and in both cases the Commission had declared the employees' applications admissible. However, in the light of the UK's new trade union legislation, the case was struck from the list.

4.10.4 Effect of the Human Rights Act 1998

Under Article 14, discrimination in the application of Convention rights is prohibited. It is submitted that the Convention makes no distinction between action and inaction in disapproving inequality of treatment. The old wording of s 146 of the TULR(C)A 1992 should therefore be interpreted differently than in *Associated Newspapers Limited v Wilson; Associated British Ports v Palmer*,[114] in the light of the HRA 1998.

---

111 (1996) 22 EHRR 409.
112 [1995] 2 AC 454.
113 [1995] 2 AC 454 *per* Lord Lloyd at p 486C–D.
114 [1995] 2 AC 454.

Secondly, the decision that there was no right to union representation in English law would also call for re-examination in the light of the clear decisions of the ECtHR in the *National Union of Belgian Police* and the *Swedish Engine Drivers* cases.

4.11   ROLE OF THE STATE IN COLLECTIVE AGREEMENTS

With regard to collective agreements, Article 11 clearly does not cover a right for trade unions to conclude collective agreements, which authorities are obliged to uphold. Nevertheless, the freedom to make collective agreements is guaranteed, and the State must help make this possible.[115]

4.12   INDUSTRIAL CONFLICT: STRIKES AND INDUSTRIAL ACTION

4.12.1   Existing UK law

Individuals
Section 246 of the TULR(C)A 1992 defines a strike as a concerted stoppage of work. As against the State, individual workers may organise and participate in strikes without being exposed to sanctions under the criminal law. As against the employer, an individual worker is free to strike: but only by leaving his or her job having given appropriate notice. A simple refusal to work is a breach of the worker's contract of employment, for which damages can be awarded by the courts. Injunctions to enforce contracts of personal service will not be granted.

Apart from a claim for damages for breach of contract, the employee may be vulnerable to other sanctions. The strike may amount to a repudiatory breach of contract, for which the employer is justified at common law summarily to dismiss the employee. An employee dismissed during unofficial strike action has no right to complain of unfair dismissal.[116] At present, also, an employee dismissed during official action can complain of unfair dismissal only if the dismissal is unfairly selective.[117]

Individuals can also commit breaches of contract by other forms of industrial action. Withdrawing co-operation, if motivated by a desire to harm the employer's undertaking, will breach the implied duty to give faithful service.[118] An employee must reasonably perform his part of a contract. Deliberately bad

---

115   *Association A v Federal Republic of Germany* Application No 9792/82, (1983) 34 DR 173 at 174.
116   TULR(C)A 1992, s 237.
117   TULR(C)A 1992, s 238.
118   *Miles v Wakefield MDC* [1987] IRLR 193, [1987] ICR 368.

performance is a breach of contract: a go-slow is therefore such a breach.[119] It seems that works-to-rule are also in breach of contract if done with an intention to disrupt the employer's business.[120] 'Blacking' or boycotting goods, services or persons will usually breach the employment contract as an employer is entitled to require its workers to carry out their contracts in full and employees break their contacts if they refuse to obey lawful, reasonable instructions.[121] Overtime bans, however, are only in breach of contract if overtime is compulsory.[122]

Again, industrial action, other than strikes, may constitute a repudiatory breach of contract, which would justify summary dismissal of the worker. Alternatively, the employer can sue for damages for the breach.

However, the new s 238A of TULR(C)A 1992 provides that an employee taking part in protected industrial action will be regarded as having been unfairly dismissed in certain specified circumstances.

Trade unions

A strike or other industrial action will usually involve the commission by individuals of an economic tort. These economic torts comprise:

– inducing a breach of contract;
– interfering with trade, business or contract by unlawful means;
– intimidation;
– conspiracy

A trade union may be made vicariously liable for a tort committed on its behalf. Statute lays down a precise test of vicarious liability; the act must have been authorised or endorsed by the union within the meaning of s 20 of the TULR(C)A 1992. Even then, the economic torts are not actionable against the union if done in 'in contemplation or furtherance of a trade dispute'.[123] Trade dispute is defined by s 244(1) of the TULR(C)A 1992. The s 219 defence can itself be lost if:

(a) the union takes official industrial action without a secret ballot of workers;[124]
(b) the union fails to give the employer seven days' notice of the industrial action;[125]
(c) the purpose of the industrial action is to enforce union membership;[126]

119 *Secretary of State for Employment v Associated Society of Locomotive Engineers and Firemen (No 2)* [1972] 2 QB 455.
120 *Ticehurst v British Telecommunications plc* [1992] IRLR 219, CA.
121 *J T Stratford & Son Ltd v Linley* [1965] AC 269.
122 *Secretary of State for Employment v Associated Society of Locomotive Engineers and Firemen (No 2)* [1972] 2 QB 455.
123 TULR(C)A 1992, s 219.
124 TULR(C)A 1992, s 226.
125 TULR(C)A 1992, s 234A.
126 TULR(C)A 1992, s 222.

(d) the industrial action is taken in response to the dismissal of 'unofficial' strikers;[127]

(e) the action is 'secondary' action as defined, apart from secondary action by workers picketing their own workplace;[128]

(f) the purpose of the industrial action is to impose 'union labour only' clauses;[129]

(g) the tort is committed by a non-statutory picket.[130] (See further **4.13.1**.)

4.12.2   Convention for the Protection of Human Rights and Fundamental Freedoms

With regard to individual exercise of the right to strike, Article 4 of the Convention provides that no one shall be held in slavery or servitude and no one shall be required to perform forced or compulsory labour. The Article confirms the English common law position that, if an individual ceases to work, his or her contract for service will not be enforced by specific performance.

The 'right' of unions to strike was considered in detail in *Schmidt and Dahlstrom.*[131] The applicants were members of a striking union and were denied certain benefits even though they were not themselves involved in the strike. They argued that the policy of denying benefits to the members of striking unions violated trade union freedom contrary to Article 11 and was also discriminatory.

The ECtHR held that strikes were not the only means for union members to protect their interests. The ECtHR referred to the European Social Charter and held that a right to strike, assuming that it is protected by Article 11, may, even so, be subjected to restrictions by national laws.[132] States must leave trade unions sufficient scope to protect the interests of affiliated employees, since trade union freedom would otherwise be illusory, but it is for States to decide what means are allowed to unions to further their interests.

A number of different themes can be identified from the ECtHR's decisions on the rights guaranteed to unions.

(1) Article 11 permits trade union activity in various forms, but States have a wide discretion as to the particular forms which they will guarantee.

(2) The ECtHR is guided and informed by other international instruments, ILO Conventions, the International Covenant on Economic, Social and Cultural Rights, the International Covenant on Civil and Political Rights, the European Social Charter and the Universal Declaration of Human Rights. In particular, the ECtHR is unwilling to go beyond the provisions of

---

127   TULR(C)A 1992, s 223.
128   TULR(C)A 1992, s 224.
129   TULR(C)A 1992, s 225.
130   TULR(C)A 1992, s 219(3).
131   Series A No 21 (1976).
132   Series A No 21 (1976) at p 16.

the European Social Charter and to read a code of industrial relations into the Convention.

(3) The purpose of the Convention is the protection of individual rights, not collective rights.

4.12.3 Impact of the Human Rights Act 1998

The compatibility of British employment law on strikes and the Convention was considered in the recent admissibility decision in *NATFHE v United Kingdom*.[133] The Commission held that the requirements contained in the TULR(C)A 1992, ss 226A and 234A that a trade union must notify an employer of, inter alia, those who will be taking part in industrial action, do not violate Article 11 in the context of other statutory protections against discrimination on the grounds of trade union membership. The Commission considered that the requirements caused little hardship to the union or its members.

The Commission's decision in *NATFHE* is a powerful indication that the exacting procedural requirements imposed by UK law on the calling of strikes are compatible with Article 11. Significantly, though, it also suggests that Article 11 does include a right to strike and that interferences with that right will be examined to ensure proportionality. National courts will not be able to apply the doctrine of margin of appreciation in considering such interferences.[134]

4.13 PICKETING AND OTHER DEMONSTRATIONS

4.13.1 Existing UK law

Picketing is essentially a form of public demonstration.

At common law, picketing can constitute the tort of trespass to the highway, or nuisance. The law of trespass to the highway was reviewed in *DPP v Jones*.[135]

The minority in the House of Lords, Lords Slynn and Hope, considered that the public's right to use the highway was confined to use *as a highway*. Demonstrators who were intent on staying in one place were not exercising a right to pass along the highway. The majority considered that the public's right to use the highway extended beyond mere passage, so that there was a limited right of peaceful assembly so long as it did not unreasonably interfere with the rights of others to pass and repass. Lord Irvine, in particular, held that, even if he were wrong in considering that English law already gave a right of peaceful assembly on the highway, the Convention required that the common law evolve to include a right of peaceful assembly on the highway. As the law stands,

---

133 (1998) 25 EHRR CD 122.
134 See *R v Director of Public Prosecutions, ex parte Kebiline* [1999] 3 WLR 972 and **2.6.4**.
135 [1999] 2 All ER 257, HL.

however, any stopping on the highway must be no more than a temporary stopping, for no more than a reasonable period (see Lord Clyde's speech). Because of this, picketing will probably fall foul of the common law.

Work-ins and sit-ins will involve a trespass against the owner of the workplace.[136]

Statute provides a defence to tortious liability arising out of mere attendance of a peaceful picket. Section 220 of the TULR(C)A 1992 provides that it is lawful for a person, in contemplation or furtherance of a trade dispute, to attend (near) his or her place of work for the purpose of peacefully obtaining or communicating information, or peacefully persuading any person to work or abstain from working. Trade union officials have a similar right to attend the workplace of a union member whom they represent or accompany. The Code of Practice on Picketing suggests that a maximum of six pickets should attend a works entrance.

The 'right' to picket in s 220 of the TULR(C)A 1992 is subject to the powers of the police to prevent breaches of the peace.

In terms of such police powers, *Jones*[137] has already had a significant impact. The case itself concerned a protest close to Stonehenge. The local authority had, pursuant to an application by the local police force, exercised its powers under s 14A of the Public Order Act 1986 to prohibit trespassory assemblies in a particular district. Section 14A defines a trespassory assembly as one which is held without the permission of the landowner or is conducted in such a way that it exceeds the public right of access. *Jones* now means that a banning order may no longer be made unless the Chief Constable reasonably believes that an assembly is likely to occur and is likely to go beyond a reasonable, peaceful assembly. If the Chief Constable has no reason to suppose that the assembly will not be peaceful, the Chief Constable cannot intervene unless he or she reasonably believes that the assembly will result in public or private nuisance or obstruct the use of the highway by others.

Other, less common and obvious, criminal and civil offences can arise out of picketing. For a full consideration of these, see *Harvey on Industrial Relations and Employment Law* (Butterworths) Division N, paras [3420]–[3480].

4.13.2   Convention for the Protection of Human Rights and Fundamental Freedoms

The first words of Article 11 provide: 'Everyone has the right of freedom of peaceful assembly and to freedom of association with others'. The Commission has held that the freedom of peaceful assembly 'is a fundamental right in a democratic society and ... is one of the foundations of such a society'.[138]

Article 11 guarantees both private and public assemblies. In the *Rassemblement Jurassien* case, the Commission described the nature of peaceful assembly and

---

136   *Collier v Sunday Referee Publishing Co Ltd* [1940] 2 KB 647, [1940] 4 All ER 234, CA.
137   *DPP v Jones* [1999] 2 All ER 257, HL.
138   *Rassemblement Jurassien v Switzerland* Application No 8191/78, (1980) 17 DR 93 at 119.

held, uncontroversially, that the existence of a prior authorisation procedure for public assemblies did not of itself infringe Article 11.

> 'The right of peaceful assembly . . . covers both private meetings and meetings in public thoroughfares. Where the latter are concerned, their subjection to an authorisation procedure does not normally encroach upon the essence of the right. Such a procedure is in keeping with the requirements of Article 11(1), if only in order that the authorities may be in a position to ensure the peaceful nature of a meeting, and accordingly does not as such constitute interference with the exercise of the right.'

On the other hand, it is by no means clear that the Convention guarantees a right of public assembly on private land, even where such land has come to be used for public purposes.

Furthermore, unsurprisingly, the freedom of assembly in Article 11 has been held only to apply to peaceful gatherings and does not encompass demonstrations 'where the organisers and participators have violent intentions which result in public disorder'.[139]

States do enjoy a wide 'margin of appreciation' in the measures they can take to protect public order and safety. Nevertheless, both the ECtHR and the Commission are astute to disapprove unnecessary restrictions on the right of peaceful assembly which have been dressed up as measures to protect national security and public safety. In its report in *The Greek Case,*[140] the Commission reviewed the restrictions applying in Greece at that time with regard to both private and public and political and non-political assemblies, for their conformity with Article 11(2) and, on the basis of the very wide discretion which the law left to authorities, concluded that they could not find a sufficient justification in any of the grounds of restriction mentioned therein.

In *Ezelin v France,*[141] the applicant, in his capacity as vice-chairman of a union of Guadeloupe *avocats*, took part in a duly authorised public demonstration. In the course of the demonstration, insulting remarks were addressed to the police and offensive graffiti, directed against the judiciary, were painted on public buildings. At the instigation of the State prosecutor, disciplinary proceedings were taken against the applicant.

The ECtHR rejected France's argument that the disciplinary proceedings taken against E after the demonstration did not come within the term 'restrictions' in Article 11(2). It considered whether the disciplinary proceedings, as interference with the exercise of his freedom of peaceful assembly was 'necessary in a democratic society'. The 'proportionality principle' demanded that a balance be struck between the requirements of public order in Article 11(2), and freedom of expression. The court felt that the pursuit of a just balance ought not to result in *avocats* being discouraged, for fear of disciplinary sanctions, from exercising their rights of free speech on such occasions. Although the ECtHR found that the penalty imposed on E was at the lower end

---

139   *G v Germany* (1989) 60 DR 256, (1989) E Com HR.
140   12 YB 1 at 161.
141   (1992) 14 EHRR 362.

of disciplinary penalties, it considered that the freedom to take part in peaceful assembly was of such importance that it could not be restricted in any way, even for an *avocat*, so long as the person concerned did not himself commit any reprehensible act on such an occasion.

The sanction complained of, however minor, was not 'necessary in a democratic society' and there had therefore been a violation of Article 11. This is a welcome result, as the protection afforded by Article 11(1) would be rendered substantially less valuable if it were removed whenever co-demonstrators engaged in criminal conduct.

In the context of Article 10, the ECtHR was willing to scrutinise the 'necessity' and 'proportionality' of restrictions on protestors' freedom of expression under English law in *Steel v UK*.[142]

4.13.3   Impact of the Human Rights Act 1998

Since Article 11(1) and (2) seeks itself to strike a balance between the rights of employees and the what is necessary in a democratic society for the prevention of disorder, s 220 of the TULR(C)A 1992 is unlikely to offend against Article 11. Section 220 grants a right to peaceful communication of information. The section and the Code of Practice on Picketing give content to the balance to be struck between freedom of assembly and prevention of civil unrest.

On the other hand, the common law may well be developed beyond the position stated in *DPP v Jones*.[143] It is submitted that Article 11 necessarily means that the views of Lords Hope and Slynn in *DPP v Jones* are incorrect. It is quite clear that Article 11 guarantees meetings in public thoroughfares (see the *Rassemblement Jurassien* case at **4.13.2**). The Convention therefore demands that some type of right to public peaceful assembly is incorporated into the common law. If all assemblies on the highway were trespassory, it would follow that the common law was incapable of performing the 'proportionality' test demanded by the Convention.

There would, naturally, remain the possibility of placing restrictions on public assemblies, 'necessary in a democratic society in the interests of national security or public safety, for the prevention of disorder or crime, for the protection of health or morals or for the protection of rights or freedoms of others'.[144] In deciding whether restrictions were, indeed, necessary, national courts would not be able to apply the 'margin of appreciation'. Rather, they would have to decide whether the measure was 'proportionate'. Proportionality would require that the interference by the State corresponded to a pressing social need and was proportionate to the legitimate aim pursued (see, for example, *Olsson v Sweden*).[145]

Arrests for behaviour likely to cause a breach of the peace or convictions for public order offences may violate Article 11 if the law is not sufficiently clear

---

142   (1999) 28 EHRR 603, ECtHR. See further, **4.13.3**.
143   [1999] 2 All ER 257, HL.
144   Article 11(2).
145   (1988) Series A No 130.

(*Steel v United Kingdom*),[146] or if the restrictions imposed are not necessary in a democratic society. On this latter point, the ECtHR observed that States do have a margin of appreciation in deciding what restrictions are 'necessary', but that the overriding consideration must be that the means used should be proportionate to the end to be achieved. Therefore, on the facts, the detention for breach of the peace of protestors who had merely held banners and distributed leaflets, was disproportionate. The protestors had not offered violence nor attempted significant disruption and had done nothing to provoke others to violence. Hence, their Article 10 right to freedom of expression had been infringed. The ECtHR did not consider complaints based on infringement of Article 11 because the issues raised thereunder had been examined under Article 10.

The application of the principles in *Steel* to picketing would mean that:

(1) picketing by way of peaceful assembly is a protected right under the Convention;
(2) picketing which is peaceful, but amounts to an obstruction, is not protected.

Pickets charged with breach of the peace who had assembled peacefully and had not obstructed the highway or other persons would have a defence that such charges were unlawful as an abuse of the process of the court under the HRA 1998.

Other police actions under the Public Order Act 1986 will be affected by the coming into force of the HRA 1998. Section 11 requires that the police be notified of a proposal to hold a procession. Sections 12, 13 and 14 give the police powers to impose conditions on, or prohibit altogether, public processions and static assemblies. The HRA 1998 will allow decisions of the police and local authorities under these sections to be challenged by way of judicial review, on the grounds that any restrictions imposed are disproportionate to the aims sought to be achieved. Again, persons charged with criminal offences arising out of organising or participating in unauthorised processions or assemblies, would have a defence that the prohibition itself was unlawful.

It has been suggested that other miscellaneous provisions of the Public Order Acts may fall foul of Convention requirements. An offence under s 5 of the Public Order Act 1986 is committed by a person who uses abusive or insulting words within the hearing of a person likely to be caused distress. It is not necessary that anyone actually is caused distress, nor, clearly, that the accused is threatening or provoking violence. So, an accused may be able to challenge the compatibility of s 5 of the Public Order Act 1986 with Articles 10 and 11 of the Convention and argue the accused's prosecution is an abuse of the process of the court. Section 1 of the Public Order Act 1936, which prohibits the wearing of a uniform, 'signifying ... association with any political organisation or with the promotion of a political object' may be subject to challenge on the basis that it is too widely drafted to be 'necessary' in a democratic society.

---

146 (1999) 28 EHRR 603, ECtHR.

4.14   ROLE OF THE STATE – POSITIVE OBLIGATIONS

More than in most other areas, the State has a vital role in ensuring the right to picket and demonstrate on behalf of trade union interests. In particular, it is the State, by way of the police force, which holds the power to permit demonstrations to take place on the public highway, to impose restrictions on public demonstrations or to ban them altogether, in accordance with Article 11(2).

The Greek Case[147] demonstrates that the Commission is willing and able to examine and disapprove restrictions imposed by States on private and public and political and non-political assemblies, if these restrictions are not genuinely imposed for the aims set out in Article 11(2).

Equally, the actions of States with respect to demonstrations is liable to scrutiny. Even if a demonstration is not banned, if a State fails to protect a group of demonstrators from physical assault, this will constitute a restriction by the State on the right to peaceful assembly.

In its decision in *Plattform 'Ärtze Für Das Leben' v Austria*,[148] the Commission rejected the claim of the Austrian Government that Article 11 does not include a right of protection of demonstrations against interference by private individuals. It referred to previous decisions of the ECtHR, which had held that the Convention does not merely oblige the contracting States themselves to honour the Convention rights and freedoms by preventing and remedying any breach of them. The obligation to secure the effective exercise of Convention rights may involve positive obligations on the State, even involving the adoption of measures which applied between individuals. The Commission therefore considered that the right to freedom of assembly must include the right to protection against counter-demonstrators, because only then can effective exercise of rights be secured to social groups wishing to demonstrate for controversial principles. If the protection provided by the authorities proves insufficient to enable free exercise of the right to freedom of assembly, this amounts to a restriction which has to be tested for justification under Article 11(2). The ECtHR concurred with this view. It stated that the participants of a demonstration must:[149]

> 'be able to hold the demonstration without having to fear that they will be subjected to physical violence by their opponents; such a fear would be liable to deter associations or other groups supporting common ideas or interests from openly expressing their opinions on highly controversial issues affecting the community. In a democracy the right to counter-demonstrate cannot extend to inhibiting the exercise of the right to demonstrate.'

Therefore:

> 'Genuine, effective freedom of peaceful assembly cannot ... be reduced to a mere duty on the part of the State not to interfere: a purely negative conception would

---

147   (1969) 12 YB.
148   (1988) Series A No 139, 13 EHRR 204.
149   (1991) 13 EHRR 204 at 210. See also *X & Y v The Netherlands* (1985) Series A No 91 at p 11.

not be compatible with the object and purposes of Art 11. Like Art 8, Art 11 sometimes requires positive measures to be taken, even in the sphere of individuals if need be.'

It should be noted that there has not been any decided case in which the ECtHR has found a breach of Article 11 by reason of inadequate protection. Nevertheless, the existence of the obligation will prevent a State from refusing to provide protection of any kind.

Thus the role of the State is to uphold the right to peaceful assembly, by permitting public and private demonstrations, but not imposing restrictions unless these are *necessary*, and by physically protecting demonstrators from attempts by third parties to prevent the exercise of their Article 11 rights.

A national court, considering the imposition of restrictions on demonstrations and counter-demonstrations, must secure this role. The national court will have to do so in the absence of the doctrine of the 'margin of appreciation', which is widely applied in the decisions of the ECtHR.

Chapter 5

DISCRIMINATION

5.1 INTRODUCTION

As an important component of an international treaty, Article 14 of the Convention (Prohibition of Discrimination) is best appreciated against the historical backdrop of the struggle for equality. It is perhaps with the French Declaration of the Rights of Man that equality became a fundamental norm in the legal sphere and it was not until the mid-nineteenth century with the adoption of the Fourteenth Amendment to the US Constitution that the principle of equal treatment became legally enforceable.[1] Freedom and equality have always been seen as two facets of the same coin and freedom is viewed as the best protection against any form of discrimination.

5.2 Protection from discrimination in the United States

Equality became of central importance in the US after the civil war, since prior to that the Constitution had recognised slavery. The emancipation of blacks led to the adoption of the Fourteenth and Fifteenth Amendments to the Constitution. However, the Supreme Court's efforts in this direction were piecemeal and the amendments were first restricted to a narow definition limited solely to racial discrimination against blacks. The case of *Yick Wo v Hopkins*[2] challenged the practice of the San Francisco city administration of refusing to grant laundry permits to Chinese applicants while accepting almost all white applications. It was the court's decision in *Brown v Board of Education*[3] which recognised the full extent of the equality clause in the Constitution and outlawed classifications based on race. This prohibition did not cover the action of private individuals but was directed against 'State action'. The Supreme Court developed the doctrine of 'public function' theory to cover private conduct which has many of the characteristics of exercising public authority. This type of analysis may prove a useful source of comparison for interpretation of the HRA 1998.

The focus in the US has been on indirect discrimination and the court developed the theory of 'adverse impact' to deal with such problems. In *Griggs v Duke*,[4] the court adumbrated a two-stage test in which the complainant had to show that the employer's practice had an adverse impact on a particular group. The burden of proof then shifted to the employer to show that such a practice

---

1   Sotirios Manolkidis 'The Principle of Equality from a Comparative Constitutional Perspective: Lessons for the EU' in *The Principle of Equal Treatment in EC Law* (Dashwood & O'Leary, eds) (Sweet & Maxwell, 1997).
2   118 US 356 (1886).
3   347 US 483 (1954).
4   401 US 424 (1971).

bore a reasonable relationship to the nature of the employment in question. This test will be familiar to discrimination lawyers and it is likely that indirect discrimination will develop under the HRA 1998. Indeed, the new Race Relations (Amendment) Act 2000 extends the scope of the existing rules on indirect discrimination to public bodies such as the police for the first time and this, coupled with the HRA 1998, will have a major impact on the legal landscape.

5.3   INTERNATIONAL PROTECTION

Freedom from discrimination and equality before the law have consistently featured on the international human rights agenda. The UN Charter speaks of the promotion and encouragement of respect for human rights without distinction as to race, sex, language or religion as one of the purposes of the organisation. The UN itself has promoted the International Convention on the Elimination of all Forms of Racial Discrimination 1966 and the International Convention on the Elimination of Discrimination against Women 1979. Article 26 of the International Convenant on Civil and Political Rights 1966 also provided for all-encompassing protection against discrimination in all activities:

> 'All persons are equal before the law and are entitled without any discrimination to the equal protection of the law. In this respect the law shall prohibit any discrimination and guarantee to all persons equal and effective protection against discrimination on any ground such as race, colour, sex, language, religion, political or other opinion, national or social origin, property, birth or other status.'

5.4   UK DOMESTIC LEGISLATION ON DISCRIMINATION

5.4.1   Introduction

The unwritten nature of the British constitution is unique in Europe and the influences on the contemporary situation are manifest and varied. It had been suggested that far from having no written constitution, it could be said with more glibness than inaccuracy, that the UK has a surfeit of written documents making up its constitution; that the uniqueness of its structure lies in too much rather than too little of that written constitution that is said so frequently to be absent.[5]

By the end of the first decade of the eighteenth century, the basic parameters of the British constitution had been laid. Extensions to the franchise were introduced by the Great Reform Act of 1832 and uniform franchise based on residence was established after the First World War for both county and borough constituencies and in 1919 the extension of the right to vote was granted to women over 30. This age limit was reduced to 21 in 1928 and it could

---

5   Conor A Gearty (ed) *European Civil Liberties and the European Convention on Human Rights – A comparative study* (Martinus Nijhoff Publishers, 1997).

then be said that universal mass suffrage had been introduced. The grand notion of 'human rights' was missing from this framework[6] and it was arguably Dicey's[7] concept of 'the rule of law' which ensured that the individual's rights and freedoms were protected from arbitrary abuse of power. There was perhaps a sense in Britain that grandiose and grandiloquent declarations were unnecessary to protect the individual. This view continued even after the signing of the Convention.[8]

Existing domestic legislation has attempted, in a piecemeal way, to deal with the issue of discrimination in society. Thus there are three related but distinct statutes in this area: the Sex Discrimination Act 1975 (SDA 1975), the Race Relations Act 1976 (RRA 1976) and the Disability Discrimination Act 1995 (DDA 1995). In mainland Britain, it is possible to discriminate on the grounds of religion but this is outlawed in Northern Ireland. The legislation targets discrimination in employment and in certain other limited sectors, for example the provision of goods and services, education and housing. There is also the pervasive influence of the law of the EC. EC law focuses primarily on equality between the sexes in employment and social security, although the Treaty of Amsterdam has for the first time empowered the Commission to introduce legislation to outlaw discrimination on the grounds of race, religion etc. The provisions of the Convention will be grafted onto this framework but litigants may find limited scope in the area of discrimination for use of Convention rights in the employment sphere.

It is proposed to examine briefly the current state of legislation and then attempt to anticipate the areas in which the Convention will add a new dimension.

5.4.2 Sex discrimination

The SDA 1975 outlaws discrimination on grounds of sex and marital status. There are three types of discrimination which are rendered unlawful: direct discrimination; indirect discrimination; and discrimination by victimisation. Victimisation can arise where a person suffers detrimental treatment after that person has threatened to bring, or has brought, or has been involved in the bringing of, proceedings under the SDA 1975 or the Equal Pay Act 1970.

Discrimination can be manifested as either direct or indirect discrimination. An applicant has to prove less favourable treatment and that such treatment has occurred because of his or her sex. In *R v Birmingham City Council, ex parte EOC*,[9] the City Council had made provision for more places for boys than girls at selective secondary schools. In so doing, girls in the area were being denied the same opportunity as boys. It was immaterial whether selective education was better or worse than non-selective: the crucial issue was that the Council had

---

6   Gearty, *op cit* p 63.
7   A.V. Dicey *An Introduction to the Study of the Law of the Constitution* (Macmillan, 1959) 10th edn.
8   Gearty, *op cit* p 65.
9   [1989] IRLR 173, HL.

deprived girls of a choice which was available to boys in the area. The motive of the discrimination is equally irrelevant:

> 'The purity of the discriminator's subjective motive intention or reason for discriminating cannot save the criterion applied from the objective taint of discrimination on the ground of sex.'

The applicant must show that his or her sex was an important or substantial reason for the treatment which has been meted out.[10] The applicant will need to show that the treatment of a given comparator of the opposite sex would have been different. Unlike the Equal Pay Act 1970 where the applicant must show an actual comparator, the applicant can rely under the SDA 1975 on the treatment of a hypothetical comparator of the opposite sex. Where the act of discrimination has occurred because of a woman's pregnancy, there is no need to identify a male comparator.

With regard to indirect discrimination, the applicant must show the existence of a practice or policy which has a disparate adverse impact on a particular class or group and is thus discriminatory. The legislation uses the term 'a requirement or condition' which has been imposed and applies equally to both sexes but the proportion of women who are able to comply with the requirement or condition is considerably smaller than the proportion of men (or vice versa). In *Jones v Chief Adjudication Officer*,[11] the tribunal identified the process for establishing discrimination:

(1) identify the criterion for selection;
(2) identify the relevant population, comprising all those who satisfy all the other criteria for selection;
(3) divide the relevant population into grounds representing those who satisfy the criterion and those who do not;
(4) predict statistically what proportion of each groups consists of women;
(5) ascertain what are the actual male/female balances in the two groups;
(6) compare the actual with the predicted imbalances;
(7) if women are found to be under-represented in the first group and over-represented in the second, it is proved that the criterion is discriminatory.

One of the difficulties in discrimination case-law has been the identification of a comparator. This problem has, for instance, arisen in the case of pregnant women and more recently in the case of disabled workers where the Court of Appeal has ruled that the appropriate comparator of a disabled person is someone to whom the disability does not apply.[12]

Another issue which has caused great controversy recently has been discrimination on the grounds of sexual orientation, where the interplay between domestic and European legislation has been at its most creative, but where even Convention case-law has been remarkably conservative. This is discussed further at **5.5.2** below.

---

10   *James v Eastleigh Borough Council* [1990] IRLR 288, HL.
11   [1990] IRLR 533.
12   *Clark v Novacold* [1999] IRLR 318, CA.

5.4.3 Race discrimination

The essential concepts of direct discrimination, indirect discrimination and victimisation are similar for race discrimination and sex discrimination. It is also unlawful to segregate anyone on racial grounds. The term segregation bears its ordinary meanings, as it is not defined in the RRA 1976. One of the key issues in the race relations legislation is that the applicant must prove that the less favourable treatment occurs on racial grounds. Section 3(1) of the RRA 1976 defines 'racial grounds' as any of the grounds of 'colour, race, nationality or ethnic or national origins'. 'Racial group' means a group of people defined by reference to their colour, race, nationality or ethnic or national origins. Where an applicant complains under the RRA 1976, the crucial first step is to identify the racial group into which the applicant falls and whether this comes within the mischief of the RRA 1976. In *Mandla v Lee*,[13] a Sikh boy was refused entry to a fee-paying school unless he agreed to stop wearing a turban. The court had to decide whether Sikhs constituted a racial group and the House of Lords determined that they did constitute such a group. A racial group will have a long, shared, history, the memory of which the group keeps alive and which consciously distinguishes it from other groups, as well as a cultural tradition of its own including family and social customs and manners, often but not necessarily associated with religious observance. Other characteristics which will be considered are whether the group shares:

- a common geographical origin or descent from a small number of common ancestors;
- a common language;
- a common literature peculiar to the group;
- a common religion different from that of neighbouring groups; and
- a sense of being a minority or being a distinctive group within a larger community.

Thus 'travellers' have been held to constitute a racial group[14] but Rastafarians have not.[15] The Court of Appeal held that although Rastafarians were a separate group with identifiable characteristics, they had no separate identity by reference to their ethnic origins.

5.4.4 Disability discrimination

The DDA 1995 is deceptively similar to the SDA 1975 and the RRA 1976. However, it has ushered in concepts which are entirely new to employers and, indeed, to employment lawyers and has caused some difficulty for employment tribunals with regard to its interpretation. It should be noted that the DDA 1995 does not distinguish explicitly between direct and indirect discrimination. It uses a different comparative basis for detecting discrimination and contains a broad defence of justification which is not present in other statutes. There is also a positive duty on employers to accommodate disabled persons. A final

---

13 [1983] ICR 385, HL.
14 *CRE v Dutton* [1989] IRLR 8.
15 *Crown Supplier (PSA) Ltd v Dawkins* [1993] IRLR 517, CA.

distinction is that the DDA 1995 does not apply to small businesses which employ less than 15 employees. Given these variations, the Court of Appeal has expressly stated that the DDA 1995 should not be approached on the basis of assumptions and concepts borrowed from the RRA 1976 or the SDA 1975.[16]

One of the key concepts is 'disability'. The complainant must prove that he or she is disabled within the meaning of the DDA 1995, which provides that a person is considered to be disabled if that person has a physical or mental impairment which has a substantial and long-term adverse effect on the ability to carry out normal day-to-day activities. Guidance had been provided by the EAT to tribunals as to how they should approach the matter.[17] The term 'physical or mental impairment' is not defined in the DDA 1995 but reference may be made to the World Health Organisation's *International Classification of Impairment, Disability and Handicap 1980*. To fall within the DDA 1995, the impairment must affect the person's:

–   mobility;
–   manual dexterity;
–   physical co-ordination;
–   continence;
–   ability to lift, carry or otherwise move everyday objects;
–   speech, hearing or eyesight;
–   memory or ability to concentrate, learn or understand;
–   perception of the risk of physical danger.

5.5   EC LEGISLATION AGAINST DISCRIMINATION

5.5.1   The fundamental rights

The European Court of Justice (ECJ) recognises those fundamental rights common to the national traditions of Member States as binding in EC law. In the words of one commentator:

> 'Equality stands alongside economic, commercial and property rights, rights of defence, traditional civil and political liberties, rights created by the community treaties and legislation, social rights and administrative law principles as fundamental rights recognised by the court.'[18]

The European ideal has seen equality as one of the oldest of the fundamental rights and principles and many seek to argue that the EU is not simply an economic union but includes the ideal of social justice. This intellectual and moral deficiency has been remedied by the Treaty of Amsterdam which enshrines human rights in the vanguard of the Treaties. One commentator has adopted the view of Kant that 'a legal order without morally generated rights is like the wooden head of a horse, beautiful but empty'.[19]

---

16   *Clark v Novacold* [1999] IRLR 318, CA.
17   *Goodwin v The Patent Office* [1999] IRLR 4.
18   Catherine Barnard "P v S: Kite Flying or a new Constitutional Approach?" in *The Principle of Equal Treatment in EC Law* (Dashwood & O'Leary, eds) (Sweet & Maxwell, 1997), p 64.
19   Quoted in Barnard, *op cit* p 69.

The ECJ has never stipulated a complete list of principles but will look to the constitutions of Member States and the international treaties when considering general norms of behaviour. Equality is one of the cornerstones of constitutional law in each of the Member States and is a fundamental tenet in economic and social legislation in the EU. In 1996, the ECJ delivered an opinion on the competence of the Community to accede to the Convention. The ECJ found that the Community lacks competence to accede to the Convention but the ECJ emphasised that it is:

> 'well settled that fundamental rights form an integral part of the general principles of law whose observance the Court ensures. For that purpose the Court draws inspiration from the constitutional traditions common to the Member States and from the guidelines supplied by international treaties for the protection of human rights on which the Member States have collaborated or of which they are signatories ... Respect for human rights is therefore a condition of lawfulness of Community acts.'[20]

The EU has itself focused on eliminating one type of social inequality, ie that between men and women. Until recently, it was only discrimination on the grounds of sex and nationality which were expressly covered by EC law.[21] The case of *Konstantinidis*[22] involved a black Dutch national who was refused employment in Greece on the basis that the employers' customers did not want to be served by a black woman. Greek law did not prohibit such discrimination. Advocate-General Jacobs argued:

> 'In my opinion, a Community national who goes to another member State as a worker or self-employed person under Articles 48, 52 or 59 of the Treaty is entitled not just to pursue his trade or profession and to enjoy the same living and working conditions of the nationals of the host State, he is in addition entitled to assume that, wherever he goes to earn his living in the European community, he will be treated in accordance with a common code of fundamental values, in particular those laid down in the European Convention on Human Rights. In other words, he is entitled to say "civis europeaus sum" and to invoke that status in order to oppose any violation of his fundamental rights.'

His position was not adopted by the ECJ. A black Greek worker would have experienced the same difficulties and therefore there was no discrimination under the Treaty of Rome. This issue will be addressed by legislation under the Treaty of Amsterdam.

Article 141 (formerly Article 119) of the Treaty of Rome contains a broad legal obligation to implement the principle of equal pay for equal work. This was supplemented by the Equal Pay Directive 75/117/EEC which was implemented in the UK by the Equal Pay Act 1970. The ECJ also makes a distinction between direct and indirect discrimination. In the field of equal pay, the ECJ in the case of *Defrenne v Sabena*[23] defined direct discrimination as

---

20   [1996] 2 CMLR 265.
21   Elspeth Guild, 'EC law and the means to combat racism and xenophobia' in *The Principles of Equal Treatment in EC Law* (Dashwood & O'Leary, eds) (Sweet & Maxwell, 1997). The Communities have largely adopted soft law to deal with the issue.
22   C–168/91 *Konstantinidis v Stadt Altensteig* [1993] 1 ECR 1191.
23   [1976] ECR 455.

situations in which a discriminatory effect can be 'identified solely with the aid of the criteria based on equal work and equal pay'. Indirect discrimination may be presumed where a measure which is apparently neutral in fact predominantly affects workers of one sex. It is not necessary to establish that discrimination was intended.

The equal pay programme was complemented by the Equal Treatment Directive 76/207/EEC which introduced the concept of equal treatment as regards access to employment, vocational training, promotion and working conditions.

Individuals have had recourse to EC law where there has been a gap in existing legislation. The ECJ has accordingly had a profound impact on employment law and increasingly individuals have had recourse to the ECtHR to enlarge on rights which are not adequately protected by either of the two bodies of legislation.

Another area where the concept of equality has been looked at by the ECJ has been in cases dealing with staff regulations, ie claims by EU officials. In such cases, the ECJ is unable to look to Article 141 (the legal basis for equal treatment legislation) because this is addressed to Member States and does not apply to Community institutions. However, in *Razzouk and Beydoun v Commission*[24] the ECJ drew on fundamental concepts of equality to deal with the issues raised by the application.

5.5.2   Sexual orientation

One particular source of difficulty for all tribunals, domestic and international, has been how to deal with discrimination faced by homosexuals, lesbians and transsexuals based on their sexual orientation. This merits closer examination.

Wintemute has identified three approaches or methods of analysis adopted by courts or applicants in dealing with the question of sexual orientation.[25]

(1) *An immutable status argument:* because gay men and lesbian women believe that their sexual orientation is unchosen, sexual orientation may be an immutable status like race or sex.

(2) *A fundamental choice argument:* because every person's sexual orientation (as direction of conduct) is chosen and is extremely important to that person's happiness, it may be a fundamental choice (or right or freedom), like religion or political opinion, and come wholly or partly within a specific 'fundamental right' such as freedom of expression, association or religion, or a residual and more general 'right of privacy' or 'right to respect for private life'.

---

24   [1984] ECR 1509.
25   For an in-depth discussion of this topic see Robert Wintemute *Sexual Orientation and Human Rights* (Clarendon Paperbacks, 1997) which is a comparative study of the US Constitution, the Convention and the Canadian Charter.

(3) *A sex discrimination argument*: because the acceptability of the direction of the person's emotional–sexual attraction or conduct depends on that person's own sex, sexual orientation discrimination may be a kind of sex discrimination, like sexual harassment or pregnancy discrimination.[26]

The ECJ has played a pivotal role in the development of EC discrimination law which reached the high water mark with the decision in *P v S and Cornwall County Council*[27] and fell away disappointingly with the *Grant v South-West Trains*[28] decision. In *P v S*, the ECJ had to consider whether the principle of equal treatment between men and women also applied to transsexuals. One year after being employed by the Council, P who at the time was a male announced his intention to undergo gender reassignment to become female. This involved a life test during which P would dress and behave as a woman, to be followed by surgery which would complete his transformation into a female. After five months of this course of treatment and after he had undergone minor surgery P was dismissed. The ECJ held this to be an act of discrimination on the basis that P was being treated unfavourably by comparison with a person of the sex P was deemed to be prior to the gender reassignment. The ECJ said that:

'to tolerate such discrimination would be tantamount as regards such a person to a failure to respect the dignity and freedom to which he or she is entitled and which the Court has a duty to safeguard.'[29]

The UK Government had argued that no discrimination had occurred because a female to male transsexual would have been treated in the same way. This was indeed the argument which succeeded in *Grant v South-West Trains*[30] which concerned a lesbian employee whose partner was denied free travel benefits enjoyed by opposite sex partners. The ECJ surprisingly declined to follow the *P v S* decision. This was the least controversial approach and the ECJ perhaps had in mind the fact that, with the coming into force of the Treaty of Amsterdam amending the EC Treaty, discrimination on the grounds of sexual orientation would be expressly outlawed. It is an issue which has been conservatively dealt with by the ECtHR as will be discussed below.

The Treaty of Amsterdam provides:

'Without prejudice to the other provisions of this Treaty and within the limits of the powers conferred by it upon the Community, the council, acting unanimously on a proposal from the Commission and after consulting the European Parliament, may take appropriate action to combat discrimination based on sex, racial or ethnic origin, religion or belief, disability, age or sexual orientation.'

The pattern for employment lawyers has hitherto been to consider, first, the domestic legislation, secondly, whether EC law provides any solutions to the

---

26   Wintemute, at p 17.
27   Case C13/94 [1996] 2 CMLR 247.
28   [1998] IRLR 206.
29   *P v S and Cornwall County Council* [1996] CMLR 247 at para 22.
30   [1998] IRLR 206.

problem, and finally, to turn to the Convention to see whether the Strasbourg jurisprudence is at all helpful. The EC has now adopted a specific race directive 2000/43/EC and a framework directive to give effect to Article 13 of the Treaty directive 2000/78/EC. Member States have three years to implement the directives which will immediately widen the scope of protection from discrimination and, with regard to existing legislation, should have a significant impact in areas such as the reversal of the burden of proof and greater flexibility in proof of indirect discrimination. To some extent, the more tortious route provided by the European Convention on Human Rights will thus be circumvented.

5.6   CONVENTION FOR THE PROTECTION OF HUMAN RIGHTS AND FUNDAMENTAL FREEDOMS

5.6.1   Article 14: its role and function[31]

Article 14 of the Convention provides:

> 'The enjoyment of the rights and freedoms set forth in this Convention shall be enjoyed without discrimination on any ground such as sex, race, colour, language, religion, political or other opinion, national or social origin, association with a minority, property, birth or other status.'

While the Article appears to be wider than the protection which currently exists under domestic law, it contains one significant restriction: Article 14 can be invoked only in association with another Convention right. It is not a free-standing prohibition against discrimination but seeks to ensure that individuals are not disadvantaged in the exercise of their Convention rights on one or more of the grounds set out. It is thus described as a parasitic right with no independent life of its own.

Article 14 imposes an obligation on States to secure the non-discriminatory enjoyment of the rights and freedoms protected by the Convention. It is, however, important to bear in mind that an individual can establish a breach of Article 14 although there has been no breach of another Convention right. The sphere of the alleged discrimination must, however, be that of another Convention right as in the case of *Inze v Austria*[32] where the applicant alleged that Austrian law affecting the succession to hereditary farms gave precedence to legitimate children at the expense of illegitimate children. This was held to be a violation of Article 14 but not a violation of Article 1 of the 1st Protocol which dealt with property rights. Another interesting point is that a State can be in violation of Article 14 where the State provides greater rights and freedoms than required by the Convention but they are not accorded equally. The most striking case is that of *Abdulaziz*[33] where the UK allowed foreign wives of British

---

31   See DJ Harris, M O'Boyle and C Warbrick *The Law of the European Convention on Human Rights* (Butterworths, 1995); *The Law and Practice of the European Convention on Human Rights and the European Social Charter* (Council of Europe Publishing, 1996).

32   (1988) 10 EHRR 394.

33   *Abdulaziz, Cabales and Balkandali v UK* (1985) 7 EHRR 471.

men a right of entry and residence which they did not accord to foreign husbands of British women. This privilege was tainted with sex discrimination and there was accordingly a violation of Article 14. The claim itself fell within the ambit of Article 8 (the right to respect for family life). Just as in existing discrimination law, a claim will fail if the State or public authority can show that the difference in treatment is objectively justified.

The concept of discrimination[34]

In the *Belgian Linguistic Case (No 1)*,[35] the ECtHR identified the steps to be taken to determine when an act of discrimination has occurred. The facts must disclose a differential treatment which has no legitimate aim, or no objective and reasonable justification having regard to the aim and effects of the measure under consideration; and that the means employed are not proportionate to the stated aim.

> 'The existence of such a justification must be assessed in relation to the aims and effects of the measure under consideration, regard being had to the principles which normally prevail in democratic societies. A difference of treatment in the exercise of a right laid down in the Convention must not only pursue a legitimate aim: art 14 is likewise violated when it is clearly established that there is not reasonable relationship of proportionality between the means employed and the aim sought to be realised.'[36]

This test is broadly similar to that contained in the SDA 1975, the RRA 1976 and the DDA 1995 and will therefore not involve a different manner of analysis in cases which arise under these provisions. In the context of these types of discrimination, it would appear that little will be added to the protection already enjoyed by individuals. However, the list of categories of discrimination contained in Article 14 is considerably wider than that encompassed in the UK statutory framework, for instance in relation to language or religion.

There is some argument for saying that autochthonous language communities such as the Welsh, Celtic or Gaelic may now be able to argue more strongly against discrimination in the workplace. The case of *Gwynedd County Council v Jones*[37] may yet be revisited. The Convention would address the question posed by the RRA 1976 as to whether such groups are racial groups. Similarly, the narrow interpretation of racial group which excluded Rastafarians would not be an obstacle to a claim by a Rastafarian of discrimination.[38] Similarly, it may be that challenges may be made to the legality of situations where jobs are reserved to persons who speak a particular language or who are from a particular ethnic group. For instance, schools which cater for teachers from a particular ethnic community may be accused of discriminating against other minority groups by failing to have similar posts for them. There would, of course, be a possible defence of justification.

---

34 Stephen Livingstone *Article 14 and the Prevention of Discrimination in the European Convention on Human Rights* [1997] EHRLR Issue 1, p 25.
35 (1979–80) 1 EHRR 252.
36 (1979–80) 1 EHRR 271.
37 [1986] ICR 833.
38 *Dawkins v Department of the Environment* [1993] IRLR 284.

The grounds of discrimination

Under the Convention the categories of discrimination are not closed and litigants will find a non-exhaustive list of grounds in Article 14. It is here that minorities who are not effectively covered by existing domestic legislation will find some assistance; for instance, those who alleged that they are accorded differential treatment on the grounds of sexual orientation, language or suffering from HIV/AIDS (although this would now be covered by the DDA 1995).

SEX

The ECtHR has emphasised that since equality of the sexes is a major goal of the contracting States there would have to be very powerful reasons to justify a difference in treatment on the ground of sex. There have been a number of cases brought by men which have been upheld; for instance an obligation on a man to pay a fire service levy in lieu of actual service based on a local tradition of male participation in the fire brigade was discrimination in conjunction with Article 1 of the 1st Protocol and Article 4(3)(d) since women neither served nor paid the levy.

MARRIAGE

Hitherto, since marriage is a special legal regime, a difference in treatment between non-married couples and married couples has been found not to amount to discrimination. It is questionable whether this distinction will persist given the reduced importance of marriage in society and the increasing willingness of society to accept alternative lifestyles as being equally valid or important.

RACE

The ECtHR has been quick to condemn discrimination on the grounds of race and the Commission has concluded that such actions amount to an affront to human dignity and could amount to degrading treatment within the meaning of Article 3 of the Convention.[39]

RELIGION

The essence of the right to believe (Article 9) is that the citizen is permitted to believe what he or she wishes, free of indoctrination by the State.[40] Thus an employee cannot be dismissed for his or her religious beliefs. The employer may be justified in asking that the employee does not manifest his or her beliefs in the workplace and this would apply to a request for time off for religious observance. Restrictions may be legitimately imposed where the requests made by the employee are incompatible with the proper performance of the job and cannot sensibly be accommodated by the employer.[41]

---

39   See *East African Asians v UK* (1973) 3 EHRR 76, which is discussed in greater detail at **5.6.2**.
40   *Angelini v Sweden* (1986) 51 DR 41.
41   *Ahmad v UK* (1981) 4 EHRR 126.

In *Hoffmann v Austria*,[42] the applicant who lost custody of her children to her divorced spouse as a result partly of her religious beliefs as a Jehovah's Witness successfully challenged that decision. The ECtHR found a violation of Article 14 and did not consider it necessary to look at Article 8 (freedom of religion).

BIRTH

The protection accorded to traditional family relationships had been favourably viewed by the ECtHR given the importance of social integration, but in *Marckx v Belgium*[43] the ECtHR challenged a rule whereby a child born out of wedlock could not inherit property from his or her mother without special steps being taken by the mother in order to do so. The ECtHR also rejected an argument based on the convictions of the local rural population. These were used to justify precedence taken by a legitimate child over one born out of wedlock for the purpose of inheriting a farm on intestacy.[44]

NATIONAL ORIGIN AND MINORITIES

In *Gaygusuz v Austria*,[45] the ECtHR held that exclusion of the applicant from emergency unemployment assistance due to his national origin was not justified where he had satisfied all the other material criteria of eligibility applicable to Austrian claimants and had worked and paid contributions.

LANGUAGE

It is important to note that there is no obligation on governments to have the same legislation applicable throughout the various regions of the State, and regional differences have generally not been successfuly challenged. The question of regional languages such as Welsh and the provision of certain services in that language or indeed any other regional language may be subject to challenge.

In *Gwynedd County Council v Jones*,[46] the EAT refused to recognise any distinction between Welsh-speaking people and English-monoglot Welsh people and rejected a claim by English-speaking Welsh claimants that reserving certain local authority jobs for Welsh speakers was a violation of their rights under the RRA 1976. One might well imagine individuals from some ethnic minorities also seeking protection of their right to receive public services in their mother tongue.

The question of use of a particular language as a barrier to employment has been examined under EC law. In *Groener v Minister for Education and City of Dublin Vocational Education Committee*,[47] the ECJ held that because of the constitutionally guaranteed official status of the Irish language in the Republic of Ireland, a Dublin college could lawfully impose an Irish language require-

---

42   (1993) 17 EHRR 293.
43   (1979–80) 2 EHRR 330.
44   *Inze v Austria* (1988) 10 EHRR 394.
45   (1997) 23 EHRR 364.
46   [1986] ICR 833.
47   [1989] ECR 3967.

ment for an art lecturing post, even though knowledge of Irish was not actually needed to perform the job. The ECJ noted that:

> 'The EEC Treaty does not prohibit the adoption of a policy for the protection and promotion of a language of a member State which is both the national language and the first official language. However, the implementation of such a policy must not encroach upon a fundamental freedom such as that of the free movement of workers. Therefore, the requirements deriving from measures intended to implement such a policy must not in any circumstances be disproportionate in relation to the aim pursued and the manner in which they are applied must not bring about discrimination against nationals of other Member States.'

The ECJ concluded that the importance of education for the implementation of such a policy had to be recognised as did the essential role that teachers had to play not only through teaching but through their participation in the daily life of the school and their privileged relationship with their pupils.[48] Using the Convention, case-law might not entail a different result in such circumstances.

Interaction of Article 14 with substantive Convention rights

An applicant who wishes to rely on Article 14 needs to show that the action of which the applicant is complaining calls into play a substantive Convention right. Article 14 has also been used to test entitlement to welfare benefits or tax concessions which are available only to one sex or one group to the detriment of others. The substantive right which is infinged is Article 1 of the 1st Protocol – the right to property.

It is proposed to consider the types of Convention rights which are more likely to come into play in conjunction with Article 14 in the employment context, namely:

- Article 3 (freedom from torture, inhuman and degrading treatment);
- Article 4 (freedom from forced labour);
- Article 6 (right to a fair trial);
- Article 8 (right to respect of private and family life);
- Articles 9 and 10 (freedom of thought and expression);
- Article 11 (freedom of association).

5.6.2   Article 3

Article 3 provides that no one shall be subjected to torture or to inhuman or degrading treatment or punishment. It is clear that Article 3 envisages the more extreme treatment which persons may receive in police States or more severe punishment meted out by branches of government, security forces and so on. In *Ireland v UK*,[49] the ECtHR examined five techniques used by the British Government to interrogate prisoners accused of being terrorists. They were deprived of food, drink and sleep, forced to stand in uncomfortable positions, hooded and subjected to loud continuous noise. Such practices were deemed to amount to degrading treatment. The ECtHR categorised 'torture' as

---

48   Wilson Mcleod, 'Autochthonous language communities and the Race Relations Act' at *Current legal issues*: http://webjcli.ncl.ac.uk/1998/issue 1.

49   (1979–80) 2 EHRR 25.

deliberate inhuman treatment causing very serious and cruel suffering; 'inhuman treatment' was treatment that caused intense physical and mental suffering; and 'degrading treatment' amounted to treatment that aroused in the victim a feeling of fear, anguish and inferiority capable of humiliating and debasing the victim and possibly breaking the victim's physical or moral resistance.

In the important case of *East African Asians v UK*,[50] the applicants were citizens of the UK and colonies who were unable to join their wives in the UK. In those cases, 25 East African Asians had retained their status as UK citizens when Kenya and Uganda became independent. They understood that in so doing they would be able to enter the UK free from immigration control. However, the UK government imposed immigration control following the adoption of a policy of Africanisation by the Kenyan and Ugandan governments. The right of entry was terminated for UK citizens lacking ancestral or 'place of birth' connections with the UK. The Commission concluded that the racial discrimination to which the applicants had been publicly subjected through immigration legislation amounted to degrading treatment within Article 3 of the Convention. While accepting that States have a right to refuse to admit persons to their territory, the Commission noted that the State's discretion cannot be exercised by implementing policies of a purely racist nature such as a policy prohibiting the entry of any persons of a particular skin colour.

This is an important decision insofar as it established that institutionalised racial discrimination can amount to 'degrading treatment' within the meaning of Article 3 of the Convention. The case of *Tyrer*[51] notes that the humiliating or degrading treatment does not necessarily have to be public.

In some circumstances, the State can be liable for the acts of its agents, such as soldiers or police authorities. In the employment context, it may be possible in case of extreme harassment or abuse to argue that Article 3 has been infringed; certainly bullying and harassment which may or may not involve physical contact is capable of amounting to *degrading treatment*. It is hoped that activities capable of amounting to 'torture' or 'inhuman treatment' would not be found in the workplace. The State will be liable if sufficient safeguards are not in place which reduce the likelihood of such events occurring.

5.6.3 Article 4

Article 4 of the Convention contains the prohibition against slavery, servitude and forced or compulsory labour. For the purposes of the Convention, forced or compulsory labour does not include:

- work required to be done while in detention;
- military service;
- any service required in case of an emergency or calamity threatening the life or well-being of the community; and

---

50   (1981) 3 EHRR 76.
51   *Tyrer v UK* (1979–80) 2 EHRR 1.

–   any work done which forms part of normal civic obligations.

Slavery and servitude are not defined in the Convention. Servitude is considered to amount to a requirement that the person working lives on the property of the employer, but there is no connotation of ownership of the worker. There should, generally speaking, be little need for the invocation of this provision of the Convention, although domestic servants who work excessive hours for low wages and whose freedom of movement is curtailed may consider that they fall within the provisions of this Article.

The question would arise, since such workers are in private employment, as to whether the UK government has taken any or any sufficient steps to ensure that such practices could not be maintained through loopholes in the existing labour legislation. For instance, the Working Time Regulations 1998[52] contain a number of exceptions so that a number of workers are denied the benefits of such legislation and it may be possible to argue that the denial of such benefits to a class of worker may be indirectly discriminatory. Domestic workers are often female and a large majority of such workers may come from a particular ethnic group.

Forced and compulsory labour refers to work exacted from a person under the threat of penalty, for which that person has not voluntarily offered himself or herself. Certain obligations to work will not violate Article 4(2) provided they are not excessive or disproportionate in the circumstances.

Article 4(3) exempts certain types of work from the term 'forced or compulsory labour':

'(a) any work required to be done in the ordinary course of detention imposed according to the provisions of Article 5 of this Convention or during conditional release from such detention;

(b) any service of military character or, in case of conscientious objectors, in countries where they are recognised, service exacted instead of compulsory military service;

(c) any service exacted in case of an emergency or calamity threatening the life or well-being of the community;

(d) any work or service which forms part of normal civic obligations.'

These exemptions are largely self-explanatory and there is little case-law on these. In *Iversen v Norway*,[53] a Norwegian dentist was compelled to work in a certain area for a year; his claim under Article 4 failed. The situation in 1956 and 1960 in relation to public dental services and school dental care in northern Norway was regarded as an emergency and Iversen's complaint that the obligatory service that he had to perform amounted to compulsory labour was rejected. The Commission had regard to the similar provisions in the ILO Convention which limited the concept of compulsory labour to work which was 'oppressive or unjust'. A similar claim by a Belgian trainee barrister who was required to represent clients *pro bono* for a certain period also failed since the ECtHR considered that the requirement was not disproportionate or excessive

---

52   SI 1998/1833.
53   Application No 1468/62 (1963) 6 YB 278.

in the circumstances. An added factor was that his services allowed the State to give effect to Article 6 of the Convention by ensuring a fair trial for his client which would not otherwise have been possible.[54]

The case of *Schmidt v Germany*[55] did establish a breach of Article 4(3) where the German municipal authorities required male citizens either to serve in the fire brigade or to pay a financial contribution in lieu of such service.

5.6.4 Article 6

Article 6 enshrines the right to a fair trial and is of equal importance for criminal and civil matters. Article 6(1) provides:

> 'In the determination of his civil rights and obligations or of any criminal charge against him, everyone is entitled to a fair and public hearing within a reasonable time by an independent and impartial tribunal established by law. Judgment shall be pronounced publicly but the press and public may be excluded from all or part of the trial in the interests of morals, public order or national security in a democratic society, where the interests of juveniles or the protection of the private life of the parties so require, or to the extent strictly necessary in the opinion of the court in special circumstances where publicity would prejudice the interests of justice.'

The first issue is what constitutes a civil right and obligation. This is fairly wide-ranging and in the employment context it is important to note that public employment is not generally considered to amount to a civil right or obligation.[56] In the case of *Balfour v UK*,[57] a former diplomat was unable to use Article 6 to challenge the use of public interest immunity certificates to exclude evidence from his case alleging unfair dismissal.

The case-law of the Convention suggests paradoxically that it will cover private employment contracts but not necessarily public law employees since the ECtHR has rejected claims by employees concerning conditions of service and discipline. There is some evidence that this is changing and in *Muyldermans v Belgium*[58] the determination of the employee's obligation to reimburse certain sums were held by the Commission to be within the scope of Article 6. The applicant worked as an accountant in a post office. On audit, it was found that she had failed to perform her duties and she was in effect surcharged. The Commission concluded that the obligation in question was mixed public and private and that the private aspects predominated.

In contrast, in *X v United Kingdom*,[59] a claim by an English policeman was held not to fall within Article 6 because police officers are exclusively subordinated to governmental authorities and do not enter into contractual relationships.

---

54 *Van der Musselle v Belgium* (1984) 6 EHRR 163.
55 (1984) 18 EHRR 513.
56 *Kosieck v Germany* (1986) 9 EHRR 328 and *Neigel v France* [1997] EHRLR 424.
57 [1997] EHRLR 665.
58 A/214–A (1991) Com Rep.
59 (1980) 21 DR 168.

Disciplinary proceedings which determine a right to practise a profession do not amount to proceedings dealing with civil rights and must conform to Article 6(1).[60] In the leading case of *Le Compte, Van Leuven and De Meyere v Belgium*[61] the ECtHR emphasised the importance of Article 6 which is really a procedural right. It does not create a new cause of action where none previously existed in domestic law and will apply only to disciplinary proceedings in 'public law proceedings' such as those before professional bodies or regulators. The recent case of *Pellegrin v France*[62] attempts to clarify the somewhat confusing case-law. Disputes excluded are those raised by public servants whose duties 'typify the specific duties of the public service', acting as 'the depository of public authority responsible for protecting the general interests of the State, eg the armed forces and the police.

Right to a fair hearing

The right to a fair hearing is interpreted in a liberal manner and with the overriding concern being to ensure that the proceedings are fair and that all evidence and submissions are properly examined. The litigant must have real and effective access to a court, should have notice of the proceedings and should have a genuine opportunity to present his or her case and be given a reasoned decision at the end of the hearing. The principle of equality of arms means that there should be no imbalance between the opportunities afforded to both parties in the presentation of their case and their representation before the court.

Hearings must also be concluded within a reasonable time, and this has been the source of much litigation. In *Maillard v France*,[63] the applicant lodged a complaint about the assessment of his service in the navy during 1983 and applied to have his career retrospectively reassessed. This matter was not resolved until March 1996 and he complained that this amounted to a breach of Article 6 in that he had a right to a trial within a reasonable time. The ECtHR held that the dispute dealt primarily with his career and as such was outside the scope of Article 6(1).

In contrast, in *Cazenave de la Roche v France*[64] the applicant contested the termination of the employment in proceedings which took eight years and nine months to reach a conclusion. The Government sought to rely on the civil service exemption but the ECtHR rejected this argument since the case concerned a reparation for damage caused by the applicant's dismissal. It was a purely economic right and was justiciable under Article 6(1).

In *Obermeier v Austria*,[65] the ECtHR held that an appeal can be considered to be sufficient for the purposes of Article 6 only if the appeal court is a judicial body

---

60   *König v Germany* (1979–80) 2 EHRR 170; *Wickramsinghe v United Kingdom* [1998] EHRLR 338 and *X v United Kingdom* (1998) EHRR 480.
61   (1982) 4 EHRR 1.
62   8 December 1999 unreported.
63   (1999) 27 EHRR 232.
64   [1998] HRCD 620.
65   (1990) 13 EHRR 290.

that has full jurisdiction. A court which can determine only whether the discretion enjoyed by administrative authorities has been used in a manner compatible with the object and purpose of the law does not comply with the requirements of Article 6. This describes, in effect, the function of the High Court in the exercise of its role in judicial review.

Independent and impartial tribunal

In *Smith v Secretary of State for Trade and Industry*,[66] the EAT questioned whether employment tribunals constitute an independent tribunal since the selection and appointment of members is carried out by the Secretary of State for Employment. This was a claim by a director and controlling shareholder of an insolvent company that he was entitled to recover a redundancy payment from the Secretary of State for Trade and Industry. Morison J concluded that it was something of an anomaly that the employment tribunals had such close links with the executive arm of the Government. In this context, it may also be questioned whether disciplinary panels can also be challenged and great care should be taken to avoid allegations of bias which could trigger a claim. It should be noted that the ECtHR has been reluctant to condemn apparent irregularities in the tribunal of first instance where there is an appeal to a properly constituted court.[67]

In *Stefan v UK*,[68] the applicant's registration as a GP was suspended after the health committee of the General Medical Council (GMC) ruled that she was not fit to practise. Of the 13 members of the GMC, two are non-medical. There is a legal assessor to advise on points of law. The applicant's Privy Council application was unsuccessful. She complained of a breach of Article 6 arguing that the GMC acted in the proceedings as investigator, prosecutor and adjudicator and as such the health committee was not an independent and impartial tribunal. She also contended that judicial review by the Privy Council did not fulfil the requirement of Article 6. The Commission accepted that the proceedings determined the applicant's civil rights and obligations for the purpose of Article 6(1) and noted that there were some safeguards lacking in the health committee of the GMC in terms of the appointment of its members and its independence from the GMC policy. However, the review by the Privy Council was held to be sufficient to cure the defects.

Access to justice

It has been argued that access to justice should also include the provision of civil legal aid. In the case of *Airey v Ireland*,[69] this question was addressed and the ECtHR stated:

> 'To hold that so far reaching an obligation exists would ... sit ill with the fact that the Convention contains no provision on legal aid for those disputes ... However, despite the absence of ... a clause for civil litigation, article 6(1) may sometimes

66   [2000] ICR 69.
67   *Adolf v Austria* Series A No 49, (1982) 4 EHRR 313 and *Edwards v UK* (1993) 15 EHRR 417.
68   Application No 11674/95, (1998) 25 EHRR CD 130.
69   (1979–80) 2 EHRR 305.

compel the state to provide for the assistance of a lawyer when such assistance proves indispensable for an effective access to the court, either because legal representation is rendered compulsory, as is done by the domestic law of certain contracting states . . . , or by reason of the complexity of the procedure of the case.'

In *Artico v Italy*,[70] the right to be provided with legal representation meant the right to be provided with genuine and effective representation and not simply to have a lawyer present.

5.6.5 Article 8[71]

Article 8 provides that everyone has the right to respect for his or her private and family life, home and correspondence. There should be no interference by a public authority with the existence of this right except such as is in accordance with the law and is necessary in a democratic society in the interests of national security, public safety or the economic well-being of the country, for the prevention of disorder or crime, for the protection of health or morals, or for the protection of the rights and freedoms of others. Private life has not received extensive interpretation by the ECtHR. The concept encompasses personal freedom and it ensures that there is a sphere within which everyone can freely pursue the development and fulfilment of their personalities. It includes the right to an identity and the right to develop relationships with other persons. A Member State must not only curb its own interference in the private lives of its citizens in keeping with Article 8 but there is a positive duty on States to protect the enjoyment of rights and secure respect for those rights in domestic law.

In the field of employment this can be important in many respects: apparent discrimination on the grounds of sexuality or sexual orientation may be considered to be a violation of Article 8 and a person's entitlement to respect for private and family life. This can manifest itself not only in the way that a person is treated but also in the nature of benefits which are provided to one class or group of persons but not to others.

In the context of general employment practices, some issues may impinge on the right to privacy, such as the collection of medical data and the maintenance of medical records, security checks and wire-tapping. The State must ensure that there are proper safeguards to ensure that respect for private and family life is guaranteed. In *Halford v UK*,[72] Alison Halford, a senior police officer, established that a breach of Article 8 occurred when her telephone at work was tapped. In *Leander v Sweden*,[73] the ECtHR held that the retention and use of information about an individual in connection with employment in national security jobs did not carry with it a positive obligation to allow the applicant to know the content of the files.[74]

---

70 (1980) 3 EHRR 1.
71 A useful commentary is provided by Dinah Rose in 'Discrimination: European Community and Competition Law, Sexual Orientation and Gender Identity' (unpublished paper presented at the Liberty conference on 22 November 1999).
72 (1997) 24 EHRR 523.
73 (1987) 9 EHRR 433.
74 Karen Reid *A Practitioner's Guide to the European Convention on Human Rights* (Sweet & Maxwell, 1998).

In the case of *Lustig-Prean and Beckett v UK*,[75] the applicants, who had been discharged from the armed services on the grounds of their homosexuality, claimed breaches of their right to a private life under Article 8, their right to free expression of their sexual identity under Article 10, their right to an effective domestic remedy under Article 13 and their right to equal enjoyment of Convention rights under Article 14. A claim that investigation into their sexuality amounted to degrading treatment within the meaning of Article 3 was not upheld, but their complaint under Article 8 was successful. The Government's contention that the ban was justified as the presence of homosexuals in the armed forces would have a substantial and negative effect on morale and the operational effectiveness of the armed forces was rejected. The ECtHR, echoing the *Obermeier*[76] decision, concluded that judicial review did not constitute an effective remedy and consequently there had been a breach of Article 13 of the Convention.

While the ECtHR and the ECJ have both been reluctant to move in advance of public opinion, homosexuals or transsexuals will be able to rely on Article 8 and Article 14 where in the course of their employment they suffer a detriment which has occurred because of their sexuality. The existing gap in legal protection will in any event be filled by the Treaty of Amsterdam, which includes protection from discrimination on the ground of sexual orientation. Lord Bingham stated:

'To dismiss a person from his or her employment on the grounds of private sexual preference ... would not appear to me to show respect for that person's private and family life. There may also be room for argument whether the interference in question answers a pressing social need and in particular is proportionate to the legitimate aim pursued ...'[77]

There has been some case-law in relation to the treatment of persons suffering from AIDS in respect of the length of time that claims for compensation have taken and differential treatment accorded to them in criminal proceedings. It is possible that a difference in treatment of such persons in the workplace may fall foul of Article 8 and Article 14. Employers will have to be sensitive to the use and storage of personal data in relation to confidential issues. Surveillance of telephone calls and e-mail correspondence will also have to be carefully implemented to ensure that there is no infringement of Article 8.

The ECtHR has had a limited contribution to resolving the problems of stigmatisation and discrimination facing persons who are homosexual since it has adopted a more conservative approach to social mores. *Dudgeon v UK*[78] established that private sexual conduct cannot be prohibited because of its propensity to shock or offend since it is an important part of an individual's private life.

The ECtHR has not clearly defined what is understood by 'private life' but the concept stands for the sphere of immediate personal autonomy. This covers

75   (2000) 29 EHRR 548.
76   *Obermeier v Austria* (1991) 13 EHRR 290.
77   *R v Ministry of Defence, ex parte Smith and Others* [1996] ICR 740 at 782.
78   (1982) 4 EHRR 149.

aspects of physical and moral integity; it ensures a sphere within which everyone can freely pursue the development and fulfilment of their personality. This means the right to an identity, and includes the right to develop relationships with other persons. Private life overlaps with family life, home and correspondence. In *Klass v Germany*,[79] interception of communication was potentially an interference with family and private life, correspondence and home.

The ability of judges of the ECtHR to interpret the Convention as a living instrument which takes into account changes in social attitudes is very clear. In the case of *López Ostra v Spain*,[80] the applicant argued that the pollution caused by a privately owned waste treatment plant affected the applicant's house and that this amounted to a violation of Article 8.

In *Horsham v UK*,[81] the ECtHR ruled that the applicant's privacy had not been breached when, for legal purposes such as court appearances or obtaining insurance and contractual documents, transsexuals were forced to show certificates revealing their previous names and gender.

5.6.6   Articles 9 and 10

Article 9 is divided into two parts – the right to believe and the right to manifest religion or belief subject to certain limitations. The general freedoms of thought, conscience and religion are absolute rights and are not subject to any limitation. It is the manifestation of such beliefs which is subject to safeguards necessary in a democratic society. The ECtHR has noted that the religious dimension is one of the most vital elements that go to make up the identity of believers and their conception of life.[82] Minority religions may enjoy the benefit of greater protection in the employment field as a result of the Convention. Muslims, for instance, may be able to argue that certain requirements or employment practices discriminate against them because they infringe Article 9. In a case before the ECJ, *Prais v EC Council*,[83] a Jewish woman complained of the holding of an examination for a job on a Saturday when the job itself was to be performed during weekdays. Her failure to disclose to her employer that she was Jewish meant that her claim failed.

Article 10 provides that everyone has the right to freedom of expression. This right includes freedom to hold opinions and to receive and impart information and ideas without interference by public authority and regardless of frontiers. The limitations on the right to freedom of expression are more detailed and Article 10(2) states:

> 'The exercise of these freedoms, since it carries with it duties and responsibilities, may be subject to such formalities, conditions, restrictions or penalties as are

79   (1979–80) 2 EHRR 214.
80   (1995) 20 EHRR 277.
81   (1998) 5 BHRC 393.
82   *Young, James and Webster v UK* (1982) 4 EHRR 38.
83   [1976] 2 CMLR 708.

prescribed by law and are necessary in a democratic society, in the interests of national security, territorial integity or public safety, for the prevention of disorder or crime, for the protection of health or morals, for the protection of the reputation or rights of others, for preventing the disclosure of information received in confidence, or for maintaining the authority and impartiality of the judiciary.'

The impact on employment may be limited as there is a general exemption from the Convention of public employment. However, in *Vogt v Germany*[84] the ECtHR held that an interference with civil servants' right to freedom of expression was not justifiable. In that case, a teacher was employed by a State school and was suspended from her post when it emerged that she was involved with the Communist party. The ECtHR accepted that a restriction on an applicant's freedom of expression could be justified on the ground that there was a need to protect the rights of others to effective political democracy. However, it found that the need to limit the applicant's freedom of expression had not been convincingly established in this case.

In *Glimmerveen and Harderbeek v The Netherlands*,[85] the Commission upheld the right to prevent the dissemination of propaganda and opinions maintaining racial supremacy or the spreading of race hatred. However, in *Grigoriades v Greece*,[86] the applicant was penalised for making allegations about a range of abusive practices which he alleged had occurred while he served in the army. He described the army as 'a criminal and terrorist apparatus' in a note to his comanding officer when refusing to serve additional time as sanction for his original comments. The ECtHR concluded that the restrictions imposed were not necessary in a democratic society and that while his comments were intemperate they had been made in the context of a lengthy discourse which had been critical of army life.

The applicant in *Rekvenyi v Hungary*[87] was a police officer and secretary of the police trade union who claimed that legislation prohibiting police and security services from joining any political party or engaging in political activities breached Articles 10, 11 and 14. This was rejected by the ECtHR which held that, given Hungary's recent history and the police force's involvement with the ruling party, there was clearly a need to achieve political neutrality of the police force.

A similar result was reached in *Ahmed v UK*[88] where political restrictions were imposed on the applicants who held posts in local government. The applicants alleged violations of Articles 10 and 11 and their right to participate fully in the electoral process, guaranteed by Article 3 of the 1st Protocol. The ECtHR held that the aim of restricting the applicant's freedom of expression could be justified on account of the need to protect the rights of others to effective political democracy.

---

84   (1996) 21 EHRR 205.
85   (1979) 18 DR 187.
86   (1998) 4 BHRC 43.
87   (2000) 30 EHRR 519.
88   (2000) 29 EHRR 1.

However, there will be no interference by the State where an individual has agreed or contracted to limit his freedom of expression. The protection from interference is not limited to prior censorship of expression and includes sanctions imposed after the act.[89] In *Lingens*, after the applicant had been successfully sued for defamation he was fined. The ECtHR concluded that the fine was a type of censure which was likely to discourage criticism in the future.

Freedom of expression can also extend to the way in which a person dresses and consequently employers will have to be careful that their dress codes do not fall foul of Article 10. The case-law tends to suggest that the requirement imposed by the employer would have to be manifestly unreasonable for such an argument to succeed.

5.6.7   Article 11

Article 11 provides:

'1.   Everyone has the right to freedom of peaceful assembly and to freedom of association with others, including the right to form and to join trade unions for the protection of his interests.

2.   ... This Article shall not prevent the imposition of lawful restrictions on the exercise of these rights by members of the armed forces, of the police or of the administration of the State.'

This Article is considered more fully in Chapter 4.[90] The right to freedom of association protects the right to join or form other associations as well as trade unions. Professional regulatory bodies set up by a State to regulate a profession do not, however, come within this definition.[91]

In *NATFHE v UK*,[92] the applicant trade union claimed that the requirement to provide lists of members who were to be balloted concerning proposed strike action amounted to a breach of the right of association. If such lists were not provided then the union could be prevented from proceeding with industrial action. The ECtHR held that the right to strike was not expressly enshrined in Article 11 and may reasonably be subject to a measure which was designed to foster debate and discussion between the parties. The application was rejected.

5.6.8   Public authorities as employers[93]

For a detailed discussion on this topic see **2.11**. While the HRA 1998 contains no definition of what is or is not a public authority, it does include a court or tribunal. However, once it is established that a body is a public authority, the employee will have directly effective rights as against his or her employer when

---

89   *Lingens v Austria* (1986) 8 EHRR 103.
90   See also John Hendy QC, 'The Human Rights Act, Article 11, and the Right to Strike' [1998] EHRLR Issue 5 at p 583 and Martin Chamberlain, 'Trade Unions and the Human Rights Act 1998' (unpublished paper).
91   *Le Compte, van Leuven and de Meyere v Belgium* (1982) 4 EHRR 1.
92   (1998) 25 EHRR CD 122.
93   Sir Gavin Lightman and John Bowers QC, 'Incorporation of the ECtHR [the Convention] and its impact on Employment Law' [1998] EHRLR Issue 5 at p 560.

it is acting in its public capacity. It is thus clear that local authorities will be covered by the HRA 1998, as will NHS trusts, education and health authorities, and large corporations carrying out a public role. The Lord Chancellor identified Railtrack as a company which would be performing a public function as a safety regulator.

However, traditionally the relationship of employer–employee has been seen as one which is a private law function and not a public law function. This potentially creates invidious distinctions between the staff and patients who deal with a consultant through the NHS and those who see him half-an-hour later at a private hospital, or indeed, in the same hospital but as private patients.

5.6.9 Private employers[94]

The Convention provides no protection from private parties' violation of Convention rights. However, a State can be liable for permitting or failing to prevent such violations. It was applied by the ECtHR in *National Union of Belgian Police v Belgium*[95] which dealt with trade union rights. The ECtHR held that the State had a duty to ensure that, under national law, trade unions should be able to strive for the protection of their members' interests in conditions compatible with Article 11 (freedom of association).

It should be remembered that the ECtHR found a violation of the Convention where caning had been permitted in a private school. Under Article 8 there is not only the requirement that the State refrain from interfering with the citizen's rights but also the positive obligation to act in order to ensure respect for these rights. In *Kroon v The Netherlands*,[96] the State had a duty to ensure that there was effective respect for family life.

It will clearly be the case that if domestic courts are willing to fuse concepts learned from domestic and EC law with protection on grounds of other statuses afforded by Article 14, there will be scope for innovative law-making under the HRA 1998.[97]

In *Mavronichis v Cyprus*,[98] the applicant claimed that the delay in determining his damages action in respect of a decision not to appoint him to a public sector post breached his right to a fair trial in reasonable time. The ECtHR did not accept the Government's argument that this was a public law issue and outside the scope of 'civil rights'. It held that the sole purpose of the compensation proceedings was to obtain financial reparation and to secure the appointment for which he had applied. It was a purely pecuniary claim which sounded in private law.

---

94 For an interesting historical analysis see Andrew Clapham, 'Human Rights in the Private Sphere' (Clarendon Press, 1993).
95 (1979–80) 1 EHRR 578.
96 (1995) 19 EHRR 263.
97 I am indebted to a paper prepared by Diane Luping, 'Discrimination: European Community Law and the European Convention' 22 November 1999, unpublished.
98 [1998] HRCD 480.

There is a proposal for a free-standing discrimination Article to be incorporated into the Convention. This will make it considerably easier for individuals to rely on the Convention to protect the right to live and work without discrimination if it is accepted by the UK government.

Chapter 6

REMEDIES, DAMAGES AND FUNDING

6.1 INTRODUCTION

6.1.1 Checklist

Where an individual's case raises facts which might involve a breach of his Convention rights, the practitioner should consider the following checklist.

(1) What are the facts of the situation engaging a Convention right (specify)?
(2) What is the act challenged by the individual?
(3) Is it an act of a wholly private nature?
    (a) If not, check to see whether the body carrying it out is a public body in the sense of being a manifestation of the State to the extent that its acts are the State's acts (for example, local government).
    (b) If not, check to see whether certain of the functions of the body (including the one manifested by the act under challenge) are of a public nature, in the sense of being a function of the State (for example, education or maintaining prison security).
    (c) If it is wholly private, and for all purposes the body is not a public authority, there is no cause of action.
(4) Is the challenge in respect of a general act (measure, policy etc) or is it in respect of particular actions of the public authority?
(5) If the body is a private body, what statutory causes of action exist?
(6) In relation to a public body, what causes of action exist:
    (a) under the HRA 1998, s 7(1)(a)?
    (b) under other legislation, interpreted to give effect to the Convention rights?
    (c) arising other than by statute?
(7) If there is a statutory cause of action, against either a public or private body, how can this be interpreted so as to give effect to the Convention rights insofar as it is possible to do so?
(8) If there is a common law remedy only, what powers of the court are involved in its administration?
    (a) Is there a statutory basis for these powers, or have they been reduced to statutory form at any stage?
    (b) How can these powers be given effect and read, so far as it is possible to do so, in a manner compatible with the Convention rights?
(9) In considering whether there is a cause of action under s 7(1)(a) of the HRA 1998: how is the act of the public authority unlawful under s 6 of the HRA 1998?
    (a) consider *prima facie* infringement;
    (b) consider possible justifications;
    (c) consider necessity and proportionality.

(10) What are the powers of the court or tribunal, read in the light of s 3 of the HRA 1998, to provide a remedy in respect of a finding that s 6 had been breached?
  (a) consider statutory remedies (construed via s 3);
  (b) consider remedies said to be exercisable (in the High Court) by s 19 of the Supreme Court Act 1981 (construed via s 3).
(11) What is the appropriate venue? Crown Office; CPR 1998, Part 8 or ordinary claim?
(12) Are the remedies already given, if any, sufficient to afford just satisfaction?
(13) Are damages necessary to afford just satisfaction?
(14) Is there non-pecuniary loss or moral damage present? Would it be just and equitable to award compensation for the moral damage?

The HRA 1998 will have an impact on the remedies available before the courts. The practitioner will need to consider the following.

(1) The effect of s 3 of the HRA 1998 on any existing remedy; and either:
  (a) in cases involving a public authority, the effect of s 6 of the HRA 1998; or
  (b) in cases involving private parties, whether reliance can be placed on an unlawful act of a public authority.
(2) If a finding is made that a public authority has acted unlawfully under s 6, whether there is a remedy available in respect of that finding before the court that made it, or whether fresh proceedings must be issued for a remedy (and/or to establish the unlawfulness of the act).
(3) The effect of s 6 on the actions of the court or tribunal.

In order to be able to consider the effects of s 3 or s 8 on remedies available to the court, it is necessary to have a clear idea of when an act of a public authority (including the court) is compatible with a Convention right.

The concept of compatibility must, it is suggested, be read with a view to the purpose of the Convention right, and not simply with a view to obtaining linguistic compatibility with the Convention right. The purpose of s 3 is to ensure practical and effective adherence to the Convention rights.

6.1.2 The effect of the Convention on disputes between private parties

It is in the area of remedies that the HRA 1998 may have greatest impact. A court or a tribunal is obliged to interpret its statutory powers so as to give effect to them in a way that is compatible with the Convention rights. This obligation applies whether the dispute is between fully private bodies or between an individual and a public authority (or in relation to the public act of a body, certain of whose functions are public). Moreover, in relation to certain Convention rights, such as those in Article 8 or Article 10, the court has a positive obligation to protect the individual's access to these rights.[1] The court will, in the context of certain factual situations invoking Articles of the

---

1   See *X & Y v The Netherlands* (1986) 8 EHRR 235.

Convention imposing a positive obligation, have to guarantee rights that are not theoretical or illusory, but rights that are practical and effective.[2] The duty under s 3 of the HRA 1998 is to give effect to statutory powers insofar as possible so as to render the exercise of those powers compatible with the Convention rights.

Against this approach is the view that a claimant in a dispute against another private party does not have a Convention right against the other party, as there is no State party to the action, and the Convention rights are enforceable against State parties only. This argument misses the point about the role of positive obligations under the Convention, but does signify a limitation on the type of rights that the court may need to take into account in claims between purely private parties. The State (in the form of a judicial body) is engaged in the administration of justice between the parties, and its actions cannot facilitate the limitation of the Convention rights to a greater extent than is permitted under the Convention. The provisions of s 3 independently point to the same conclusion in respect of the powers of the court in the context of the long title of the HRA 1998 (ie its purpose is to give further effect to the Convention rights).

The Government's view of the way in which the duty to act compatibly with Convention rights will affect the functions of the court was set out at, among other places, Hansard HL Debs, 24 November 1997, col 783. The Lord Chancellor stated:

> 'We also believe that it is right as a matter of principle for the courts to have a duty of acting compatibly with the convention not only in cases involving other public authorities but also in developing the common law in deciding cases between individuals.'

From this view of the effect of the Convention rights, it is clear that the duty of compatibility (which is to give effect so far as it is possible to do so) requires the courts to apply the Convention rights where they would be applied in cases between individuals by the Strasbourg authorities. However, not every right imposes the positive obligation on the State to ensure protection for the individual against the acts of other persons which infringe the individual's right to protection under the Convention.

It is submitted, therefore, that in relation to remedies available to the individual by statute, the individual has the right to require them to be exercised in such a way that the *final outcome* is compatible with the Convention rights. This has two consequences, depending on whether or not the right relied upon is one that imports a positive obligation on the State to protect an individual against another individual.

In considering remedies, of whatever nature, the practitioner should adopt the following process.

(1) Identify the basis of jurisdiction of the court/tribunal in relation to the remedy (for example, s 19 of the Supreme Court Act 1981).

---

2   See *Artico v Italy* (1981) 3 EHRR 1.

(2) Identify the Convention right in question:
    (a) would the Convention right be engaged by the facts if the other party was a State party?
    (b) would the infringement be justified if the other party was a State party?
    (c) does the right import a positive obligation on the State to ensure protection between individuals?
    (d) if so, is there sufficient State protection for the right by alternative means?

(3) If there is no sufficient State protection for the right by alternative means available to the party claiming infringement of the right, how can the court exercise its remedial powers (within its jurisdiction) to ensure the effective protection of the Convention right?

(4) If the Convention right in issue does not give rise to a positive obligation on the State to provide protection, then the court must have regard to the Convention rights in giving effect to its powers and in its interpetation of statutory provisions. It must reach a conclusion which does not limit the application of the Convention rights further than is permitted under the Convention itself.

Section 7 of the HRA 1998 permits a further use of the Convention rights. In a dispute between private individuals, a party may rely upon his or her Convention rights insofar as he or she alleges that a public authority has carried out an unlawful act under s 6 of the HRA 1998. This right is independent of the duty of the court under s 3 of the HRA 1998. In disputes between purely private bodies, it is open to the court hearing the matter to make a finding under s 8 that a public authority has committed an act rendered unlawful under s 6. If the public authority is not a party to proceedings, that finding may form the basis of a claim under s 6 against the public authority. However, the public authority in those proceedings may dispute the factual and legal basis of the finding.[3] The court or tribunal that made such a finding would not have jurisdiction to make an award against the public authority.[4] Further, in a dispute in the civil courts, there may be scope for the public authority to be joined as a third party in respect of its unlawful act, insofar as the damage suffered by the private individuals may be attributed to its unlawful act.

6.1.3   Disputes between an individual and a public authority

The position in relation to disputes between individuals and public authorities is more straightforward. Section 6 of the HRA 1998 renders unlawful any act of a public authority which is not compatible with a Convention right. Proceedings may be brought under s 7(1)(a) of the HRA 1998 if the allegation is only that s 6 has been breached by the public authority. However, in employment tribunals, the individual may rely on an act of his or her public authority employer which is rendered unlawful under s 6.[5]

---

3   See CPR 1998, r 7.11. The claim is brought in any court.
4   See s 8(1) of the HRA 1998.
5   HRA 1998, s 7(1)(b).

The question of whether an act is unlawful under s 6 is to be determined, it is suggested, by reference to the outcome of the act. If the effect of the act is to infringe Convention rights, without justification, it is unlawful. Where the public authority is before the employment tribunal as a result of that unlawful act (for example because it dismissed an employee in a manner that breaches the employee's right to respect for his or her family life or private life), the tribunal will be able to make a finding to that effect, and under s 8(1) of the HRA 1998 give such remedy within its jurisdiction as it considers just and appropriate in relation to that unlawful act.

Note that the public authority whose every act is an act of the State cannot rely on its Convention rights as against the tribunal as it is not a 'victim' for the purposes of the Convention, but it can rely on s 3 for the proper interpretation of statutory powers. For the purposes of interpretation, the court or tribunal must render legislation compatible with the Convention rights. For these purposes, the authority does not have to show that its own Convention rights would be breached, but simply that a certain interpretation must be given to the provision to protect Convention rights of individuals.

6.1.4 Disputes between a private individual and a hybrid body

An individual may rely on the Convention rights in respect of a public act of a hybrid body. A body is a 'hybrid body' if some of its acts are public acts. Public acts are those engaging State authority. The hybrid body may be a public authority in the act of defending itself from litigation. Therefore it may rely on its Convention rights as against the court or tribunal.

6.2 SECTION 7 – PROCEEDINGS

6.2.1 Introduction

Section 7 of the HRA 1998 envisages two types of proceedings. First, there are those between private individuals. Secondly, there are those between a public authority and a private individual. The scope of actions brought by individuals against public authorities or the reliance placed on the Convention rights is purely confined to civil remedies against the public authority. Section 7(8) provides that nothing in the HRA 1998 creates a criminal offence. By virtue of the definition of legal proceedings as including proceedings instigated by a public authority, the Convention rights may be relied upon in the criminal courts in defence. Where private prosecutions are brought against a public authority, the individual prosecutor will be able to rely on the principles of interpretation in s 3 of the HRA 1998 and on the Convention rights.

By s 7(1) of the HRA 1998, a person who claims that a public authority has acted (or proposes to act) in a way which is made unlawful by s 6(1) of the HRA 1998 may:

(a) bring proceedings against the authority under the HRA 1998 in the appropriate court or tribunal; or

(b) rely on the Convention right or rights concerned in any legal proceedings,

but only if that person is (or would be) a victim of the unlawful act.

The phrase 'appropriate court or tribunal' means such court or tribunal as may be determined in accordance with rules.[6] As yet, the employment tribunals have not been determined as appropriate tribunals. Thus the employment tribunal cannot hear stand-alone proceedings against a public authority for breach of s 6. 'Proceedings against' an authority include a counterclaim or similar proceeding. The 'legal proceedings' in which the person may rely on the Convention rights include proceedings brought by or at the instigation of a public authority and an appeal against the decision of a court or tribunal.[7] This definition of legal proceedings is not exhaustive. The purpose of this provision appears to be to include in the definition of legal proceedings those cases in which the public authority is not the named litigant, but has 'instigated' the litigation. The intention is that legal proceedings should include criminal proceedings brought by the prosecuting authorities of the State. As such, this seems unnecessary, given the breadth of the definition of 'legal proceedings' even when considered without the inclusion of claims instigated by the public authority. The inclusive definition must be treated as giving clarification of the concept of 'legal proceedings' and nothing more. The fact that the claim has been instigated by a public authority does not give the individual any greater right to allege as against the named claimant a breach of s 6 or for the court to treat that act as an unlawful act of the individual. If reliance is on any unlawful act of the public authority, albeit that the public authority is not a party to the action, it may be joined to the action since s 7(1)(a) entitles the aggrieved party to bring proceedings against the public authority directly in the appropriate court or tribunal. In such an action, the claim against the public authority would be that it is liable for any damages which the individual defendant becomes liable to pay to the individual claimant due to its unlawful act under s 6. However, this cumbersome route to redress may be avoided altogether if it is accepted that the concept of 'act' under s 6 includes the instigation of a person to commit an act that would be in breach of the Convention rights of another person.

Section 7 was debated during the course of the passage of the Human Rights Bill. Although s 7 is probably not ambiguous, it may be useful to consider the intention behind it. An amendment had been moved, the effect of which would be to exclude tribunals from taking account of the Convention rights. To the limited extent that the amendment would have achieved that end, the Government opposed it.

The Minister stated:[8]

> 'one of the Bill's key principles is that all courts and tribunals should take account of convention rights whenever they are relevant to the case before them. Otherwise, people would have no access to their rights unless they went to the European Court of Human Rights or to the Commission. We shall ensure that

---

6   See procedural rules for bringing claims, CPR 1998, r 7.11.

7   See HRA 1998, s 7(6).

8   HC Debs, 24 June 1998, col 1056.

individuals can rely on their convention rights and have access to them at the earliest opportunity. We shall also make the convention rights an integral part of our legal system.

We want everyone in Britain to view the basic principles set out in the convention as part of their national heritage. We shall not achieve that by practising an internal system of apartheid, keeping the convention rights as the exclusive preserve of the courts. ...

It is in keeping with that principle that tribunals as well as courts are required by clause 3 to read and give effect to legislation as far as possible in a way that is compatible with the convention rights. It is also in keeping with that principle that tribunals should be able to take account of the convention rights when a person alleges that he or she has been the victim of an unlawful act by a public authority. ...

... It is our expectation that the great majority of cases in which the convention arguments are raised will fall within the scope of ... proceedings [in which Convention rights may be relied upon]. That is because, in most cases, it is likely that a victim of an act made unlawful by clause 6(1) will have available to him an existing course of action or other means of legal challenge, such as a judicial review.

Furthermore, in a significant proportion of such cases, a tribunal, not a court, will be the forum in which a case is brought. Social security, employment, housing and immigration are but a few of the many areas where tribunals handle the bulk of cases. ...

To prevent individuals from raising convention points in tribunals would cause unnecessary delay, expense and frustration.

... cases brought under clause 7(1)(a) that is, cases brought solely on convention grounds. As I have said, we expect that such cases will be relatively infrequent, but where they do arise, it is likely that a tribunal will sometimes be the most appropriate forum for hearing the case.

If the case concerns a subject which is usually heard, in the first instance, by a tribunal, there is a good prima facie case for assuming that a tribunal will be the correct place in which to hear the convention case. The two amendments will prevent a tribunal from being designated for such a purpose.'

The amendment, which was clearly exploratory, was withdrawn after this explanation. It is submitted that the intention behind s 7 cannot clearly be derived from this passage, as the Minister used the word 'sometimes' in relation to the question of whether the tribunal would be the most appropriate forum for hearing the s 7(1)(a) case. However, the presumption that a tribunal could hear a s 7(1)(a) claim ('a stand-alone' claim) is not borne out by consideration of the HRA 1998 and the subsequent CPR 1998. The correct view is, therefore, probably that where a finding of an unlawful act is made the applicant will have to take further proceedings in the courts to enforce the finding under s 7(1)(a).

6.2.2 The nature of the claim under s 7(1)(a) – private law/ public law challenge

Where the individual is seeking to assert that a particular act of a public authority employer constituted an infringement of the individual's rights under s 6 of the HRA 1998, but is not challenging the validity of a policy, it is suggested that the cause of action is in private law, and judicial review would not be appropriate. Where the challenge is to a policy on the basis that the individual has been affected by it or is likely to be affected by it, the appropriate course is an application for judicial review.

The courts will adopt a flexible approach to the issue of venue, but the provisions of the CPR 1998[9] should be taken into account in determining where to start the claim.

6.2.3   Secondary and alternative claims: torts of inducement

A person may commit the tort of inducing a breach of the HRA 1998 where that person induces a public authority, by information, advice or other means, to commit a breach of s 6 of the HRA 1998.[10]

> 'There are, in my opinion, two grounds only upon which a person who procures the act of another can be made legally responsible for its consequences. In the first place, he will incur liability if he knowingly and for his own ends induces that other person to commit an actionable wrong. In the second place, when the act induced is within the right of the immediate actor, and is therefore not wrongful in so far as he is concerned, it may be to the detriment of a third party; and in that case, according to the law laid down by the majority in *Lumley v Gye* (1853) 2 E & B 216, the inducer may be held liable if he can be shown to have procured his object by the use of illegal means directed against the third party.'[11]

In such cases there will be an element of persuasion by the tortfeasor to do the acts constituting the breach. Although the same principle applies, in theory, to the acts of a public authority, the victim of the public authority's unlawful act under s 6 of the HRA 1998 will have a remedy against the public authority under s 7(1)(a) of the HRA 1998 by bringing an action for breach of s 6 in respect of that act of inducement. The public authority's act of inducement will itself be such an unlawful act.

These torts may cover unlawful means of inducing a breach of contract, contempt of court and breach of statutory duty.[12]

In *Wilson v Housing Corp*,[13] Dyson J held that the tort of inducing unfair dismissal did not exist in law because the ERA 1996 established a code in respect of unfair dismissal remedies and set out certain safeguards, which might be bypassed if the tort of inducing unfair dismissal was recognised. It is likely that the same reasoning would apply to all claims which must be brought before the employment tribunals. Where the unfair dismissal action is based on a breach of the Convention rights, and the employer was induced to dismiss the applicant by the public authority's breach of s 6, there will be an independent action against the public authority for this unlawful act.

---

9   See **6.3.2**.
10   See by analogy *Lumley v Gye* (1853) 2 E & B 216.
11   *Allen v Flood* [1898] AC 1 at 96, *per* Lord Watson.
12   *J T Stratford & Son Ltd v Lindley* [1965] AC 269, *Merkur Island Shipping Corp v Laughton* [1983] 2 AC 570 and *Lonrho plc v Fayed* [1989] 3 WLR 631.
13   [1998] ICR 151.

By contrast, where a private individual induces the public authority to act in breach of the Convention rights there is a cause of action for inducing breach of s 6 against the private individual. Such claims may be predicated on a claim which can be brought before the courts, against the public authority under s 7. The private individual may be made liable in damages for inducing the unlawful act where that person knew what he or she was doing and that it was wrong, and had no legal justification for so doing.

6.2.4 Secondary and alternative claims: misfeasance in public office

Misfeasance in public office is another cause of action which may apply where the public authority's liability may arise under the HRA 1998 or because of some other unlawful act. Misfeasance should be considered as a second line of attack in potential HRA 1998 claims, or where officials of the public authority have acted recklessly as to the consequences of their actions for a person or known group of persons. In addition to considering whether they have a remedy for breaches of the HRA 1998 towards them, the employee's family members may be able to claim that a local authority employer's dismissal of a member of the family was an act of misfeasance towards members of the family if it was performed with reckless indifference as to the outcome of the act. Until recently, it was necessary to show that the public official acted with a deliberate dishonest intent to injure the applicant and with knowledge that the action was beyond its powers.

In *R v Chief Constable of North Wales Police, ex parte AB*,[14] the applicants for judicial review were released from prison after serving sentences for serious paedophilic offences. Whenever they attempted to settle they were met by adverse local press publicity and angry responses from local residents. They eventually obtained a caravan and located themselves on a caravan site where they intended to remain. They were notified, about four months later, to the local police authority as presenting a considerable risk to children and vulnerable people within the community where they had settled. There were a number of meetings of the child protection unit together with members of the local authority social services department and the probation service to consider the appropriate response to the applicants' continued presence on the site during the forthcoming Easter holidays. The concern was that there would be a considerable number of children at the site during that time. They sought to persuade the applicants to move from the site before then, and warned them that if they did not do so the site owner would be told of their records. Information acquired by the police about such offenders could be released only on a 'need to know' basis to protect a potential victim and only after specific consideration of the particular case and with the agreement of senior officers and advisers according to the relevant police policy document. Eventually an officer, after discussion with senior officers, showed the site owner material from the local press relating to the applicants' convictions, and the owner told them to move on. They immediately did so.

---

14   [1997] 3 WLR 724.

The applicants then sought judicial review by way of declarations that the policy and the decision to inform the site owner of their convictions were unlawful and that the conduct of the police amounted to harassment contrary to the Caravan Sites Act 1968, breach of confidence, misfeasance in public office and a breach of Article 8 of the Convention.

The application for misfeasance was rejected by the Divisional Court in the course of the application for judicial review. As the police could not be shown to have acted with a deliberate and dishonest intention to injure the applicants or with the knowledge that they had no power to make the disclosure, there could be no complaint of misfeasance in public office. On the issue of Article 8, the court stated that the disclosure made would have fallen within the specified exception. The court held that:

> 'the disclosure which the N.W.P. made was within the exception specified in the article, provided that the disclosure was made in good faith and in the exercise of a careful professional judgment, and provided that the disclosure was limited to that reasonably judged necessary for the public purpose which the N.W.P. sought to protect.'

When the case came before the Court of Appeal,[15] the Court of Appeal approved this reasoning.[16] Such an officer will be a public body for the purposes of s 6 and where the HRA 1998 has application to the officer's acts there will be no need to go on to consider misfeasance. However, where the HRA 1998 claim fails, the court may still consider the argument based on misfeasance.

The ingredients of the tort of misfeasance in public office were recently clarified in *Three Rivers District Council and Others v Governor and Company of the Bank of England*.[17] Lord Steyn set out the ingredients for this tort:

> '*The ingredients of the tort*
>
> It is now possible to consider the ingredients of the tort. That can conveniently be done by stating the requirements of the tort in a logical sequence of numbered paragraphs.
>
> *(1) The defendant must be a public officer*
>
> It is the office in a relatively wide sense on which everything depends. Thus a local authority exercising private-law functions as a landlord is potentially capable of being sued: *Jones v Swansea City Council* [1990] 1 WLR 1453.
>
> *(2) The second requirement is the exercise of power as a public officer*
>
> This ingredient is also not in issue. The conduct of the named senior officials of the Banking Supervision Department of the Bank was in the exercise of public functions. Moreover, it is not disputed that the principles of vicarious liability apply as much to misfeasance in public office as to other torts involving malice, knowledge or intention: *Racz v Home Office* [1994] 2 A.C. 45.'[18]

---

15   [1998] 3 WLR 57.
16   [1998] 3 WLR 57 at p 69.
17   [2000] 2 WLR 1220 at p 1230, HL.
18   [2000] 2 WLR 1220 at p 1231.

Thus, where an officer of a public authority acts in breach of s 6, it may be necessary to join that officer as a named defendant to the action under s 7(1)(a) to which a claim of misfeasance may be added in the alternative.

'*(3) The third requirement concerns the state of mind of the defendant*

It can therefore now be regarded as settled law that an act performed in reckless indifference as to the outcome is sufficient to ground the tort in its second form.'[19]

The element of reckless indifference is not necessary for there to be a breach of s 6 of the HRA 1998.

'*(4) Duty to the plaintiff*

The question is who can sue in respect of an abuse of power by a public officer. . . . What can be said is that, of course, any plaintiff must have a sufficient interest to found a legal standing to sue. Subject to this qualification, principle does not require the introduction of proximity as a controlling mechanism in this corner of the law. The state of mind required to establish the tort, as already explained, as well as the special rule of remoteness hereafter discussed, keeps the tort within reasonable bounds. There is no reason why such an action cannot be brought by a particular class of persons, such as depositors at a bank, even if their precise identities were not known to the bank. . . .'[20]

An interesting question is the scope of the duty that a public authority owes in the light of the HRA 1998. In respect of an act rendered unlawful by the HRA 1998, would the family of a person whose right to respect for family life had been infringed have sufficient standing to bring a claim for misfeasance or indeed directly under the HRA 1998? For the purposes of remedies for a public authority's employees, it is unlikely that recourse to misfeasance would be necessary. The action could simply be founded on contract. However, where the act was non-contractual, but likely to affect only the employees of a public authority, there is nothing to suggest that such a class may not be owed a duty. Where an unlawful act is likely to have an impact on the families of the employees, it may be that the families would be able to claim under s 7(1)(a) in respect of any failure of the public authority employer to respect their family life. However, if the HRA 1998 challenge failed, the family members of employees might exceptionally establish misfeasance.

'*(5) Causation*

Causation is an essential element of the plaintiff's cause of action. It is a question of fact.

. . .

(6) Damage and remoteness

The claims by the plaintiffs are in respect of financial losses they suffered. These are, of course, claims for recovery of consequential economic losses. The question is when such losses are recoverable. . . .

. . . in both forms of the tort the intent required must be directed at the harm complained of, or at least to harm of the type suffered by the plaintiffs. This results

---

19   [2000] 2 WLR 1220 at p 1231, HL.
20   [2000] 2 WLR 1220 at p 1233.

in the rule that a plaintiff must establish not only that the defendant acted in the knowledge that the act was beyond his powers but also in the knowledge that his act would probably injure the plaintiff or person of a class of which the plaintiff was a member. In presenting a sustained argument for a rule allowing recovery of all foreseeable losses counsel for the plaintiffs argued that such a more liberal rule is necessary in a democracy as a constraint upon abuse of executive and administrative power. The force of this argument is, however, substantially reduced by the recognition that subjective recklessness on the part of a public officer in acting in excess of his powers is sufficient. Recklessness about the consequences of his act, in the sense of not caring whether the consequences happen or not, is therefore sufficient in law. . . .

It is undoubtedly right, as counsel for the plaintiffs pointed out, that the mental element required for the tort of misfeasance in public office means that it is not an effective remedy to deal with state liability for breaches of Community law: *Brasserie du Pêcheur S.A. v Federal Republic of Germany; Reg. v. Secretary of State for Transport, Ex parte Factortame (No. 4)* Joined Cases C-46/93 and C-48/93 [1996] Q.B. 404.'[21]

Considerable quotations from Lord Steyn's judgment are set out above as this represents the most recent and authoritative statement of principle on this point. The implications of the existence of this tort in the context of the HRA 1998 are potentially great.

For example, where the public authority dismisses a person despite being aware that the dismissal is unfair and knowing that person to be the main breadwinner of the family, the family may have a cause of action against the public authority for misfeasance. The family would have to be able to show that it had suffered foreseeable loss as a result of the unlawful act. Where the loss to the family is economic, such as contributions to the mortgage, this may be a foreseeable consequence of the unfair dismissal. Where the family's loss exceeded the statutory limit on compensation for unfair dismissal, a claim based on their rights under the HRA 1998 or for misfeasance may be relevant, but would only be available in the ordinary courts.

Where the actions of the public authority leading up to dismissal constituted a breach of the HRA 1988 in respect of the family of the employee, the family would have a remedy in respect of these actions in the courts under the HRA 1998. However, in relation to family life, the actions would have to be very serious for the court to accept that they struck at the ability of the persons involved to have a family life. It is unlikely that a court would accept that a minor impairment of the quality of the family life enjoyed would constitute an infringement of the right to respect for family life. The act of the public authority would have to constitute an infringement of that family life, and not merely an act which had repercussions on how that family life is conducted. It would thus apply only to situations in which the effect of the unlawful act of the employer was the effective break up of the family relationship or situations in which the maintenance of family relationships was rendered considerably more difficult.

21　[2000] 2 WLR 1220 at pp 1233–1235, HL.

Thus if the way in which the employee is treated is such as to cause severe psychological stress resulting in the break up of his or her marriage, the public authority may have to answer a claim for infringement of the right to respect for family life. If the employer's act was found to be in breach of Article 3, the family would be able to bring a claim based on misfeasance in public office as regards the economic consequences of that treatment for the family.

The situation does not need to be as extreme as regards a failure to respect private life. For example, if covert surveillance is found to have been an unlawful infringement of the right to respect for private life, involving interference with the private life of other members of the employee's family, a claim could be brought by those family members. Thus where the fact of unlawful surveillance has resulted in distress and anxiety to the employee's partner, that partner would have a right to claim damages against the public authority.

The family of an employee may have such claims directly under s 7(1)(a) of the HRA 1998 if they can show that they are victims of an unlawful act of the public authority. It is possible for such persons to be indirect victims of the unlawful act for the purposes of the Convention.[22]

6.2.5 Requirement that the person be a victim of the unlawful act

In order to succeed in establishing a breach of s 6 of the HRA 1998, the individual must show that he or she has been directly affected by the act of the public authority. By s 7(7), a person is a victim of an unlawful act only if that person would be a victim for the purposes of Article 34 of the Convention if proceedings were brought in the ECtHR in respect of that act. Article 34 permits the ECtHR to receive applications from 'any person, non-governmental organisation or group of individuals claiming to be the victim of a violation' of the Convention. Thus public authorities cannot satisfy this criterion so as to be able to claim the protection of s 6 against another public body or to rely on s 7(1)(b) rights in the course of proceedings.

The court must identify whether the person is a victim or not, from the facts placed before it by the individual. As it is part of the procedural provisions of the Convention, the concept of 'victim' must be applied in a manner serving to make the system of individual reliance efficacious.[23]

In the *Guzzardi* case,[24] the Italian government argued that the applicant was not a victim in relation to a breach of Article 5 in addition to the claims he had expressly made when the Commission had identified him as an arguable victim of a breach of Article 5. The State argued that Article 25 (now Article 34) identified both the persons empowered to lodge an application and the object of the proceedings instituted before the Commission and then, if appropriate, before the ECtHR, namely a finding that the breach alleged by the applicant

---

22   *McCann v UK* (1996) 21 EHRR 97.
23   *Klass v FRG* (1979–80) 2 EHRR 214.
24   *Guzzardi v Italy* (1981) 3 EHRR 333.

did occur. The State argued that there is an obligation to limit the decision to facts adduced by the litigant. However, the ECtHR stated that Article 25 requires that individual applicants should claim to be the victim 'of a violation of the rights set forth in the Convention'. It does not oblige them to specify which Article, paragraph or sub-paragraph or even which right they are praying in aid. The ECtHR has an inherent power to decide upon the characterisation in law to be given to a matter. The court or tribunal must therefore examine the situation impugned by an applicant in the light of the Convention as a whole. In the performance of this task it is free to give to the facts of the case, as found to be established by the material before it,[25] a characterisation in law different from that given to them by the applicant. Thus the duty is on a court to establish whether the person is a victim on all the material before it. This means that a court must take a pro-active role in relation to the identification of Convention issues in a case, even if the applicant does not assert that he or she is a victim of breach of the Convention rights, or rely on the most appropriate Convention right. Such a duty is consistent with the duty on a court to construe its powers so as to give them an effect that is compatible with the Convention rights. However, the individual must raise the facts on which that conclusion can be based.

The case-law of ECtHR is not consistent on the concept of when a body constitutes a victim. The ECtHR will consider the facts and merits of the case. However:

(a) it is not enough to allege that someone's rights have been violated. There is no right to take an '*actio popularis*';

(b) the act must be to the person's detriment or prejudice. However, detriment or prejudice may arise simply from the existence of a rule or policy or criminalising act. A person may cease to be a victim in these circumstances if the State acknowledges fault in criminalising the applicant's actions and affords the applicant redress;[26]

(c) a detriment may exist (and the victim criterion may be satisfied) where there is a serious risk of the person claiming to be a victim being directly affected by the act;[27]

(d) if the person has not previously asserted the right previously on which reliance is now sought to be placed, that person may possibly not fulfil the 'victim' requirement.

The first of these propositions means that the ECtHR must determine whether the manner in which the system of rules (for example, laws) of the public authority was applied to or affected the particular applicants before the court gave rise to a violation of the Convention rights.[28] The last of these propositions could be of importance in employment law cases. Thus in *Guenon v France*[29] the

---

25   *Ireland v UK*, judgment of 18 January 1978, Series A, No 25, p 64 at para 160.
26   *Eckle v FRG* (1983) 5 EHRR 1.
27   *Marckx v Belgium* (1979–80) 2 EHRR 330.
28   *Hakansson v Sweden* (1991) 13 EHRR 1.
29   (1990) 66 DR 181.

applicant claimed that he had been denied a public hearing before a professional disciplinary tribunal. However, he had not asserted his right to have a public hearing at the time of the hearing. It is suggested that that assertion will only be necessary in such procedural cases where there could be some doubt, and not in cases dealing with the fundamental rights such as respect for family life or privacy.

Some associations may not have sufficient connection with the rights involved for them to be considered to be victims. Thus unions cannot claim to be victims simply because they represent their members.[30] In *Mobin Ahmed and Others v UK*,[31] the union UNISON represented the local government employees who worked in politically restricted posts. UNISON claimed to be a victim of substantially the same violations of the Convention as the individual applicants. It argued that because the State's act in restricting the political activities of its members affected local authority employees both as employees and as members of their trade union, it could claim to be directly affected by this act. It argued that the act of the State inhibited individuals from engaging in, and expressing views on, trade union matters. The Commission rejected this analysis, but its reasoning shows the general approach to the concept of 'victim'.

The word 'victim' refers to the person or persons directly affected by the act or omission in issue.[32] The Commission has found, for example, that the loss of employment by journalists on closure by the State of the press agency which employed them did not suffice to permit the journalists to claim to be victims of alleged violations of the Convention in respect of the closure.[33]

The ECtHR will consider the content of the rights under the Convention by which the body claiming to be a victim may claim to be protected. Thus in *Ahmed* the Commission noted the express inclusion in Article 11(1) of the Convention, of the right 'to form and to join trade unions'. It referred to the fact that a trade union may claim to be a victim of alleged violations of its own rights.[34]

A trade union may be able to claim to be the victim of a violation of Article 11 of the Convention where the right to join a trade union is completely removed.[35]

The Commission noted in *Ahmed* that the State's act in issue did not affect any rights which UNISON might have under Article 11 of the Convention, and that UNISON's freedom of expression was not limited in any way by the State's act. The act in that case was a statutory instrument which was not addressed to trade unions but to local authority employees, and did not refer to limitations on union activity by individuals.

In *Ahmed* the Commission stated:

---

30   *Purcell v Ireland* (1991) 70 DR 262.
31   Application No 22954/93.
32   *Corigliano v Italy* (1982) Series A, No 57, p 12 at para 31.
33   *MS and PS v Switzerland* (1985) 44 DR 175, at p 190.
34   *National Union of Belgian Police v Belgium*, judgment of 27 October 1975, Series A, No 19, p 18 at para 39.
35   *Council of Civil Service Unions et al v the UK* Application No 11603/85, (1987) 50 DR 2.

'To the extent that an individual may be affected by the Regulations in the exercise of his Convention rights, for example in his freedom of expression by speaking in public in a union context, he is the person affected and not the union.'

UNISON was not directly affected by the provisions of the regulations within the meaning of the Convention and could not claim to be a victim of a violation of the Convention within the meaning of Article 25.

In considering whether the putative victim of a breach of s 6 of the HRA 1998 can rely on the breach of his Convention rights, it is suggested that the following approach may be useful.

(1) What rights are said to be invoked by the situation?
(2) In considering the extent to which a person may be said to suffer a detriment from the act of which complaint is made, to what extent is there secrecy or privacy involved on the facts? How intimate a right is in issue? The more 'intimate' the right is to the person, the slighter the risk will need to be before the court will be prepared to say that there is sufficient (risk of) detriment for that person to claim to be a potential victim of the infringement. Can it be said that the public authority has made it difficult to identify victims of a particular act?
(3) What detriment is identified as a result of considerations under item (2)?
(4) Is there anything in the other Articles of the Convention indicating a limitation on the nature of bodies that can claim to be a victim of the rights invoked by the situation?
(5) How serious a detriment is the detriment identified in item (3)? If the risk or effect is very small it may not qualify the subject of it to victim status.[36] This question must be answered in the context of the rights the Convention seeks to protect.
(6) What are the merits of the substantive case? The slighter the merits of the case the less likely it is that it will be accepted that the person is a victim of any alleged breach.
(7) The purpose of the Convention is the protection of the rights of individuals, so that an inclusive approach to 'victim' should be taken subject to the limitation that it must be possible to say that the person is directly affected by the act or omission in question.
(8) In considering employment rights, the international context of the Convention should be considered. In the context of ILO Conventions etc (see **1.6**), is the situation attracting potential protection regarded as fundamental or less than fundamental?

Thus a person might be the victim of a law which breaches the Convention, even where there is no specific implementing measure.[37] One factor in that case was the risk that a system of secret surveillance for the protection of national security poses of undermining or even destroying democracy on the ground of defending it. The application was by five German lawyers claiming

---

36   See *Hilton v UK* (1988) 57 DR 108.
37   *Klass v Germany* (1979–80) 2 EHRR 214 at para 34.

that legislation allowing the inspection of mail and of telephone tapping, infringed Article 6 as a breach of the right to fair hearing and Article 8 as a breach of the right to respect for correspondence.

An association cannot be given authority to make a complaint retrospectively by the execution of powers of attorney by individual victims in favour of the association.[38] Thus the person relying on an infringement must, at the time of the alleged infringement, have had sufficient connection to the situation and the right allegedly infringed to constitute a victim.

6.2.6   Examples of 'victim' in the context of particular Articles

In relation to Article 3 rights: in *Vijayanathan and Pusparajah v France*,[39] Tamils who were refused refugee status by the French authorities were ordered to leave the country. They remained unlawfully after the period permitted in their departure orders and were thus liable to arrest and expulsion proceedings. They argued that the possibility that they would be returned to Sri Lanka with a real risk of torture violated Article 3. The Commission upheld the State's preliminary objection and held that it was unable to consider the case on its merits. As no expulsion orders had yet been made against them they could not currently claim victim status. Further, if such orders were made there was a right of appeal.

In relation to Article 5 rights: see *Guzzardi*.[40] In *Amuur v France*,[41] the ECtHR held that the word 'victim' denotes the person directly affected by the act or omission in issue. Consequently, a decision or measure favourable to the applicant is not in principle sufficient to deprive the applicant of his or her status as a 'victim' unless the public authority acknowledged (either expressly or in substance), and then afforded redress for, the breach of the Convention.[42]

In relation to Article 8 rights: in *Norris v Ireland*,[43] it was held that an active homosexual, who attacked legislation penalising buggery and acts of gross indecency between males was a victim (and was successful in his challenge). The State contended that he was not a 'victim' of a violation as the legislation had never been enforced against him. The ECtHR held that he could be a 'victim' as he ran the risk of being directly affected by the legislation. However, the National Gay Federation was not a victim in those circumstances. In relation to the existence of such legislation, the maintenance in force of the legislation could constitute a continuing interference with his rights under Article 8(1). The same would apply to a policy maintained by a public authority which constitutes a continuing breach of the victim's rights in the sense that the individual either has to abide by the policy or leave employment or be subjected to a detriment as a result of breaching the policy. In *Dudgeon v UK*,[44] the ECtHR

---

38   *S Association v Sweden* (1984) 37 DR 87.
39   (1993) 15 EHRR 62.
40   *Guzzardi v Italy* (1981) 3 EHRR 333.
41   (1996) 22 EHRR 533.
42   See also *Ludi v Switzerland* (1993) 15 EHRR 173.
43   (1985) 44 DR 132.
44   (1982) 4 EHRR 149.

also had held that the existence of legislation criminalising homosexual conduct 'continuously and directly affects' the private life of a gay man. The reason for this is that: 'either he respects the law and refrains from engaging in prohibited sexual acts to which he is disposed by reason of his homosexual tendencies, or he commits such acts and thereby becomes liable to prosecution', and it was a contravention of his right to respect for his private life.

In relation to Article 9 rights: a church or organisation may be a victim of an interference with the rights under Article 9, as well as an individual.[45]

In relation to Article 10 rights: in *Open Door Counselling and Dublin Well Woman Clinic v Ireland*,[46] the ECtHR held that women of childbearing age were 'victims' of an injunction giving effect to restrictions on abortion, as they 'may be adversely affected by the restrictions imposed' and 'run a risk of being directly prejudiced by the measure complained of'. The organisation itself, however, successfully complained of infringement of its own right to free expression.

In relation to Article 1 of the 1st Protocol: the rights of corporate bodies are protected by Article 1 of the 1st Protocol, provided that the applicant is the real victim of a violation of the Article. Thus in *Yarrow v UK*,[47] shareholders were held not to be victims when the value of their shares was affected by reason of damage to the company. However, where a substantial majority shareholder made an application under Article 1 of the 1st Protocol he was regarded as a victim when the company in which held those shares suffered damage.[48] In *Guillemin v France*,[49] the domestic courts' acknowledgement of G's right to compensation did not mean that she ceased to be a 'victim' for the purposes of Article 25 of the Convention since she had not been afforded effective redress to the alleged violation of Article 1 of the 1st Protocol.[50] In *Agrotexim v Greece*,[51] the applicants were shareholders in a brewery which wanted to develop two of its sites. The State adopted measures in order to expropriate the sites. The ECtHR held that the shareholders were not 'victims' and had not complained of a violation of rights vested in them as shareholders of the company. Their complaint was based solely on violation of the brewery's right and that this had adversely affected their own financial interests. The ECtHR stated that the Commission's view that a fall in the value of the shares resulting from the attempt to expropriate the sites automatically gave rise to an infringement of shareholders' rights was an unacccptable criterion for giving shareholders 'victim' status as normally there would be differences of views between shareholders. Disregarding the corporate personality could be justified only in exceptional circumstances. One such exceptional circumstance might be where it was proved that it was impossible for the company to apply to the court, as a result of its articles of incorporation. In such cases, whilst the company has a

---

45   *X and Church of Scientology v Sweden* (1979) 16 DR 68 and *Chappell v UK* (1987) 53 DR 241.
46   (1993) 15 EHRR 244.
47   (1983) 30 DR 155 at 185.
48   *X v Austria* (1966) 21 CD 34 at 44.
49   (1998) 25 EHRR 435.
50   *Eckle v Germany* (1983) 5 EHRR 1 and *Inze v Austria* (1988) 10 EHRR 394.
51   (1996) 21 EHRR 250.

personality of its own it must be clearly proved that it could not have made the application itself before shareholders may make such an application.

6.2.7 Sufficient interest and judicial review claims for breaches of s 6

Where the proceedings are brought on an application for judicial review, the applicant is to be taken to have a sufficient interest (in Scotland 'title and interest to sue') in relation to the unlawful act only if that person is, or would be, a victim of that act.[52] Note that the converse does not hold. Thus in the case of a trade union, it might in theory be able to show that it had sufficient interest for the purposes of challenging regulations, without being able to show that it was a victim for the purposes of s 7 of a public authority's unlawful act in making or applying those regulations. The concept of 'sufficient interest' is, in this context, wider than that of 'victim' (see **6.13.4**).

6.3 PROCEDURE FOR BRINGING CLAIMS AND APPEALS

6.3.1 Time-limit for the claim

Proceedings against a public authority under s 7(1)(a) of the HRA 1998 must be brought before the end of:

(a) the period of one year beginning with the date on which the act complained of took place; or

(b) such longer period as the court or tribunal considers equitable having regard to all the circumstances, but that is subject to any rule imposing a stricter time-limit in relation to the procedure in question (s 7(5)).

The reference to a rule imposing a stricter time-limit to the procedure in question is a reference to judicial review proceedings or any other proceedings in which there is uniform time-limit. It would not apply to proceedings before a tribunal as these are not subject to a uniform time-limit. The time-limit will vary according to the nature of the statutory right being enforced.

Where a tribunal makes a finding that an act of a public authority was unlawful under s 6 of the HRA 1998, but has no power to give a remedy for the breach (for example, because the public authority was not a party to the case), the time for bringing proceedings against the public authority will run from the date of the unlawful act, rather than the date on which the finding of unlawfulness is made. Practitioners may need to ensure that proceedings are issued independently against the public authority within the time-limit.

Section 7 of the HRA 1998 allows for the fixing of a longer period where the court or tribunal considers it equitable having regard to all the circumstances. The discretion may be exercised to override the technical defence of limitation and to enable the court to allow the action if that would be fair and just in all the circumstances of the case. It is the widest possible term that can be used to

---

52   HRA 1998, s 7(3) and (4).

confer such a discretion on the court.[53] Section 33 of the Limitation Act 1980 also permits the time-limits under s 11 or s 12 of that Act to be disapplied where it appears to the court that it would be equitable to allow the action to proceed having regard both: (a) to the degree to which the provisions of these sections prejudice the plaintiff; and (b) to the extent to which a decision to allow the action to proceed would prejudice the defendant.[54] Section 33 requires that the court have regard to all the circumstances of the case.[55]

Such a challenge to a claim may be dealt with as a preliminary issue.[56] However, the substantive issues may be so intimately and inextricably bound up with the questions involved in considering extension of the limitation period as to make any summary resolution impracticable.[57]

Under s 33 of the Limitation Act 1980, certain specific considerations are regarded as guides to whether the time-limit should be extended.[58] Whilst these do not place a fetter on the generality of the discretion of the court, they are clearly important factors in any consideration of whether it is equitable to extend time-limits. In the context of employment law, it is suggested that these guidelines can be reconstructed in the following way. The court or tribunal will take account of:

(a) the length and reasons for delay between the expiry of the limitation period and the issue of the claim on the part of the claimant;

(b) the effect of any delay on the evidence, for example prejudice to the respondent if the claim is allowed to proceed (but not simply that involved in defending proceedings). Where the allegation of breach of the Convention rights is based on the memories of witnesses to a much greater extent than on documentation, this will indicate that the respondent may be prejudiced in its defence;

(c) the conduct of the respondent from the act to the application for extension may also be taken into account;

(d) the duration of any disability of the claimant arising after accrual of the cause of action; in the context of employment cases this may be broadened to any medical condition which might have inhibited the making of a claim;

(e) the claimant's conduct. Did the claimant seek legal advice? If so, the nature of the advice will be taken into account to the extent that it is relevant to whether the claimant acted promptly and reasonably after the claimant had knowledge of the information which might give rise to the cause of action.[59] If the delay was caused by a misunderstanding of the law which was understandable at the time, it may be just and equitable to extend time;[60]

---

53   *Dudley (Lord) v Dudley (Lady)* (1705) Prec Ch 241 at 244.
54   Limitation Act 1980, s 33(1).
55   Limitation Act 1980, s 33(3).
56   *Buck v English Electric Co Ltd* [1977] 1 WLR 806.
57   *Walkley v Precision Forgings Ltd* [1978] 1 WLR 1228.
58   See *Donovan v Gwentoys Ltd* [1990] 1 WLR 472.
59   *Jones v G D Searle & Co Ltd* [1979] 1 WLR 101.
60   *British Coal Corporation v Keeble and Others* [1997] IRLR 336.

(f) whether another remedy is available to the claimant if the claim is not allowed to proceed. However, this must be seen simply as a factor, and not as conclusive of whether the claim should be permitted to proceed;

(g) the diligence on the part of the claimant in obtaining medical, legal or other expert advice;

(h) whether the claimant was awaiting the outcome of an internal appeal or grievance procedure. Did this make it more difficult for the claimant to be able to identify the detriment to which he or she was subjected?[61] Where the breach alleged relates to the guarantees under Article 6, this may be a significant factor.

In applying the test under s 7 of the HRA 1998, the court will consider the conduct of the claimant in delaying. It will consider whether a reasonable person in the position of the claimant would have done as the claimant did. Thus it will generally be reasonable to follow the advice of a trade union of which the claimant is a member.[62] The test is broad enough to permit an extension if the claimant, not knowing his or her legal rights, delayed before bringing an action but could not be criticised for doing so, although the claimant knew facts on which a claim could be based.[63]

The power to extend time under s 7 of the HRA 1998 is also similar to that in the DDA 1995, the RRA 1976 and the SDA 1975. The case-law under those provisions suggests that it is the circumstances surrounding the delay that should be taken into account rather than the merits of the claim. The similar test for extending time where a tribunal considers it just and equitable to do so under s 76(5) of the SDA 1975 was considered by the EAT in *Hutchinson v Westward Television Ltd.*[64] There the union decided that the applicant had no case when she had to leave her job due to the employer's policy of not employing married couples. She read a newspaper article suggesting she might have a claim just before expiry of the limitation period. Outside the time-limit she consulted a solicitor who presented a claim at once on her behalf.

On her appeal against the refusal of the industrial tribunal (as it then was) to extend the time in which she could present her claim, the EAT held that the tribunal had a discretion to extend the limit if it thought it just and equitable in all the circumstances of the case. However, the tribunal did not have to investigate the facts of the complaint, but it had a discretion as to whether and if so how far it wanted to hear the grounds of complaint before deciding the question of whether the time should be extended.

In order to succeed on appeal, the applicant has to show that the tribunal took a demonstrably wrong approach or left relevant facts out of account, or took irrelevant facts into account, or that the decision was so perverse that no reasonable tribunal could have reached that conclusion on the evidence before it. It is important, therefore, to ensure that all the factors are properly dealt with at first instance.

---

61   *Aniagwu v London Borough of Hackney* [1999] IRLR 303.
62   *Dale v British Coal Corporation (No 2)* (1992) *The Times,* July 2.
63   *Halford v Brookes* [1991] 1 WLR 428.
64   [1977] ICR 279.

6.3.2   Procedural rules for bringing claims

Provision is made in s 7 of the HRA 1998 for rules of court and for rules of procedure for the tribunals to be made.[65] Thus 'rules' means:

'(a)   in relation to proceedings before a court or tribunal outside Scotland, rules made by the Lord Chancellor or the Secretary of State for the purposes of s 7 or rules of court;

(b)   in relation to proceedings before a court or tribunal in Scotland, rules made by the Secretary of State for those purposes;

(c)   in relation to proceedings before a tribunal in Northern Ireland:
(i)   which deals with transferred matters; and
(ii)   for which no rules made under (a) are in force, rules made by a Northern Ireland department for those purposes,
and includes provision made by order under s 1 of the Courts and Legal Services Act 1990.'

In making rules, regard must be had to s 9 of the HRA 1998 which deals with claims made against the court as a public body for unlawful judicial acts.

The Minister who has power to make rules in relation to a particular tribunal may, to the extent that the Minister considers it necessary to ensure that the tribunal can provide an appropriate remedy in relation to an act (or proposed act) of a public authority which is (or would be) unlawful as a result of s 6(1), by order add to:

(a)   the relief or remedies which the tribunal may grant; or
(b)   the grounds on which it may grant any of them.

The order made by the Minister may contain such incidental, supplemental, consequential or transitional provision as the Minister making it considers appropriate. 'The Minister' includes the Northern Ireland department concerned.[66]

The CPR 1998 have been amended to provide for:

(a)   claims in the courts for breaches of s 6 by a public authority (CPR 1998, r 7.11);
(b)   appeals in which a breach of s 6 is raised in respect of a judicial authority's act (CPR 1998, r 19.4A);
(c)   claims in respect of a judicial act which is alleged to have infringed the claimant's rights under Article 5 and which is based on a finding that the claimant's Convention rights have been infringed (CPR 1998, r 33.9).

6.3.3   Procedure for claims in the courts

A claimant who is bringing proceedings against a public authority under s 7(1)(a) of the HRA 1998 (which entitles the claimant to bring a claim relying solely on the public authority's breach of s 6 of the HRA 1998):

(1)   must state that fact in the claim form; and

---

65   HRA 1998, s 7(9).
66   HRA 1998, s 7(11)–(13).

(2) must in the claim form or particulars of claim:
   (a) give details of the Convention right which its is alleged has been infringed and of the infringement, and
   (b) where the claim is founded on a finding of unlawfulness by another court or tribunal, give details of the finding.[67]

By CPR 1998, Practice Direction 2B – Allocation of Cases to Levels of Judiciary, para 7A, a deputy High Court judge, a master or a district judge may not try:

(1) a case in a claim regarding a judicial act; or
(2) a claim for a declaration of incompatibility.

The Practice Direction to CPR 1998, Part 19, para 6.6, provides for the Lord Chancellor to be joined as a party where the claim is in respect of a judicial act.[68]

6.3.4 Procedure for appeals in the courts

The Practice Direction to CPR 1998, Part 52 requires that where the appellant is adding a claim against a public authority under s 7(1)(a) of the HRA 1998 in an appeal, the appellant must in the appeal notice:

(1) state that fact; and
(2) give details of:
   (a) the Convention right which it is alleged has been infringed and of the infringement; and
   (b) the finding of the court or tribunal, where there is a finding of unlawfulness by another court or tribunal; or
   (c) the judicial act and the court or tribunal which made it, where it is the act of that court or tribunal which is complained of as provided by s 9 of the HRA 1998.

Note that this requirement for an appeal does not apply to notices of appeal to the EAT. The EAT does not have jurisdiction over s 7(1)(a) claims, and therefore where the sole issue remaining after a tribunal claim is whether damages ought to be awarded for a finding of breach of the Convention rights, the appropriate vehicle will be a fresh claim in the court. The tribunal cannot entertain a s 7(1)(a) claim.

6.3.5 Procedure for tribunal claims

There is no procedure for bringing a claim for breach of the HRA 1998 in the tribunals. The parties can rely on their Convention rights (s 7(1)(b)) but cannot found an action solely on the breach of those rights before the tribunal.

Section 7(11) of the HRA 1998 provides that the Minister who has power to make rules in relation to the employment tribunal may, to the extent that the Minister considers it necessary to ensure that the tribunal can provide an appropriate remedy in relation to an act (or proposed act) of a public authority which is (or would be) unlawful as a result of s 6(1), by order add to:

---

67   See Practice Direction to CPR 1998, Part 16, para 16.1 and Practice Direction to CPR 1998, Part 54, para 5.3.
68   HRA 1998, s 9(3)–(5), and Practice Direction to Part 54, para 8.2.

(a) the relief or remedies which the tribunal may grant; or

(b) the grounds on which it may grant any of them.

These powers might be used to extend the powers of the tribunal to ensure that it did have power to award damages for breach of Convention rights in claims including a breach of s 6 for the breach of s 6 alone. The provisions of s 8(1) of the HRA 1998 appear to permit the tribunal take account of a breach of s 6 in the remedy for any existing breach of statutory duty within its jurisdiction in order to reflect the breach of the Convention. Section 8(1) does not permit the tribunal to act outside its powers.

The employment tribunals have over the course of their existence developed many 'barnacles' of interpretation by the EAT. The combined effect of ss 3, 6 and 8(1) of the HRA 1998 is the following.

(a) Where the tribunal reads the legislative provisions of the statute permitting it to give a remedy for a breach of one of the statutes within its jurisdiction, it must start with the wording of the legislation, shorn of pre-HRA 1998 interpretations by the EAT or higher courts.

(b) The wording of the legislative provision must then be read and given effect, so far as it is possible, so as to give effect to the Convention rights.

(c) The provisions of s 8(1) of the HRA 1998 must then be taken into account, so that the tribunal will give effect to its powers to award a remedy read without the interpretation placed upon those powers pre-HRA 1998.

(d) The scope of the 'powers' within which the tribunal must act will be the statutory provision interpreted by s 3 of the HRA 1998.

(e) In relation to the unlawful act under s 6, if the facts giving rise to the finding of unlawfulness also constituted an unlawful act under a provision giving the tribunal powers of remedy, the tribunal may award such remedy as seems just and appropriate to it.

In the absence of rules extending the power to entertain s 7(1)(a) claims, the claimant who succeeds only in establishing a finding that an unlawful act has occurred under s 6(1) will have to start fresh proceedings in the court, relying on that finding, before he or she may obtain a remedy. Theoretically, this would result in a multiplicity of proceedings but a finding of an HRA 1998 breach without a breach of other employment legislation will be rare.

The limitation of the power of the tribunal to give a remedy for breach of the Convention rights under s 6 to those remedies that are within its powers, gives rise to the following problem. If causation is a necessary element in proving loss in terms of the host statutory provision, and it cannot be shown that the loss flowed from the breach of the host provision, but the tribunal concludes that it has been shown that the unlawful act under s 6 gave rise to the loss, it would be acting outside its powers if it were to award any damages in respect of that breach (see **6.4.1**).

6.3.6   Proceedings under s 7(1)(a) and estoppel

Where the applicant loses the host statute claim, but there is a finding that the Convention was breached, the tribunal will have no power, in the absence of rules under s 7(11) of the HRA 1998, to give compensation for that breach.

In Convention practice, where the State does not mount an argument on an issue on the admissibility hearing an estoppel may arise, but if the issue emerges as a result of the proceedings before the Commission, it is unlikely to arise.[69] Thus if a tribunal took the Convention point itself, as opposed to it being fully argued between the parties, it is unlikely to be an abuse of process for the public authority to seek go behind the finding made.

Where the tribunal considered whether there was a breach of the Convention and rejected the idea, the domestic doctrines of '*res judicata*' or 'issue estoppel' may apply to s 6 claims. The respondent could plead an estoppel to the entire cause of action on the basis that the whole of the legal rights and obligations in relation to that cause of action have already been determined as between the parties by an earlier final judgment (*res judicata*). Such cause of action estoppel may arise where the facts before the tribunal disclosed a breach of the Convention.[70]

If the applicant could have raised a breach of the Convention rights in the tribunal proceedings, estoppel may bar the applicant from raising a claim for breach of Convention rights under s 7(1)(a). This species of abuse of process (issue estoppel) arises where subject-matter of the new claim must be related to the earlier action. The estoppel will arise if the claim is one which could have been put forward, with reasonable diligence, in the previous proceedings.[71] There is a 'special circumstances' exception.[72] Note that the over-rigid application of the doctrine may itself contravene Article 6(1).

Thus where the applicant could, on the facts before the tribunal, have alleged that a breach of the Convention had occurred, and could have sought to rely on them, it may be considered an abuse of process if the applicant brings a s 7(1)(a) claim which has to be determined on its facts where those facts are substantially the same as in the tribunal claim. When a public authority seeks to rely on fresh material in the course of a claim under s 7(1)(a), it is likely to be estopped because it could have brought forward its whole defence before the tribunal to avoid the finding that an unlawful act under s 6 had occurred. The fact that the tribunal did not have jurisdiction to award a remedy in respect of that breach would not prevent the estoppel arising, any more than the inability of tribunals to award damages in respect of wrongful dismissal prevented an estoppel arising in *O'Laoire*.[73] In *O'Laoire v Jackel Ltd (No 2)*,[74] the Court of

---

69   See *Guzzardi v Italy* (1981) 3 EHRR 333 and, *mutatis, Artico v Italy* (1980) Series A, No 37, pp 13–14, 27.
70   See *Munir v Jang Publications Ltd* [1989] ICR 1.
71   *Henderson v Henderson* (1843) 3 Hare 100 and *Talbot v Berkshire County Council* [1994] QB 290 at 294.
72   *Divine-Bortey v Brent London Borough* [1998] IRLR 525.
73   [1990] ICR 197.
74   [1991] ICR 718.

Appeal considered it well established that the findings of a tribunal could bind another court so as to give rise to an issue estoppel. By s 8 of the HRA 1998, the tribunal has the power to make a finding that s 6 has been breached by the public authority. Where the tribunal has made a finding that a Convention right has been breached, therefore, the court considering the s 7(1)(a) claim arising from that finding (in which the claimant is seeking damages for breach of Convention rights) will be bound by the findings of the court. The claimant will be able to rely on the facts found by the tribunal in his claim against the public authority, which will be estopped from denying those facts. The fact that the tribunal cannot award a remedy in respect of that breach is irrelevant.

Thus in the case of reliance on Convention rights in cases where there is a finding made under the host statute that an unlawful act under s 6 was committed, the matter may be determined in such a way that the public authority cannot defend the issue of liability for the unlawful act, although it may defend the issue of damages for the unlawful act on the basis that just satisfaction does not require a remedy other than the finding which has already been made.

The concept of abuse of process is at the heart of issue estoppel. In *Hancock v Doncaster MBC*,[75] the EAT held that the pleas of *res judicata* and issue estoppel were equitable concepts designed to ensure that justice was done (see also *Talbot v Berkshire CC*).[76] The Privy Council in *Yat Tung Investment Co v Dao Heng Bank*[77] took the view that if the strict principle of *res judicata* did not apply to a case it was possible to argue that it was an abuse of the process of the court to raise in subsequent proceedings matters which could and should have been litigated in previous proceedings. The court may take the view that, where breach of Convention rights was fully argued, it would be an abuse of process for the matter to be relitigated in the s 7(1)(a) proceedings. However, where the finding of an unlawful act was made in proceedings to which the public authority was not a party, the issues will not have been ventilated, and no estoppel will arise.

6.4 SECTION 8: REMEDIES

6.4.1 Introduction

The first point to note is that the courts are obliged by s 3 of the HRA 1998, taken with s 19 of the Supreme Court Act 1981 or s 38 of the County Courts Act 1984, to give effect to all of their remedial powers in a way which is compatible with the Convention rights. Thus, in cases between private individuals, the court must interpret its powers under those sections in such a way that the application of these powers does not conflict with the Convention rights. This means that if there is a possible interpretation of the circumstances in which those powers may be exercised which conflicts with the Convention rights, the

---

75   [1998] ICR 900.
76   [1994] QB 290, and *Barber v Staffordshire CC* [1996] ICR 379.
77   [1975] 2 WLR 690.

court is obliged to reject that option. Conversely, if it is possible to find an interpretation of the circumstances in which those powers may be exercised which is compatible with the Convention rights, the court is obliged to give effect to the powers. Primary legislation is to be given effect, so far as it is possible to do so, in a way which is compatible with the Convention rights.

By s 8 of the HRA 1998, in relation to any act (or proposed act) of a public authority which the court finds is (or would be) unlawful (as in breach of s 6), it may grant such relief or remedy, or make such order, within its powers as it considers just and appropriate.[78] Note that the following definitions apply by s 8(6) to judicial remedies:

– 'court' includes a tribunal;
– 'damages' means damages for an unlawful act of a public authority; and
– 'unlawful' means unlawful under s 6(1) of the HRA 1998.

Damages, therefore, appear to be distinguished from compensation. Tribunals have powers to award compensation, and not damages, although s 56 of the RRA 1976 refers to 'compensation of an amount corresponding to any damages [the respondent] could have been ordered by a county court ...'.

6.4.2 Effect of s 8(1) on real remedies

Section 8 of the HRA 1998 does not require the court to take account of the principles of just satisfaction in determining the nature of the remedy to be awarded, save where contemplating awarding damages for breach of s 6 unlawful acts by a public authority. This reflects the practice in Strasbourg of not requiring States to take particular steps in relation to a judgment. The court does have to consider whether a remedy will be 'just and appropriate'.[79] It is submitted that this does not mean that the court can simply exercise its pre-existing powers as before, as the phrase 'just and appropriate' must be construed in the context of the purpose of the HRA 1998 as set out in its long title, namely 'to give further effect to rights and freedoms guaranteed under the European Convention on Human Rights' and in the light of the duty of the court under s 3 of the HRA 1998 to give effect to its statutory powers in such a way as is compatible with the Sch 1 rights.

In a case where a person has been dismissed by a public authority in breach of the principles in Article 6, for example, the court could order that the employment be continued so that the breach of Article 6 could be rectified. Other Articles of the Convention, such as Article 10, envisage certain standards of tolerance for (in that case) freedom of expression. A person whose dismissal was due to the employer's breach of Article 10 might be able to argue that this purpose of the Article could be rendered effective and practical rather than theoretical and illusory only by making an order for his or her continued employment. This is particularly the case where the information that the individual was seeking to impart related to the workplace or concerned his or her employment.

---

78   HRA 1998, s 8(1).
79   HRA 1998, s 8(1).

The court, considering whether to grant an injunction, will not be excluded from considering the availability of the remedy of reinstatement in the context of unfair dismissal. This, whilst not a real remedy, provides for compensation should the employer refuse to comply in situations in which it is practicable for it to comply. The question in such cases will be whether the remedy of ordering the public authority to re-employ the person it has dismissed is just and appropriate given that the employee may obtain a monetary award should the employer refuse to reinstate him or her. If the employee can show that the remedy of compensation for non-reinstatement does not serve properly to protect the Convention right because, for example, it permits the defaulting employer to purchase a breach of the Convention, the court should consider granting an injunction to continue employment as the most just and appropriate means of protecting the employee's rights in a real and effective way.

A court can order an account of profits from a public authority found to be in breach of a Convention right. In certain cases, perhaps where the breach by the public authority is analogous to a breach of trust, this may be the most just and appropriate remedy.

It should be noted, however, that s 8(1) gives the court power to grant the remedy that it considers to be just and appropriate in respect of a breach of s 6. It is not a requirement for it to do so. Provided that the court has considered the question, it will be difficult to challenge the refusal of an injunction or other remedy on the basis that the court did not observe the provisions of s 8.

6.5 INJUNCTIONS

The general rule is that equity will not order specific performance of a contract for personal services on the basis that it is impossible for the court to supervise such a contract.[80] If the contract requires the parties to work together, importing a high level of mutual trust, the court is unlikely to order its performance.[81] However, the court will now have to take account of the fact that tolerance is one of the underlying features of the democratic society in determining whether to issue or refuse an injunction. The mere fact that the employer expresses a lack of trust in the employee may therefore no longer be sufficient in certain cases to prevent an order being made.

One of the questions raised by the HRA 1998 in this context is the extent to which a person who is not able to bring a claim under one of the pieces of discrimination legislation in respect of that person's failure to obtain a job may be protected by injunction. In *Wishart v National Association of Citizens Advice Bureaux Ltd*,[82] the interlocutory injunction sought was in that context. The

---

80   *C H Giles & Co Ltd v Morris* [1972] 1 WLR 307.
81   *Warren v Mendy* [1989] ICR 525.
82   [1990] ICR 794, CA.

plaintiff had been offered a post 'subject to receipt of satisfactory written references'. When these were taken up they disclosed absence for reason of illness on a number of occasions. This was before the introduction of the DDA 1995. The defendants, who viewed the advertised post as a demanding one requiring constant attendance, consequently withdrew the offer of employment.

The plaintiff issued a writ and sought an injunction to restrain them from re-advertising the post or appointing any person other than the plaintiff. On the employer's appeal, the Court of Appeal held that there was no established employment relationship between the parties. It was clear that the employers did not have trust and confidence in the plaintiff so the normal rule concerning specific performance of a contract of employment applied.

The Court said that if the question is whether there is an enforceable contract of employment, it was highly unlikely that the plaintiff would succeed at trial in establishing that there was an objective test involving a notional reasonable prospective employer for determining whether a reference is satisfactory. It was said that probably all that the employer was required to do was consider the references in good faith.

However, if the employer is a public authority, and has a selection procedure, can that be said to be a process determinative of civil rights attracting the guarantees of Article 6? Such a process may be said to be determinative of the rights of the parties in respect of the employment, particularly if the procedure is adopted so as to avoid discrimination on the grounds of sex, race or disability. If so, the employer would act unlawfully if it did not provide the would-be employee with a fair trial. In those circumstances, an injunction to provide the employee with the opportunity to make representations on the references and to prevent the decision being to his or her detriment would stand some prospect of success. Where the reason for non-appointment is the exercise, past or present, of a Convention right, it is submitted that the domestic court would have to consider issuing the injunction on the basis that it was the most just and appropriate means of giving the job applicant a remedy and giving effect to the powers of the court so far as it is possible to do so, so as to be compatible with effective and practical Convention rights.

Such injunctions would not be granted where no such selection procedure had been embarked upon, and it is submitted that it would not be proportionate, at an early stage of selection proceedings, for each candidate to be given the full guarantees of Article 6. Nevertheless, in the circumstances taken from the *Wishart* case, an injunction could now be sought. In the actual case, the employers did speak to the job applicant concerning the references before refusing to appoint him, and he might now have an adequate remedy under the DDA 1995.

Given that the domestic court's obligation under s 8 is to consider only whether to make such order within its powers as it considers just and appropriate, the general rule that a court will not enforce a contract for personal services is unlikely to alter in relation to public bodies which require the working relationship to be a close one, provided the reasons for the lack of trust and confidence do not themselves show a disregard for the individual's Convention rights. However, there is no reason in principle why the court should not order an injunction to keep a contract for personal services alive. Where the detriment to the person claiming breach of s 6 by a public authority employer is that he or she has been dismissed, and the employer is a large one, there is no reason why the court cannot in principle monitor for breaches and, in effect, supervise enforcement. It may be argued that in order to give an interpretation to the Convention rights that renders them practical and effective, the domestic court should remove the detriment so far as it can.

Pre-HRA 1998, it was only in special circumstances that a court would grant an injunction preventing a threatened wrongful dismissal. In *Hill v Parsons*, the domestic court needed to be satisfied that the employer and employee were themselves willing to continue with the contract before it was willing to grant an injunction where a third party brought pressure to bear on the employer to dismiss.[83] That requirement altered in *Irani v Southampton and South-West Hampshire Health Authority*,[84] in which an employee sought an interlocutory injunction that the employers should not dismiss him, by notice, without applying and exhausting the procedures laid down in his conditions of service. The domestic court accepted that the defendants still had faith in the honesty, integrity and loyalty of the plaintiff. Termination of the contract would lead to him being denied access to NHS facilities so that damages would not be an adequate remedy. Essentially, the injunction would prevent an abuse of power. Thus the element of the *continuation* of the contract being a voluntary matter was not regarded as an essential requirement for the grant of such an injunction, where there was admitted confidence in the employee to carry on doing the job honestly, and loyally. However, the domestic courts have viewed the question as being essentially one of whether the employer has 'sufficient confidence' in the employee for the employment relationship to continue, and this is a matter of fact for the particular case so that in a redundancy situation dismissals could not be restrained where the employer had employed a skills-based selection procedure, thus indicating that it had less confidence in those selected for redundancy than those retained to carry out the work.[85]

In *Powell v London Borough of Brent*,[86] the dispute concerned whether the claimant had been promoted. She had been undertaking the duties of her new position for two months and was required by her employers to revert to her previous duties. The Court of Appeal granted an injunction to restrain the employers from advertising the post to which she claimed to have been appointed and requiring them to treat her as if she were properly employed by them in that post. Applying the *American Cyanamid Co v Ethicon Ltd*[87] principles, it concluded that she had a real prospect of succeeding with her claim for a permanent injunction at trial. There was no doubt about her competence to do the job in question and there was no friction at work.

---

83   *Hill v C A Parsons & Co Ltd* [1972] Ch 305.
84   [1985] ICR 590.
85   *Alexander v Standard Telephones and Cables plc* [1990] ICR 291.
86   [1988] ICR 176, CA.
87   [1975] AC 396.

In *Wadcock v London Borough of Brent*,[88] a social worker objected to being transferred to a new post and refused to co-operate or perform his new duties. He was dismissed. He sought an injunction restraining his employer from acting on its purported determination of his contract. By the time of the grant of the order he had changed his mind and was prepared to work normally in the post to which he had been transferred and obey the orders of his superior pending the trial of the action. This was made a condition of the injunction. In *Robb v London Borough of Hammersmith and Fulham*,[89] the Director of Finance was the subject of the local authority's contractual disciplinary procedure on grounds of capability. He was told to take paid special leave. He was later summarily dismissed before the process was complete. The court granted an injunction preventing the employer effecting dismissal until the procedure had been completed. The court applied *American Cyanamid* principles. Where there is such a procedure and the employee does not need to attend work, the question of whether the court is enforcing a contract so as to require the parties to work together is irrelevant. The existence of the procedure suggests that there is a mechanism for resolving conflicts between the employer and employee relating to their ability to work together. One important factor in deciding to grant the injunction in *Robb* was that the procedure gave the employee the opportunity to put his case and justify himself at the hearings and enquiries required by it.

In cases where there is a 'public' element involved such as the employer's right to dismiss being regulated by statute, the court could, under pre-HRA 1998 law, grant an injunction to prevent the unlawful action of the employer.[90] In that case the appellant entered the employment of an education authority as a teacher qualified by certification. In March 1969 the education committee, to whom the authority delegated its powers, passed a resolution to dismiss him, as he was not 'registered' in terms of para 2 of Sch 2 to the Teachers (Education, Training and Registration) (Scotland) Regulations 1967.[91] The committee thought therefore that his continued employment would be unlawful. He brought an action against the authority arguing that the purported dismissal was a nullity because it was contrary to natural justice. He had not been given a hearing. He also argued that the resolution was passed under an error of law as the committee had a discretion which it had failed to exercise. The House of Lords held that teachers in Scotland had in general a right to be heard before they were dismissed. As the regulations were ambiguous the appellant might have had an arguable case before the committee, which might have influenced sufficient members to vote against his dismissal. In denying him a hearing, the committee had breached its duty, and the resolution and dismissal were declared nullities.

Injunctions may be issued to restrain disclosure of confidential information, and to enforce restrictive covenants in the contract of employment. When seeking an injunction to restrain these acts, the employer will require the court

---

88   [1990] IRLR 223.
89   [1991] ICR 514.
90   *Malloch v Aberdeen Corpn* [1971] 1 WLR 158.
91   SI 1967/1162.

to construe its powers to give effect to its rights under Article 1 of the 1st Protocol. *Anton Piller*[92] orders (now search orders under the Civil Procedure Act 1997, s 7 and the CPR 1998, Part 25) were challenged in the ECtHR, and were found to be legitimate interferences with the right of privacy.[93]

In *Middlebrook Mushrooms Ltd v TGWU*,[94] the Court of Appeal had regard to the provisions of Article 10 when considering whether an injunction should be issued to restrain the distribution of the leaflets outside the doors of certain supermarkets in order to persuade customers not to buy a product when there was a dispute between the producer and its employees. The employer's complaint was that the union was inducing a breach of contract. To constitute the tort from *Lumley v Gye*[95] the persuasion had to be directed at one of the parties to the contract. It was therefore necessary in every case to examine the form or nature of the communication on which a claimant relied. The suggested influence was exerted through the actions or the anticipated actions of third parties who were free to make up their own minds. In that context, Article 10 was considered to be relevant in all cases which involve a proposed restriction on the right of free speech. In the exercise of its discretion, the court would consider whether the suggested restraint was necessary. In the light of the HRA 1998, the court would need to ask whether the restraint was necessary having regard to the nature of a democratic society and whether it was proportionate to the infringement it represents of the right to freedom of expression. The restraint being an injunction, the court would be obliged to interpret its powers so as to give them effect in a way which is compatible with the Convention right of freedom of expression.

6.6   DECLARATORY RELIEF

6.6.1   Determination without full trial

In certain cases, declaratory relief may be all that is necessary to terminate the dispute. In *Jones v Gwent County Council*,[96] a lecturer at a college had been the subject of two disciplinary enquiries. A decision was taken to dismiss the employee at a hearing concerning her return to work after the suspension relating to these enquiries. The court used its power under RSC Ord 14A (to determine any question of law or construction of any document arising in any cause or matter at any stage in the proceedings (now CPR 1998, r 1.4(2)(c) and Part 24)) to determine that the letter of dismissal was not a valid dismissal. In order to be able to use this power, it must appear to the court that: (a) the question is suitable for determination without a full trial of the action; and (b) its determination will finally determine the entire matter or any issue in the action.

---

92   *Anton Piller KG v Manufacturing Processes Ltd* [1976] Ch 55.
93   *Chappell v UK* (1990) 12 EHRR 1.
94   [1993] ICR 612.
95   (1853) 2 E & B 216.
96   [1992] IRLR 521.

6.7 DAMAGES FOR BREACH OF SECTION 6

Damages for breach of s 6 of the HRA 1998 may be awarded only by a court (or tribunal) which has power to award damages, or to order the payment of compensation in civil proceedings.[97] Tribunals as creations of statute only have the powers conferred by statute on them. There is no power in the tribunal to award compensation other than for the specific employment legislation breaches over which it has jurisdiction. The tribunal having found that there has been a breach of s 6 would seem to be doomed to use existing powers of compensation to provide a remedy. However, it might be argued that HRA 1998, s 8 provides jurisdiction in the tribunal to award damages in respect of breaches of the Convention because the tribunal has powers to award compensation in civil proceedings. The problem with this argument is that s 8(2) is limiting the scope of the power to award damages, and not creating jurisdiction to award damages. The wording of the subsection indicates that it is a contrast from s 8(1). Section 8(1) indicates that remedies must be within the powers of the tribunal. The limiting nature of subsection (2) can be seen from the use of the word 'only'.

By s 8(3), no award of damages is to be made unless, taking account of all the circumstances of the case, including:

(a) any other relief or remedy granted, or order made, in relation to the act in question (by that or any other court); and

(b) the consequences of any decision (of that or any other court) in respect of that act,

the court is satisfied that the award is necessary to afford just satisfaction to the person in whose favour it is made.

In determining whether to award damages and, if so, the amount of an award, the court must take into account the principles applied by the ECtHR in relation to the award of compensation under Article 41 of the Convention.

6.7.1 Principles on which damages may be awarded for breach of s 6

The court must ask itself whether it is 'necessary' to make an award of compensation. This involves consideration and weighing of a number of factors and the particular facts of the case.[98] The ECtHR stated in *Guzzardi v Italy*:

> 'as is borne out by the adjective "just" and the phrase "if necessary", the Court enjoys a certain discretion in the exercise of the power conferred by Article 50 (art. 50). Mr. Guzzardi has furnished no particulars and no prima facie evidence of the nature and scope of his alleged damage; in effect, he leaves the matter to the Court's discretion. Above all, his enforced stay at Cala Reale was markedly different from detention of the classic kind and involved far less serious hardships. What is more, in July 1976 – even before the Commission had accepted the application –

---

97 HRA 1998, s 8(2).
98 *Guzzardi v Italy* (1980) Series A, No 39, 3 EHRR 333.

the Milan Regional Court brought that stay to an end by ordering Mr. Guzzardi's transfer to the mainland; in August 1977, that is without awaiting the adoption of the report (7 December 1978), the Ministry of the Interior deleted Asinara from the list of districts used for compulsory residence, a decision which was apparently influenced by the proceedings pending in Strasbourg (see paragraph 95 above). On the other hand, Mr. Guzzardi had to bear certain costs in connection with the submission of his complaints to the Italian courts and to the Commission, especially as he did not have the benefit of free legal aid before the latter.'[99]

Thus the court will look at the nature and extent of the breach as well as the consequences of the breach.

The principle on which damages are to be awarded for breach of a Convention right is that 'the applicant should as far as possible be put in the position he would have been in had the requirements of [the Convention] not been disregarded'.[100] This may mean that the applicant should be placed in the position he or she would have been in had the applicant not been dismissed if the dismissal was an act in breach of a Convention right. Further, it would permit an unfair dismissal award to reflect the injury to the applicant's feelings. However, there must be a causal link between the damage suffered and the violation.[101] Therefore, it would be necessary for an applicant to show that the violation of his or her rights in particular had caused injury to feelings. In unfair dismissal cases, when considering the compensatory award, the tribunal must award such sum as it considers just and equitable having regard to the loss suffered by the applicant as a result of the dismissal. It will only be if the violation of the Convention right and the dismissal are the same act that it could be argued that there was a loss caused by the dismissal in the form of injury to feelings. On the other hand, if the applicant has required medical treatment as a result of the effect of the dismissal on his or her feelings, it would be appropriate to award compensation either under the ordinary principles for unfair dismissal cases or applying the HRA 1998 provisions.

The court will be able to award compensation for pecuniary loss under the principle of just satisfaction. Under the Convention, the ECtHR has not always insisted on a causal link between the violation and the pecuniary loss being proved on a balance of probabilities. Damages based on loss of opportunities may also be more freely available.[102]

Any court or tribunal will have to apply the principles of the ECtHR in determining whether an award in just satisfaction should be made. The principle of 'just satisfaction' in Convention law is predicated on the following conditions:

(a) if a decision or a measure taken by a legal authority or any other authority of a State is:
     (a) completely, or
     (b) partially,

---

99   *Guzzardi v Italy* (1980) Series A, No 39, 3 EHRR 333, at para 114.
100   *Piersack v Belgium (Compensation)* (1984) Series A, No 85, 7 EHRR 251 at para 12.
101   *Philis v Greece (No 2)* (1998) 25 EHRR 417 at para 58.
102   *Weeks v UK* (1988) Series A, No 145–A, para 13.

in conflict with the obligations arising from the Convention; and

(b) if the internal law of the State allows only partial reparation to be made for the consequences of this decision or measure,

the decision of the court shall, if necessary, afford just satisfaction to the injured party.

These principles were formerly found in Article 50, but now are in Article 41.

The process which a court or tribunal will need to go through is as follows.

6.7.2 Is a declaration sufficient?

The court or tribunal must consider whether damages for breach of s 6 of the HRA 1998 are necessary. One option available to the court is a declaration that the act was an unlawful violation of the Convention. Sometimes the ECtHR will simply declare that a violation has occurred. In such cases, it may consider that an award of costs and expenses relating to the case may be sufficient.

The court or tribunal will need to consider whether the other remedies, including any power it has to make declarations, are sufficient to afford just satisfaction to the person whose rights under the Convention have been breached. The ECtHR often reaches the conclusion that the finding of a violation of Convention rights constitutes just satisfaction, for example where the challenge is to primary legislation under the guarantee of freedom of expression in Article 10.

In *Zimmerman & Steiner v Switzerland*,[103] the ECtHR considered what would constitute just satisfaction for delay in legal proceedings (Article 6). The State contended that the pronouncement of, and the publicity attaching to, the ECtHR judgment would constitute sufficient just satisfaction. In *Zimmerman*, the ECtHR assumed that the applicants suffered some degree of prejudice in the form of mental strain as a result of the delay, but found that adequate compensation for this, on the facts of that case, would be furnished by the finding that the reasonable time was exceeded (see *Corigliano*[104]). However, the ECtHR also considered the question of whether an award of the applicants' costs and expenses should be made.

In *Brogan v UK*,[105] the ECtHR looked at the reasoning leading to the finding of breach. In that case, a breach of Article 5 was found. This related to not being brought promptly before a judge or other officer authorised by law to exercise judicial power and also to having no enforceable claim for compensation before the domestic courts for the breach of Article 5(3).

A respondent to a claim for just satisfaction can argue that the award of damages is not 'necessary'. In considering this question, the Strasbourg authorities suggest that the court will need to consider whether there is evidence of the alleged damage. It will also need to know whether it had been proved that any damage was the result of the violations found by the ECtHR.

---

103 (1984) 6 EHRR 17.
104 (1982) Series A, No 57, p 17 at para 53.
105 (1989) 11 EHRR 117.

The applicant can argue for just satisfaction damages including compensation for non-pecuniary damage in the form of distress, humiliation and anxiety. The nature of the interference complained of will be relevant. So, for example, the fact that sex discrimination is universally condemned and the fact that the existence of a practice in breach of the Convention is an aggravating factor will both be relevant factors.[106]

The adverse effects on the ability of the applicant to foster the rights in the Convention Article will be relevant, and any threat hanging over the applicant will also be relevant. So, for example, the fact that a person had criminal proceedings hanging over him or her as a result of a dismissal (constituting a breach of a Convention right) would be considered an aggravating factor.

In *Abdulaziz*, the ECtHR noted that by reason of its nature, non-pecuniary damage cannot always be the object of concrete proof. However, it said that it was reasonable to assume that persons who, like the applicants, found themselves faced with problems relating to the continuation or inception of their married life might suffer distress and anxiety. In cases relating to degrading treatment, this will clearly be an assumption that the court or tribunal will readily make; it is submitted that any interference with private or family life also carries this assumption. However, even where that factor is present on the particular facts of a case, the finding of violation can constitute sufficient just satisfaction. If a respondent has agreed to take action on the finding of violation so as to remedy the violation's effects, it is likely that the court will not go further than declaring the violation. Similarly, an award of a declaration and costs may suffice to afford just satisfaction, and therefore the court would not need to make an order for damages.

Under the HRA 1998, where an unlawful act by a public authority is established, damages may be awarded for a breach of statutory right. Such damages will be awarded on the above principles in relation to non-pecuniary damages, and on tortious principles in relation to pecuniary damages caused by the unlawful act.

The equitable assessment of non-pecuniary loss will be influenced by the court's assessment of the seriousness of the violation.[107]

Awards for compensation for non-pecuniary loss are modest, and involve a large element of discretion. Evidence of some such loss having occurred will be necessary and the tribunal will be able to make its own assessment, as the ECtHR would do 'on an equitable basis'.[108] The court will not automatically make an award under this head even if anxiety or distress have been suffered as the finding of violation may be sufficient compensation. (This was the case in the immigration/family life case *Abdulaziz, Cabales & Balkandali v UK*.[109])

The Law Commission's Report 'Damages under the Human Rights Act 1998' gives the case-law on damages broken down by Articles of the Convention.

---

106   *Abdulaziz, Cabales and Balkandali v UK* (1985) 7 EHRR 471.
107   *Halford v UK* (1997) 24 EHRR 523 at para 76.
108   *Philis v Greece (No 2)* (1998) 25 EHRR 417.
109   (1985) 7 EHRR 471.

6.7.3   The status of damages for breach of s 6 in actions for a contribution

By s 8(5), a public authority against which damages are awarded is to be treated:

(a) in Scotland, for the purposes of s 3 of the Law Reform (Miscellaneous Provisions)(Scotland) Act 1940 as if the award were made in an action of damages in which the authority has been found liable in respect of loss or damage to the person to whom the award is made;

(b) for the purposes of the Civil Liability (Contribution) Act 1978 as liable in respect of damage suffered by the person to whom the award is made.

This enables a public authority against which an award of damages is made to claim contribution from any other person liable in respect of the same damage. This will permit recovery of damages, but not necessarily any costs of remedial action ordered by the court. In s 1(1) of the Civil Liability (Contribution) Act 1978, 'the same damage' is the damage suffered by the person to whom the party seeking contribution was liable. In *Birse Construction Ltd v Haiste Ltd,*[110] the damage suffered by a water authority, namely the physical defects in a reservoir, and the damage suffered by the plaintiff seeking contribution (the financial loss of having to construct a second reservoir for the water authority) were not 'the same damage' within the meaning of the section. Section 8(5) is restricted to damages awarded under s 8 for breach of s 6. Where a public authority is found liable (as in *X & Y v The Netherlands*[111]) for having failed to protect the Convention rights of an individual, it may use this section to seek contribution for the damages awarded by the court from the individual who actually perpetrated the acts which constituted the infringement of the Convention rights.

6.8   LEGAL HELP IN THE COURTS

Human rights cases may raise matters of general importance. Section 8 of the Access to Justice Act 1999 provides for a code for funding of services as part of the community legal service. Section 13 of that code deals with decisions of principle. Where the Legal Services Commission is considering granting an application relating to proceedings with a significant wider public interest, the Commission may require the client, as a condition of providing funding, to agree not to settle the proceedings without the consent of the Commission. A decision of principle under the code must specify the cases or the description of cases to which it applies and the date on which it takes effect.[112] Where an issue arises as to whether a case has a significant wider public interest, or as to the nature and extent of that public interest, the Regional Director may refer the matter to the Public Interest Advisory Panel, whose report must be sent to the applicant's solicitor. The solicitor may make such further representations arising from the Panel's report as the solicitor thinks fit.

---

110   [1996] 1 WLR 695.
111   (1985) Series A, No 91, 8 EHRR 235.
112   Paragraph 46.3.

6.9   SECTION 9: JUDICIAL ACTS

6.9.1   Bringing a claim for an unlawful judicial act

The court is a public authority, and therefore may be liable for breaches of s 6 of the HRA 1998. However, there is a restriction on where a claim for an unlawful judicial act may be brought. Section 9 of the HRA 1998 provides that proceedings under s 7(1)(a) in respect of a judicial act may be brought only:

(a)   by exercising a right of appeal; or

(b)   on an application (in Scotland a petition) for judicial review; or

(c)   in such other forum as may be prescribed by rules.

The provisions of s 9(1) do not affect a rule of law which prevents a court from being the subject of judicial review.[113] Thus the Crown Court, in the context of a trial on indictment, and the High Court are immune from judicial review. Where the Crown Court is acting outside that context, it may be susceptible to judicial review.

Section 9(3) provides that, in proceedings under the HRA 1998 in respect of a judicial act done in good faith, damages may not be awarded otherwise than to compensate a person to the extent required by Article 5(5) of the Convention. Such an award of damages is to be made against the Crown; but no award may be made unless the Minister responsible for the court concerned, or a person or government department nominated by the Minister ('the appropriate person'), if not a party to the proceedings, is joined.

For the purposes of remedies for judicial acts, a 'court' includes a tribunal and 'judge' includes a member of a tribunal, a justice of the peace and a clerk or other officer entitled to exercise the jurisdiction of a court. The term 'judicial act' means a judicial act of a court and includes an act done on the instructions, or on behalf, of a judge.

6.9.2   Exercising a right of appeal

Section 9(1) of the HRA 1998 provides that proceedings in respect of an unlawful judicial act may be brought only by way of an appeal or on application for judicial review. Where there is a right of appeal, the court will probably not entertain an application for judicial review as, absent special circumstances, the applicant must have exhausted his alternative remedies.[114] Thus where the unlawful act consists of a refusal to protect the Convention rights of the individual before it, it is likely that the individual will have an argument that the tribunal erred in law and would therefore have to bring the matter by way of an appeal. It is only where the unlawful judicial act is one which does not found an appeal that judicial review would be appropriate.

The reference to 'exercising a right of appeal' must be a reference to an existing right of appeal or a right, and the HRA 1998 does not confer fresh jurisdiction on the EAT in respect of appeals. The individual may rely on the

---

113   HRA 1998, s 9(2).

114   *R v Secretary of State for the Home Department, ex parte Swati* [1986] 1 All ER 717.

Convention rights in an appeal involving a public authority where there is also an appeal against an issue in respect of another matter under employment legislation. However, the individual may not appeal simply on the basis that the employment tribunal committed an unlawful act of its own. This is because s 21 of the Employment Tribunals Act 1996 does not confer jurisdiction on the EAT in respect of decisions made under the HRA 1998 and s 21(2) confines rights of appeals to those statutes listed in subs (1) (see **6.10.1**).

Thus where a respondent wishes to challenge a finding that an act was unlawful under s 6, the respondent will have to bring judicial review proceedings of the tribunal in which the finding was made (provided that this finding does not give rise to a finding of unlawful action under a provision over which the EAT does have jurisdiction). Similarly, where an applicant wishes to challenge a failure of the tribunal to make a finding that the applicant's Convention rights were breached (or to challenge a finding that the Convention rights were not breached) where there is no other ground of appeal under the employment legislation in issue, the applicant will have to bring judicial review proceedings of the decision of the tribunal.

6.10 APPEALS FROM EMPLOYMENT TRIBUNALS

6.10.1 Jurisdiction of employment tribunals

In relation to the employment tribunals, the EAT has its jurisdiction defined by s 21 of the Employment Tribunals Act 1996:

'(1) An appeal lies to the Appeal Tribunal on any question of law arising from any decision of, or arising in any proceedings before, an employment tribunal under or by virtue of:

    (a)   the Equal Pay Act 1970,
    (b)   the Sex Discrimination Act 1975,
    (c)   the Race Relations Act 1976,
    (d)   the Trade Union and Labour Relations (Consolidation) Act 1992,
    (e)   the Disability Discrimination Act 1995,
    (f)   the Employment Rights Act 1996,
   (ff)   the National Minimum Wage Act 1998, or
   (fg)   the Tax Credits Act 1999, or
    (g)   this Act or under the Working Time Regulations 1998.

(2) No appeal shall lie except to the Appeal Tribunal from any decision of an employment tribunal under or by virtue of the Acts listed in subsection (1).

(3) Subsection (1) does not affect any provision contained in, or made under, any Act which provides for an appeal to lie to the Appeal Tribunal (whether from an employment tribunal, the Certification Officer or any other person or body) otherwise than on a question to which that subsection applies.

(4) The Appeal Tribunal also has any jurisdiction in respect of matters other than appeals which is conferred on it by or under –

    (a)   the Trade Union and Labour Relations (Consolidation) Act 1992,

    (b)   this Act, or

    (c)   any other Act.'

An individual may rely on the Convention rights as regards the unlawful activities of a public authority in any appeal as these are legal proceedings.[115] There appears to be nothing to prevent the EAT from considering whether the tribunal, in making a finding that an unlawful act had occurred, had exceeded its powers under one of the Acts listed in s 21 of the ETA 1996. By s 8, jurisdiction is conferred on the EAT to make a finding that a breach has occurred. The EAT will have jurisdiction to deal with the question of interpretation of existing legislation in the light of the HRA 1998, and whether the interpretation of the listed legislation by the tribunal gives effect to the Convention rights.

What is not clear is whether the EAT can entertain an appeal where the sole issue is the failure to find a breach of the Convention under s 8 or a finding of a breach. In *Pendragon plc v Jackson*,[116] the EAT ruled that it did not have jurisdiction in respect of certain contract appeals as the power had not been conferred on it. On the face of s 21, the EAT would appear not to have this jurisdiction, as the power to make a finding that an unlawful act has occurred is not the power to determine that a tribunal erred in law in its application of the HRA 1998 in order to make or not make a finding that a breach had occurred. If this argument is right, parties whose sole complaint is that a finding of a breach of the Convention rights was or was not made by the tribunal would have to challenge that finding by way of judicial review proceedings against the employment tribunal.

The EAT is not a branch of the High Court, although such judges sit there. It cannot therefore make a finding of incompatibility under s 4 of the HRA 1998. The proper procedure for the EAT where an issue of incompatibility arises will be to apply the employment legislation despite the fact that it is incompatible. It is likely that in such cases it would grant leave to appeal to the Court of Appeal, which can make such a declaration.

6.10.2   Judicial review of unlawful judicial acts by employment tribunals

A public body will not be deemed to have sufficient interest in proceedings by virtue of s 7 of the HRA 1998. This is because a public authority cannot be regarded in Convention law as a victim. It is the State. However, the domestic concept of sufficient interest will clearly apply and, where a public authority seeks to quash a finding that it has acted unlawfully, it will have sufficient standing as a body directly affected by the tribunal's finding of unlawfulness.

A private individual will have to show that he or she is a victim of the unlawful act of the tribunal (see **6.2.5**).

---

115   HRA 1998, s 7(1)(b).

116   [1998] ICR 215.

6.11 JUDICIAL REVIEW

6.11.1 Judicial review generally

Judicial review is the most appropriate vehicle for the challenge if there is a general challenge to the legal basis of a policy or other measure or a question as to whether it complies with the statutory intention. Where essentially the claim is for money, the questions which might arise can be dealt with by a judge on the hearing of an ordinary claim. It is suggested that even if discretionary elements are present in a decision by a public authority, the generally appropriate course, where the application of powers is challenged as unlawful under s 6 of the HRA 1998, will be by way of action for breach of the statutory duty on the public authority and for damages, rather than by way of judicial review.[117]

Where there is a challenge to the compatibility of legislation with the Convention rights, the proper course will be to bring an application for judicial review.

6.11.2 Special provisions relating to detention claims

Compensation for unlawful detention

Under the CPR 1998, Part 33 (miscellaneous rules about evidence), provision is made for the findings on which a claim of breach is based to be admitted in evidence by the court dealing with breaches based on judicial acts. The rule applies where a claim is:

(a) for a remedy under s 7 of the HRA 1998 in respect of a judicial act which is alleged to have infringed the claimant's Article 5 Convention rights; and
(b) based on a finding by a Crown Court.

The rules permit the court hearing the claim to reconsider the evidence of the alleged infringement and the finding of the Crown Court. This rule deals with the consequences of infringements of the right to liberty of the person such as in an action for false imprisonment as a result of a judicial act.

Unlawful orders for committal etc

By para 14 of Practice Direction 40B to CPR 1998 (judgments and orders), on any application or appeal concerning:

(a) a committal order;
(b) a refusal to grant habeas corpus; or
(c) a secure accommodation order made under s 25 of the Children Act 1989,

the judgment or order must, if the court orders the release of the person, state whether or not the original order was made in circumstances which infringed that person's Convention rights. This provision may apply where a person has

---

117 See *Steed v Home Office* [2000] 1 WLR 1169, HL.

been committed for breach of an injunction, for example in an industrial action case or in cases concerning restraint of trade.

6.12   REMEDIAL ACTION FOLLOWING A DECLARATION OF INCOMPATIBILITY BY THE HIGH COURT, COURT OF APPEAL, OR HOUSE OF LORDS

Remedial action under s 10 of the HRA 1998 may be taken where one or more of the following conditions are satisfied:

(a) a provision of legislation has been declared under s 4 of the HRA 1998 to be incompatible with a Convention right and, if an appeal lies:
    (i)   all persons who may appeal have stated in writing that they do not intend to do so;
    (ii) the time for bringing an appeal has expired and no appeal has been brought within that time; or
    (iii) an appeal brought within that time has been determined or abandoned; or
(b) it appears to a Minister of the Crown or Her Majesty in Council that, having regard to a finding of the ECtHR made after the coming into force of s 10 in proceedings against the UK, a provision of legislation is incompatible with an obligation of the UK arising from the Convention.

If a Minister of the Crown considers that there are compelling reasons for proceeding by way of remedial action, the Minister may make such amendments to the legislation by order as the Minister considers necessary to remove the incompatibility.[118] Amendment includes repeal.[119]

In the case of subordinate legislation, if a Minister of the Crown considers the following conditions satisfied, the Minister may by order make such amendments to the primary legislation as the Minister considers necessary.[120] Those conditions are:

(a) that it is necessary to amend the primary legislation under which the subordinate legislation in question was made, in order to enable the incompatibility to be removed; and
(b) that there are compelling reasons for proceeding under s 10.

If the legislation is an Order in Council, the power conferred by s 10(2) or (3) is exercisable by Her Majesty in Council.[121]

Remedial action may also be taken where the provision in question is in subordinate legislation and has been quashed, or declared invalid, by reason of incompatibility with a Convention right and the Minister proposes to proceed under para 2(b) of Sch 2 to the HRA 1998. Schedule 2 makes further provision

---

118 HRA 1998, s 10(2).
119 HRA 1998, s 21.
120 HRA 1998, s 10(3).
121 HRA 1998, s 10(6).

about remedial orders.[122] Paragraph 2(b) of Sch 2 provides that no remedial order may be made unless it is declared in the order that it appears to the person making it that, because of the urgency of the matter, it is necessary to make the order without a draft being approved by Parliament by means of resolution of both Houses.

The remedial order, by para 1(3) of Sch 2, may be made so as to have the same extent as the legislation which it affects. Finally, no person is to be guilty of an offence solely as a result of the retrospective effect of a remedial order.[123]

Paragraph 2 of Sch 2 provides a procedure to be followed in making remedial order. No remedial order may be made unless:

(a) a draft of the order has been approved by a resolution of each House of Parliament made after the end of the period of 60 days beginning with the day on which the draft was laid; or
(b) it is declared in the order that it appears to the person making it that, because of the urgency of the matter, it is necessary to make the order without a draft being so approved.

Paragraph 3 makes provisions for the remedial order to be laid before Parliament in draft and requires the following conditions to be satisfied before a draft may be laid before Parliament:

(a) the person proposing to make the order has laid before Parliament a document which contains a draft of the proposed order and the required information; and
(b) the period of 60 days, beginning with the day on which the document required was laid, has ended.

Representations made during the period of 60 days during which the document containing a draft of the proposed order and the required information was before Parliament are considered. The draft of the order laid under para 2(a) must be accompanied by a statement containing:

(a) a summary of the representations; and
(b) if, as a result of the representations, the proposed order has been changed, details of the changes.

It is at that stage that the order may be laid before Parliament for resolution within 60 days. However, the HRA 1998 envisages that there may be occasions when this procedural timetable would be inappropriate due to the urgency of the situation to be addressed. Paragraph 4 of Sch 2 makes provision that if a remedial order ('the original order') is made without being approved in draft, the person making it must lay it before Parliament, accompanied by the required information, after it is made. If representations have been made during the period of 60 days beginning with the day on which the original order

---

122 HRA 1998, s 10(7).
123 HRA 1998, Sch 2, para 1(4).

was made, the person making it must (after the end of that period) lay before Parliament a statement containing:

(a) a summary of the representations; and
(b) if, as a result of the representations, he or she considers it appropriate to make changes to the original order, details of the changes.

Where such a statement is required the person making it must:

(a) make a further remedial order replacing the original order; and
(b) lay the replacement order before Parliament.

If, at the end of the period of 120 days beginning with the day on which the original order was made, a resolution has not been passed by each House approving the original or replacement order, the order ceases to have effect (but without that affecting anything previously done under either order or the power to make a fresh remedial order).

For the purposes of Sch 2, 'representations' means representations about a remedial order (or proposed remedial order) made to the person making (or proposing to make) it and includes any relevant Parliamentary report or resolution, and 'required information' means:

(a) an explanation of the incompatibility which the order (or proposed order) seeks to remove, including particulars of the relevant declaration, finding or order; and
(b) a statement of the reasons for proceeding under s 10 of the HRA 1998 and for making an order in those terms.

Schedule 2 makes provision for the computation of time in relation to the passing of remedial orders which are outside the scope of this book.

'Legislation' for the purposes of remedial action does not include a Measure of the Church Assembly or of the General Synod of the Church of England. Thus the Government cannot intervene in these measures by means of a remedial order.

By para 1(1) of Sch 2, a remedial order may contain such incidental, supplemental, consequential or transitional provision as the person making it considers appropriate. It may also be made so as to have effect from a date earlier than that on which it is made and make provision for the delegation of specific functions. The Minister may make different provision for different cases.

Paragraph 1(2) of Sch 2 provides that the power to contain such incidental, supplemental, consequential or transitional provision as the person making the order considers appropriate includes:

–   power to amend primary legislation (including primary legislation other than that which contains the incompatible provision); and
–   power to amend or revoke subordinate legislation (including subordinate legislation other than that which contains the incompatible provision).

6.13 JUDICIAL REVIEW AND HUMAN RIGHTS IN EMPLOYMENT CASES

6.13.1 Introduction

The rights of employees of a public authority may arise either by the employment contract, or by statute, or by the common law. Traditionally, contracts of employment have been seen as enforceable by ordinary action and not by means of judicial review. Thus in *R v BBC, ex parte Lavelle*,[124] the court converted a judicial review application into an ordinary action for this reason.

Woolf J said:

> 'Ord. 53, r. 1(2) ... merely requires that the court should have regard to the nature of the matter in respect of which such relief may be granted. However, although applications for judicial review are not confined to those cases where relief could be granted by way of prerogative order, I regard the wording of Ord. 53, r. 1(2) and s 31(2) of the Act of 1981 as making it clear that the application for judicial review is confined to reviewing activities of a public nature as opposed to those of a purely private or domestic character. The disciplinary appeal procedure set up by the B.B.C. depends purely upon the contract of employment between the applicant and the B.B.C., and therefore it is a procedure of a purely private or domestic character.'[125]

Under s 6 of the HRA 1998, the act impugned may be any act of a public authority. Where the intention of the proceedings is to impugn the validity of the legal basis of the action of the public authority as a whole, the elements of domestic public law in the case outweigh any element of private right and therefore an application for judicial review would be appropriate. In a case under s 6, which arises because it is alleged that specific acts of the public authority infringed the Convention right in issue, thus causing harm to the individual, it is suggested that it creates a domestic private law right in the individual.

An employee of, or office holder in, a public authority pre-HRA 1998 might have had to consider whether he or she needed to bring a claim in private or public law. The effect of the HRA 1998 is to diminish the scope for such judicial review applications, in particular in relation to procedural issues that might be covered by Article 6, as the employee or office holder will either have access to an employment tribunal or will be able to bring a claim in the courts for the private law remedy of breach of s 6 of the HRA 1998.

The analysis of the occasions on which an employee of a public body might or might not be able to bring judicial review proceedings is nonetheless useful. The following principles need to be considered (based on remarks in *McLaren v Home Office*[126]).

(1) There is no reason why an injunction should not be granted against the Crown.

---

124 [1983] 1 WLR 23.
125 [1983] 1 WLR 23 at p 31.
126 [1990] ICR 824.

(2) The employee can bring proceedings for damages, a declaration or an injunction in the court and for this remedy will not need to resort to judicial review.

(3) There is no reason why, after the HRA 1998, a claim in respect of a disciplinary or other body established under the prerogative or by statute to which the public authority or the employee may or must refer employment-related disputes, should not be brought in the courts without needing to be assigned to the Crown Office list. The remedies available to the employee are no more extensive in judicial review than in an action for breach of statutory duty under the HRA 1998.

(4) Thus where an employee of the public authority is adversely affected by a decision of general application by the public authority, and wishes to argue that the decision is flawed by reference to the Convention rights, the employee will no longer be entitled to challenge that decision by way of judicial review, as the claim will fall to be considered under s 8 of the HRA 1998.

(5) Where, of course, the HRA 1998 does not give rise to an issue of breach of s 6, the public authority employee will have to consider whether the two situations mentioned in *Maclaren* in which judicial review may be available to the employee obtain:
    (a) claims in respect of a disciplinary body (see item (3) above);
    (b) adverse effect on the claimant by a decision of general application.

(6) It is difficult to conceive of situations in which the HRA 1998 will not subsume the issues that have been raised in employment judicial review claims into the ordinary court system.

A point of general principle (the principle being pragmatism) in relation to the choice of venue for claims under s 7(1)(a) of the HRA 1998 may be derived from *Steed v Home Office*.[127] The House of Lords started by considering *O'Reilly v Mackman*[128] and in particular the passage in the speech of Lord Diplock:

> 'it would in my view as a general rule be contrary to public policy, and as such an abuse of the process of the court, to permit a person seeking to establish that a decision of a public authority infringed rights to which he was entitled to protection under public law to proceed by way of an ordinary action and by this means to evade the provisions of Order 53 for the protection of such authorities.'[129]

Note that in relation to the HRA 1998 any court is under an obligation to consider the justification of an act of a public authority, which is, on the facts established by the claimant, on the face of it, an infringement of a Convention right. Thus the protection afforded to public authorities in relation to the discretionary nature of some of their acts is to be provided by the balancing exercise required by issues of justification. The House of Lords, in *Steed*, stated that *O'Reilly v Mackman* has had an important influence on the regulation of court proceedings where an individual seeks to assert his or her rights against a

---

127   [2000] 1 WLR 1169, HL.
128   [1983] 2 AC 237.
129   [1983] 2 AC 237 at p 285D.

public authority. But it noted that Lord Diplock set out the position 'as a general rule'. Earlier in his speech he said that Parliament and the Rules Committee (formulating Order 53) had been:

> 'content to rely upon the express and the inherent power of the High Court, exercised upon a case to case basis, to prevent abuse of its process whatever might be the form taken by that abuse. Accordingly I do not think that your lordships would be wise to use this as an occasion to lay down categories of cases in which it would necessarily always be an abuse to seek in an action begun by a writ or originating summons a remedy against infringement or rights of the individual that are entitled to protection in public law.'[130]

He accepted further that although striking out may be appropriate 'normally':

> 'there may be exceptions, particularly where the invalidity of the decision arises as a collateral issue in a claim for infringement of a right of the plaintiff arising under private law, or where none of the parties objects to the adoption of the procedure by writ or originating summons.'[131]

Other exceptions, if any, were to be decided on a case-to-case basis. One such exception was *Roy v Kensington and Chelsea and Westminster Family Practitioner Committee*,[132] when it was accepted that a claim for private rights could be made by action even if that involved a challenge to a 'public law act or decision'. Another exception is *Mercury Communications Ltd v Director General of Telecommunications*[133]:

> 'The recognition by Lord Diplock that exceptions exist to the general rule may introduce some uncertainty but it is a small price to pay to avoid the over-rigid demarcation between procedures reminiscent of earlier disputes as to the forms of action and of disputes as to the competence of jurisdictions apparently encountered in civil law countries where a distinction between public and private law has been recognised ...
>
> The experience of other countries seems to show that the working out of this distinction is not always an easy matter. In the absence of the single procedure allowing all remedies – quashing, injunctive and declaratory relief, damages – some flexibility as to the use of different procedures is necessary. It has to be borne in mind that the overriding question is whether the proceedings constitute an abuse of the process of the court.'[134]

In *Trustees of the Dennis Rye Pension Fund v Sheffield City Council*,[135] Lord Woolf said that the guidelines he gave (see below) involved:

> 'not only considering the technical questions of the distinctions between public and private rights and bodies but also looking at the practical consequences of the choice of procedure which has been made. If the choice has no significant disadvantage for the parties, the public or the court, then it should not normally be regarded as constituting an abuse.'[136]

---

130 [1983] 2 AC 237 at p 285A.
131 [1983] 2 AC 237 at p 285E–F.
132 [1992] 1 AC 624.
133 [1996] 1 WLR 48.
134 [1996] 1 WLR 48 *per* Lord Slynn at p 57.
135 [1998] 1 WLR 840.
136 [1998] 1 WLR 840 at p 849.

In that case, the claimants were served by the local authority with a repair notice under s 189 of the Housing Act 1985. This required work to be carried out to a number of premises to render them fit for human habitation. The works were carried out and the council approved applications for improvement grants under s 101 of the Local Government and Housing Act 1989. It then refused to pay the grants on the ground that the works had not been completed to its satisfaction under s 117(3) of that Act. The claimants' private law claims against the council for payment of the sums withheld were initially struck out as an abuse of the process of the court as the decision could be challenged only by way of judicial review. The Court of Appeal held that the council was performing a public function in making grants. In general, this function did not give rise to private rights. However, once the council had approved an application for an improvement grant it was under a duty to make payment upon the applicant's compliance with the statutory conditions and any amount unpaid could be recovered as an ordinary debt in a private law action. Since the challenge to the council's refusal to express satisfaction with the repairs depended largely on issues of fact, these were more appropriately determined in the course of ordinary proceedings than on an application for judicial review.

Lord Woolf MR stated:

'What I would suggest is necessary is to begin by going back to first principles and remind oneself of the guidance which Lord Diplock gave in *O'Reilly v Mackman*. This guidance involves recognising:

(a) that remedies for protecting both private and public rights can be given in both private law proceedings and on an application for judicial review;

(b) that judicial review provides, in the interest of the public, protection for public bodies which are not available in private law proceedings (namely the requirement of leave and the protection against delay). The proceedings will be heard by a High Court judge and will be managed by the Crown Office which has the necessary experience of public law proceedings to ensure that questions, such as expedition, are dealt with in a manner which is appropriate;

(c) that for these reasons it is a *general rule* that it is contrary to public policy "and as such an abuse of the process of the court, to permit a person seeking to establish that a decision of a public authority infringed rights to which he was entitled to protection under public law to proceed by way of an ordinary action and by this means to evade the provisions of Order 53 for the protection of such authorities:" p 285.

Having established the foundation of the general rule it seems to me that there will be a reduction in the difficulties which are apparently being experienced at present by practitioners and the courts, if it is remembered that:

(1) If it is not clear whether judicial review or an ordinary action is the correct procedure it will be safer to make an application for judicial review than commence an ordinary action since there then should be no question of being treated as abusing the process of the court by avoiding the protection provided by judicial review. In the majority of cases it should not be necessary *for purely procedural reasons* to become involved in arid arguments as to whether the issues are correctly treated as involving public or private law or both. (For reasons of

substantive law it may be necessary to consider this issue.) If judicial review is used when it should not, the court can protect its resources either by directing that the application should continue as if begun by writ or by directing it should be heard by a judge who is not nominated to hear cases in the Crown Office List. It is difficult to see how a respondent can be prejudiced by the adoption of this course and little risk that anything more damaging could happen than a refusal of leave.

(2) If a case is brought by an ordinary action and there is an application to strike out the case, the court should, at least if it is unclear whether the case should have been brought by judicial review, ask itself whether, if the case had been brought by judicial review when the action was commenced, it is clear leave would have been granted. If it would, then that is at least an indication that there has been no harm to the interests judicial review is designed to protect. In addition the court should consider by which procedure the case could be appropriately tried. If the answer is that an ordinary action is equally or more appropriate than an application for judicial review that again should be an indication the action should not be struck out.

(3) Finally, in cases where it is unclear whether proceedings have been correctly brought by an ordinary action it should be remembered that after consulting the Crown Office a case can always be transferred to the Crown Office List as an alternative to being struck out.'

For most acts of a public authority which the claimant wishes to establish are unlawful under s 6 of the HRA 1998 there will be no reason to commence proceedings by way of judicial review, as the establishment of a factual situation will be central to the claim. Once that factual situation is established there will be argument concerning whether the facts established constitute an infringe-ment or an unjustified infringement of the claimant's rights under the HRA 1998. This will involve the court in considering whether the discretion of the public authority was properly exercised by reference to the legal basis of the act, whether the infringement of the claimant's rights was necessary in a demo-cratic society and whether the interference was proportionate to the legitimate aim sought by the act.

6.13.2 Judicial review v CPR 1998, Part 8 claims

The overriding question is whether the procedure adopted is as well suited to the issue between the individual and public authority as judicial review would be (see *Mercury*[137]). Given that the CPR 1998 are amended in such a way as to make the issuing of claims under s 7(1)(a) of the HRA 1998 in the general courts the most usual course (save where there is a question of a challenge to a judicial act), the action under s 7(1)(a) will rarely need to be transferred to the Crown Office. Further, even where there is a challenge to the validity of a policy of general application, it may still be appropriate to commence an action rather than bring proceedings for judicial review. Where claims under s 7(1)(a) involve a challenge to a policy of a public authority employer, there seems no reason why the claim should not be commenced under Part 8 of the CPR 1998 by the issue of a Part 8 claim form (claim form N208). Supporting evidence is filed immediately on issue and service of the claim form. The public authority

---

137 *Mercury Communications Ltd v Director-General of Telecommunications* [1996] 1 WLR 48.

will serve an acknowledgment of service and its opposing evidence. The claimant may then serve evidence in reply. There will then be directions given and the final hearing will be based on written evidence only. The procedure is inappropriate for significant factual disputes.

CPR 1998, Parts 6 and 7 governing issue and service apply to Part 8 claims. However, only the form for acknowledging service should be served on the defendant with the claim form. There is no need under r 7.8(2) for forms for defending or admitting the claim. Requirements for Part 8 claim forms are contained in r 8.2, but in HRA 1998 cases the modifications referred to at **6.3.2–6.3.4** will also apply. It must be served within four months after issue by r 7.5.

Part 16 does not apply to Part 8 claims by r 8.9(a)(i), but the above procedure for service of written evidence will apply. Witness statements or affidavits may be used. The matters included in the claim form may stand as the claimant's evidence, if the form has a statement of truth.[138]

If the public authority believes that the Part 8 procedure should not be used, it must file an acknowledgment of service, and should (at the same time) file and serve a statement of reasons for opposing the procedure.[139]

It is unlikely that such opposition would result in a claim being struck out even if successful, because the court has power to order the claim to continue as if it were an ordinary claim not governed by Part 8, and give appropriate directions by r 8.1(3). By r 8.8(2), the court can give directions for the future conduct of the case in such a situation, and the powers of the court would extend to making an order for transfer to the Crown Office where the issues warranted this course.

All Part 8 claims are allocated to the multi-track,[140] but Part 26 does not apply. There is no requirement for parties to complete allocation questionnaires.

The court has a discretion to deal with claims without a hearing under the Practice Direction to Part 8, para 4.3.

6.13.3   Standing in judicial review cases under the Human Rights Act 1998

Where judicial review is the route adopted for the challenge under s 7 of the HRA 1998, the claimant will be deemed to have sufficient interest (in Scotland interest to sue) once the victim requirement is satisfied. In relation to the unlawful act, the applicant must show that he or she is or would be a victim of that act.[141]

It is likely that the only employment-related claims which will, initially, need to be dealt with by way of judicial review, are those relating to judicial acts. The proposed Practice Direction provides that where an issue arises in a claim or appeal relating to breach of a Convention right as a result of a judicial act under

---

138   Practice Direction to Part 8, para 5.2.
139   CPR 1998, r 8.8(1) and Practice Direction to Part 8, para 3.6.
140   CPR 1998, r 8.9(c).
141   HRA 1998, s 7(1), (3) and (4).

s 7(1)(a) and s 9(3) of the HRA 1998 which would be heard in the county court then that claim or appeal will be transferred to the Crown Office in the High Court. Other claims, it is submitted, will be dealt with as claims for breach of s 6 of the HRA 1998.

6.13.4 Victim v sufficient interest

An application for judicial review may be brought by any person with sufficient interest in the matters in issue.

The starting point for the concept of standing in judicial review is *Inland Revenue Commissioners v National Federation of Self-Employed and Small Businesses.*[142] Since the introduction of RSC Ord 53, r 3, standing is achieved if the applicant has sufficient interest in the matter to which the application relates. A decision of the court on standing is a mixed decision of fact and law, which the court must decide on legal principles. The greater the remedy sought, the greater the interest required. The interest of a person seeking to compel an authority to carry out a duty is different from that of a person complaining that a judicial or administrative body has, to that person's detriment, exceeded its powers.

In the *National Federation of Self-Employed and Small Businesses* case, the court was concerned with an alleged failure to perform a duty. The House of Lords was guided by the definition of the statutory duty and asked whether expressly, or by implication, the applicant was within the scope of the duty. In relation to s 9 of the HRA 1998 (complaints about judicial acts), the court will have to consider that the parties before it have sufficient interest in an application for judicial review, as they will be the parties before the inferior court or tribunal, and the tribunal itself.

This test of 'standing' is affected by s 7(3) of the HRA 1998 in cases involving judicial review based on s 6 unlawfulness. What is now necessary is that the applicant prove that he or she would be directly affected by the measure about which the complaint is made, or would otherwise be a victim of the unlawful acts.

In *R v Bow County Court, ex parte Pelling*,[143] the applicant tried to attend a chambers hearing in the county court to act as a litigation friend by sitting with and providing assistance and advice to a litigant in person who was making an application, without notice to the other party, concerning contact arrangements. The judge refused to allow him to attend the hearing, and gave no reasons for refusal. The applicant applied for judicial review. The Court of Appeal considered his appeal from the Divisional Court. They rejected it as the form of assistance he offered was for the benefit of the litigant in person. He had no right to provide the services and the nature of proceedings in private might mean that it was undesirable in the interests of justice for such an assistant to be present. The Divisional Court held that:

> 'where the hearing is in open court there is a right to a *McKenzie* friend. That right is vested solely in the litigant in person; there is no correlative right vested in the

---

142 [1982] AC 617.
143 [1999] 1 WLR 1807.

McKenzie friend. Where the hearing is in chambers there is a discretion in the judge whether to permit the presence of a *McKenzie* friend. Any challenge to the exercise of the judge's discretion can only be made by the litigant in person, he alone seeks redress from the court. The *McKenzie* friend has neither the right to be present in chambers nor to impugn the exercise of judicial discretion to exclude him. In my judgment it must follow that he has no locus standi to bring these proceedings.'[144]

The court considered also that Article 6 of the Convention did not assist in the question of the applicant's standing:

'The precise terms of article 6 do not, in my judgment, support the applicant's case. The Convention clearly recognises an exception that the public may be excluded where the interests of juveniles or protection of the private life of the parties so requires. As explained, the applicant is a member of the public, nothing more. Accordingly there is no breach of the Convention. Moreover, the proviso in article 6 is consistent with article 8(1) which guarantees the right to respect for private and family life. Nowhere in the Convention is it suggested that there is a right to a *McKenzie* friend or someone similar, as distinct from the litigant. As I am not persuaded that the common law position is not in conformity with the Convention, I see no obligation on this court to consider or apply its implications.'[145]

The Divisional Court appears to have considered first whether the assistant has a right to be present and then gone on to consider whether he had sufficient interest in the decision of the judge. Looked at from the point of view of the Convention, an assistant might be able to argue that he was directly affected by the decision. In the case of *Pelling* he acted as a litigation friend for reward, and thus it is arguable that the decision had an impact on his livelihood. Clearly, he was directly affected by the decision, and would probably be able to argue that he would be directly affected if that decision had been taken in breach of a Convention right. In the particular case, the analysis of Article 6 pragmatically dealt with whether there had been a breach of the Convention, rather than with the question of whether the applicant was directly affected so as to be a victim of any alleged breach. It was not necessary therefore to go on to consider whether the litigation friend was a victim of any breach.

R v Secretary of State for Foreign and Commonwealth Affairs, ex parte World Development Movement Ltd[146] is a good example of the concept of standing in judicial review cases, and illustrates the way it differs from the 'victim' requirement. There the applicant was a pressure group which asked for an assurance from the Secretary of State that no further funds for the project of the Pergau Dam would be furnished. This was refused. They claimed judicial review of the Secretary of State's decision to grant funding.

The court identified the merits of the challenge as being an important factor when considering standing. The court held that the following factors supported the conclusion that the organisation had sufficient interest for the purposes of standing:

---

144   [1999] 1 WLR 1807 at p 1817.
145   [1999] 1 WLR 1807 at pp 1815–16.
146   [1995] 1 WLR 386.

(a) the importance of vindicating the rule of law;

(b) the importance of the issue raised;

(c) the likely absence of any other responsible challenger;

(d) the nature of the breach of duty against which relief was sought; and

(e) the prominent role of the applicants in giving advice, guidance and assistance regarding aid.

Other examples of groups held to have standing include *R v Secretary of State for Social Services, ex parte Child Poverty Action Group*[147] and *R v Inspectorate of Pollution, ex parte Greenpeace Ltd (No 2)*.[148] The scope of the concept of standing can also be illustrated by reference to *R v Secretary of State for Foreign and Commonwealth Affairs, ex parte Rees-Mogg*,[149] where the applicant was held to have standing 'because of his sincere concern for constitutional issues'. The requirements of standing will vary from case to case and that the court may accord standing to someone who would not otherwise qualify where exceptionally grave or widespread illegality is alleged. The concept of 'victim' is more narrowly circumscribed (see **6.2.5**).

6.13.5 Procedure for judicial review applications

No application for judicial review may be made unless the permission of the court has been obtained in accordance with CPR 1998, r 54.3(1). If an oral hearing is required, it must be sought in the written application.[150]

In practice, an applicant for judicial review has the choice of making a 'paper application' or of seeking a hearing for permission. Where the case is one of urgency the applicant is probably best advised to apply for an oral hearing immediately, as this is likely to be determined much earlier than the paper application.

The Crown Office has over recent years tended towards a practice of asking respondents to attend and either to give their views on the application or to resist permission being granted. The judge may adjourn the notice without hearing to allow the respondents to attend. Equally, if the application is made on paper, it may be refused. The applicant must then review the application to the Divisional Court single judge.

In *R v Inland Revenue Commissioners, ex parte National Federation of Self-Employed and Small Businesses*[151] Lord Diplock stated that the purpose of the leave stage, now known as the permission stage, was to prevent the time of the court being wasted by busybodies with misguided or trivial complaints of administrative error and to remove the uncertainty in which public officers and authorities might be left as to whether they could safely proceed with administrative action while misconceived proceedings for judicial review of that action were actually pending.

---

147 [1990] 2 QB 540.

148 [1994] 4 All ER 329.

149 [1994] QB 552 at 562A.

150 CPR 1998, r 54.3(3).

151 [1982] AC 617 at p 642.

The court is not supposed to look into the matter in any depth, but is supposed to make a quick perusal of what is before it and, if it thinks that this material discloses what might, on further consideration, turn out to be an arguable case in favour of granting the relief that the applicant claims, it should (exercising judicial discretion) grant leave or permission. However, the practice of the court is very different and will depend on the nature of the case before it.

Judicial review of employment decisions will be very rare. It is difficult to say how the Crown Office will deal with the issues raised by applications claiming that there has been a violation of a Convention right. They will involve consideration of whether, on the face of it, there is an infringement of a Convention right. A respondent to an application may seek to demonstrate that the action was justified even at the permission stage. It is submitted that there will be no hard-and-fast rule on whether a person who can show that the Convention right is engaged by the facts of the case will obtain permission to bring a full application. In certain cases, the respondent will be able to produce clear justification and, it is submitted, in this situation the court will have no hesitation in declaring that there there is no arguable case. The public authority may find a device, adopted by the Home Office in relation to immigration cases, useful when it becomes aware at that it is likely to face an application for judicial review. In immigration cases, the Home Office will send to the applicants a letter setting out the reasoning for the decision that is being challenged, and will ask for this letter to be placed before the court when and if the applicant seeks permission for judicial review.

The applicant for permission for judicial review is under a duty to disclose to the court all relevant material. A letter setting out the respondent's case is obviously relevant. The respondents therefore should attempt to give details of any available justification for the decision in this sort of letter. Such pre-emptive action may lead the applicant to decide not to make the claim in the first place, or, if an application is made, to the court rejecting the application for permission.

Having said that, in cases when it is not possible to demonstrate that the justification available or the decision provides a 'knockout' blow to the prospects of success of the applicant, justification should be considered when the full merits of the case are dealt with. Where this is the case, the respondent will need to provide evidence of the justification involved, if necessary by witness statements.

Both parties to an action for judicial review will need to deal with the issues of whether the apparent infringement of the Convention right is necessary in a democratic society. The question will be whether the interference with the applicant's right corresponds to a pressing social need. A witness statement dealing with the question of justification should therefore devote a subheading to the question of whether there is a pressing social need. Likewise, part of the witness statement should deal with the question of whether interference is in proportion to the aim that the interference pursues. At the least the chain of reasoning concerning proportionality should be covered.

6.14 FUNDING AND RELATED ISSUES: ACCESS TO JUSTICE ACT 1999

6.14.1 The Funding Code

Section 7 of the Access to Justice Act 1999 provides for a code for funding for judicial review. It applies to applications for legal representation in relation to court proceedings concerning public law challenges to the acts, omissions or decisions of public bodies, including in particular challenges by way of judicial review or *habeas corpus* and proceedings under Part VII of the Housing Act 1996.

The General Funding Code Criteria 5.6.1 (potential for a conditional fee agreement) and 5.6.3 (minimum damages level) do not apply to applications for investigative help under s 7. The solicitor must first ascertain whether judicial review is an available remedy, as an application may be refused if the act or decision complained of in the proposed proceedings does not appear to be susceptible to challenge by way of judicial review. It may also be refused if there are administrative appeals or other procedures which should be pursued before proceedings are considered. This requirement corresponds to the idea developed in the case-law that alternative remedies should be exhausted before judicial review is sought.[152]

6.14.2 Full representation

If, at the time the application for funding is made, the court has not yet granted permission to bring the proceedings, or if according to rules of court such permission is not required, the following criteria apply.

(1) The application may be refused if the act or decision complained of in the proposed proceedings does not appear to be susceptible to challenge.

(2) Full representation may be refused if there are administrative appeals or other procedures which should be pursued before proceedings are considered.

(3) Full representation will be refused unless the proposed respondent has been given a reasonable opportunity to respond to the challenge or deal with the applicant's complaint, save where this is impracticable in the circumstances.

(4) Full representation will be refused if the prospects of successfully obtaining the substantive order sought in the proceedings are:
   (a) unclear;
   (b) borderline and the case does not appear to have significant wider public interest, to be of overwhelming importance to the client or to raise significant human rights issues; or

---

152 *R v Secretary of State for the Home Department, ex parte Swati* [1986] 1 WLR 477 and *R v Epping & Harlow General Commissioners, ex parte Goldstraw* [1983] 3 All ER 257.

(c) poor.

(5) Full representation may be refused unless the likely benefits of the proceedings justify the likely costs, having regard to the prospects of success and all other circumstances.

6.14.3   Post-permission criteria

If at the time the application for legal help is made the court has granted permission, the following criteria apply.

(1) If the case has a significant wider public interest, is of overwhelming importance to the client or raises significant human rights issues, then, provided the standard criteria in s 4 of the Access to Justice Act 1999 are satisfied, funding shall be granted save where, in light of information which was not before the court at the permission stage or has subsequently come to light, it appears unreasonable for legal representation to be granted.

(2) Where the case does not appear to have a significant wider public interest, to be of overwhelming importance to the client or to raise significant human rights issues, legal representation will be refused if:
(a) prospects of success are borderline or poor; or
(b) the likely benefits of the proceedings do not appear to justify the likely costs having regard to the prospects of success and all the circumstances.

6.15   COSTS IN JUDICIAL REVIEW CASES UNDER THE HUMAN RIGHTS ACT 1998

6.15.1   Pre-emptive costs orders

In *Joseph Owen Davies v Eli Lilly & Co*[153] an order was made that any costs that were ordered or fell to be borne by any plaintiff in the lead actions should be borne proportionately by all plaintiffs. This was appealed on the grounds that making prospective orders as to costs was not within the jurisdiction of s 51 of the Supreme Court Act 1981 and RSC Ord 62. The Court of Appeal held that there was jurisdiction to make anticipatory costs orders. Lloyd LJ said:

> 'In the normal way, of course, the discretion is exercised at the conclusion of the proceedings, whether final or interlocutory. But there is nothing in the language of Ord 62, r. 3(3) to prohibit the exercise of the discretion at an earlier stage where the interests of justice so require.'[154]

Such orders have become known as 'pre-emptive costs orders'. The discretion to make pre-emptive orders, in cases involving public interest challenges, will be exercised only in the most exceptional circumstances. The court must be satisfied that:

---

153   [1987] 1 WLR 1136.
154   [1987] 1 WLR 1136 at p 1144.

(a) the issues raised are truly ones of general public importance; and
(b) it has a sufficient appreciation of the merits of the claim to conclude that it is in the public interest to make the order.

Unless the court is satisfied of these points by brief argument it is unlikely to make the order as there is a risk that these applications would become dress rehearsals of the substantive applications. The court will have regard to the financial resources of the applicant and respondent, and the amount of costs likely to be in issue. It is more likely to make an order where the respondent clearly has superior ability to bear the costs than the applicant and it is satisfied that the applicant would discontinue the proceedings if the order is not made.[155]

In the context of an application for judicial review of a decision of public authority, it is open to the public authority to change the decision it reached which is the subject of the judicial review proceedings. However, in those circumstances the applicant may obtain his or her costs.[156]

6.15.2 Costs

The normal rule under the CPR 1998, Parts 43 and 44 is that the court has a discretion in relation to costs and the person who loses normally pays the costs incurred by the winner. The CPR 1998 allow the judge to allocate costs on a proportionate basis. Thus if the person who wins succeeds on only one issue out of many which have involved substantial costs to the other party, the losing side may argue that it should obtain the costs of winning those other issues. This may result in the winning party bearing the majority of the costs of the case. One area which may cause difficulty arises when a declaration of incompatibility is made under s 4 of the HRA 1998. If the applicant succeeds only in establishing that the law is incompatible with the Convention he or she will have lost on all the other points and, if the CPR 1998 are applied in full, will pay all of the costs. The discretion of the court may be exercised so as to order no costs or in ordering the respondent to pay the applicant's costs. However, if there were a prospect of a remedial order being made, another option for the court would be to assess costs to be paid by the applicant in the normal way. One of the consequential issues that may be dealt with in the case of a statutory instrument which remedies incompatibility between legislation and the Convention rights, is the removal of any prejudice which the party has suffered as a result of the incompatibility. It is submitted that the Minister would be able to ensure that the public fund covered the costs of the applicant who had established the incompatibility by drawing the court's attention to the provision. The court would also be able to suspend a decision on costs until it was known whether a remedial order would compensate the pyrrhic victor in the case or to make an order that the costs should not be enforced without leave of the court under its powers to stay matters.[157]

---

155 *R v Lord Chancellor, ex parte CPAG* [1999] 1 WLR 347.
156 *R v Central Criminal Court, ex parte Newman* [1993] COD 65.
157 See CPR 1998, r 3.1(2)(f) and in the furtherance of the overriding objective.

6.15.3   Public funding

Where an individual seeks to assert Convention rights by means of judicial review proceedings, in many cases the availability of funding from the Legal Services Commission will be a crucial element in that person's access to justice. In order to be able to obtain public funding, the individual has to show the specific, identifiable, and personal interest he or she has in the case. The Legal Aid Act 1988, ss 15 and 1 and the several legal aid notes for guidance result in a scheme which sets quite a high threshold against which the merits of a potential challenge will be judged. In *UDT v Bycroft*,[158] Lord Evershed MR stated 'The Legal Aid Act was devised to assist those whom it finances in the course of litigation and not indirectly to assist other parties, or even the general public, in determining points of interest'. Whilst this proposition remains true, the provisions of the funding legislation must themselves be construed so as to give effect to the Convention rights including the rights guaranteed under Article 6. The concept of a sufficient interest in judicial review proceedings now involves the concept of 'victim' under the HRA 1998. This requires the person to be directly affected by an act in breach of Convention rights. Further, it is open to doubt whether obtaining legal help, and the decision-making process leading to the decision to grant or refuse public funding, is a process by which the private civil rights of the applicant are determined.

Under the Funding Code established pursuant to the Access to Justice Act 1999, cases involving a wider public interest are regarded as areas of high priority for funding. The kinds of cases that it was intended to benefit include social welfare cases. These relate to a person's basic entitlements such as housing or social security benefits and cases involving children or protection from violence. Cases involving the wider public interest were said to be those involving 'protection of life or other basic human rights – for example a challenge to government immigration policy concerning a class of asylum seekers who allege that they face persecution if not allowed to remain in this country'. It also included 'cases concerning intangible benefits such as a health, safety and quality of life'.

6.15.4   Conditional fee agreements

In the context of judicial review claims, the fact that there is a possibility of entry into a conditional fee agreement does not prevent the claimant from obtaining legal help from the Legal Services Commission. This is set out in paras 7.5 and 5.7.1 of the Funding Code summarised above.

6.16   PRACTICAL EFFECT OF THE HUMAN RIGHTS ACT 1998 ON TRIBUNALS' REMEDIAL POWERS

When considering cases before the employment tribunals involving a breach of s 6 of the HRA 1998, it is necessary to distinguish between:

---

158   [1954] 1 WLR 1345 at p 1351.

(a) cases against a public authority employer in which a finding of an unlawful act is made from facts which also constitute a breach of a statute giving the tribunal jurisdiction;

(b) cases against a public authority employer in which a finding is made that an unlawful act was committed by it on the basis of facts which do not fall within the jurisdictional scope of the tribunal;

(c) cases against a private employer in which a finding is made that a public authority has acted in a way which is (or would be) unlawful under s 6 whether or not the facts are within the jurisdiction of the tribunal to give a remedy.

Section 7(1)(b) permits a private individual to rely on the unlawful act of the public authority in any legal proceedings. Section 8(1) permits a tribunal in relation to any act (or proposed act) of a public authority which it finds is (or would be) unlawful, to grant such relief or remedy, or make such order, within its powers as it considers just and appropriate.

6.17 THE TRIBUNALS' JURISDICTION AND THE HUMAN RIGHTS ACT 1998

6.17.1 Introduction

The right to rely on the Convention means that the tribunal has jurisdiction to deal with s 6 claims against the public authority in proceedings before it. However, an individual may not bring a claim solely in respect of a breach of Convention rights unless and until tribunals are specified as an appropriate tribunal or the Minister makes an order permitting such claims to be brought before them. Section 7(1)(a) entitles a person to bring proceedings against a public authority under the HRA 1998. The right is limited to appropriate courts and tribunals. The right is to bring a claim without reference to any other claim. 'Appropriate court or tribunal' means the court or tribunal determined in accordance with rules.

Section 2 of the ETA 1996 confers jurisdiction on employment tribunals describing it as 'the jurisdiction conferred on them by or by virtue of this Act or any other Act, whether passed before or after this Act'. The question arises therefore whether the HRA 1998 confers on employment tribunals any jurisdiction and, if so, what. Section 8(1) envisages a tribunal making a finding that an act is unlawful under s 6, and this, it is suggested, confers jurisdiction on the tribunal to make such a finding. However, the tribunal does not have the right to grant a remedy in respect of a breach of s 6 considered alone. It can grant a remedy only if the facts also give rise to a finding under employment legislation which gives the tribunal powers to award a remedy under employment legislation.

6.17.2 Cases in which an act is unlawful under s 6 of the Human Rights Act 1998 and under an employment statute

In an employment tribunal case against a public authority, if the act is unlawful both under a statutory provision giving jurisdiction to the employment tribunals (for example, unfair dismissal) and under s 6 of the HRA 1998 (for example, because it was or involved an unjustified infringement of privacy), the tribunal may consider making a finding that the dismissal was unfair under s 112 of the ERA 1996 and a finding that it was unfair because the public authority employer acted in breach of Article 8 and therefore s 6 of the HRA 1998.

Under s 113 of the ERA 1996, the tribunal has a discretion as to whether an order for reinstatement or re-engagement should be made. Section 116 of the ERA 1996 provides guidance on the factors to be taken into account. Suppose that the applicant wishes to be reinstated and did not contribute to his or her dismissal. The question then becomes whether it is practicable for the employer to reinstate. Where the dismissal was also an act in breach of s 6 of the HRA 1998, the tribunal must consider s 8(1) of the HRA 1998. In relation to the act of dismissal it must consider whether the remedy of reinstatement is within its powers. Section 116 gives power to the tribunal to make an order where, in its discretion, it considers that it would be practicable for the employer to reinstate the employee. The concept of whether it is practicable for the employer to reinstate the employee must be given effect so far as it is possible to do so, so as to give effect to the applicant's right not to have the right to privacy infringed. Given that the tribunal has a positive obligation to protect the applicant's right to privacy in an effective and practicable way, and that the aim is to ensure that the applicant is in the position that the applicant would have been had the unlawful act not taken place, it may be that the concept of practicability must be given a meaning which is nearer 'physically possible' rather than merely 'feasible'.

Such an interpretation would recast the concept of practicability. Pre-HRA 1998, many cases have considered it and given interpretations to it. These interpretations remain relevant in respect of non-HRA 1998 cases.[159] The approach has been that the standard is not to be set too high. The employer cannot be expected to explore every possible avenue which ingenuity might suggest. The employer does not have to show that reinstatement or re-engagement was impossible. It is a matter of what is practicable in the circumstances of the employer's business at the relevant time. *Coleman* suggested that it was necessary for the tribunal to consider the industrial relations realities of the situation. Where the consequences of reinstatement are likely to be serious industrial relations problems, it will not generally be ordered. However, in a case where the industrial relations problems would arise because of intolerance by the other workers towards the exercise by the applicant of a right protected under the Convention, such as freedom of expression, the tribunal will have to consider whether this could justify not

---

159   See *Port of London v Payne* [1994] IRLR 9 and *Coleman v Magnet Joinery Ltd* [1975] ICR 46.

protecting the applicant's Convention right by not ordering reinstatement where it would be possible.

Shorn of interpretation by the courts, the concept of 'practicable' can be interpreted using s 3 so as to give effect in a real and practical way to the Convention rights of the applicant even where the atmosphere in the workplace is said to have been poisoned.[160] Where the atmosphere has been poisoned by the insistence of the applicant on rights under the Convention, it is hard to see how the tribunal could state that reinstatement was not practicable and give effect to the applicant's Convention rights in a real and practical way, as opposed to a theoretical and illusory manner.[161]

Where a right of respect for private life has been infringed, it is likely that the employee will exhibit some distrust of the employer. Such distrust may still prevent reinstatement being practicable, where it has spread to all aspects of the employment relationship, but if the distrust is limited to the facts showing a breach of the right to respect for private life, the tribunal will have to consider whether ordering reinstatement best protects that right to privacy, given the finding against the employer and the fact that the effect of the infringement will remain unless the employee is reinstated. Where the employee considers that he or she has been the victim of a conspiracy by the employer to dismiss him or her, that may not be enough to prevent reinstatement if in fact it is true.[162]

It is likely, however, that there would be no change in cases raising issues such as those raised in *ILEA v Gravett*.[163] ILEA dismissed a swimming instructor on the basis that he had been convicted of indecent exposure and indecent assault. The job required contact with a section of the public, and ILEA no longer trusted the applicant. In cases such as *Saunders*,[164] however, where the ground for dismissal was the private sexual activities of the applicant which did not indicate any real risk to the group he worked with, the absence of trust from the employer may be based on little more than prejudice. The tribunal would now have to consider whether reinstatement was practicable disregarding the distrustful prejudice which resulted in an infringement of the applicant's right to respect for his private life.

Tribunals have been unwilling to order reinstatement where that would be tantamount to ordering the employer to reverse a policy which resulted in the employee's dismissal.[165] However, where that policy was itself in breach of s 6, the tribunal would be entitled to make an order. It would have to disregard the suggestion that the policy rendered the remedy impracticable.

It is unlikely that the HRA 1998 will have any effect on the restrictions on ordering reinstatement in ERA 1996, s 116(5) and (6), ie that the fact that the

---

160   Cf pre-HRA 1998 approach in *Meridian Ltd v Gomersall* [1977] ICR 597.
161   See *Artico v Italy* (1981) 3 EHRR 1.
162   Cf *Northman v London Borough of Barnet (No 2)* [1980] IRLR 65.
163   [1988] IRLR 497.
164   *Saunders v Scottish National Camps Association* [1981] IRLR 277.
165   See the tribunal decision appealed in *Redbridge London Borough Council v Fishman* [1978] ICR 569 at p 573.

employer engaged a permanent replacement cannot be taken into account in considering practicability unless the employer can show that:

(a) it was not practicable for the employer to arrange for the dismissed employee's work to be done without engaging a permanent replacement; or

(b) the employer engaged the replacement after the lapse of a reasonable period, without having heard from the dismissed employee that he or she wished to be reinstated or re-engaged, and that when the employer engaged the replacement it was no longer reasonable for the employer to arrange for the dismissed employee's work to be done except by a permanent replacement.

In those circumstances, it is submitted that it would not be just or appropriate to award the remedy of reinstatement in order to give further effect to the Convention rights.

The effect of s 8(2) of the Human Rights Act 1998

Section 8(2) of the HRA 1998 permits damages for an unlawful act under s 6 to be awarded by a tribunal that has power to award compensation in civil proceedings. The concept of civil proceedings is undefined in the HRA 1998 but this is the way in which employment tribunal proceedings are viewed. Thus in *Langdale v Hannibal*,[166] the EAT thought that the tribunal should have considered a piece of evidence by virtue of s 1(1) of the Civil Evidence Act 1995 which provides: 'In civil proceedings evidence shall not be excluded on the ground that it is hearsay'. Also, where other Acts refer to 'civil proceedings' they envisage proceedings before the tribunals as included as civil proceedings. Thus s 18 of the Civil Evidence Act 1968 has the effect that proceedings before the tribunal are not governed by its provisions. This is because, although proceedings before the tribunal are civil proceedings, the proceedings before an employment tribunal are not 'proceedings in relation to which the strict rules of evidence apply'.[167] Employment tribunals are clearly tribunals having the power to award compensation in civil proceedings, however.

When considering whether to award damages for breach of the Convention rights, the tribunal will have to consider the requirement of 'just satisfaction' in s 8(3) (see **6.7.1**). The purpose of s 8(2) is clearly to restrict the power to award damages for a finding of unlawful acts under s 6, hence the restrictive use of the word 'only'. Section 8(2) characterises those tribunals that have the power to award damages as those which have the power to award compensation or damages in civil proceedings. Thus it excludes SENT, VAT tribunals and the like, which do not. It says, in the context of s 8(1), that if a tribunal has a power to award compensation, then within that power is also the power to award damages for an unlawful act under s 6. The principles of interpretation of a constitutional provision such as the HRA 1998 require the language of s 8(1) to

---

166 EAT, unreported, 1382/96.
167 See also Civil Evidence Act 1972, s 5 and Civil Evidence Act 1995, s 11.

be interpreted in such a way as to permit tribunals to make awards of damages for breach of s 6, providing at the same time they are making awards for breaches of employment legislation. In effect, such discretion as is brought to the question of compensation must be exercised to afford compensation for the breach of Convention rights contained within the breach of employment law.

6.17.3   Public authority employer; finding of unlawful act; facts not within the jurisdictional scope of the tribunal

Where the tribunal makes a finding that a public authority employer has committed an unlawful act, but also finds that the unlawful act is not connected with the case over which it has jurisdiction, it is submitted that the terms of s 8(1) of the HRA 1998 permit it to make this finding. Section 8(1) permits a tribunal to make a finding that an act is or would be unlawful. The employee must take that finding to the court under s 7(1)(a) if the employee wishes to obtain a remedy. On this interpretation, the jurisdiction of the tribunal would not extend to giving a remedy, as all of its powers are predicated upon pre-existing statutory provisions in respect of the employment rights protected by the statutes within its jurisdiction. The extent to which the facts must overlap before a tribunal has the power to award damages in respect of the unlawful act is unclear, but it is submitted that the facts must be such as to allow the tribunal also to make an award under the relevant employment legislation. Section 8(2) does not extend the powers of the tribunal. It provides that damages for an unlawful act under s 6 may only be awarded if the tribunal has powers to award compensation in a civil matter. However, by s 8(1) that power must be exercised within the scope of the tribunal's powers. Thus where a tribunal makes a finding that there was an unlawful act by a public authority, but also finds that the allegation made under the employment legislation is not made out, it has no powers to make any award of compensation or damages as it has exhausted its jurisdiction.

6.17.4   Cases against a private employer; finding of public authority's unlawful act

Where the employer is a private body, the tribunal is entitled to make a finding that a public authority acted unlawfully, or failed to act lawfully, under s 6 of the HRA 1998. The public authority in question might not be a party to the proceedings. Further, the employer may be a public body only by virtue of certain of its functions being public. The act over which the tribunal has jurisdiction may have been a private act. It would be open to the tribunal to make a finding that on a particular occasion the employer was acting as a public authority and that its act on that occasion was unlawful under s 6. However, the employee would not be able to recover damages via the tribunal against the public authority for breach of s 6, as the tribunal would have no jurisdiction over that act. The employee would have to commence proceedings under s 7(1)(a) against the public authority in respect of the particular act in which it was a public authority.

6.18   THE EFFECT OF THE HUMAN RIGHTS ACT 1998 ON COMPENSATION FOR UNFAIR DISMISSAL

6.18.1   Compensation

We will now consider the ways in which remedies will be affected by ss 3 and 8 of the HRA 1998. Section 123 of the ERA 1996 provides the tribunal with powers to order payment of a compensatory award. The amount of the compensatory award is 'such amount as the tribunal considers just and equitable in all the circumstances having regard to the loss sustained by the complainant in consequence of the dismissal in so far as that loss is attributable to action taken by the employer'. The concept of loss is the subject of a non-exhaustive definition in s 123(2) of the ERA 1996 and includes:

(a) any expenses reasonably incurred by the complainant in consequence of the dismissal; and
(b) loss of any benefit which the complainant might reasonably be expected to have had but for the dismissal.

The tribunal's ability to award a remedy in respect of an unlawful act under s 6 of the HRA 1998 in respect of an unfair dismissal case includes such compensation within its powers as it considers just and appropriate. However, those powers are limited by the following concepts:

(a) the loss sustained in consequence of the dismissal; and
(b) attribution of the loss to action taken by the employer.

6.18.2   Loss

The concept of loss has traditionally been limited to financial loss. In particular, the manner of dismissal cannot be compensated under this heading.[168] The NIRC held in that case, that on the true construction of ERA 1996, s 123, such loss did not include injury to the employee's feelings or pride, and, therefore, the manner of his dismissal was irrelevant, unless it was likely to cause the employee future financial loss.[169] In considering s 123 of the ERA 1996 in the light of s 3 of the HRA 1998, the tribunal would have to consider how to give effect, so far as it is possible to do so, to the section so as to render the Convention rights effective and practical. Looking at the terms of s 123(1) it is possible to interpret it so as to permit the infringement (of, for example, the right to respect for privacy) to be protected by means of an award of a sum which is just and equitable in all the circumstances of the case. The tribunal must have regard to the loss sustained by the employee in consequence of the dismissal, but s 123(1) can be interpreted to permit the tribunal to award compensation for injury to feelings, as the subsection does not expressly restrict the tribunal to financial loss. It is submitted that s 8(1) of the HRA 1998 permits the tribunal to consider whether it may compensate the applicant for the injury to feelings arising out of the dismissal.

---

168   *Norton Tool Co Ltd v Tewson* [1972] ICR 501.
169   *Norton Tool Co Ltd v Tewson* [1972] ICR 501 at pp 504F–H.

On this point, the reasoning of the NIRC in *Tewson* was as follows:

'The court or tribunal is enjoined to assess compensation in an amount which is just and equitable in all the circumstances, and there is neither justice nor equity in a failure to act in accordance with principle. The principles to be adopted emerge from s 116 of the Act of 1971 [now s 123 of the ERA 1996]. First, the object is to compensate, and compensate fully, but not to award a bonus; save possibly in the special case of a refusal by an employer to make an offer of employment in accordance with the recommendation of the court or a tribunal. Secondly, the amount to be awarded is that which is just and equitable in all the circumstances, having regard to the loss sustained by the complainant. "Loss" in the context of s 116 does not include injury to pride or feelings. In its natural meaning the word is not to be so construed, and that this meaning is intended seems to us to be clear from the elaboration contained in s 116(2). The discretionary element is introduced by the words "having regard to the loss." This does not mean that the court or tribunal can have regard to other matters, but rather that the amount of the compensation is not precisely and arithmetically related to the proved loss. Such a provision will be seen to be natural and possibly essential, when it is remembered that the claims with which the court and tribunals are concerned are more often than not presented by claimants in person and in condition of informality.'

The following points may be noted about this reasoning.

(1) It is based on the perceived parliamentary intention behind the section; post-HRA 1998, in applicable cases, the approach must be to interpret the words so as to give effect to them, so far as it is possible to do so, compatibly with the Convention rights. Such rights are to be interpreted so that the guarantees are real and effective. Although a person denied compensation for injury to feelings may take the case against the public authority to a court under s 7(1)(a), the tribunal will have to consider whether that course of action renders the protection given to the rights under the Convention theoretical and illusory. Most claims for injury to feeling will not be substantial and an applicant would have to engage in potentially costly proceedings.

(2) The NIRC construed 'having regard to' not as indicating that the tribunal might have regard to other matters. Construed so as to give effect to s 8(1) and to the Convention rights in accordance with s 3, it is open to the tribunal to regard these words as inclusive of matters to which it must have regard.

(3) In referring to s 123(2) of the ERA 1996, the NIRC regarded it as an elaboration of the concept of loss. However, the actual wording of the subsection indicates that the concept of loss includes certain financial matters, and broadens the scope of financial loss beyond merely matters that would be taken into account in an action based solely on contract. Thus it includes benefits of which there is a legitimate expectation.[170]

---

170 Cf the wrongful dismissal position: no compensation for discretionary matters; the court assumes that the contract breaker would have performed the contract in a way most favourable to himself: *Lavarack v Woods of Colchester* [1967] 1 QB 278.

6.18.3   Contributory fault

Section 123(6) of the ERA 1996 provides that where the tribunal finds that the dismissal was to any extent caused, or contributed to, by any action of the complainant, it shall reduce the amount of the compensatory award by such proportion as it considers just and equitable having regard to that finding. It is submitted that action which manifests a Convention right cannot generally be construed as contributory fault. An exception might arise in respect of freedom of expression under Article 10, as this makes explicit reference to the responsibilities attaching to the exercise of that freedom. In relation to respect for family life, in addition, the tribunal might regard it as incompatible with respect for family life that blame be attached to conduct referable to family life.

6.19   THE EFFECT OF THE HUMAN RIGHTS ACT 1998 ON REMEDIES FOR DISCRIMINATION

6.19.1   Recommendations

The tribunal is entitled to make a recommendation for the purpose of removing the effect of discrimination against an applicant. Thus the tribunal may recommend that the respondent take, within a specified period, action appearing to the tribunal to be reasonable, in all the circumstances of the case, for the purpose of obviating or reducing the adverse effect on the complainant of any matter to which the complaint relates.[171]

A tribunal does not have the power to recommend that a successful applicant be promoted to the next available suitable vacancy as this would amount to unlawful discrimination.[172] Where the discrimination took the form of the discriminatory application of a procedure for determining the civil rights of the individual, it may be that the scope for matters of recommendation may be increased to include a recommendation of promotion to the next available position. Where the discrimination was a failure to appoint, the tribunal may have to make a recommendation that the person be given the job for which that person applied.

In *Irvine v Prestcold Ltd*,[173] the applicant was twice passed over for promotion. The tribunal recommended that she be seriously considered for the post to which she had not been appointed. It also recommended that she should be given career development opportunities. The recommendation that she should receive the salary for the higher post until promoted was struck out. It amounted to compensation and did not fall within the powers of the tribunal because it failed to specify a time by which action had to have taken place. There is nothing in the legislation that requires a recommendation to be made

---

171   SDA 1975, s 65; RRA 1976, s 56; and DDA 1995, s 8(2)(c).
172   *British Gas plc v Sharma* [1991] IRLR 101.
173   [1981] IRLR 281.

as an alternative to an order for compensation, so that a recommendation amounting to a recommendation to pay compensation is not incompatible with a recommendation to remove the effects of discrimination.

A tribunal considering similar facts where a Convention right is in issue would have to consider making such a recommendation in order to remove the discriminatory effects. It is in any event open to the tribunal to award compensation on the basis of the loss flowing from the failure to appoint.

Appendix

Human Rights Act 1998

(1998 c 42)

ARRANGEMENT OF SECTIONS

An Act to give further effect to rights and freedoms guaranteed under the European Convention on Human Rights; to make provision with respect to holders of certain judicial offices who become judges of the European Court of Human Rights; and for connected purposes.

[9th November 1998]

Introduction

1   The Convention Rights

(1)   In this Act, 'the Convention rights' means the rights and fundamental freedoms set out in—

(a)   Articles 2 to 12 and 14 of the Convention,
(b)   Articles 1 to 3 of the First Protocol, and
(c)   Articles 1 and 2 of the Sixth Protocol,

as read with Articles 16 to 18 of the Convention.

(2)   Those Articles are to have effect for the purposes of this Act subject to any designated derogation or reservation (as to which see sections 14 and 15).

(3)   The Articles are set out in Schedule 1.

(4)   The Secretary of State may by order make such amendments to this Act as he considers appropriate to reflect the effect, in relation to the United Kingdom, of a protocol.

(5)   In subsection (4) 'protocol' means a protocol to the Convention—

(a)   which the United Kingdom has ratified; or
(b)   which the United Kingdom has signed with a view to ratification.

(6)   No amendment may be made by an order under subsection (4) so as to come into force before the protocol concerned is in force in relation to the United Kingdom.

2   Interpretation of Convention rights

(1)   A court or tribunal determining a question which has arisen in connection with a Convention right must take into account any—

(a) judgment, decision, declaration or advisory opinion of the European Court of Human Rights,
(b) opinion of the Commission given in a report adopted under Article 31 of the Convention,
(c) decision of the Commission in connection with Article 26 or 27(2) of the Convention, or
(d) decision of the Committee of Ministers taken under Article 46 of the Convention,

whenever made or given, so far as, in the opinion of the court or tribunal, it is relevant to the proceedings in which that question has arisen.

(2)   Evidence of any judgment, decision, declaration or opinion of which account may have to be taken under this section is to be given in proceedings before any court or tribunal in such manner as may be provided by rules.

(3)   In this section 'rules' means rules of court or, in the case of proceedings before a tribunal, rules made for the purposes of this section—

(a) by the Lord Chancellor or the Secretary of State, in relation to proceedings outside Scotland;
(b) by the Secretary of State, in relation to proceedings in Scotland; or
(c) by a Northern Ireland department, in relation to proceedings before a Tribunal in Northern Ireland—
    (i)   which deals with transferred matters; and
    (ii) for which no rules made under paragraph (a) are in force.

Legislation

3   Interpretation of legislation

(1)   So far as it is possible to do so, primary legislation and subordinate legislation must be read and given effect in a way which is compatible with the Convention rights.

(2)   This section—

(a) applies to primary legislation and subordinate legislation whenever enacted;
(b) does not affect the validity, continuing operation or enforcement of any incompatible primary legislation; and
(c) does not affect the validity, continuing operation or enforcement of any incompatible subordinate legislation if (disregarding any possibility of revocation) primary legislation prevents removal of the incompatibility.

4   Declaration of incompatibility

(1)   Subsection (2) applies in any proceedings in which a court determines whether a provision of primary legislation is compatible with a Convention right.

(2)   If the court is satisfied that the provision is incompatible with a Convention right, it may make a declaration of that incompatibility.

(3)   Subsection (4) applies in any proceedings in which a court determines whether a provision of subordinate legislation, made in the exercise of a power conferred by primary legislation, is compatible with a Convention right.

(4)   If the court is satisfied—

(a) that the provision is incompatible with a Convention right, and

(b) that (disregarding any possibility of revocation) the primary legislation concerned prevents removal of the incompatibility,

it may make a declaration of that incompatibility.

(5)   In this section 'court' means—

(a) the House of Lords;
(b) the Judicial Committee of the Privy Council;
(c) the Courts-Martial Appeal Court;
(d) in Scotland, the High Court of Justiciary sitting otherwise than as a trial court or the Court of Session;
(e) in England and Wales or Northern Ireland, the High Court or the Court of Appeal.

(6)   A declaration under this section ('a declaration of incompatibility')—

(a) does not affect the validity, continuing operation or enforcement of the provision in respect of which it is given; and
(b) is not binding on the parties to the proceedings in which it is made.

5 Right of Crown to intervene

(1)   Where a court is considering whether to make a declaration of incompatibility, the Crown is entitled to notice in accordance with rules of court.

(2)   In any case to which subsection (1) applies—

(a) a Minister of the Crown (or a person nominated by him),
(b) a member of the Scottish Executive,
(c) a Northern Ireland Minister,
(d) a Northern Ireland department,

is entitled, on giving notice in accordance with rules of court, to be joined as a party to the proceedings.

(3)   Notice under subsection (2) may be given at any time during the proceedings.

(4)   A person who has been made a party to criminal proceedings (other than in Scotland) as the result of a notice under subsection (2) may, with leave, appeal to the House of Lords against any declaration of incompatibility made in the proceedings.

(5)   In subsection (4)—

'criminal proceedings' includes all proceedings before the Courts-Martial Appeal Court; and
'leave' means leave granted by the court making the declaration of incompatibility or by the House of Lords.

Public authorities

6 Acts of public authorities

(1)   It is unlawful for a public authority to act in a way which is incompatible with a Convention right.

(2)   Subsection (1) does not apply to an act if—

(a) as the result of one or more provisions of primary legislation, the authority could not have acted differently; or

(b) in the case of one or more provisions of, or made under, primary legislation which cannot be read or given effect in a way which is compatible with the Convention rights, the authority was acting so as to give effect to or enforce those provisions.

(3) In this section, 'public authority' includes—

(a) a court or tribunal, and
(b) any person certain of whose functions are functions of a public nature,

but does not include either House of Parliament or a person exercising functions in connection with proceedings in Parliament.

(4) In subsection (3) 'Parliament' does not include the House of Lords in its judicial capacity.

(5) In relation to a particular act, a person is not a public authority by virtue only of subsection (3)(b) if the nature of the act is private.

(6) 'An act' includes a failure to act but does not include a failure to—

(a) introduce in, or lay before, Parliament a proposal for legislation; or
(b) make any primary legislation or remedial order.

7 Proceedings

(1) A person who claims that a public authority has acted (or proposes to act) in a way which is made unlawful by section 6(1) may—

(a) bring proceedings against the authority under this Act in the appropriate court or tribunal, or
(b) rely on the Convention right or rights concerned in any legal proceedings,

but only if he is (or would be) a victim of the unlawful act.

(2) In subsection (1)(a) 'appropriate court or tribunal' means such court or tribunal as may be determined in accordance with rules; and proceedings against an authority include a counterclaim or similar proceeding.

(3) If the proceedings are brought on an application for judicial review, the applicant is to be taken to have a sufficient interest in relation to the unlawful act only if he is, or would be, a victim of that act.

(4) If the proceedings are made by way of a petition for judicial review in Scotland, the applicant shall be taken to have title and interest to sue in relation to the unlawful act only if he is, or would be, a victim of that act.

(5) Proceedings under subsection (1)(a) must be brought before the end of—

(a) the period of one year beginning with the date on which the act complained of took place; or
(b) such longer period as the court or tribunal considers equitable having regard to all the circumstances,

but that is subject to any rule imposing a stricter time limit in relation to the procedure in question.

(6) In subsection (1)(b) 'legal proceedings' includes—

(a) proceedings brought by or at the instigation of a public authority; and
(b) an appeal against the decision of a court or tribunal.

(7)   For the purposes of this section, a person is a victim of an unlawful act only if he would be a victim for the purposes of Article 34 of the Convention if proceedings were brought in the European Court of Human Rights in respect of that act.

(8)   Nothing in this Act creates a criminal offence.

(9)   In this section 'rules' means—

  (a) in relation to proceedings before a court or tribunal outside Scotland, rules made by the Lord Chancellor or the Secretary of State for the purposes of this section or rules of court,
  (b) in relation to proceedings before a court or tribunal in Scotland, rules made by the Secretary of State for those purposes,
  (c) in relation to proceedings before a tribunal in Northern Ireland—
       (i)   which deals with transferred matters; and
       (ii) for which no rules made under paragraph (a) are in force,
       rules made by a Northern Ireland department for those purposes,

and includes provision made by order under section 1 of the Courts and Legal Services Act 1990.

(10)   In making rules regard must be had to section 9.

(11)   The Minister who has power to make rules in relation to a particular tribunal may, to the extent he considers it necessary to ensure that the tribunal can provide an appropriate remedy in relation to an act (or proposed act) of a public authority which is (or would be) unlawful as a result of section 6(1), by order add to—

  (a) the relief or remedies which the tribunal may grant; or
  (b) the grounds on which it may grant any of them.

(12)   An order made under subsection (13) may contain such incidental, supplemental, consequential or transitional provision as the Minister making it considers appropriate.

(13)   'The Minister' includes the Northern Ireland department concerned.

8   Judicial remedies

(1)   In relation to any act (or proposed act) of a public authority which the court finds is (or would be) unlawful, it may grant such relief or remedy, or make such order, within its powers as it considers just and appropriate.

(2)   But damages may be awarded only by a court which has power to award damages, or to order the payment of compensation, in civil proceedings.

(3)   No award of damages is to be made unless, taking account of all the circumstances of the case, including—

  (a) any other relief or remedy granted, or order made, in relation to the act in question (by that or any other court), and
  (b) the consequences of any decision (of that or any other court) in respect of that act,

the court is satisfied that the award is necessary to afford just satisfaction to the person in whose favour it is made.

(4)   In determining—

  (a) whether to award damages, or

(b) the amount of an award,

the court must take into account the principles applied by the European Court of Human Rights in relation to the award of compensation under Article 41 of the Convention.

(5) A public authority against which damages are awarded is to be treated—

    (a) in Scotland, for the purposes of section 3 of the Law Reform (Miscellaneous Provisions) (Scotland) Act 1940 as if the award were made in an action of damages in which the authority has been found liable in respect of loss or damage to the person to whom the award is made;

    (b) for the purposes of the Civil Liability (Contribution) Act 1978 as liable in respect of damage suffered by the person to whom the award is made.

(6) In this section—

'court' includes a tribunal;
'damages' means damages for an unlawful act of a public authority; and
'unlawful' means unlawful under section 6(1).

9 Judicial acts

(1) Proceedings under section 7(1)(a) in respect of a judicial act may be brought only—

    (a) by exercising a right of appeal;

    (b) on an application (in Scotland a petition) for judicial review; or

    (c) in such other forum as may be prescribed by rules.

(2) That does not affect any rule of law which prevents a court from being the subject of judicial review.

(3) In proceedings under this Act in respect of a judicial act done in good faith, damages may not be awarded otherwise than to compensate a person to the extent required by Article 5(5) of the Convention.

(4) An award of damages permitted by subsection (3) is to be made against the Crown; but no award may be made unless the appropriate person, if not a party to the proceedings, is joined.

(5) In this section—

'appropriate person' means the Minister responsible for the court concerned, or a person or government department nominated by him;
'court' includes a tribunal;
'judge' includes a member of a tribunal, a justice of the peace and a clerk or other officer entitled to exercise the jurisdiction of a court;
'judicial act' means a judicial act of a court and includes an act done on the instructions, or on behalf, of a judge; and
'rules' has the same meaning as in section 7(11).

Remedial action

10 Power to take remedial action

(1) This section applies if—

    (a) a provision of legislation has been declared under section 4 to be incompatible with a Convention right and, if an appeal lies—

    (i) all persons who may appeal have stated in writing that they do not intend to do so;

    (ii) the time for bringing an appeal has expired and no appeal has been brought within that time; or

    (iii) an appeal brought within that time has been determined or abandoned; or

(b) it appears to a Minister of the Crown or Her Majesty in Council that, having regard to a finding of the European Court of Human Rights made after the coming into force of this section in proceedings against the United Kingdom, a provision of legislation is incompatible with an obligation of the United Kingdom arising from the Convention.

(2)   If a Minister of the Crown considers that there are compelling reasons for proceeding under this section, he may by order make such amendments to the legislation as he considers necessary to remove the incompatibility.

(3)   If, in the case of subordinate legislation, a Minister of the Crown considers—

(a) that it is necessary to amend the primary legislation under which the subordinate legislation in question was made, in order to enable the incompatibility to be removed, and

(b) that there are compelling reasons for proceeding under this section,

he may by order make such amendments to the primary legislation as he considers necessary.

(4)   This section also applies where the provision in question is in subordinate legislation and has been quashed, or declared invalid, by reason of incompatibility with a Convention right and the Minister proposes to proceed under paragraph 2(b) of Schedule 2.

(5)   If the legislation is an Order in Council, the power conferred by subsection (2) or (3) is exercisable by Her Majesty in Council.

(6)   In this section 'legislation' does not include a Measure of the Church Assembly or of the General Synod of the Church of England.

(7)   Schedule 2 makes further provision about remedial orders.

Other rights and proceedings

11 Safeguard for existing human rights

A person's reliance on a Convention right does not restrict—

(a) any other right or freedom conferred on him by or under any law having effect in any part of the United Kingdom; or

(b) his right to make any claim or bring any proceedings which he could make or bring apart from sections 7 to 9.

12 Freedom of expression

(1)   This section applies if a court is considering whether to grant any relief which, if granted, might affect the exercise of the Convention right to freedom of expression.

(2)   If the person against whom the application for relief is made ('the respondent') is neither present nor represented, no such relief is to be granted unless the court is satisfied—

(a) that the applicant has taken all practicable steps to notify the respondent; or

(b) that there are compelling reasons why the respondent should not be notified.

(3) No such relief is to be granted so as to restrain publication before trial unless the court is satisfied that the applicant is likely to establish that publication should not be allowed.

(4) The court must have particular regard to the importance of the Convention right to freedom of expression and, where the proceedings relate to material which the respondent claims, or which appears to the court, to be journalistic, literary or artistic material (or to conduct connected with such material), to—

(a) the extent to which—

(i) the material has, or is about to, become available to the public; or

(ii) it is, or would be, in the public interest for the material to be published;

(b) any relevant privacy code.

(5) In this section—

'court' includes a tribunal; and

'relief' includes any remedy or order (other than in criminal proceedings).

13 Freedom of thought, conscience and religion

(1) If a court's determination of any question arising under this Act might affect the exercise by a religious organisation (itself or its members collectively) of the Convention right to freedom of thought, conscience and religion, it must have particular regard to the importance of that right.

(2) In this section 'court' includes a tribunal.

Derogations and reservations

14 Derogations

(1) In this Act, 'designated derogation' means—

(a) the United Kingdom's derogation from Article 5(3) of the Convention; and

(b) any derogation by the United Kingdom from an Article of the Convention, or of any protocol to the Convention, which is designated for the purposes of this Act in an order made by the Secretary of State.

(2) The derogation referred to in subsection (1)(a) is set out in Part I of Schedule 3.

(3) If a designated derogation is amended or replaced it ceases to be a designated derogation.

(4) But subsection (3) does not prevent the Secretary of State from exercising his power under subsection (1)(b) to make a fresh designation order in respect of the Article concerned.

(5) The Secretary of State must by order make such amendments to Schedule 3 as he considers appropriate to reflect—

(a) any designation order; or

(b) the effect of subsection (3).

(6) A designation order may be made in anticipation of the making by the United Kingdom of a proposed derogation.

15   Reservations

(1)   In this Act, 'designated reservation' means—

(a)   the United Kingdom's reservation to Article 2 of the First Protocol to the Convention; and

(b)   any other reservation by the United Kingdom to an Article of the Convention, or of any protocol to the Convention, which is designated for the purposes of this Act in an order made by the Secretary of State.

(2)   The text of the reservation referred to in subsection (1)(a) is set out in Part II of Schedule 3.

(3)   If a designated reservation is withdrawn wholly or in part it ceases to be a designated reservation.

(4)   But subsection (3) does not prevent the Secretary of State from exercising his power under subsection (1)(b) to make a fresh designation order in respect of the Article concerned.

(5)   The Secretary of State must by order make such amendments to this Act as he considers appropriate to reflect—

(a)   any designation order; or

(b)   the effect of subsection (3).

16   Period for which designated derogations have effect

(1)   If it has not already been withdrawn by the United Kingdom, a designated derogation ceases to have effect for the purposes of this Act—

(a)   in the case of the derogation referred to in section 14(1)(a), at the end of the period of five years beginning with the date on which section 1(2) came into force;

(b)   in the case of any other derogation, at the end of the period of five years beginning with the date on which the order designating it was made.

(2)   At any time before the period—

(a)   fixed by subsection (1)(a) or (b), or

(b)   extended by an order under this subsection,

comes to an end, the Secretary of State may by order extend it by a further period of five years.

(3)   An order under section 14(1)(b) ceases to have effect at the end of the period for consideration, unless a resolution has been passed by each House approving the order.

(4)   Subsection (3) does not affect—

(a)   anything done in reliance on the order; or

(b)   the power to make a fresh order under section 14(1)(b).

(5)   In subsection (3) 'period for consideration' means the period of forty days beginning with the day on which the order was made.

(6)   In calculating the period for consideration, no account is to be taken of any time during which—

(a)   Parliament is dissolved or prorogued; or

(b)   both Houses are adjourned for more than four days.

(7)   If a designated derogation is withdrawn by the United Kingdom, the Secretary of State must by order make such amendments to this Act as he considers are required to reflect that withdrawal.

17   Periodic review of designated reservations

(1)   The appropriate Minister must review the designated reservation referred to in section 15(1)(a)—

- (a)   before the end of the period of five years beginning with the date on which section 1(2) came into force; and
- (b)   if that designation is still in force, before the end of the period of five years beginning with the date on which the last report relating to it was laid under subsection (3).

(2)   The appropriate Minister must review each of the other designated reservations (if any)—

- (a)   before the end of the period of five years beginning with the date on which the order designating the reservation first came into force; and
- (b)   if the designation is still in force, before the end of the period of five years beginning with the date on which the last report relating to it was laid under subsection (3).

(3)   The Minister conducting a review under this section must prepare a report on the result of the review and lay a copy of it before each House of Parliament.

Judges of the European Court of Human Rights

18   Appointment to European Court of Human Rights

(1)   In this section 'judicial office' means the office of—

- (a)   Lord Justice of Appeal, Justice of the High Court or Circuit judge, in England and Wales;
- (b)   judge of the Court of Session or sheriff, in Scotland;
- (c)   Lord Justice of Appeal, judge of the High Court or county court judge, in Northern Ireland.

(2)   The holder of a judicial office may become a judge of the European Court of Human Rights ('the Court') without being required to relinquish his office.

(3)   But he is not required to perform the duties of his judicial office while he is a judge of the Court.

(4)   In respect of any period during which he is a judge of the Court—

- (a)   a Lord Justice of Appeal or Justice of the High Court is not to count as a judge of the relevant court for the purposes of section 2(1) or 4(1) of the Supreme Court Act 1981 (maximum number of judges) nor as a judge of the Supreme Court for the purposes of section 12(1) to (6) of that Act (salaries etc);
- (b)   a judge of the Court of Session is not to count as a judge of that court for the purposes of section 1(1) of the Court of Session Act 1988 (maximum number of judges) or of section 9(1)(c) of the Administration of Justice Act 1973 ('the 1973 Act') (salaries etc);
- (c)   a Lord Justice of Appeal or a judge of the High Court in Northern Ireland is not to count as a judge of the relevant court for the purposes of section 2(1) or 3(1) of the Judicature (Northern Ireland) Act 1978 (maximum number of judges) nor

as a judge of the Supreme Court of Northern Ireland for the purposes of section 9(1)(d) of the 1973 Act (salaries etc);

(d) a Circuit judge is not to count as such for the purposes of section 18 of the Courts Act 1971 (salaries etc);

(e) a sheriff is not to count as such for the purposes of section 14 of the Sheriff Courts (Scotland) Act 1907 (salaries etc);

(f) a county court judge of Northern Ireland is not to count as such for the purposes of section 106 of the County Courts Act (Northern Ireland) 1959 (salaries etc).

(5)   If a sheriff principal is appointed a judge of the Court, section 11(1) of the Sheriff Courts (Scotland) Act 1971 (temporary appointment of sheriff principal) applies, while he holds that appointment, as if his office is vacant.

(6)   Schedule 3 makes provision about judicial pensions in relation to the holder of a judicial office who serves as a judge of the Court.

(7)   The Lord Chancellor or the Secretary of State may by order make such transitional provision (including, in particular, provision for a temporary increase in the maximum number of judges) as he considers appropriate in relation to any holder of a judicial office who has completed his service as a judge of the Court.

Parliamentary procedure

19   Statements of compatibility

(1)   A Minister of the Crown in charge of a Bill in either House of Parliament must, before Second Reading of the Bill—

(a) make a statement to the effect that in his view the provisions of the Bill are compatible with the Convention rights ('a statement of compatibility'); or

(b) make a statement to the effect that although he is unable to make a statement of compatibility the government nevertheless wishes the House to proceed with the Bill.

(2)   The statement must be in writing and be published in such manner as the Minister making it considers appropriate.

Supplemental

20   Orders etc under this Act

(1)   Any power of a Minister of the Crown to make an order under this Act is exercisable by statutory instrument.

(2)   The power of the Lord Chancellor or the Secretary of State to make rules (other than rules of court) under section 2(3) or 7(9) is exercisable by statutory instrument.

(3)   Any statutory instrument made under section 14, 15 or 16(7) must be laid before Parliament.

(4)   No order may be made by the Lord Chancellor or the Secretary of State under section 1(4), 7(13) or 16(2) unless a draft of the order has been laid before, and approved by, each House of Parliament.

(5)   Any statutory instrument made under section 18(7) or Schedule 4, or to which subsection (2) applies, shall be subject to annulment in pursuance of a resolution of either House of Parliament.

(6)   The power of a Northern Ireland department to make—

(a) rules under section 2(3)(c) or 7(9)(c), or
(b) an order under section 7(11),

is exercisable by statutory rule for the purposes of the Statutory Rules (Northern Ireland) Order 1979.

(7)   Any rules made under section 2(3)(c) or 7(9)(c) shall be subject to negative resolution; and section 41(6) of the Interpretation Act (Northern Ireland) 1954 (meaning of 'subject to negative resolution') shall apply as if the power to make the rules were conferred by an Act of the Northern Ireland Assembly.

(8)   No order may be made by a Northern Ireland department under section 7(11) unless a draft of the order has been laid before, and approved by, the Northern Ireland Assembly.

21   Interpretation, etc

(1)   In this Act—

'amend' includes repeal and apply (with or without modifications);
'the appropriate Minister' means the Minister of the Crown having charge of the appropriate authorised government department (within the meaning of the Crown Proceedings Act 1947);
'the Commission' means the European Commission of Human Rights;
'the Convention' means the Convention for the Protection of Human Rights and Fundamental Freedoms, agreed by the Council of Europe at Rome on 4th November 1950 as it has effect for the time being in relation to the United Kingdom;
'declaration of incompatibility' means a declaration under section 4;
'Minister of the Crown' has the same meaning as in the Ministers of the Crown Act 1975;
'Northern Ireland Minister' includes the First Minister and the deputy First Minister in Northern Ireland;
'primary legislation' means any—

(a) public general Act;
(b) local and personal Act;
(c) private Act;
(d) Measure of the Church Assembly;
(e) Measure of the General Synod of the Church of England;
(f) Order in Council—
    (i)   made in exercise of Her Majesty's Royal Prerogative;
    (ii) made under section 38(1)(a) of the Northern Ireland Constitution Act 1973 or the corresponding provision of the Northern Ireland Act 1998; or
    (iii) amending an Act of a kind mentioned in paragraph (a), (b) or (c);

and includes an order or other instrument made under primary legislation (otherwise than by the National Assembly for Wales, a member of the Scottish Executive, a Northern Ireland Minister or a Northern Ireland department) to the extent to which it operates to bring one or more provisions of that legislation into force or amends any primary legislation;

'the First Protocol' means the protocol to the Convention agreed at Paris on 20th March 1952;
'the Sixth Protocol' means the protocol to the Convention agreed at Strasbourg on 28th April 1983;

'the Eleventh Protocol' means the protocol to the Convention (restructuring the control machinery established by the Convention) agreed at Strasbourg on 11th May 1994;

'remedial order' means an order under section 10;

'subordinate legislation' means any—

(a) Order in Council other than one—
   (i) made in exercise of Her Majesty's Royal Prerogative;
   (ii) made under section 38(1)(a) of the Northern Ireland Constitution Act 1973 or the corresponding provision of the Northern Ireland Act 1998; or
   (iii) amending an Act of a kind mentioned in the definition of primary legislation;
(b) Act of the Scottish Parliament;
(c) Act of the Parliament of Northern Ireland;
(d) Measure of the Assembly established under section 1 of the Northern Ireland Assembly Act 1973;
(e) Act of the Northern Ireland Assembly;
(f) order, rules, regulations, scheme, warrant, byelaw or other instrument made under primary legislation (except to the extent to which it operates to bring one or more provisions of that legislation into force or amends any primary legislation);
(g) order, rules, regulations, scheme, warrant, byelaw or other instrument made under legislation mentioned in paragraph (b), (c), (d) or (e) or made under an Order in Council applying only to Northern Ireland;
(h) order, rules, regulations, scheme, warrant, byelaw or other instrument made by a member of the Scotish Executive, a Northern Ireland Minister or a Northern Ireland department in exercise of prerogative or other executive functions of Her Majesty which are exercisable by such a person on behalf of Her Majesty;

'transferred matters' has the same meaning as in the Northern Ireland Act 1998; and 'tribunal' means any tribunal in which legal proceedings may be brought.

(2) The references in paragraphs (b) and (c) of section 2(1) to Articles are to Articles of the Convention as they had effect immediately before the coming into force of the Eleventh Protocol.

(3) The reference in paragraph (d) of section 2(1) to Article 46 includes a reference to Articles 32 and 54 of the Convention as they had effect immediately before the coming into force of the Eleventh Protocol.

(4) The references in section 2(1) to a report or decision of the Commission or a decision of the Committee of Ministers include references to a report or decision made as provided by paragraphs 3, 4 and 6 of Article 5 of the Eleventh Protocol (transitional provisions).

(5) Any liability under the Army Act 1955, the Air Force Act 1955 or the Naval Discipline Act 1957 to suffer death for an offence is replaced by a liability to imprisonment for life or any less punishment authorised by those Acts; and those Acts shall accordingly have effect with the necessary modifications.

22 Short title, commencement, application and extent

(1) This Act may be cited as the Human Rights Act 1998.

(2) Sections 18 and 20 and this section come into force on the passing of this Act.

(3)   The other provisions of this Act come into force on such day as the Secretary of State may by order appoint; and different days may be appointed for different purposes.

(4)   Paragraph (b) of subsection (1) of section 7 applies to proceedings brought by or at the instigation of a public authority whenever the act in question took place; but otherwise that subsection does not apply to an act taking place before the coming into force of that section.

(5)   This Act binds the Crown.

(6)   This Act extends to Northern Ireland.

(7)   Section 21(5), so far as it relates to any provision contained in the Army Act 1955, the Air Force Act 1955 or the Naval Discipline Act 1957, extends to any place to which that provision extends.

SCHEDULES

SCHEDULE 1

THE ARTICLES

PART I

THE CONVENTION

Rights and Freedoms

Article 2

Right to life

1.   Everyone's right to life shall be protected by law. No one shall be deprived of his life intentionally save in the execution of a sentence of a court following his conviction of a crime for which this penalty is provided by law.

2.   Deprivation of life shall not be regarded as inflicted in contravention of this Article when it results from the use of force which is no more than absolutely necessary:

   (a) in defence of any person from unlawful violence;
   (b) in order to effect a lawful arrest or to prevent the escape of a person lawfully detained;
   (c) in action lawfully taken for the purpose of quelling a riot or insurrection.

Article 3

Prohibition of torture

No one shall be subjected to torture or to inhuman or degrading treatment or punishment.

Article 4

Prohibition of slavery and forced labour

1.   No one shall be held in slavery or servitude.

2.   No one shall be required to perform forced or compulsory labour.

3.   For the purpose of this Article the term 'forced or compulsory labour' shall not include:

   (a) any work required to be done in the ordinary course of detention imposed according to the provisions of Article 5 of this Convention or during conditional release from such detention;
   (b) any service of a military character or, in case of conscientious objectors in countries where they are recognised, service exacted instead of compulsory military service;
   (c) any service exacted in case of an emergency or calamity threatening the life or well-being of the community;

(d) any work or service which forms part of normal civic obligations.

Article 5

Right to liberty and security

1.   Everyone has the right to liberty and security of person. No one shall be deprived of his liberty save in the following cases and in accordance with a procedure prescribed by law:

(a) the lawful detention of a person after conviction by a competent court;

(b) the lawful arrest or detention of a person for non-compliance with the lawful order of a court or in order to secure the fulfilment of any obligation prescribed by law;

(c) the lawful arrest or detention of a person effected for the purpose of bringing him before the competent legal authority on reasonable suspicion of having committed an offence or when it is reasonably considered necessary to prevent his committing an offence or fleeing after having done so;

(d) the detention of a minor by lawful order for the purpose of educational supervision or his lawful detention for the purpose of bringing him before the competent legal authority;

(e) the lawful detention of persons for the prevention of the spreading of infectious diseases, of persons of unsound mind, alcoholics or drug addicts or vagrants;

(f) the lawful arrest or detention of a person to prevent his effecting an unauthorised entry into the country or of a person against whom action is being taken with a view to deportation or extradition.

2.   Everyone who is arrested shall be informed promptly, in a language which he understands, of the reasons for his arrest and of any charge against him.

3.   Everyone arrested or detained in accordance with the provisions of paragraph 1(c) of this Article shall be brought promptly before a judge or other officer authorised by law to exercise judicial power and shall be entitled to trial within a reasonable time or to release pending trial. Release may be conditioned by guarantees to appear for trial.

4.   Everyone who is deprived of his liberty by arrest or detention shall be entitled to take proceedings by which the lawfulness of his detention shall be decided speedily by a court and his release ordered if the detention is not lawful.

5.   Everyone who has been the victim of arrest or detention in contravention of the provisions of this Article shall have an enforceable right to compensation.

Article 6

Right to a fair trial

1.   In the determination of his civil rights and obligations or of any criminal charge against him, everyone is entitled to a fair and public hearing within a reasonable time by an independent and impartial tribunal established by law. Judgment shall be pronounced publicly but the press and public may be excluded from all or part of the trial in the interest of morals, public order or national security in a democratic society, where the interests of juveniles or the protection of the private life of the parties so require, or to the extent strictly necessary in the opinion of the court in special circumstances where publicity would prejudice the interests of justice.

2.   Everyone charged with a criminal offence shall be presumed innocent until proved guilty according to law.

3.   Everyone charged with a criminal offence has the following minimum rights:

(a) to be informed promptly, in a language which he understands and in detail, of the nature and cause of the accusation against him;

(b) to have adequate time and facilities for the preparation of his defence;

(c) to defend himself in person or through legal assistance of his own choosing or, if he has not sufficient means to pay for legal assistance, to be given it free when the interests of justice so require;

(d) to examine or have examined witnesses against him and to obtain the attendance and examination of witnesses on his behalf under the same conditions as witnesses against him;

(e) to have the free assistance of an interpreter if he cannot understand or speak the language used in court.

Article 7

No punishment without law

1.   No one shall be held guilty of any criminal offence on account of any act or omission which did not constitute a criminal offence under national or international law at the time when it was committed. Nor shall a heavier penalty be imposed than the one that was applicable at the time the criminal offence was committed.

2.   This Article shall not prejudice the trial and punishment of any person for any act or omission which, at the time when it was committed, was criminal according to the general principles of law recognised by civilised nations.

Article 8

Right to respect for private and family life

1.   Everyone has the right to respect for his private and family life, his home and his correspondence.

2.   There shall be no interference by a public authority with the exercise of this right except such as is in accordance with the law and is necessary in a democratic society in the interests of national security, public safety or the economic well-being of the country, for the prevention of disorder or crime, for the protection of health or morals, or for the protection of the rights and freedoms of others.

Article 9

Freedom of thought, conscience and religion

1.   Everyone has the right to freedom of thought, conscience and religion; this right includes freedom to change his religion or belief and freedom, either alone or in community with others and in public or private, to manifest his religion or belief, in worship, teaching, practice and observance.

2.   Freedom to manifest one's religion or beliefs shall be subject only to such limitations as are prescribed by law and are necessary in a democratic society in the interests of public safety, for the protection of public order, health or morals, or for the protection of the rights and freedoms of others.

Article 10

Freedom of expression

1.   Everyone has the right to freedom of expression. This right shall include freedom to hold opinions and to receive and impart information and ideas without interference by public authority and regardless of frontiers. This Article shall not prevent States from requiring the licensing of broadcasting, television or cinema enterprises.

2.   The exercise of these freedoms, since it carries with it duties and responsibilities, may be subject to such formalities, conditions, restrictions or penalties as are prescribed by law and are necessary in a democratic society, in the interests of national security, territorial integrity or public safety, for the prevention of disorder or crime, for the protection of health or morals, for the protection of the reputation or rights of others, for preventing the disclosure of information received in confidence, or for maintaining the authority and impartiality of the judiciary.

Article 11

Freedom of assembly and association

1.   Everyone has the right to freedom of peaceful assembly and to freedom of association with others, including the right to form and to join trade unions for the protection of his interests.

2.   No restrictions shall be placed on the exercise of these rights other than such as are prescribed by law and are necessary in a democratic society in the interests of national security or public safety, for the prevention of disorder or crime, for the protection of health or morals or for the protection of the rights and freedoms of others. This Article shall not prevent the imposition of lawful restrictions on the exercise of these rights by members of the armed forces, of the police or of the administration of the State.

Article 12

Right to marry

Men and women of marriageable age have the right to marry and to found a family, according to the national laws governing the exercise of this right.

Article 14

Prohibition of discrimination

The enjoyment of the rights and freedoms set forth in this Convention shall be secured without discrimination on any ground such as sex, race, colour, language, religion, political or other opinion, national or social origin, association with a national minority, property, birth or other status.

Article 16

Restrictions on political activity of aliens

Nothing in Articles 10, 11 and 14 shall be regarded as preventing the High Contracting Parties from imposing restrictions on the political activity of aliens.

Article 17

Prohibition of abuse of rights

Nothing in this Convention may be interpreted as implying for any State, group or person any right to engage in any activity or perform any act aimed at the destruction of any of the rights and freedoms set forth herein or at their limitation to a greater extent than is provided for in the Convention.

Article 18

Limitation on use of restrictions on rights

The restrictions permitted under this Convention to the said rights and freedoms shall not be applied for any purpose other than those for which they have been prescribed.

PART II

THE FIRST PROTOCOL

Article 1

Protection of property

Every natural or legal person is entitled to the peaceful enjoyment of his possessions. No one shall be deprived of his possessions except in the public interest and subject to the conditions provided for by law and by the general principles of international law.

The preceding provisions shall not, however, in any way impair the right of a State to enforce such laws as it deems necessary to control the use of property in accordance with the general interest or to secure the payment of taxes or other contributions or penalties.

Article 2

Right to education

No person shall be denied the right to education. In the exercise of any functions which it assumes in relation to education and to teaching, the State shall respect the right of parents to ensure such education and teaching in conformity with their own religious and philosophical convictions.

Article 3

Right to free elections

The High Contracting Parties undertake to hold free elections at reasonable intervals by secret ballot, under conditions which will ensure the free expression of the opinion of the people in the choice of the legislature.

PART III

THE SIXTH PROTOCOL

Article 1

Abolition of the death penalty

The death penalty shall be abolished. No one shall be condemned to such penalty or executed.

Article 2

Death penalty in time of war

A State may make provisions in its law for the death penalty in respect of acts committed in time of war or of imminent threat of war; such penalty shall be applied only in the instances laid down in the law and in accordance with its provisions. The State shall communicate to the Secretary of the Council of Europe the relevant provisions of that law.

SCHEDULE 2

REMEDIAL ORDERS

Orders

1.—(1)   A remedial order may—

   (a)   contain such incidental, supplemental, consequential or transitional provision as the person making it considers appropriate;
   (b)   be made so as to have effect from a date earlier than that on which it is made;
   (c)   make provision for the delegation of specific functions;
   (d)   make different provision for different cases.

(2)   The power conferred by sub-paragraph (1)(a) includes—

   (a)   power to amend primary legislation (including primary legislation other than that which contains the incompatible provision); and
   (b)   power to amend or revoke subordinate legislation (including subordinate legislation other than that which contains the incompatible provision).

(3)   A remedial order may be made so as to have the same extent as the legislation which it affects.

(4)   No person is to be guilty of an offence solely as a result of the retrospective effect of a remedial order.

Procedure

2.   No remedial order may be made unless—

   (a)   a draft of the order has been approved by a resolution of each House of Parliament made after the end of the period of 60 days beginning with the day on which the draft was laid; or
   (b)   it is declared in the order that it appears to the person making it that, because of the urgency of the matter, it is necessary to make the order without a draft being so approved.

Orders laid in draft

3.—(1)   No draft may be laid under paragraph 2(a) unless—

   (a)   the person proposing to make the order has laid before Parliament a document which contains a draft of the proposed order and the required information; and
   (b)   the period of 60 days, beginning with the day on which the document required by this sub-paragraph was laid, has ended.

(2)   If representations have been made during that period, the draft laid under paragraph 2(a) must be accompanied by a statement containing—

(a) a summary of the representations; and
(b) if, as a result of the representations, the proposed order has been changed, details of the changes.

Urgent cases

4.—(1)   If a remedial order ('the original order') is made without being approved in draft, the person making it must lay it before Parliament, accompanied by the required information, after it is made.

(2) If representations have been made during the period of 60 days beginning with the day on which the original order was made, the person making it must (after the end of that period) lay before Parliament a statement containing—

(a) a summary of the representations; and
(b) if, as a result of the representations, he considers it appropriate to make changes to the original order, details of the changes.

(3)   If sub-paragraph (2)(b) applies, the person making the statement must—

(a) make a further remedial order replacing the original order; and
(b) lay the replacement order before Parliament.

(4)   If, at the end of the period of 120 days beginning with the day on which the original order was made, a resolution has not been passed by each House approving the original or replacement order, the order ceases to have effect (but without that affecting anything previously done under either order or the power to make a fresh remedial order).

Definitions

5.   In this Schedule—

'representations' means representations about a remedial order (or proposed remedial order) made to the person making (or proposing to make) it and includes any relevant Parliamentary report or resolution; and
'required information' means—

(a) an explanation of the incompatibility which the order (or proposed order) seeks to remove, including particulars of the relevant declaration, finding or order; and
(b) a statement of the reasons for proceeding under section 10 and for making an order in those terms.

Calculating periods

6.   In calculating any period for the purposes of this Schedule, no account is to be taken of any time during which—

(a) Parliament is dissolved or prorogued; or
(b) both Houses are adjourned for more than four days.

SCHEDULE 3

DEROGATION AND RESERVATION

PART I

DEROGATION

The 1988 notification

The United Kingdom Permanent Representative to the Council of Europe presents his compliments to the Secretary General of the Council, and has the honour to convey the following information in order to ensure compliance with the obligations of Her Majesty's Government in the United Kingdom under Article 15(3) of the Convention for the Protection of Human Rights and Fundamental Freedoms signed at Rome on 4 November 1950.

There have been in the United Kingdom in recent years campaigns of organised terrorism connected with the affairs of Northern Ireland which have manifested themselves in activities which have included repeated murder, attempted murder, maiming, intimidation and violent civil disturbance and in bombing and fire raising which have resulted in death, injury and widespread destruction of property. As a result, a public emergency within the meaning of Article 15(1) of the Convention exists in the United Kingdom.

The Government found it necessary in 1974 to introduce and since then, in cases concerning persons reasonably suspected of involvement in terrorism connected with the affairs of Northern Ireland, or of certain offences under the legislation, who have been detained for 48 hours, to exercise powers enabling further detention without charge, for periods of up to five days, on the authority of the Secretary of State. These powers are at present to be found in Section 12 of the Prevention of Terrorism (Temporary Provisions) Act 1984, Article 9 of the Prevention of Terrorism (Supplemental Temporary Provisions) Order 1984 and Article 10 of the Prevention of Terrorism (Supplemental Temporary Provisions) (Northern Ireland) Order 1984.

Section 12 of the Prevention of Terrorism (Temporary Provisions) Act 1984 provides for a person whom a constable has arrested on reasonable grounds of suspecting him to be guilty of an offence under Section 1, 9 or 10 of the Act, or to be or to have been involved in terrorism connected with the affairs of Northern Ireland, to be detained in right of the arrest for up to 48 hours and thereafter, where the Secretary of State extends the detention period, for up to a further five days. Section 12 substantially re-enacted Section 12 of the Prevention of Terrorism (Temporary Provisions) Act 1976 which, in turn, substantially re-enacted Section 7 of the Prevention of Terrorism (Temporary Provisions) Act 1974.

Article 10 of the Prevention of Terrorism (Supplemental Temporary Provisions) (Northern Ireland) Order 1984 (SI 1984/417) and Article 9 of the Prevention of Terrorism (Supplemental Temporary Provisions) Order 1984 (SI 1984/418) were both made under Sections 13 and 14 of and Schedule 3 to the 1984 Act and substantially re-enacted powers of detention in Orders made under the 1974 and 1976 Acts. A person who is being examined under Article 4 of either Order on his arrival in, or on seeking to leave, Northern Ireland or Great Britain for the purpose of determining whether he is or has been involved in terrorism connected with the affairs of Northern Ireland, or whether there are grounds for suspecting that he has committed an offence under Section 9 of the 1984 Act, may be detained under Article 4 or 10, as appropriate, pending the conclusion of his examination. The period of this examination may exceed

12 hours if an examining officer has reasonable grounds for suspecting him to be or to have been involved in acts of terrorism connected with the affairs of Northern Ireland.

Where such a person is detained under the said Article 9 or 10 he may be detained for up to 48 hours on the authority of an examining officer and thereafter, where the Secretary of State extends the detention period, for up to a further five days.

In its judgment of 29 November 1988 in the Case of *Brogan and Others*, the European Court of Human Rights held that there had been a violation of Article 5(3) in respect of each of the applicants, all of whom had been detained under Section 12 of the 1984 Act. The Court held that even the shortest of the four periods of detention concerned, namely four days and six hours, fell outside the constraints as to time permitted by the first part of Article 5(3). In addition, the Court held that there had been a violation of Article 5(3) in the case of each applicant.

Following this judgment, the Secretary of State for the Home Department informed Parliament on 6 December 1988 that, against the background of the terrorist campaign, and the over-riding need to bring terrorists to justice, the Government did not believe that the maximum period of detention should be reduced. He informed Parliament that the Government were examining the matter with a view to responding to the judgment. On 22 December 1988, the Secretary of State further informed Parliament that it remained the Government's wish, if it could be achieved, to find a judicial process under which extended detention might be reviewed and where appropriate authorised by a judge or other judicial officer. But a further period of reflection and consultation was necessary before the Government could bring forward a firm and final view.

Since the judgment of 29 November as well as previously, the Government have found it necessary to continue to exercise, in relation to terrorism connected with the affairs of Northern Ireland, the powers described above enabling further detention without charge for periods of up to 5 days, on the authority of the Secretary of State, to the extent strictly required by the exigencies of the situation to enable necessary enquiries and investigations properly to be completed in order to decide whether criminal proceedings should be instituted. To the extent that the exercise of these powers may be inconsistent with the obligations imposed by the Convention the Government has availed itself of the right of derogation conferred by Article 15(1) of the Convention and will continue to do so until further notice.

Dated 23 December 1988.

The 1989 notification

The United Kingdom Permanent Representative to the Council of Europe presents his compliments to the Secretary General of the Council, and has the honour to convey the following information.

In his communication to the Secretary General of 23 December 1988, reference was made to the introduction and exercise of certain powers under section 12 of the Prevention of Terrorism (Temporary Provisions) Act 1984, Article 9 of the Prevention of Terrorism (Supplemental Temporary Provisions) Order 1984 and Article 10 of the Prevention of Terrorism (Supplemental Temporary Provisions) (Northern Ireland) Order 1984.

These provisions have been replaced by section 14 of and paragraph 6 of Schedule 5 to the Prevention of Terrorism (Temporary Provisions) Act 1989, which make comparable provision. They came into force on 22 March 1989. A copy of these provisions is enclosed.

The United Kingdom Permanent Representative avails himself of this opportunity to renew to the Secretary General the assurance of his highest consideration.

23 March 1989.

PART II

RESERVATION

At the time of signing the present (First) Protocol, I declare that, in view of certain provisions of the Education Acts in the United Kingdom, the principle affirmed in the second sentence of Article 2 is accepted by the United Kingdom only so far as it is compatible with the provision of efficient instruction and training, and the avoidance of unreasonable public expenditure.

Dated 20 March 1952. Made by the United Kingdom Permanent Representative to the Council of Europe.

SCHEDULE 4

JUDICIAL PENSIONS

Duty to make orders about pensions

1.—(1) The appropriate Minister must by order make provision with respect to pensions payable to or in respect of any holder of a judicial office who serves as an ECHR judge.

(2) A pensions order must include such provision as the Minister making it considers is necessary to secure that—

(a) an ECHR judge who was, immediately before his appointment as an ECHR judge, a member of a judicial pension scheme is entitled to remain as a member of that scheme;
(b) the terms on which he remains a member of the scheme are those which would have been applicable had he not been appointed as an ECHR judge; and
(c) entitlement to benefits payable in accordance with the scheme continues to be determined as if, while serving as an ECHR judge, his salary was that which would (but for section 18(4)) have been payable to him in respect of his continuing service as the holder of his judicial office.

Contributions

2. A pensions order may, in particular, make provision—

(a) for any contributions which are payable by a person who remains a member of a scheme as a result of the order, and which would otherwise be payable by deduction from his salary, to be made otherwise than by deduction from his salary as an ECHR judge; and
(b) for such contributions to be collected in such manner as may be determined by the administrators of the scheme.

Amendments of other enactments

3. A pensions order may amend any provision of, or made under, a pensions Act in such manner and to such extent as the Minister making the order considers necessary or expedient to ensure the proper administration of any scheme to which it relates.

Definitions

4.   In this Schedule—

'appropriate Minister' means—

(a) in relation to any judicial office whose jurisdiction is exercisable exclusively in relation to Scotland, the Secretary of State; and

(b) otherwise, the Lord Chancellor;

'ECHR judge' means the holder of a judicial office who is serving as a judge of the Court;
'judicial pension scheme' means a scheme established by and in accordance with a pensions Act;
'pensions Act' means—

(a) the County Courts Act (Northern Ireland) 1959;

(b) the Sheriffs' Pensions (Scotland) Act 1961;

(c) the Judicial Pensions Act 1981; or

(d) the Judicial Pensions and Retirement Act 1993; and

'pensions order' means an order made under paragraph 1.

INDEX

References are to paragraph numbers.